STUDIES IN
CHEREMIS: THE SUPERNATURAL

VIKING FUND
PUBLICATIONS IN ANTHROPOLOGY
Number Twenty-Two

STUDIES IN CHEREMIS: THE SUPERNATURAL

THOMAS A. SEBEOK
and
FRANCES J. INGEMANN

New York · 1956
Published by
WENNER-GREN FOUNDATION FOR ANTHROPOLOGICAL RESEARCH, INCORPORATED

A. IRVING HALLOWELL

Editor

"The only legitimate mode of approach will then correspond to the modern linguist's: considering each religion from the point of view of its votaries, let us ascertain what are their concepts of the Supernatural, how they are interrelated and weighted with reference to one another."

ROBERT H. LOWIE, *Primitive Religion,* p. xviii.

This monograph is Volume 2 of a series, *Studies in Cheremis*. Other volumes, published or in press, include: Volume 1, by Sebeok and others, *Studies in Cheremis Folklore*, Indiana University Publications, Folklore Series, Number 6, 1952; Volume 3, by Sebeok and Alo Raun, *The 1775 Cheremis Grammar*, The Newberry Library, 1955; Volume 4, by Eeva K. Minn, *Derivation*, Publication Two, Indiana University Research Center in Anthropology, Folklore and Linguistics, 1956; and Volume 5, by Sebeok, *The Cheremis*, Human Relations Area Files, Inc., Subcontractor's Monograph HRAF-2 Indiana-2, 1955.

PREFACE

THE development of the Cheremis project through the end of 1949 was sketched in the Preface to the first volume of this series, and the task there begun was brought up to 1952 in an article published that year in the *Journal of American Folklore.*

In February 1952, Iwan Jewskij, a native speaker of Cheremis, landed in the United States, and we were immediately put in touch with him through the kind offices of Gerald F. P. Dooher, then Chief of the Soviet East and Transcaucasian Section of the International Broadcasting Service in the Department of State. With the aid of a substantial grant from the Overhead Fund, Research Division of Indiana University—here gratefully acknowledged—it became possible later in the spring of that year to bring Mr. Jewskij to our campus where he has been available as an informant continuously since then. Mr. Jewskij is undoubtedly the first member of his culture and the first native speaker of his language ever to have come to America, a fact which immediately gave our project new direction. Our expectation from this unique happening was evidently shared by the U. S. Air Force, at least to the extent of their awarding us Contract No. 01(600)–314, for the preparation of a monograph, completed in June 1953, entitled, "Ethnic and Area Analysis of Mari U.S.S.R." It is a pleasure in this connection to acknowledge the co-operation of Paul H. Nesbitt, Chief; Deric O'Bryan, Chief of the Arctic Section, and Moreau S. Maxwell, Research and Editorial Specialist of the Arctic, Desert, Tropic Information Center of the Research Studies Institute, Maxwell Air Force Base.

During the first semester of the 1953–1954 academic year, the senior author was Visiting Research Professor in the Department of Anthropology of the University of New Mexico. W. W. Hill and Stanley S. Newman made working conditions perfect, and our appreciation for the many courtesies extended, as well as for the climate—intellectual and other—is boundless.

Completion of this second volume became possible with the support of the American Philosophical Society, for which we wish to express our thanks.

We are indebted to Felix J. Oinas, of our Department of Slavic Studies, for the note on the Russian etymologies used in Appendix A. We are grateful to Eeva Kangasmaa Minn both for her help in connection with the secondary Finnish sources of this book, and her advice on several portions of the manuscript. Nicholas Michailov-Shelly assisted with translations and abstracts of secondary sources from Russian, and interpreted for Mr. Jewskij who, when we first met him, spoke, beside his native tongue, only Tatar and Russian adequate for our purpose. Alo Raun, of the Linguistics group at Indiana University, was good enough to call some additional Soviet sources to our attention and to advise us with respect to occasional problems involving Turkic contacts. Teresa Carterette elicited and helped organize a part of the materials used in the Introduction, and we most gratefully record her valued collaboration.

Erkki Itkonen, Secretary of the Finno-Ugric Society, granted us the privilege of reproducing illustrations from a work of A. O. Heikel, previously published by that society.

Some of the materials in Part Two of this book were reworked from articles originally published in the *Southwestern Journal of Anthropology,* vol. 6 (1950), and *Anthropos,* vol. 48 (1953), respectively. To Leslie Spier, Editor of the former, and to Fritz Bornemann, Editor of the latter journal, we are beholden for permission for the use of some of these materials here. Louis H. Orzack collaborated on the first version of the section on "Content" in the Chapter "Charms." Portions of Part Two were read in manuscript by John Lotz and Fred W. Householder, Jr., for whose constructive criticisms we are extremely grateful.

Part Three was read in manuscript by the late Ralph Linton, who made a number of suggestions, now incorporated in the final version. We are sorry that he will not be reading these lines of appreciation for his kindness.

Our Gazetteer was prepared in close consultation with Lois S. Headings, a former Librarian of the Department of Geography, at Indiana University. Readers who would care to examine a map delineating the general area inhabited by the Cheremis, may find one in our *Studies in Cheremis Folklore,* Vol. 1. In the present volume, we chose to pinpoint geographic features by providing our readers with precise coordinates by means of which any particular location can be found when the coordinates are superimposed upon a detailed map of the Soviet Union. Among the reasons for using this method of presentation was our wish, first, to provide historical depth—and it is a well-known fact that place names in Russia have a way of changing with disturbing frequency: for example, the principal, and now capital city of the Cheremis has itself undergone three name changes within this century alone, having been called Tsarevokokshaisk until 1918, Krasnokokshaisk from 1918 through 1929, and Yoshkar-Ola since 1929. Second, a given place is not infrequently referred to in the literature by entirely different names in Russian, in Cheremis, and in a variety of Turkic languages. Problems of transcription were still a further complicating factor here. These difficulties, added to the more general problems of charting these fairly remote areas of Russia, persuaded us that we could be of greatest service to our readers by supplying our references, based on rather specialized research, by way of an exact Gazetteer instead of projecting them onto a crowded and therefore confusing map.

These studies of the folktale, the proverb, the riddle, and the supernatural elements in Cheremis culture having now appeared, the next volume, partially completed, will center upon the folksongs and games of this people. It will include analyses of the formal structure and content of the song texts, as well as an examination of the musical style and musical instruments. Other publications under preparation will contain our texts, and a phonology and grammar of the Cheremis language.

This book owes much to the creative editing of A. Irving and Maude F. Hallowell, who, by some magic alchemy, have succeeded in converting a manuscript replete with problems of typography, cross referencing, indexing, and the like, into this published form.

This book having been already planned in 1949, it would be untrue to say that it would not have been feasible for us to write it, in some sense, without our informant. However, with Mr. Jewskij's help, it became possible not only to check every piece of information available from other sources, thereby insuring its accuracy and bringing it up to date wherever possible, but it also became possible to add new parts to the whole and to supply a sounder perspective of the religious life of the Cheremis. We thank him for his patient cooperation cheerfully tendered in spite of frequent and perhaps just complaints that work with the head is almost unbearably fatiguing as opposed to work with the hands.

THOMAS A. SEBEOK
FRANCES J. INGEMANN

Albuquerque, N. M.
Christmas, 1953.

CONTENTS

ILLUSTRATIONS

TEXT FIGURES

13

ABBREVIATIONS

B	BEKE, 1931; Be—BEKE, 1939; Bj—BEKE, 1937; Bk—BEKE, 1951a; Bu—BEKE, 1938
G	GENETZ
H	HARVA (OR HOLMBERG)
Häm	HÄMÄLÄINEN
J	JEWSKIJ
L	LEWY
P	PAASONEN
PG	PORKKA
R	RAMSTEDT
S	SMIRNOV
Sz	SZILASI
Uj, Up, Ucj; FB, FT, S	Unpublished texts; Folk Beliefs, Folk Tales, Superstitions (see Sebeok, 1952, p. 6)
V	VASILJEV, 1926
W, Wj, Wju, Wm, Wt, Wu	WICHMANN, 1931 (see Sebeok, 1952, pp. 4–5)

INTRODUCTION

SOURCES

DATA for the encyclopedic sections, in Part One, and for the description of the "Big Candle" movement in Part Three of this monograph came from three sources. All available studies of aspects of Cheremis religious life were scanned and excerpted. Likewise, all available texts, whether published or unpublished, were read and abstracted. Then the informant told us of his experiences with supernatural elements of his culture. This he did partly by giving us texts, at random; partly by commenting upon and giving free associations to the data obtained from written sources and presented to him systematically; and partly by responding to miscellaneous direct questions. Only a minor proportion of the texts analyzed in Part Two of this book was, however, elicited from him. Thus, whatever the merits of Nadel's generalization—"working through 'appointed' informants is an auxiliary operation, and sometimes a control, but never the sole or main line of attack"[1]—may be, in our particular case of studying culture at a distance it was adopted through sheer necessity.

PRIMARY SOURCES

TEXTS

The catalogue of the texts used, with a description of their scope and provenience, appeared in Sebeok (1952, pp. 3–6); followed by Sebeok, Balys, Roberts and Taylor (1952, pp. 167ff.). For convenience, each reference is repeated in the Bibliography of this volume as well, and each code letter or combination is listed again among the Abbreviations.

One small group of texts not utilized in the preparation of the previous volume (but listed in the Bibliography there), must be added here, as we intend to return to it in Part Two: [Bud] Budenz, Jószef. *Erdei cseremiszség. Mondat- és szövegközlés* [The Forest Cheremis. Sentences and Texts]. Nyk 3.97–156 (1864). Of the three parts of this publication, the first is irrelevant for our purposes. The second consists of two sermons—one preached on Easter Day, the other after Holy Communion—both rendered from Russian into Cheremis by an unknown translator from the district of Tsarevokokshaisk, and found by Budenz among the manuscripts left by Antal Reguly, a pioneer explorer of the Finno-Ugric peoples

---

[1] Nadel, p. 36.

of Russia, whose early nineteenth century collections were a great incentive for Finno-Ugric studies in Hungary.[2] The third is a single text, a Cheremis prayer, found by Budenz among the letters of a Madame Alexandra Fuks, which dealt with the Chuvash and the Cheremis peoples and which was published in Kazan in 1840.[3]

THE INFORMANT AND HIS BACKGROUND

Our informant, Mr. Iwan Jewskij, was born in 1919, and raised in Apšat-jal, a Cheremis village located approximately ten kilometers from the Balayev government mill between Birsk and Burayevo in the Bashkir Autonomous Soviet Socialist Republic. Although the Cheremis do not constitute a majority in the population of the Bashkir A.S.S.R., the informant's birthplace was inhabited almost exclusively by Cheremis. In the Bashkir A.S.S.R., there are about 85,000 Cheremis in the area between 55° to 56° north and 55° to 57° east, with more in the Mishkino region than near Birsk. Near Ufa there are four or five villages, and the number decreases as one approaches the Ural mountains. To the west of Birsk, there are several Cheremis villages, but there are probably none from Birsk to the Balaiev government mill. Along the northern side of the Bir River there are more Cheremis villages than on the right bank where there are two or three of fifty to seventy houses each, some about ten kilometers from Balayev, including Apšat-jal. Most Cheremis live between the Volga and Vyatka Rivers to the northeast and northwest of the Volga bend, though a small remnant still exists on the right bank of the Volga where most of them were located formerly. Fifty-one and four-tenths per cent of the population of Mari A.S.S.R., the area situated between 55° 35′ to 57° 20′ north and 45° 35′ to 50° 15′ east, is Cheremis. There are also about 20,000 in the Tartar A.S.S.R., and about 41,000 inhabit various parts of the Ural region. The total number of Cheremis thus is in the neighborhood of half a million.

The informant's recollections of the city of Birsk—in the vicinity of which he was born—and its environs are summarized in the following paragraphs. The city of Birsk, which is a river port, is the center of the Birsk district in the Bashkir A.S.S.R. on the Belaya River. Buildings have been constructed for processing local

[2] Reguly settled in St. Petersburg, in 1841, and, after intensive study of source materials relating to the Finno-Ugric peoples of Russia, including the Cheremis, visited the Volga-Finnic peoples briefly, in 1843, en route to the Voguls and Ostyaks, intending to return to the Volga regions from Siberia for more intensive studies on his way back west. In 1845, he returned to Kazan, where, though confined to bed much of the time by serious illness, he collected Cheremis materials. In 1846, he returned to St. Petersburg where he made plans, before his total collapse, to publish an extensive series of books based on his field trip; but it remained for Budenz to publish Reguly's materials in the collection cited above. Cf. Zsirai.

[3] Fuks, pp. 209–217. Madame Fuks, who died in Kazan in 1853, was a writer of miscellaneous prose and verse. Her interest in ethnography was fostered by her husband, the well-known writer and historian, K. F. Fuks. For further details about Madame Fuks, see Agafonov, p. 242. On the prayer text, see further pp. 306–7, below.

agricultural and forest raw materials, that is, for flour milling, meat processing, and saw milling. There is a teachers' institute, a pedagogical school, and two medical schools. Birsk is famed for her gardens; and in the surrounding area of the city there are agricultural testing fields. The region has the principal vineyards in the Bashkir A.S.S.R.

There is in Birsk an old two-story brick hospital with even rows of windows. A brick kiln about six hundred feet from the Belaya River produces bricks from the local red clay. Toward the south margin of the town, near the wharfs, there are fifty or more grain elevators. There is a brewery that processes and bottles vodka. The MTS (tractor station) in Birsk, which supplies farm machines for the surrounding area, had, during the informant's youth, about thirty combines and tractors and numerous pick-up and heavier trucks for transporting grain or supplies. Gasoline, kerosene, and lube-oils in steel drums are all brought to the *kolkhoz* by truck. Near the corner of Kazarma Street and Lenin Street there is a soldiers' barracks on a hill to the south of town. The red brick barracks has an enclosed drill yard and appears to be quite old. The informant does not remember seeing any great number of soldiers or any open transport of munitions in Birsk.

The Bir River is navigable only near its mouth where it empties into the Beloi River above the town of Birsk. The town stands on high ground which gradually slopes to the east. On both sides of the Bir there is meadowland for about a third of a mile. It is possible to travel by launch (a twenty-foot craft with a twelve-inch draft and five- to seven-foot beam) for a distance of six to nine miles. At this point one reaches a large two-story brick and sheet-iron roof building, the Balaiev government mill. Beyond this point, the hills are about a third of a mile from the river banks and are separated by valleys of three to ten miles. The Balaiev mill is comparable to a fair-sized factory. As one faces the mill from the road there is a barracks on the left side. This barracks, an unpainted, yellowish-white, weathered structure, is for workers, since five or six families live at the mill. There are many poplars around the mill. Wherever there is a mill there is also a bridge—or, usually two in case one should collapse during the spring floods. Beyond Balaiev there are three or four more mills; but these are attached to the *kolkhoz* and are much smaller.

Opposite the mill a forest comes almost to the river's edge. From Birsk to the first mill there is meadowland with very few swamps; and on the right side as one goes upstream, there is a forest of oak, birch, maple, and a few pine. There are some swamps in this forest, but none is of any great extent. Soon after leaving the first mill, the Bir narrows into a sluggish stream which may be stepped over in some places. There is red clay along the banks, gray forest soil on the hill ridges, and black chestnut soil in the valley bottoms. Because of the rich soil and gentle land roll, grain is the principal product.

The Bir, Ufa, and Belaya Rivers freeze about December first and thaw in late March or April. During the freeze the ice is more than three feet thick, and the rivers are employed as roads. After March, one is not allowed to cross the ice with horses. There is a saying that if the wild ducks are still swimming in places in the river, it is not safe for transport or communication. Along the right side of the river going to the Balayev mill from Birsk, there is a road. The government mill is the only mill in the area which has electric power and a telephone. Approaching the mill the road is illuminated on both sides for a quarter of a mile. At the Balaiev mill the road then crosses a single lane wooden bridge. This road goes to Burayevo, a Tatar settlement. It is paved with fist-sized gravel, and, since it is old, it is constantly being repaired. Small trucks carry grain and supplies over it a great deal; the bus from Birsk to Burayevo also travels over it. In addition, three buses traverse this crooked road daily. Along the road there are also telegraph poles and wires connecting Birsk with Burayevo.

A mile away from the government mill the Burayevo road goes through a Russian village. Along this road, as in the case of others in the area, there are few trees and bushes. Most of the land, except where the road passes through woods, is cultivated in grains. On the main road between Birsk and Burayevo, there are more Cheremis villages after it crosses the Bir at Balayev mill than there are on the right side. Along the road toward Burai, there are on the right side two or three Cheremis villages of fifty to seventy houses each. At the Balayev mill there are three or four uniformed policemen who carry pistols and rifles and travel on horseback. The soil of this area as a whole is very soft, and people do not drive a heavy truck out onto the fields lest it become mired. In the forests there are few pines but many aspen, maple, birch and oak on the highlands.

Mr. Jewskij's impressionistic account of the physical appearance of the men and women of his community is this: Most men are taller than he (five feet six inches), but some are as much as three to four inches shorter. Ten percent are muscular; the rest are of average weight, like the informant. Those who are tall are "dry," i.e., lean. Women are shorter than men, approximately five feet two inches tall. They are heavy and thickset. The skin color of the men is not clear white. Women have lighter complexions than men; but that is "because they wash more frequently." Hair is mostly brown; and more people are blonde than red haired. Very few people have black hair. Men shave every two to three days. Unlike the Russians, almost no one, except old men, grows a beard; but married men grow fairly large mustaches. Most married women wear their hair down the back in two waist-long braids woven from three to four strands of hair with red, blue or green ribbons. Married women roll their braids into a bun worn at the nape of the neck. Many women have their ears pierced for earrings.

According to Coon[4]—though, admittedly, observations of statistical value which describe the Cheremis are scarce—while these people "preserve their original

---

[4] Coon, pp. 345–47. Detailed anthropometric measurements of Mr. Jewskij will be published elsewhere. Here it may be noted, however, that, on basis of Coon's data, except for his fine hair texture, Mr. Jewskij is a very typical specimen of his group.

Finnic type with considerable fidelity, the infiltration of Mongol and Tatar peoples into their country since the time that the ancestors of the Carelians and other western tribes departed has had some recognizable effect upon them." Coon concludes that the Cheremis deviate but little, anthropometrically, from the standard established by his study of the Carelians, except in pigmentation and soft part morphology.

The everyday work clothes of the men in Mr. Jewskij's community are made of thick homespun white linen. Some shirts are made of checkered homespun, dyed by the women with commercial or domestic dyes. Homemade dyes are manufactured from tree bark: a dark yellow is produced from alder; a dark blue, from oak; green, from a grass he could not name. Red dye is always purchased. Unless a man is wearing a jacket, the shirt always hangs out and is bound with a belt. The collar is round and the sleeves are usually long. The neck opening down the front is fastened with buttons which go almost to the waist. Embroidery, designed by the woman who does the sewing, includes roosters, butterflies, and flowers; and it is used to decorate the front of the shirt on the left side of the neck opening and the tight shirtcuffs.[5] This shirt is used in all seasons, but in summer it may be made of calico.

Winter trousers may be of heavy homespun or purchased quilted material. Colors used include white, grey, light grey, and greenish shades. Some black and a little yellow is used but no red or other bright colors. Summer trousers are home sewn from purchased chintz or homespun linen which may be a solid color or thinly striped but not checkered. The colors include white or greyish stripes on a black background.

In winter, during the warmer weather, men wear a wool tweed-like visored cap. During the colder months of December, January, and February they wear a sheepskin cap with earflaps which may be tied under the chin. Men wear the woolen cap at home all the time. Summer hats, made of straw, have narrow brims and flattened crowns. Cotton visored caps are worn a great deal.

In very cold weather the men use thick felt boots without socks, or they bind their feet and calves with linen or cotton binding and over this wear white homemade woolen socks and woven bast shoes. Knee-high leather boots are used in spring and autumn. These are purchased in town because the *kolkhoz* cobblers usually cannot do this sort of work. For milder winter weather a thinner felt boot is used with or without a rubber boot. These lighter boots are also worn in spring and autumn. Summer footwear consists of brown or yellow leather sandals made by the *kolkhoz* cobbler or woven bast shoes worn over linen strips, bound ankle height. During the muddy spring season ankle-height galoshes are worn over the thin felt boot or the linen binding.

A fur coat, usually of sheepskin, with the fur inside or out, is worn in a cut

---

[5] On Cheremis embroidery patterns, cf. Heikel, 1910–1915.

just above the knees; and a hip length padded coat made of cotton cloth batting is added on the coldest days. Both men and women use the sheepskin coats, but the women's coats are usually covered with a strong, dark fabric.

The women, he tells us, wear long dresses of checkered homespun linen in winter and chintz in summer. The neck opening is fastened with buttons which go down to the waist, and a reddish ribbon with tassels at the ends serves as a belt. Their shoes are of soft thin leather with a small heel. The women do not bind their legs. Sometimes they wear thick felt boots with socks. In spring they use the same footgear as the men but without the binding; and in the summer they wear sandals or bast shoes and work barefooted, something which the men never do. Women's headgear consists of woolen kerchiefs or shawls which are not worn very much during the summer.[6]

Men and women, alike, dress in white for prayer meetings. For holidays, men wear western style coatsuits which they have made by a tailor.

The informant, who was born into a family of farmers—he had one brother and one sister—has learned two trades, that of baker and that of barber. During the war, the Russians drafted him into a labor battalion and late in the war he was captured by the Germans. Eventually, the camp in which he was held came to be in the American Zone, and he elected to come to the United States as a displaced person. He arrived early in 1952 and, after a few months spent in a factory in Newark, New Jersey, came to Indiana University where he has now enrolled to study English. Mr. Jewskij, besides his native language, speaks Tatar best, and has spoken it since his childhood. His Russian is adequate but distinctly "foreign," his English poor. He was, on arrival, practically illiterate, though he had some slight practice in reading and writing Russian. He is a young man of a good deal of intelligence and wit, as well as shrewdness, but he was haunted by considerable, not

---

[6] The standard study of feminine garments among the Cheremis is to be found in Part One of Julie Wichmann. Cf. also Pokshishevskiĭ, pp. 64–65: "The national costumes of the Mari, especially those of the women, are very lovely. One can see these clothes even now in every village, although life under the Soviets has brought many changes. The classic Mari costume is a dress of bleached linen. Wonderful embroidery decorates the collar, the long sleeves, the shoulders, and the hem (of the skirt). Often the dress is knee length, and below this is sewn a wide embroidered, red or other colored, strip of bunting; the hem is sewn with home-made lace. Over the dress very often an apron is worn made either of the same carefully bleached linen or from some dark colored material. In the lovely individual embroidery one often sees the stylized fir branch, or leaves and flowers, or plain stripes, and a multitude of geometric designs. Red is the predominant color in the embroidery, and is contrasted with black and green. The Mari women wear a smooth white kerchief, tied under the chin. On their feet they wear thick wool socks, often colored; sometimes red. . . . Earlier, a cloth had been wrapped around the feet and was used instead of the socks before putting on bast shoes. Now, of course, everyone has boots and shoes. One cannot admire fully enough the pretty scene when there is a *kolkhoz* holiday, and all the young girls dance to the music of the dulcimer in their white, embroidered dresses and the men in white, embroidered shirts."

to say abnormal, fear of strangers and new situations, to which he reacted characteristically by wringing his hands, fidgeting, and sweating profusely. He was reticent in the extreme, and especially shy of giving information about his life and history. In brief, he saw police agents everywhere and refused to talk until reassured on this point since he expected reprisals upon his family and himself. ("Jewskij" is the name he adopted and it is not, of course, his own.) Correlated with this form of disorientation and all its attendant anxieties is a high degree of economic insecurity manifested by frequent and apparently insatiable demands for a higher rate of pay, by complaints that he is not saving enough money for future use, and by an often expressed desire for much lower living standards than any available in a University dormitory or indeed in a town. The informant has remained single all his life and is exceptionally awkward with American women. However, his adjustment to life in America seems to be satisfactory in other respects.

If we should attempt to place Mr. Jewskij among the three types of individuals arranged by Paul Radin in the order of their religious intensity, "the truly religious, the intermittently religious, and the indifferently religious," we should be inclined to assign him among the second type. Now Radin adds that "the intermittently religious really fall into two groups—those who may be weakly religious at almost any moment; and those who may be strongly religious at certain moments, such as temperamental upheavals and crises"—and Mr. Jewskij seems clearly to be an individual who is weakly religious at almost any moment. Radin further asserts that "in the intermittently and indifferently religious groups are included by far the large majority of people, but since so many extra-religious factors enter into their religious consciousness, they are actually the most poorly adapted for the study of religion. . . . The only way of avoiding confusion is to start [the analysis of a primitive religion] with the markedly religious individual and then study the expressions of religion among the intermittently and indifferently religious with reference to him."[7] We recognize that our informant is not possessed by a marked degree of religious susceptibility and we tried to minimize the confusion to which Radin points by a careful and systematic collation of our primary and secondary sources.

SECONDARY SOURCES

The secondary sources used are listed in the Bibliography under "Sources for the Text." The more important of them were commented upon in Sebeok (1952, p. 7); these include, most prominently, the works of Uno Harva (Holmberg) and Albert Hämäläinen. Any author attempting to write a book on Cheremis religion must inevitably draw deeply upon Harva's work. In addition to his extensive and intensive study of the written sources, Harva based his publications on this subject upon his field notes, collected in the course of his sojourn among

[7] Radin, 1937, pp. 9–10.

this people for two summers, 1911 and 1913. Another Finnish ethnographer, Hämäläinen, was quite probably the last western anthropologist to study Cheremis religion in the field, shortly after the turn of the century. He stayed, first, in the village of Ruš-roda, in the district of Tsarevokokshaisk, investigating marriage ceremonies, agriculture and apiculture, as well as sacrifice rituals. He reported to the Finno-Ugric Society: "I had time to study thoroughly the individual sacrifices to the high or heavenly gods (*buj ümbal jumə, küšəl tülə*). It is considered necessary for each individual to perform four series of sacrifices to *küšəl tülə*, the first of which has to be performed when the young man has grown up and begins to live the life of an independent adult. With the help of some educated Cheremis I succeeded before long in getting some personal acquaintances in the village, so that I was in no way hampered in my investigations. I worked in a barn where the Cheremis used to gather to chatter; with their remarks and additions they, in a way, participated in my work."[8]

THE HISTORICAL BACKGROUND

In the latter half of the fifteenth century, there already were Cheremis living around the Vyatka River. Their villages were robbed by the Voivodes of the Grand Duke Ivan III (1462–1505), in 1468, when passing down the Vyatka to the Kama. In the sixteenth and seventeenth centuries there were Cheremis living on the mountainous south side of the Volga and eastwards to the Sviyaga River, evidence for which comes from both historical data and the study of place names. When the Volga Bulgarian Empire was overthrown by the Tatars under Batu Khan, in 1236–37, the Cheremis came under their rule. The strong influence of Tatar culture is clearly illustrated by the numerous Tatar loanwords in the Cheremis language.[9] Tatar influence left its traces especially on handicraft, dress, housebuilding, food, social conditions, and, in some regions, on religion, although the Tatars were exceptionally tolerant in religious matters.[10] (The information in Nestor's chronicle about the Cheremis being under tribute to Rus might refer to some western Cheremis tribe.)

In the fourteenth century, the Cheremis began to be more closely connected with the Russians, who were mostly represented by the principality of Nizhni-Novgorod in the west, and the republic of Vyatka in the north. In the area of the province of Kostroma, the Cheremis at that time probably came under the influence of Russian settlements. At the same time they took part in the fights between the Russian princes of Kostroma and the rich city of Galich, northeast of Kostroma beyond the Volga, as allies of the latter. But in the long conflict between the Tatars and the Russians they faithfully remained on the side of the Tatars and with them bravely fought the over-powering Russians during three centuries.

[8] Hämäläinen, 1908 b.
[9] Sebeok, 1952, p. 2, and note 4.
[10] Platanov, p. 76; and note 3 on p. 332 below.

Under Tatar rule, the Cheremis still had their own princes. Duties to the Tatars consisted of paying tribute (*yasak*) and other taxes, and helping them in the war. Thus the Cheremis, in 1455, sent supposedly 30,000 infantry soldiers against the Russians. Early in the next century they fought the Russians from the fortress they had built outside Kazan and often fought back the assaulting Voivodes.[11] In 1530, for example, they caused Prince Fedor Obolensky-Lopata to

[11] The following passages from the important mid-sixteenth century work of Herberstein bearing upon the Cheremis appeared worth quoting rather fully: "Lower Novogorod is a large wood-built city, situated on a rock at the confluence of the Volga and the Occa, with a stone fortification, built by the present monarch, Vasiley. They say that it is forty German miles east from Murom; and if so, Novogorod will be a hundred miles from Moscow. The country equals Vladimir in fertility and abundance. It forms the boundary, in this direction, of the Christian religion; for although the Prince of Muscovy has beyond this Novogorod a fortress named Sura, yet the intermediate people, who are called Czeremissi, do not follow the Christian, but the Mahometan religion. Moreover, there are other people, called Mordwa, mixed with the Czeremissi, who occupy a great part of the country this side of the Volga, as far as Sura. The Czeremissi live northwards beyond the Volga, and to make a distinction from them, those that live above Novogorod are called Upper or Mountain Czeremissi; not, indeed, from any mountains, for there are none, but rather from the hills which they inhabit." [Herberstein, vol. 2, p. 8.]

"The province of Viatka lies beyond the river Kama, at a distance of nearly a hundred and fifty miles southeast of Moscow; the shortest road to which is by Castromovgorod and Galitz; but this road is the most difficult, not only on account of the marshes and forests which lie between Galitz and Viatka, but on account of the tribes of Czeremisse, which rove about in search of plunder. Hence the road by Vologda and Ustyug, though longer, presents greater facilities and security for traveling." [*Ibid.,* vol. 2, pp. 44–45.]

"The people of Czeremissi dwell in the woods below Lower Novogorod. They have their own dialect, and follow the tenets of Mahomet. They are now subservient to the King of Kazan, although the greatest part of them were formerly tributaries of the Duke of Muscovy, whence they are still reckoned as Russian subjects. The prince had several of these people brought to Moscow on suspicion of rebellion, whom I saw when I was there; but as they were afterwards sent back to the borders toward Lithuania, they at length dispersed themselves into various parts. These people, who have no fixed abodes, inhabit a region stretching far and wide, from Viatka and Vologda as far as the river Kama. All of them, both men and women, are exceedingly swift in running, and very skillful archers, never laying down the bow out of their hands; and so great is the delight which they take in this exercise, that they will not give their children food until they hit a mark with their arrows." [*Ibid.,* pp. 47–48.]

"But on the twenty-eighth day of the same month [July 1523] he crossed the Volga, at that point where the fortress lay, and encamped with his army on the river Kazanca, and waited twenty days for a favorable opportunity of accomplishing his object. While stationed there, the *Regulus* of the Kazan army pitched his tent not far from him, and often annoyed the Russians, though fruitlessly, with skirmishes of Czeremissian infantry. Upon this, King Scheale, who had come with his vessels to engage in that way, sent letters to him to demand his surrender to his hereditary sovereign. To which the latter briefly replied: 'If you wish to have my kingdom, take it by the sword; let us settle it between ourselves, and let him to whom fortune gives it, hold it.'

"While the Russians thus uselessly delayed, they began to suffer hunger from having

lose his entire transport and seventy cannons. But after Ivan the Terrible had become Prince of Moscow (1533–1588), things turned against the Cheremis. As the Tatar rule was getting weaker and weaker because of internal quarrels, the Cheremis who lived south of the Volga, the so-called Mountain Cheremis, thought it wiser to begin making alliances with their western neighbor. They sent deputies to Moscow in 1546, explaining that they would be ready to help the Russians against the Tatars. Ivan the Terrible immediately sent Prince Alexander Gorbatyj to the Mountain Cheremis, who delivered to him one hundred hostages as pledge for their loyalty. But the so-called Meadow Cheremis north of the Volga remained

---

sent away the provisions which they had brought with them; for as the Czeremissi had laid waste all the surrounding territory, and diligently watched the track of the enemy, there was nothing left to be seized upon; so that the prince was unable to gain information respecting the scarcity which oppressed his army, nor could they make any communication to him. Two governors had been appointed by Vasiley to attend to this business, one of whom, the Knes Ivan Palitzki, after loading the vessels with provisions from Novogorod, had to descend the river to join the army; but he, after depositing the provisions, returned home rather precipitately, considering the existing state of affairs. The other had been sent for the same purpose with five hundred soldiers over land, but was slaughtered with his men by the Czeremissi, into whose hands he fell, scarcely nine of them escaping by flight amidst the confusion. The governor himself, being severely wounded, fell three days after into the hands of the enemy and died. When the rumour of this slaughter reached the army, so great a consternation arose in the camp, increased by a groundless report that the whole cavalry were slain to a man, that nothing was thought of but flight; and though all were agreed on this point, the only subject of doubt was whether they should return against the tide, which was very difficult, or wait to descend the river then the time served, so as to enable them to reach other rivers, from which they might afterwards return home by a circuitous land journey.

"During these consultations, the army meanwhile suffering under extreme famine, the nine men whom I have described as escaping from the slaughter of the five hundred, happened to arrive, and announced that Ivan Palitzki was come with provisions; but although the latter had hastened his journey, he had had the misfortune to lose the greater part of his vessels, and had but few remaining when he reached the camp. For, being weary with his daily labour, he had laid up one night to rest himself on the shore of the Volga, but was hailed by the Czeremissi, who came upon him with great clamour, inquiring who sailed by that way; they were answered by the servants of Palitzki, who took them for servants a-ship-board, and with much abuse threatened them with stripes on the following day for disturbing their master's sleep with their unreasonable vociferations. The Czeremissi replied: 'You and we shall have other business to attend to tomorrow.' . . . before the sun was up, and while the entire bank of the river was covered with a thick fog, the Czeremissi made a sudden attack upon the ships, and threw such terror amongst the Russians, that Palitzki, the commander of the fleet, left ninety of his largest vessels, and loosing his vessel from the shore, and taking the Volga in midstream, escaped under cover of the mist, and reached the army almost in a state of nudity. A similar misfortune afterwards occurred to him in returning with several vessels in his train, when he again fell into the snares of the Czeremissi, and not only lost his vessels, but himself escaped only with great difficulty, and with very few of his men." [Ibid., pp. 68–70.]

allies of the Tatars and successfully fought the Russian armies pressing on Kazan from the direction of Galichi. It was not until Kazan had fallen in 1552 that the Meadow Cheremis were brought to acknowledge the Moscovian rule. Enormous tracts of fertile land on the Volga and Kama were now opened up to Russian colonization. The first triumph of Christianity over Islam had been achieved.

The Russians immediately began to tax the Cheremis and Votyaks heavily, trying to convert them to Christianity and usurping their lands. The result was that these related tribes made an alliance in 1553; refusing to pay taxes, they rose to fight against Moscow for their liberty. The rebellion was not subdued until 1557. By 1572, the Cheremis had begun a new rebellion hoping for help from the Tatar Khan of Crimea, but, as no help arrived, the rebels had to put down their arms. Of longer duration was the attempt of 1582, which the Russian Voivodes in Kazan were not able to subdue; they had to ask for troops from Moscow which had to occupy the Cheremis area anew step by step. Now the Russians built several fortresses in the Cheremis area (Koz'modem'yansk, Cheboksary, Yaransk, Malmyzh, Kokshayskoye, Sanchursk, Urzhum and, the farthest, Ufa), and used them to subdue easily the rebellion of 1592. During the troubled first decade of the seventeenth century, characterized by famine and highway robbery under Boris Godunov, the western Meadow Cheremis joined in support of the second Pseudo-Dimitri in 1609; the easternmost Meadow Cheremis however remained loyal to Vasilij Shuiskij. In 1611, there were Cheremis among the recruits that were being gathered to free Moscow from the Poles.

During the seventeenth century, the Cheremis began to accept the Moscovian supremacy. On behalf of the Russian rule they acted as guards far east in the Bashkir territory; these soldiers, and the Cheremis escaping from heavy taxes, were the founders of the Cheremis colonies in the provinces of Perm and Ufa.

In the Golden Horde, the Mongols had constituted a small minority, and the "numerical preponderance of the Turks made it natural that the Mongols should be gradually Turkicized, and the Mongol language, even among the ruling classes, gave way to Turkish." These Turks were remnants of the Bulgars and Bashkirs living east of the middle course of the Volga, in the Kama River basin. "On a lower political level than the Turks were the Russians, the Alans, and the Circassians. . . . Tribes of Finno-Ugric extraction like the Cheremissians, the Mordvinians, and the Meshcherians lived in the lower Oka basin. . . ."[12] During the "Tatar" rule, the Cheremis people were divided into several classes: peasants paying the taxes, small landowners doing military service and exempted from taxes (the tarkhans),[13] owners of estates, and princes who were trusted with the immediate rule of the people. During the Russian rule, this division was first preserved, except that the government was taken from the native princes and given to Russian

[12] Vernadsky, pp. 208–9.
[13] Ibid., p. 106, and note 169.

Voivodes. Towards the end of the seventeenth century, the profession of Christianity was made a condition for land ownership, and thus the Cheremis landowners changed religion and became Russianized. The class of the *tarkhans,* doing military service and exempted from taxes, was eliminated in 1718, and its members were included in the big group of taxed peasants, which in its turn had to begin doing military service.[14] Serfdom was extended mainly to the Mountain Cheremis living south of the Volga.

Beginning in the sixteenth century, the Russians tried to convert the Cheremis to Christianity using, under the guidance of the government, all kinds of temptations, especially tax exemption. Towards the middle of the eighteenth century, especially during the reign of Empress Elizabeth (1741–1761), great numbers of the Cheremis changed to Christianity. Before long, however, the material advantages failed to satisfy them. The new Christians were not able to practice freely pagan rituals; they had to support the Russian priests and were compelled by police force to attend church. The pagan population was also dissatisfied, since they were taxed the more heavily the more new Christians received tax exemption. Thus the pagan as well as the Christian Cheremis were ready to take part in Pugachev's rebellion, which started in 1773.[15]

Russian officials also tried from the beginning of the eighteenth century to promote Russianization of the Cheremis through Russian schools. These attempts, however, failed but were resumed with new force towards the middle of the nineteenth century. Russian colonization, however, has proved much more fatal to Cheremis nationality than the Russian Church or Russian schools. The flood of Russian colonization began in the eighteenth century, rose to its height in the nineteenth century, and is still going on. It is most strongly recognizable in the western Cheremis area; eastwards, Russian influence diminishes.

Our information on Cheremis history since the turn of the century is based largely on Soviet sources and the following summary must therefore be interpreted with due caution. According to Russian historians, in the course of the numerous peasant riots of 1905 the best support against the oppression of a certain landlord named Cheremetev and the owners of the leather factories in the Mari region came from the workers' settlement of Yurino. This rebellion was directed by the local Social-Democratic group under the leadership of one Kasatkin. At the end of the 1905 rebellion among the Cheremis peasants, P. A. Stolypin's agrarian reforms strengthened the land holdings among the kulaks (i.e., petty capitalist farmers employing hired labor), and aggravated the class struggle in the Mari region. Before World War I, foreign capital, especially French and English, was invested

[14] ". . . when tribute is regularized into taxation, a tribal people is on the way to becoming peasantry." (Redfield, p. 32.)

[15] Emelyan Pugachev was a Russian Cossack whose formidable revolt in East Russia ended (he having been captured by Suvorov) in his execution in Moscow in 1775.

in the lumber industry, and the competition between Russian and foreign capital "intensified the exploitation of the workers." Class conflict in town and village was sharpened by World War I. After the revolution of February, 1917, the national liberation movement, which at the beginning was headed by the "nationalistic counter-revolutionary intelligentsia,"[16] expanded. In accord with the interests of the Mari kulaks, steps were taken to support the Provisional Government.

The First All Russian Mari Convention was held in Birsk, Bashkir A.S.S.R., from June 5 to 25, 1917,[17] and was conducted by the Social Revolutionary intelligentsia. Its resolutions expressed confidence in the Provisional Government, and it directed all its energies to suppressing the peasants' movement. The peasants of the Mari region, however, expressed their dissatisfaction with World War I, and requested the immediate seizure of land belonging to the landowners, the state, and monasteries; the agrarian program of the Bolsheviks had reached the peasants of the Mari region. The bourgeois Socialist Revolutionaries and Mensheviks, who were members of the Committee of Public Safety, voiced approval for crushing the peasant movement with armed force and disapproved the seizure of lands by the peasants. The Workers Soviet, the soldier deputies in Koz'modem'yansk, and the Soviet of Peasant Deputies in Tsarevokokshaisk, because of the predominance of Socialist Revolutionaries and Mensheviks, carried out the same program. Only the Yurinsk Soviet of Soldier Deputies, guided by the Bolshevik Party, obtained the nationalization of the landowners' meadows and forests and divided them among the communities. This gained the confidence of the peasants for the Yurino Soviet of Worker Deputies. On November 7, power came into the hands of the proletariat in Kazan; and under the leadership of the Russian proletariat and its party the Mari peasants defended the conquest of October.

In the spring and summer of 1918, the kulaks in the Mari region, encouraged by the Czech offensive on Kazan, engaged in a series of counter-revolutionary uprisings. (According to Carr, "this period, unlike its predecessor, was marked by vigorous attacks on the Muslim religion and its traditions and practices, partly, no doubt, on ideological grounds, but partly also to destroy the influence of the mullahs, who had often been the backbone of the 'bourgeois' national movement.")[18] In March, 1918, a joint "Tatar-Bashkir Soviet Republic of the Russian

---

[16] Toynbee's definition of "intelligentsia" may be appropriately quoted here: "The intelligentsia is a class of liaison officers who have learnt the tricks of the intrusive civilization's trade so far as may be necessary to enable their own community, through their agency, just to hold its own in a social environment in which life is ceasing to be lived in accordance with the local tradition and is coming more and more to be lived in the style imposed by the intrusive civilization upon the aliens who fall under its dominion" (p. 394).

[17] Dimanshtein, vol. 3, pp. 414–28, is our source for the miscellaneous congresses of the smaller Muslim nationalities of the Volga basin in the summer of 1917. It is interesting to note that each of these congresses has rather a religious than a revolutionary flavor.

[18] Carr, vol. 1, p. 320.

Soviet Federation" was proclaimed, which was to have embraced the Mari as well. This republic never came into being. The Mari kulaks and the nationalistic intelligentsia, hostile to the transfer of power to the proletariat, intensified their anti-Soviet propaganda. In August, Czechoslovak forces seized Kazan; kulaks rose in the Tsarevokokshaisk district. The downfall of Kazan rallied the Tsarevo-kokshaisk bourgeoisie; and the District Soviet, containing a majority of Socialist Revolutionaries, voluntarily turned power over to the bourgeoisie. In the bordering areas of Tsarevokokshaisk, in the Urzhumsk and Yaransk districts, there were also counter-revolutionary bourgeois and kulak uprisings. The Bolshevik organization in Koz'modem'yansk fought tenaciously with the local counter-revolutionaries. In August, a Bolshevik organization was set up in Tsarevokokshaisk. In the battle with the town bourgeoisie and kulaks the First Nizhegorodski and Lettish regiments rendered support to the Mari working class. After the taking of Kazan by the Red Army, the government party and the district committee strengthened the government organs of the dictatorship of the proletariat, intensified the fight with the kulaks, and organized committees of poor peasants. Cells of sympathizers and district committees were formed in the villages. The middle of the road peasants joined the Soviets; and the Soviet machinery was strengthened.

On November 4, 1920, the Mari Autonomous Province was organized. The Mari Autonomous Province was to include the Koz'modem'yansk district of the Nizhegorod province, the Krasnokokshaisk district, and the Vasileva Sloboda district of the Nizhni Novgorod province. On June 21, 1921, the First Consti-tutional Regional Congress of Soviets of the Mari Autonomous Province took place. According to the 1936 Stalin Constitution, the Mari Autonomous Province was reorganized into the Mari Autonomous Soviet Socialist Republic on De-cember 5, 1936.

THE CULTURAL MATRIX
VILLAGE SOCIAL ORGANIZATION

The local group among the Cheremis is the village, ranging in size from large villages of one hundred to two hundred households to small villages of approximately twenty-five households. The informant's birthplace, for example, had a population of seven-hundred persons, representing about seventy nuclear families, each occupying its own house. A village may vary in racial, linguistic, and ethnic composition so that Russians, Chuvash, and Tatars, besides Cheremis, reside in it; or, like the informant's birthplace, a Cheremis village may be near a Tatar village. Almost everyone speaks Russian as well as the language of any immediate neighbors, except that elderly Cheremis people may speak only their native language.

With the establishment of the Soviet form of government a cooperative econ-omy was introduced which organized every village into a *kolkhoz,* a cooperative corporation. While retaining the traditional modes of residence and kinship, the *kolkhoz* organization transformed economic relations within the villages by requiring members to work on the cooperative farm associated with the *kolkhoz*. The term *kolkhoz* refers to the village which is also the economic and administrative unit.

Within the *kolkhoz* the unit of residence and procreation is the nuclear family. While married offspring may reside with the husband's parents, this arrangement ends as soon as the couple can afford a house. Aged parents also live with their grown children, and any person having no family of his own will go to live with his closest kin.

Usually, the married son does not remain in his parents' house very long, since his father may help him establish his own household. Residence, once the couple sets up its own household, is determined by convenience and inclination.

After her marriage, the bride's father presents her with cattle, the number being determined by his generosity. The bridegroom's father may give his son a house, property, or cattle. Girls marry at about seventeen; and almost everyone over twenty-five is married. Because the older people will not allow "blood mixture between close relatives," first and second cousins do not marry each other.

The man is the head of the family, and, on his death, his older brother, married or unmarried, assumes this role. If, however, he is "an evil person," he is turned out. Although he is not required to do so, the older brother may marry the widow.[19] Personal property is inherited by the younger sons or daughters; but if these are not old enough, it goes to the widow. As head of the family, the man controls the money and assigns the economic duties in the household.[20] So long as the son and his wife live with his father, the latter acts as head of his son's family also.

When asked for a general statement concerning kin obligations, the informant replied that good relatives give aid in times of harvest failure, fire, sickness, and death. Brothers behave toward each other as "conscience dictates," helping each other with money, food, and loans. In cases of such misfortunes as fire, sickness, and death, a brother may help a man with a large gift rather than a loan. Sisters, too, behave toward each other according to the dictates of conscience. Even when they do not live in the same *kolkhoz*, sisters visit each other every two weeks or once a month.

The oldest son is responsible for housing and looking after his parents in their old age. Uncles and aunts give presents to small children, and, when nieces and nephews marry, the uncles and aunts from both lines promise them gifts of cattle which have to be delivered anywhere from a week to a year after the ceremony. These cattle may be sold.

According to the informant, a good man is one who does not cheat others,

[19] Cf. Sebeok, 1951.
[20] Cf. Sebeok, 1950 b.

refrains from gossiping, is truthful, does not destroy property when intoxicated, does not swear, and helps the poor. Although people do not fight when sober, they may do so when intoxicated. When he is intoxicated, a man will sometimes strike his wife with his hands, "not a whip." Housebreaking does not occur despite the fact that the doors are left open, but people do steal property left in the house yard and field. Similarly, people will steal from the *kolkhoz*, but they will not break into the granary; nor do people ever steal from the store, ". . . just from the outside. If you can't look after your things, other people will look after them for you." A good woman does not cheat; she says the right things; and, when asked to do something, she gives a proper reply without hedging. She is not promiscuous.

When people pass each other on the road, even strangers exchange greetings such as "good morning" and "good afternoon," depending on the hour. While house doors are not locked, it is customary to knock at the door or window for admission. Since every household has a medium-sized mongrel, it is usually the dog's barking which announces a visitor's arrival. In entering the house, the man precedes and the wife follows. The informant reports that neither children or adults are shy in the presence of strangers, though this seems not to apply to his own case.

After the revolution of 1917, the peasantry were forced to merge their small holdings into the larger *kolkhoz* units. Tractor stations (MTS) were set up in every region to provide the *kolkhoz* with state-owned heavy mechanical equipment and agricultural experts. Operating directly through state-owned collective farms, *sovkhoz,* the Soviet government also brought much land under cultivation.

With the decrees of 1930, kulak land renting and employment of hired labor in individual peasant enterprises were abolished. This same decree provided for wholesale expropriation and deportation of kulaks by decision of the regional executive committee. To protect the *kolkhoz* against plunder and arson by the former kulaks and their supporters, a law of August 7, 1932, introduced extreme sanctions including capital punishment in most serious cases. The decrees of April 2 and 12, 1930, had established the minimum degree of collectivization which a cooperative has to observe in order to insure its members' tax and debt privileges. The labor day as a unit of remuneration was instituted in 1931, and, on May 27, 1939, a decree established the minimum amounts of labor units which every *kolkhoz* member was obliged to perform. Failure to participate in common work was to result in expulsion from the *kolkhoz,* thus depriving the individual of an opportunity to earn a living. While a general management framework is provided by the Model Articles for Agricultural Artels of 1930 and 1935, it will be seen that many issues are left to the individual *kolkhoz's* decision.

An average *kolkhoz,* covers five hundred to six hundred hectares, each person being allotted one and a quarter acres for independent attention.[21] No one is allowed to keep horses or mules, but every person is permitted to keep two cows and other farm animals so long as he is able to care for them as well as for his family.

Members of the *kolkhoz* who are over seventeen to eighteen years of age must work cooperatively on the *kolkhoz* land in groups of thirty to fifty persons with a supervisor, called a brigadier. Except for the harvest season when people work seven days a week, the normal work week is six days with Friday as the holiday. A decision as to the quota which members must produce of each crop is made during the winter meetings of the entire *kolkhoz* membership. The villagers elect three members from their midst; and, under the supervision of the regional agent, these representatives decide each year's quota of production and taxes for the *kolkhoz*. The conflict in the preceeding statements of the informant may to some extent be reconciled by his explanation that in the *kolkhoz* meeting there is one person in the membership who acts in the interests of the regional agent and suggests increases if the quota does not comply with his wishes. The MTS has its own plan for plowing, and the chairman of the *kolkhoz* cannot say when the tractors will come to plow or to harvest. Orchards and gardens are hand sprayed. One can never get permission to use a tractor for oneself; and, in the fall, regional inspectors come to inspect the crops and to determine the anticipated yield. According to the informant, one may transfer from one *kolkhoz* to another or to a *sovkhoz;* but it is only with the greatest difficulty that one may transfer to a factory, since mobility among unskilled and semiskilled laborers is discouraged by the government for reasons of efficiency.

The brigadier, selected by the *kolkhoz* representatives—i.e., the chairman, assistant chairman, and secretary—is an older literate workman of good reputation. If he does not do a good job, he is removed; however, the failure of his group to fulfill the quota does not necessarily lead to his dismissal. In the *kolkhoz* clubhouse there are two blackboards, a red and a black one. The names of members who are considered good workers, that is, have high production standards, appear on the red blackboard; and those of poor workers, on the black. Those workers whose names appear on the latter are subjected to the ridicule of other *kolkhoz* members.

In addition to individual family dwellings, the *kolkhoz* buildings include a general store, a firehouse, a school, a clubhouse, a blacksmith and machine shop, a mill, grain storage bins, a storehouse, and various yards for domestic animals.

The general store is usually in the center of the village. It carries a wide variety of merchandise ranging from aspirin to harnesses, including kerosene, cigarettes, cloth, lamps, matches, needles, and canned fish. The storekeeper is elected from the village and does not have to work in the fields.

[21] For the description of a particular *kolkhoz*, "Smena," of some hundred households, see Pokshishevskiĭ, pp. 62–63.

Every village has a fire brigade charged with the full time job of watching for fires. Two or three men are selected from the village to be trained at special regional schools. Since the firehouse is open twenty-four hours a day, these men do no other work in the *kolkhoz*. The fire fighting equipment consists of a horse-drawn hand pump and water barrels. The firehouse usually has a tall tower. While village fires are frequent, forest fires are fairly rare. In the center of the village, as well as at other appropriate points, such as animal and grain yards, water holes are dug or streams dammed up. Most of the time one does not need

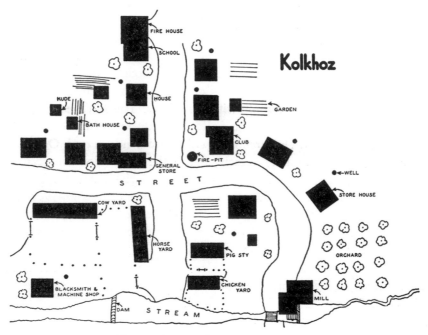

FIG. 1. GROUND PLAN OF *KOLKHOZ*

to dig deeper than six feet before striking water. Fowl swim in these waterholes, though these function mainly as sources of water in case of fires.

There is a four-year school which children may begin at the age of seven. The teacher is sent to the *kolkhoz* by the regional office.

People make it a practice to visit the *kolkhoz* clubhouse and recreation room which is open most of the day. Here they find newspapers (especially *Izvestia*), books, magazines, and musical instruments such as harmonicas, fiddles, gramaphones, and radios. The director of the clubhouse, an elected member, reviews and explains the news to *kolkhoz* members. Movies are shown on hand operated projectors. Dances are held, but card playing is not allowed because it leads to fights. Here, too, policy meetings regarding the *kolkhoz* are held almost every week; and anyone who wishes to attend may do so.

There is a blacksmith shop for shoeing horses and repairing machinery, since the *kolkhoz* may have a three-ton truck, and a quarter-ton truck. The blacksmith, too, is specially trained and is not required to work in the fields. However, the carpenter is simply someone who can do carpentry of acceptable quality; and, if there is nothing else for him to do, he is assigned to work in the fields.

The flour mill is located on a creek which is sometimes stocked with fish; and the miller, who does no work in the fields, is selected from the villagers and trained on the job. Both the tailor and cobbler work at their trade during the winter; however, during the summer they, too, work in the fields.

Russian or mixed villages, unlike Cheremis villages, have churches. These are usually old buildings constructed of logs or brick with copper or sheet iron roofs and cupolas painted in red, green, or blue. Commonly they are located on a high rise of ground. The mosque, found in Tatar villages, is constructed of logs or brick and has a tall, steep roof. Sometimes there is a balcony onto which the *molla* comes out to pray. There is always a half moon at the peak of the roof of this building.

Cheremis houses are made of horizontally stacked logs with a thatch roof; or the walls may be woven of wooden poles and plastered thickly with red clay which is then whitewashed. Around the individual houses there may be a *kudə*, 'summer house,' a bathhouse, and a well. Every household plants a kitchen garden in the area adjacent to its dwelling.

Almost every house in the village has its own bathhouse in back, some fifty to one hundred yards from the house. This bathhouse is approximately fifteen feet square with a small high window so that even in daytime artificial lighting is necessary. Friday is the Cheremis Sabbath, and the entire family uses the bathhouse Thursday evening after work; however, they may also use it during the rest of the week. Water for the steam bath may be drawn from the family's well, that of a neighbor, or the public well.

Although the *kudə* is not as common as in former times, ten or fifteen out of every hundred house yards will have one. It, too, stands at the back of the house. This dwelling, constructed of the same materials as the regular house, is smaller and has only one small window located high up on the wall. The roof is sometimes made of boards. Although the family lives in the *kudə* in the summer because it is cooler, people sleep in the regular house all year round. The *kudə* is used as a storehouse throughout the year; but nowadays there is usually a small cellar in the main house. Usually the *kudə* is not locked; however, if something valuable is stored there, it may be locked.

There are many more trees in the village itself than in the area surrounding it. The village orchard usually consists of apple trees, a few cherry trees, and peach trees. Poplar, birch, pussy willow, apple, and acacia trees are planted in the village by individual households.

In almost every village there is a secret policeman, and one can never be sure exactly who it is. If there is trouble, such as a fight in the village, the police arrive a few days later and apprehend the guilty persons. If there is some disagreement, a report of the dispute suddenly and unexpectedly appears, for example, on the third page of the *Krestinskia Gazeta*, Russian language regional newspaper pub-

FIG. 2. CHEREMIS HOUSE NEAR KAZAN (FROM HEIKEL, 1888, FIG. 107)

FIG. 3. CHEREMIS HOUSE NEAR KAZAN (FROM HEIKEL, 1888, FIG. 77)

lished in Birsk. There is also a Cheremis language newspaper of two pages, *Yoshkar Geche* (*joškar* 'red' and *keče~geče* 'sun, day'), and a Tatar language newspaper of the same size published weekly in Birsk.

A guard patrols the village at night, a job rotated among the male adults; but the informant does not recall anyone's having been apprehended stealing. At the *kolkhoz* storehouse an old man, armed with a club, is appointed as night watchman. Once the grain is ripened, a young man patrols the fields on horseback to keep out the cattle.

There is no electric power or telephone communication at the *kolkhoz*.

FIG. 4. SUMMER HOUSE EXTERIOR (FROM HEIKEL, 1888, FIG. 13)

FIG. 5. SUMMER HOUSE INTERIOR (FROM HEIKEL, 1888, FIG. 17)

ECONOMIC ORGANIZATION

The principal source of subsistence is agriculture combined with animal husbandry. Part of the *kolkhoz* harvest is purchased by the government and the proceeds are either used for purchasing and maintaining *kolkhoz* equipment or distributed among the workers. The balance of the quota is divided among the workers who can keep it for their own consumption or sell it at the nearest town or to the *kolkhoz* general store. Distribution of the harvest and proceeds is based on the amount of work done by the individual in producing the quota.

Seeding is begun on the first of May. Grain and vegetables are planted in order of their importance: wheat, oats, barley, buckwheat, millet, potatoes, and beets (the latter are planted only after the grains have been planted). The sowing lasts from two to three weeks. Wheat and clover are sown together; and when the wheat is harvested, the clover is left in the field to improve the soil's fertility. The soil may be plowed in the autumn and again in the spring; or it need only be cultivated in the spring before planting. Rye and winter wheat are planted in September and harvested in July or August. The informant reports that in each *kolkhoz* there are the following livestock: stables with approximately sixty work horses and two or three horses used for transportation and traveling; a cow yard with more than a hundred cows; a pig sty with more than forty pigs; a sheep yard with five hundred to a thousand sheep; a chicken yard with more than five hundred chickens; and around a thousand rabbits, which are kept for their fur.

Apiculture is an important economic activity among the Cheremis which nowadays comes under the management of the *kolkhoz*. The hives are kept in a wood or orchard away from the village, and the work is done by old men who are familiar with the details of caving, cleaning, and feeding. While most of the wax is donated to the government, the honey is divided among *kolkhoz* members.

The successful introduction of silkworm culture has also been reported recently.[22]

In addition to these cooperative economic activities, each family maintains a garden adjacent to the house. The size of this garden varies and may be as large as an acre. If the area around a man's house is not sufficiently large to accommodate all of his garden, he may be assigned a plot in the *kolkhoz* field. While almost every family owns its own smaller gardening equipment, such as sickles, hoes, and rakes, the horse and plow must be borrowed from the *kolkhoz*. Once a man has done the plowing, his wife and children are responsible for the planting and care of the garden, with the women generally deciding what will be grown, viz., potatoes, carrots, beets, cabbage, or cucumbers. In the fall, the husband helps with the harvesting. (No prayers or ceremonies are performed in conjunction with this garden.) While individual families are not permitted to own horses, they may keep other domestic animals so long as the family can afford them.

Every household is also responsible for obtaining its own firewood. Formally, the procedure requires that permission be obtained by the individual from the forestry division in the region. He then goes to the forest ranger who assigns him a spot where he may cut and collect dry wood. However, in practice, the *kolkhoz* chairman applies for a blanket permit for the entire *kolkhoz*.

Although regular hunting is limited principally to the old men who do little

[22] *Ibid.*, p. 62.

or no work in the *kolkhoz,* some people do secure hunting permits to shoot and trap such small game as rabbits, foxes, wolves, and pheasants. No license is necessary for pole fishing; but one is required for setting fish nets. Few forest products are gathered. Wild mushrooms are collected and used, fresh or dried, in cooking. Oak bark is used for tanning cowhide, and the bark of several other trees as well is used for dyes. Linden flowers are used to make a tea for curing a cough, and a flower similar to the daisy is used for a tea to cure head colds.

Money and produce are both used as media of exchange. The general store accepts only money, wool, grain, or eggs; however, even when they need some item badly, people dislike parting with wool which they like to keep for winter clothing. Transactions with the tailor and the cobbler are effected through bargaining; and almost every item including labor in the tradesman's garden may be exchanged for the cost of work and materials. The purchaser may either supply his own leather or buy it from the artisan.

The informant recalls that people in the *kolkhoz* visited and borrowed from each other a great deal and were more friendly with each other than are people in German villages or in the United States. In his life history he reported that when he was about fifteen years of age, he began to attend weekly gatherings and outings on the banks of the Belaya where he met people from other towns. "We said hello to each other, were getting to know each other; and we asked each other what sort of village they came from, how people lived there—so we learned all the latest news of the other villages. Some of them praised their *kolkhoz,* the others cursed it."

The usual diet of a *kolkhoz* worker is bread, soup, potatoes, buckwheat groats, sour milk, meat, wild game, kvass, fish, pickles, quartered salted cabbage heads, berries, and eggs. A Cheremis worker is very likely to breakfast on tea made from dried raspberry leaves or, rarely, Chinese tea with bread and sugar. In the afternoon he may have soup, groats, or potatoes, and bread. Usually before lunch he may have a small glass of vodka "as an appetizer." For the evening meal he may have a light soup, *kəsal,* and tea. On a holiday he may have pancakes, buns made from white flour, fat, and milk for his morning meal; and an afternoon meal of borsht, boiled or roasted chicken or rooster, groats, pancakes, vodka, kvass, cookies, and cakes. The evening meal, if anything is desired, is usually very light and is made up of leftovers from the afternoon's fare. Honey is used as a spread and to manufacture a fermented beverage.

NOTE ON TRANSPORTATION

In winter, travel and transportation are by horsedrawn sleds and skis. Dogs and oxen are not used; but the informant recalls having seen one- and two-humped camels pulling sleds in Birsk. Much of winter travel is on the frozen rivers. Sleds are made of maple, birch, or alder. Nowadays sleds are owned by the *kolkhoz* and lent to individual families. They are the only *kolkhoz* property which individuals keep at home. Skis are used for travel over open places and fields where the snow is two or three feet deep. They are of the long variety and are manufactured out of maple in the home. Ski poles are also used.

In summer, trucks are used in the large towns; but they are found rarely, if at all, in the *kolkhoz,* where draft horses and wagons are used to traverse the dirt roads. Men travel on horseback, but women rarely do so. Rivers are important arteries for transport; and the government has worked to improve these facilities. Railroads, tractor and automobile roads also transect the country of the Cheremis.

From 1925 to 1935, some ten million rubles were spent on improving river transportation. Leveling, channeling, and blasting operations of the varieties of soft rock around the stream banks resulted in the discovery of numerous chalk deposits. Timber transport roads and seventy-six miles of broad gauge and seventeen miles of narrow gauge track had been improved as of 1936. In addition to ice paths and other forms of land transport, thirteen miles of tractor road and eleven miles of automobile road have also been improved.[23]

Yoshkar-Ola, the terminus of the railroad branch from Stary Zeleny Dol on the Moscow-Kazan line, is the transportation as well as the political center of the Mari A.S.S.R.[24] The railway lines from Kazan to Yoshkar-Ola were built in 1923.

[23] *Ibid.*

[24] See, *ibid.,* pp. 66ff.: The city of Yoshkar-Ola "has grown up overnight. . . . On its main street, the Soviet, stands a row of white, many-storied buildings. The Government Building is built near the new city park in splendid Soviet style. There are three institutions of higher education, many movie houses, and many department stores. The factories produce not only for the domestic market, but for the whole U.S.S.R., e.g., such things as movie cameras. . . . There is a vitamin plant, which also produces many complicated pharmaceutical preparations, and there is also a new cooler of the meat combine.

"Yoshkar-Ola is the center of the new culture, national in form, socialistic in content. . . . Here is located the Mari Scientific Research Institute, working on questions of the national language, literature, history, and art. The Mari Government Publishing House releases many books in Russian and Mari (in both the Meadow and Hill Mari, which differ as Ukrainian and Russian do). In the Pedagogical Institute, in the special department of the literary faculty, there are professors of Mari language teaching. The number of schools in Mari A.S.S.R. approaches 1,000. There are seven pedagogical schools and many technical schools in animal husbandry, forestry, optics, paper making, medicine, and others.

"The city stands at the juncture of the rather well populated north-eastern part of the Republic and the wild forests, which occupy the western part almost to the Volga. The great forest wealth is seen everywhere. One of the larger schools in Yoshkar-Ola, the Lesotehnicheski (Forestry) Institute, trains cadres for work all along the Volga. In several villages, the houses look like country-cottages, the roofs and porches decorated with intricate woodwork. Many of the streets are paved with wooden blocks and the sidewalks are wooden footways. . . . And, in Yoshkar-Ola, the streets are also paved with wooden blocks, which are round pieces cut from the log and are in their natural form. In this endlessly changing pattern can be seen what the forests of the Mari A.S.S.R. consist of, for there are pieces of

The whole area of the Upper Volga Region is served by rail truck lines of the Moscow-Gor'kiy-Kirov, Moscow-Kazan, and the Leningrad-Kirov lines. The waterways and rail lines are equally important in transportation and radiate from the chief communications hub of Gor'kiy. The principal transportation artery is the Volga, which is more important in the southwest forest region than in the northeast agricultural area; and there is steam navigation on the Volga and Vetluga. Second in importance in this area is the railroad built by the Soviets connecting Yoshkar-Ola with the Kazan rail line at the Stary Zeleny Dol station. This line, as well as the special log transport lines, also serves the southern forest region. Only the transportation lines in the northeastern outlying districts gravitate toward the Vyatka River. Especially in the northeastern parts, cart transportation is of prime importance.

---

three meters in diameter testifying to the size of the trees: trees of this type make up about two thirds of the Republic's forest reserves.

"The growth of Yoshkar-Ola can be largely credited to the extention of the railroad to the town. The rail line came from the South, from Zeleny Dol, in 1927."

PART ONE
ENCYCLOPEDIA OF THE SACRED

ENCYCLOPEDIA OF THE SACRED

EXPLANATORY KEY

IN Section A, supernaturals are entered alphabetically according to their Cheremis name. If the name of a supernatural consists of more than one word, it is entered under the last word and then alphabetized according to the preceding word: thus, for example, *kaba jumə* and *pujərˇsə jumə* are both entered under *jumə;* however, they are also listed under *kaba* and *pujərˇsə,* each, with a reference to the entry in which they are discussed. English translations of each Cheremis word or phrase will also be found in the Index, in the proper alphabetical location. Each entry is given a separate code number. When two names are said to refer to the same supernatural, they are coded by a single number. It is sometimes uncertain whether two similar names refer to one or two supernaturals; in such doubtful cases, there are two separate entries with appropriate cross references.

Sections B through F follow the same general style of Section A, with the exception that alphabetical order is not adhered to so strictly. All major entries are listed alphabetically but sub-headings are listed by subject, so that *kon keˇcə,* for example, is listed under *kueˇcə* because it is part of the *kueˇcə* holidays. All such words appear in their proper alphabetical order with the number of the entry where they are discussed.

Entries in Section G are listed according to the omens, in Section H according to the effect the magic is intended to produce, and in Section I according to the cure.

All Cheremis forms known by our informant are transcribed phonemically in his dialect; other forms are taken from the sources with slight modifications in the transcription to conform to the style of the book: thus, for instance, the bilabial fricative, in the sources usually written β or *w,* has regularly been changed to *b,* since these symbols all represent allophones of one and the same phoneme.

At the end of each entry are given the sources from which the information was taken; abbreviations used are explained in Abbreviations. Embedded in the text are many internal cross references. Source references are distinguished from internal cross references by the fact that they are the final references in an entry.

We have used the present tense throughout as a noncommittal tense meaning that there is no information that the practices described have been abandoned. Supernaturals are referred to as "it" to reflect Cheremis usage, which does not distinguish grammatical gender. Because this was meant to be a descriptive study, historical and comparative materials have been kept to a minimum; it is hoped that these will appear at a later date in a separate volume.

Notes on pronunciation: the phonemes /b, d, g/ are pronounced, between vowels and in certain other positions, as [β, δ, γ], respectively, elsewhere as [b, d, g]; /ˇc/ is a slightly palatalized alveolar affricate, its closest English equivalent being *ch,* as in 'cheese'; /ə/ is a reduced and unstressed vowel, the quality of which is generally conditioned by preceding vowels and consonants; /'/ indicates that the preceding consonant is palatalized; /š, ž/ are similar to English *s*, as in 'sugar,' and as in 'pleasure,' respectively; /x/ is a voiceless velar fricative, and /ŋ/ a velar nasal; /ü, ö/ are, respectively, high- and mid-front-rounded vowels.

A. PERSONIFIED SUPERNATURALS

A.1.   *aba* 'mother'

Female deities of no distinct shape and of vague connotations are grouped here. These are often personifications of natural phenomena and are then preceded by the appropriate qualifying term. Sometimes an *aba* is merely a member of the household of a god or spirit. That these deities are considered to be females is indicated not only by the use of the common word for mother, but also by the fact that the animals sacrificed to them are usually female, whereas male animals are usually sacrificed to other deities.

(H[1913], 121, 131.)

A.1.1.   *büt aba* 'water mother'

In some sources this water spirit is contrasted with others by the fact that it is to be found anywhere that there is water, whereas the others dwell only in deep water. According to other sources, 'water mother' inhabits only deep water.

The most common cause for a public ceremony dedicated to *büt aba* (B.6.) is the need for rain during a long summer drought. At such a time all the inhabitants of a town gather at the bank of a river and, with a great deal of merrymaking, throw water on each other and on nearby animals, especially black sheep and black hens. In some places a little of the *jür pučəməš* 'rain porridge' (for *pučəməš*, see C.8.), which is prepared on the bank of the river, is poured into the water as an offering, and the rest is eaten by those present. In other places a black animal, either an ox or a sheep, is slaughtered, cooked, and eaten on the river bank. The bones and other uneaten parts are wrapped in the skin of the sacrificed animal and sunk in the water. If too much rain falls as a result, these remains are taken out of the water and buried in the earth. Sometimes the thunder god (A.26.22.), as well as *büt aba*, is mentioned in the prayer for rain. In some regions, however, the sprinkling of water to produce rain has no religious connotations.

Büt aba, sometimes also called *büt kuba*, 'water old woman,' also inhabits springs where it regulates the quality of the water. In the springtime it stirs up mud so that the water tastes bad; in the fall, however, the water is very good because this deity mixes in honey. A spring which has bad-tasting water is sometimes purified by means of an offering of porridge, the barley for which is contributed by all the families in town.

When a Cheremis bride goes to her husband's house, she must sacrifice to *büt aba* before she can draw water from the spring or brook. Accompanied by someone who is known to *büt aba*, the bride throws a few coins or beads into the water as an offering and prays for a blessing on this, and every other time she comes for water; this protects her from any illness the strange water might have caused. In some places, before taking water back to the house, the bride also pours out to the four points of the compass the first four bucketfuls which she draws. In other places she washes her feet when she fetches water for the first time.

The Cheremis pray for the water mother's protection when there is danger from the water; for example, when swimming. Sometimes children are warned not to go into deep water lest *büt aba* pull them down.

Since fish are under the jurisdiction of *büt aba*, some Cheremis pour vodka and porridge into the water so that this deity will provide them an abundant catch. In other regions they believe that *büt aba* gives fish freely, but that it would be angry if it knew what men were doing. Consequently, fishermen not only refrain from praying, but are very careful not to make any disturbance while fishing. If a man shouts or uses improper language, the spirit becomes angry and may cause him to drown or catch *büt ajar*, a skin disease appearing first on the hands and feet and characterized by a great amount of pus. A soothsayer can tell from which body of water the disease has come and advises a sick person how to propitiate the angry water. Usually the person first makes a vow by throwing barley, eggs, or other food into the water, asking for forgiveness and promising to make a sacrifice. Later, on the bank of the offended water, he kills a goat, a grouse, a duck, or some other waterfowl. After the meat is cooked, the bones and little pieces of meat from different parts of the animal are thrown into the water; the rest of the meat is eaten by the sick person and his family. Sometimes, before drinking water, a person prays to *büt aba* to cleanse out all evil within him.

For other water spirits, see A.9.1., A.16.1., A.26.7., A.26.29.1., A.52.2., A.58.2., A.70.3., A.84.4, and A.96.2.

(B, 23, 25; G, 55[148]; H[1913], 120–24; H[1926], 73–77; H[1927], 212; J; R, 202; S, 162; Uj[FB], 18.)

A.1.2.   *jumən aba* 'god's mother'

One of the most important deities to receive sacrifices at the same time as *jumə* 'god' (A.26.) is its mother, in some regions the deity of marriage and childbirth. A cow is sacrificed to it at the *küsə* ceremony (B.9.); an offering is also made at *aga pajram* (B.2.). The Christian Virgin Mary is also called *jumən aba*.

(G, 55[148]; H[1926], 64–65; H[1927], 258; Häm. [1908a], 8; P, 187, 203.)

A.1.3.   *kečə aba* 'sun mother'

This deity, also called *oš kečə aba* 'white sun mother' because of the brilliance of the sun, lives in the sun. It is the goddess of family, good fortune, and wealth. Earlier accounts mention sun worship as being particularly strong among the Cheremis. Houses were built facing east and prayers were said each morning at the open door.

Kečə aba has its own tree in the *küsə* grove (E.2.1.) where a white animal, usually a cow, is sacrificed to it at the *küsə* ceremony (B.9.). At certain times, such as when the grass and grain have been turned brown by heat, a special sacrifice of a white cow or sheep may be made. An offering is also made at *aga pajram* (B.2.). A calf or sheep is sacrificed to *kečə aba* at a public ceremony held by women—one of the rare instances when Cheremis women take an active part in religious functions. The bones and other remains of the animals sacrificed to this spirit are then burned.

The 'sun mother' can give people good health. When a child has become very pale, an egg and three pancakes are placed on a tree stump and *keča aba* is beseeched to restore the child's color.

Sometimes the term *keča aba* is used by the Cheremis in contexts not specifically religious: when referring to the sun, they may say, "the sun mother rises," or "the sun mother is burning the earth."

For other sun spirits, see A.1.10.3.1., A.26.15., A.26.15.1., A.26.31.2., and A.52.6.

(G, 55[148]; H[1926], 68–69; Häm.[1908a], 9; Häm.[1936–1937], 67, 71; P, 187, 203; S, 83, 162, 169.)

A.1.4.   *mardəž aba* 'wind mother'

At the *küsə* ceremony (B.9.), a cow of any color except black or white is sacrificed to the 'wind mother'; beer and pancakes are offered at *aga pajram* (B.2.). Occasionally, the Cheremis make an offering to this spirit during a destructive windstorm. Small offerings are also brought to the 'wind mother' to cure an illness which a soothsayer affirms is caused by the wind.

(G, 55[148]; H[1926], 71; P, 187, 189, 203; S, 162.)

A.1.5.   *məlandə aba* 'earth mother'

The earth is considered animate because it lets things grow; it understands the speech of men and knows their needs. *Məlandə aba* is one of the personifications of the earth. This is reflected both in the color black for the animals sacrificed to it and in the burial of the bones and remains in contrast with the burning of the remains of most other sacrifices. The most suitable animal for a sacrifice to *məlandə aba* is a black cow. Customary sacrifices to 'earth mother' consist of a cow at the *küsə* ceremony (B.9.) every three years; a sheep at the *məlandə jer* (B.10.), a ceremony dedicated to the earth deities; and beer and pancakes at *aga pajram* (B.2.). A sheep or cow may be sacrificed every fall and, in addition, special sacrifices may be made when the grain is not growing well or when devastating insects threaten to harm the crops. Sometimes, after the ceremony dedicated to the earth spirits, each person goes to his own fields and puts an egg and a spoonful of porridge on the ground for the earth to eat. This is done so that the earth will let the grain grow. Sometimes an iron or copper object is put on the place where animals are butchered and the earth mother is asked to drive the evil spirits away.

For other earth spirits, see A.1.10.5., A.9.10., A.15.4., A.26.25., A.52.10., A.58.5., A.65.2., A.67.11., A.68.8., A.70.12., A.76.6., A.79.2., A.82.7., and A.84.14.

(H[1926], 71–73; H[1927], 239; P, 189, 203, 207; PG, 20[83]; S, 162.)

A.1.5.1.   *taškəm məlandə aba* 'yard mother'

This spirit protects men and livestock in the farmyard.

(H[1926], 62; H[1927], 239.)

A.1.6.   *mükš aba* 'bee mother'

The term *mükš aba* is used to designate both a bee spirit and the queen bee.

For other bee spirits, see A.1.10.6., A.15.6., A.26.1.2., A.26.28., A.26.38.2., A.27.1., A.28.3., A.29.3., A.52.11., A.58.6., A.65.3., A.67.13., A.68.9., A.70.13., A.76.7., A.78.3., A.79.1.2., A.82.8., and A.84.15. See also A.67.12.

(Häm.[1936–37], 64; J.)

A.1.7.1.1. *kaba jumən onən abazə* 'heaven god's lord's mother'

See A.26.13. and A.27.

(V, 57.)

A.1.8. *perke aba* 'blessing mother'

A sheep is sacrificed to this spirit at the ceremony made by a young man when he assumes adult responsibilities (B.34.), as well as on miscellaneous other occasions.

For *perke,* see A.67.

(H[1926], 90; Häm.[1908a], 8–10; S, 162.)

A.1.8.1.1. *kaba jumən perke aba* 'heaven god's blessing mother'

See also A.26.13 and A.27.

(V, 57.)

A.1.8.2. *kində perke aba* 'grain blessing mother'

For other grain spirits see A.26.1.1., A.26.1.3.1., A.26.16., A.26.34.1., A.29.2., A.52.7., A.52.12.1., A.70.18., A.82.6., and A.84.13.

(B, 24; Uj[FB], 26.)

A.1.9. *pəl aba* 'cloud mother'

This spirit is worshipped both at the great sacrifice ceremonies and when there is a great drought or hailstorm.

(H[1926], 70; H[1927], 234; S, 162.)

A.1.10. *šočən aba* 'fructifier mother'

This spirit grants increase to men and animals and, along with numerous other spirits and deities, is invoked in prayer for the general welfare of the people. During the *šorək šočən* ceremony (B.20.), the Cheremis pray that this spirit increase the sheep. An offering is also made to it at *aga pajram* (B.2.). The help of *šočən aba,* which literally means 'bearing mother,' is often prayed for at births; to make a difficult birth easier, a white lamb is sometimes sacrificed. The third of the sacrifices required of each man during his lifetime (B.34.) is dedicated to *šočən aba;* a cow and six smaller animals are then sacrificed.

For *šočən,* see A.82.

(H[1926], 61, 90, 156, 189; Häm.[1908a], 9; J; P, 203; Uj[FB], 33; Up[FB], 11.)

A.1.10.1. *bol'ək šočən aba* 'livestock fructifier mother'

This spirit helps the livestock to bring forth their young easily.

For other livestock spirits, see A.26.5., A.26.38.1., A.28.1., A.52.1., A.67.2., A.68.1., A.70.2., A.76.2., A.78.1., A.79.1.1., A.82.2., and A.84.3.

(B, 24; S, 162; Uj[FB], 34; Up[FB], 12.)

A.1.10.2. *jeη šočən aba* 'man fructifier mother'

Some Cheremis pray to this spirit to help them raise good children. See also A.26.31.1., A.70.4., and A.82.3.

(B, 23.)

A.1.10.3.1. *oš ketə šočən aba* 'white sun fructifier mother'
For other sun spirits, see A.1.3., A.1.26.15., A.26.15.1., A.26.31.2., and A.52.6.
(Häm.[1936–37], 71; S, 162.)

A.1.10.4. *kajək šočən aba* 'bird fructifier mother'
For another bird spirit, see A.26.14.
(Uj[FB], 22; Up[FB], 7.)

A.1.10.5. *məlandə šočən aba* 'earth fructifier mother'
Prayers are addressed to *məlandə šočən aba* both to make the grain grow well and to make the grass grow so that the cows will give an abundant supply of milk.
For other earth spirits, see A.5., A.9.10., A.15.4., A.26.25., A.52.10., A.58.5., A.65.2., A.67.11., A.68.8., A.70.12., A.76.6., A.79.2., A.82.7., and A.84.14.
(B, 24; Uj[FB], 37.)

A.1.10.6. *mükš šočən aba* 'bee fructifier mother'
This spirit is worshipped by beekeepers who sometimes sacrifice a sheep to it (B.11.). In some places there is a special grove dedicated to it.
For other bee spirits, see A.1.6., A.15.6., A.26.1.2., A.26.28., A.26.38.2., A.27.1., A.28.3., A.29.3., A.52.11., A.58.6., A.65.3., A.67.13., A.68.9., A.70.13., A.76.7., A.78.3., A.79.1.2., A.82.8., and A.84.15. See also A.67.12.
(Häm.[1909], 5; Häm.[1936–37], 64.)

A.1.10.7. *šorək šočən aba* 'sheep fructifier mother'
Some Cheremis pray to *šorək šočən aba* both for good lambs and that the sheep may lamb easily. See also *šorək šočən* (A.82.10.)
(Be, 24; Uj[FB], 35.)

A.1.10.8. *tul šočən aba* 'fire fructifier mother'
For other fire spirits, see A.1.15., A.9.14., A.26.29.3., A.26.42., A.52.18., A.58.10., A.70.20., A.84.20., and A.88.1.
(Uj[FB], 38.)

A.1.10.9. *tüńča ümbal šočən aba* 'fructifier mother over the world'
See also A.26.31.3., A.70.21., A.76.9., A.84.21., and A.91.
(S, 162.)

A.1.10.10. *uškal šočən aba* 'cow fructifier mother'
This spirit helps the cows to calve easily.
For other spirits which aid at the time of birth, see A.1.10., A.1.10.1., and A.1.10.7.
(Uj[FB], 36.)

A.1.11. *šokšə aba* 'warmth mother'
For another warmth spirit, see A.38.26.
(H[1926], 70; S, 162.)

A.1.12. *šüdər aba* 'star mother'
For other star spirits, see A.26.39., A.52.15.
(H[1926], 69; S, 162.)

A.1.13.   *teŋəz aba* 'sea mother'

For other sea spirits, see A.26.29.2., A.26.40., A.52.16., and A.70.19.

(H[1913], 121; H[1926], 73; S, 162.)

A.1.14.   *tələzə aba* 'moon mother'

A cow or sheep is sacrificed to the 'moon mother' under the tree dedicated to it in the sacred grove.

For other moon spirits, see A.26.41., and A.52.17.

(G, 55[148]; H[1926], 69, 112; S, 162.)

A.1.15.   *tul aba* 'fire mother'

When a fire is in a friendly mood, it burns quietly. Since fire is pure, it does not tolerate impurity. Fire may be angered if someone pokes it with a dirty poker, spits into it, throws wood onto it too hard, or reprimands it. When it is angry, it leaves the hearth and burns down houses or causes the offender *tul ajar* (either burns or a skin disease resembling *büt ajar* [see A.1.1.] but with less pus in the blisters). During a conflagration the Cheremis throw a black hen, or milk from a black cow into the fire and pray the *tul aba* not to burn down the town. At sacrifice ceremonies, the priest sometimes prays *tul aba* to take the sacrifice to the gods, i.e., to be the means by which the sacrifice reaches the gods. Prayers asking it to act as intermediary usually include the formula, "Thy smoke is long, and thy tongue sharp." The priest may also ask the fire mother to correct the prayer if he has inadvertently made a mistake without realizing it. This same intermediary function is performed elsewhere by *tul bodəz* 'fire spirit' (A.9.14.). Hunters, when they spend the night in the forest, pray to *tul aba* to protect them from *targəldəš* (A.86.).

For other fire spirits, see A.1.10.8., A.9.14., A.26.29.3., A.26.42., A.52.18., A.58.10., A.70.20., A.84.20., and A.88.1.

(H[1926], 55, 79–80; H[1927], 235, 237; Häm.[1936–37], 71, 75; S, 162.)

For *kində aba jumə*, see A.26.1.1.; *mükš aba jumə*, A.26.1.2.; *perke aba jumə*, A.26.1.3.; *kində perke aba jumə*, A.26.1.3.1., *šočən aba juməšaməč*, A.26.1.4.; *šočən aban šočənzə*, A.82.1.1., *pokšəm ača*, A.38.22.; *ademe targəldəš*, A.86.; *aga pajram jumə*, A.26.2.; *kugə aga keremet*, A.31.1.; *aga kurman*, A.41.; *aga orman*, A.54.; *aga saus*, A.76.1.; *agun kuguza*, A.38.1.; *ajməldəs*, A.86.; *alak jumə*, A.26.3.

A.2.   *albasta* or *labasta*

This spirit, which inhabits bathhouses, is said to have its origin from the soul of an illegitimate child that died without having been baptized. It may appear either as a man or as a woman, or again as a giant with long flowing hair; it also has the power to change itself into an animal. When it travels about, it looks like a star shooting off sparks (cf. A.10.). The main activity of *albasta* is to have sexual relations with humans. The kiss of an *albasta* causes a sore to appear on a person's lip. An *albasta* may also punish a woman who has had many lovers by coming to her as a young man and gradually causing her to die. A man who has sexual relations with a woman visited by an *albasta* will also become sick. An *albasta* cannot go through a door on which there is a cross (H.4.6.); it loses all its power when the little finger on its left hand is broken. *Albasta* is sometimes said to be the same as *šukšəndal* (A.85.), and sometimes to be a forest spirit living in swamps and ravines.

(Be, 56; Bk, 44–45; H[1926], 56; H[1927], 184; J; R, 199–200; Up[FB], 19.)

A.3. *araptes̆*

The ghosts of murderers or their victims which harass a region are sometimes so called. A forest spirit, sometimes identified with *jekšuk* (A.20.), is also called *araptes̆*. It also appears at night in abandoned bathhouses in the form of a pretty girl (cf. A.85.).

(Beke[1949], 120; Beke[1951b], 249; L, 13; S, 149.)

For *aren patər*, see A.64.1.; *arəmdəš*, A.86.; *arńagečən šukčə*, A.84.1.

A.4. *asəra*

The personification of colic in horses is called *asəra* (cf. charm 1.2., and p. 283, below). The term *asəra* is borrowed from a Tatar word meaning an evil spirit.

(G[143]; P,75; P[1948], 6.)

A.5. *aš*

The meaning of *aš* is not altogether clear. It has been said to mean 'strength,' 'nourishment that brings health,' and 'food preparer.' An *aš* is a helper of god (A.26.) and the *keremet* spirits (A.31.) whose exact function is also not known. Nevertheless, when a sacrifice is made to a god, a smaller animal is also sacrificed to its *aš*. At the *küsə* ceremony (B.9.) a black sheep is sacrificed to *jumən aš*, 'god's *aš*'; an offering is also made at *aga pajram* (B.2.).

(Be, 63; H[1913], 123; H[1926], 64, 110, 169; Häm.[1908a], 8–10; P, 188, 203; S, 155.)

A.6. *azren* 'angel of death'

The angel of death was once visible to all men but now is seen only by those who are dying. It also appears in dreams announcing the death of a sick person. It looks like a Tatar, is thin and so tall that its head reaches the roof. According to a folk tale (for type and motif analysis, see Sebeok, 1952, p. 58) it once was taken prisoner and at that time no one died. Sometimes the angel of death is also called *azren kuba* and *azren kuguza*, '*azren* old woman' and '*azren* old man.'

The angel of death carries a long knife with which it kills people by cutting their throats. If it cuts a person's neck from behind, the person dies a year later. Sometimes it strangles a person with a wire or stabs him with a chisel. If it cuts with a scythe or an ax, the person dies quickly. If it hits the person's head with a mallet, he loses consciousness. If *azren* pricks the soles of a person's feet with an awl or strikes them with a shovel, or cuts his neck with a sickle or a dull knife, the person dies a slow painful death. Children are sometimes said to be crushed to death between boards.

In some places *azren* is considered to be the helping spirit of a *keremet* (A.31.); in others it is a *keremet* in its own right. A chicken is sacrificed to it.

(B, 11; Be, 63, 371–76; H[1925], 75; H[1926], 169; S, 154; Uj[FB], 71; Uj[T], 43.)

For *bakš ia*, see A.38.2.; *bakš kuguza* and *kuba*, A.38.2.; *bakš oza*, A.38.2; *basli kuguza* and *kuba*, A.38.3.

A.7.   *b'es* 'devil'

For other devils, see A.15., A.16., A.18., A.75., and A.81.

(Sz, 14.)

For *biča ia*, see A.38.4.; *biča kuguza* and *kuba*, A.38.4.; *biča oza*, A.38.4.; *biča ört*, A.58.1.; *biča perke*, A.67.1.; *biča pujəršə*, A.70.1.; *biča šukčə*, A.84.2.

A.8.   *bitnəzə* 'reporter'

The function of this spirit is to report to a god the sacrifices which are made. At the *mir küsə* (B.9.1.2.) a sheep, a goose, or other small animal is sacrificed to *jumən bitnəzə* 'god's reporter' so that this spirit will report favorably to god the sacrifices performed. The same priest who sacrifices to *kugə jumə* (A.26.) also sacrifices to this spirit under the tree dedicated to *kugə jumə*. An offering is also made at *aga pajram* (B.2.). An *aba* (A.1.), a *pujəršə* (A.70.), a *keremet* (A.31.), and other deities may also have a *bitnəzə* which receives sacrifices. When a vow is made to *kugə jeη nemdə kurak* 'great man Nemda Mountain' (A.21.2.1.), for example, a duck is also promised to his *bitnəzə*. As a member of the retinue of *kugərak* (A.21.2.1.), a duck is sacrificed to this spirit in the summer and a hare in the winter.

(Be, 63; H[1926], 64–65, 132, 140, 144; Häm.[1908a], 9–10; Häm.[1909], 5; P, 72, 188, 189, 203, 206; V, 36.)

A.9.   *bodəž* 'spirit'

The principal use of this term is to designate nature spirits of lesser importance than *jumə* 'god' (A.26.). However, in some places, *bodəž* means more specifically a water spirit; in still others it is used for a *keremet* spirit (A.31.) or the helper of a *keremet*. As a *keremet*, it is an evil being which is said to have originated from an evil or murdered man. Black animals are sacrificed to such a *keremet*.

(Be, 63; H[1913], 127–28; H[1926], 95, 173; P, 188; V, 37.)

A.9.1.   *büt bodəž* 'water spirit'

This water spirit, which lives in rivers and springs, may punish anyone who offends it. A sore on the lip is the penalty for drinking directly from a spring, a sore on the penis for urinating into the water. If a person who has crossed a river gets a pain in his hand or foot, it is attributed to *büt bodəž*. This spirit may also cause infected ulcers or a skin disease named after the river or spring that causes it, e.g., *amše bodəž čer* is the disease caused by the spirit of Amse Brook. To cure a disease caused by *büt bodəž*, an offering must be made either by throwing porridge into the water or by killing a fowl or goat on the bank.

For other water spirits, see A.1.1., A.9.4., A.16.1., A.26.7., A.26.29.1., A.52.2., A.58.2., A.70.3., A.84.4., and A.96.2.

(Bk, 46; H[1913], 126; H[1926], 95–96; Usj[FB], 2.)

A.9.2.   *eŋer bodəž* 'river spirit'

This spirit originated when a man threw groats and salt into a river and said that the river was to have a spirit which would punish anyone who offended it. Ever since, the river spirit has caused an offender to have swollen hands and feet or to lose his eyesight. To be cured, the sick person sprinkles groats and salt into the river and promises to make an offering of porridge when he is cured. One evening, after he has recovered, he fulfills his vow (cf. A.9.1.).

(Be, 380–82.)

A.9.3.   *jal(x)ter bodəž*

A duck is sacrificed to this *keremet* (A.31.).

(S, 155.)

A.9.4.   *jer bodəž* 'lake spirit'

The fishermen of some regions pray to *jer bodəž* for fish, throwing an offering of bread and vodka into both a fire and the water.

For other lake spirits, see A.22., A.38.10., A.51. See also A.1.1., A.9.1., and A.16.1.

(H[1913], 127; H[1926], 95; S, 149.)

A.9.5.   *jüt bodəž* 'night spirit'

A prayer is sometimes said to this spirit asking it to chase away evil.

(Uj[FB], 41.)

A.9.6.   *kərtńə bodəž* 'iron spirit'

kərtnə bodəž is a *keremet* (A.31.) known because of its legendary battles. Richly dressed, it drives about in a troika drawn by bay horses. Sacrifices are made to it and its retinue of helping spirits.

According to another account, it is believed to have been a renegade soldier who, together with his brother, became a robber in the forest. When pursued, the two took refuge in a tall tree and, after threatening to revenge their death by sending disease, threw themselves down into the water below. When many people in the neighborhood began to fall ill, the townspeople were forced to make sacrifices to appease them. Some Cheremis who have had contact with Christianity identify St. Michael Archangel with this *keremet*.

(H[1926], 173; S, 149–51, 156.)

A.9.7.   *korna bodəž* 'road spirit'

For another road spirit, see A.70.10.

(H[1913], 128.)

A.9.8.   *kudə bodəž* 'hut spirit'

The *kudə* (E.1.), particularly the holy corner there, is inhabited by the family deity. Since the holy part is sometimes separated from the rest of the hut by a partition and called *izə kudə* 'little hut,' the spirit is also called *izə kudə bodəž* 'little hut spirit.' The term *kudə bodəž* is also applied to the dried twigs which are sometimes kept in the holy corner. Once a year the old twigs are taken out and new ones brought in. In older accounts there are reports of coarse little wooden figurines which were regarded as family gods. However, no investigator within the past seventy-five years has found any trace of such an idol. At times this spirit appears in human form to members of the family in dreams. This family spirit is sometimes worshipped by members of the family who live elsewhere but who return to their parents' home to worship it. A newly married woman returns to her parents' *kudə*; an older woman worships her husband's *kudə*.

Sacrifices to the *kudə bodəž* are placed on the shelf in the holy corner or in *kudə bodəž kalta* 'hut spirit box,' (F.6.). Both cereal and blood offerings are made. The usual sacrifice is a black sheep, but a duck, hen, or even a hare will suffice if there is nothing better available. When food is placed on the sacrifice shelf, the head of the house begs for forgiveness for himself and his family and prays for the protection of the whole household. In some places there is an annual sacrifice in the fall. The bones of the sacrificed animal are not burned but buried under the hut. A little piece of many of the organs of the animal is laid on the holy shelf. More often, sacrifices are made to the *kudə bodəž* when some misfortune or illness occurs in the family and a soothsayer traces it back to the neglect of this spirit. In some places a hen or duck is sacrificed when a person has trachoma. First a vow is made by putting on the sacrifice shelf a little meal, honey, pieces of cake, or other food; later the promised fowl is sacrificed and a loaf of bread is made from the honey and meal set aside at the time of the vow. The sacrifice feast, which only the family may eat, is prepared and consumed in the *kudə;* a stranger is never permitted to eat this food.

In some places there is the custom of taking a house spirit which wants a sacrifice over to a neighbor. If a man does not want to make a sacrifice, he tells the *kudə bodəž* that his neighbor will be hospitable, takes a bit of the remains of a sacrifice from the holy box and goes to a neighbor's house. When he is invited to take a seat and is served bread and salt, the spirit is also considered to have been received hospitably. Unnoticed, the guest throws what he has brought with him into a corner of the house and leaves without saying good-bye or inviting his neighbor to return the visit.

The *kudə bodəž* also inhabits the place on which a *kudə* stood formerly. Anyone who quarrels there or dirties the spot will become sick.

For other *kudə* spirits, see A.38.20. and A.58.4.

(Bk, 47; H[1913], 128; H[1926], 44–49, 95; H[1927], 135–37; Müller, 363; R, 206; Ränk[1949], 87–97; Ränk[1949–51], 117–19; S, 158–59; V, 82.)

A.9.9. *kurək bodəž* 'mountain spirit'

For other mountain spirits, see A.15.3., A.16.2., A.21.2.1., A.26.21., A.38.14., A.68.6.

(V, 86.)

A.9.10. *məlandə bodəž* 'earth spirit'

Sacrifices to the earth spirit are usually black animals whose bones and remains are buried in the earth instead of being burned. At the *küsə* ceremony (B.9.) a cow is sacrificed every third year; at *məlandə jər* 'earth offering' (B.10.), a sheep is sacrificed; at *aga pajram* (B.2.) the customary offering of beer and pancakes is made to *məlandə bodəž*. In cases of illness caused by a fall, the sick person pours salt water on the place where he fell and prays to the earth spirit to be healed.

For other earth spirits, see A.1.5., A.1.10.5., A.15.4., A.26.25., A.52.10., A.58.5.,

A.65.2., A.67.11., A.68.8., A.70.12., A.76.6., A.79.2., A.82.7., and A.84.14.

(H[1913], 128; H[1926], 95–97, 111; P, 189, 203, 207.)

A.9.10.1. *surt(lə) məlandə bodəž* 'house earth spirit'

Some Cheremis pray to the spirit of the earth on which the house stands to give peace within the house and to protect it from fire.

(G, 55 [148]; H[1926], 96; J.)

A.9.11. *nur bodəž* 'field spirit'

A cock and hen are sacrificed to this *keremet* (A.31.).

(S, 155.)

A.9.12. *pört bodəž* 'house spirit'

For other house spirits, see A.38.23. and A.58.9.

(H[1913], 128.)

A.9.13. *šərt bodəž* 'devil spirit'

A sacrifice of a ram is made to this *keremet* (A.31.).

For *šərt*, see A.15.

(S, 155.)

A.9.14. *tul bodəž* 'fire spirit'

Fire personified is capable of being either man's friend or his enemy. One of the most important functions of *tul bodəž* is to act as intermediary between man and other deities at sacrifice ceremonies. The priest throws the sacrifice into the fire and asks the fire spirit to take it to the one for whom it is intended. This request is usually accompanied by the formula, "thy smoke is long and thy tongue sharp." In order to exorcise evil both from a house and a person, a lighted forked pine branch is waved about to smoke up the house and, at the same time, prayers are said to *tul bodəž* to drive out the evil. People also pray to the *tul bodəž* for protection from conflagrations. When angered, fire may send disease to those who offend it. If a person suffers from a disease which is believed to be caused by the fire, he throws a sacrifice into the fire, asks forgiveness for his offense and prays that his health be restored.

For other fire spirits, see A.1.10.8., A.15., A.26.29.3., A.26.42., A.52.18., A.58.10., A.70.20., A.84.20., and A.88.1.

(Be, 62, 382–83; Bk, 47; H[1913], 128; H[1926], 95–96, 129, 140, 185; Häm.[1936–37], 73; J; S, 166; Uj[FB], 40.)

For *tul bodəž təlmaze*, see A.88.1.; *bol'ək jumə*, A.26.5.; *bol'ək kazna*, A.28.1.; *bol'ək kazna sərabočəš*, A.79.1.1.; *bol'ək on*, A.52.1.; *bol'ək perke*, A.67.2.; *bol'ək piambar*, A.68.1.; *bol'ək pujəršə*, A.70.2.; *bol'ək saus*, A.76.2.; *bol'ək serlagəš*, A.78.1.; *bol'ək šočən* or *bol'ək šačəktšə*, A.82.2.; *bol'ək šočən aba*, A.1.10.1.; *bol'ək šočən jumə*, A.26.38.1.; *bol'ək šukčə*, A.84.3.; *bolgenčə jumə*, A.26.4.; *er bolgaster*, A.26.10.

A.10. *buber* or *uber*

An evil spirit combining the features of a vampire, a will-o'-the-wisp, and a witch is designated by this term. A *buber* is most often seen as fire which travels through the air not far above the ground shooting off sparks. The fire may be small or large; often it is described as being a line of fire about six feet in length. When people try to approach it, it flees. A *buber* may also have human form. As a woman, it has long hair and has been described as flying along a little above the ground shooting off sparks; as a man it may have a long beard. In the form of a bird it pecks at trees so that they dry up and become hollow. In folk tales *buber kuba* is a term used for a witch and *buber kuguza* for an ogre. Without knowing about it, a person may be possessed by a *buber* spirit while he is living; he thinks that what he does as the *buber* is a dream. If he tells people about the dream, the *buber* spirit leaves him.

A *buber* originating from a dead person frequents the cemetery, returning to the grave in the morning. At the foot of the grave in which there is a *buber,* there is a hole which allows the *buber* to go in and out. The corpse of a *buber* has a red face and does not decay. In some places there is the belief that if the coffin is opened, the corpse, covered with blood, may sit up and speak. To prevent such a *buber* from continuing its evil deeds, a spell is spoken, the corpse is beaten with mountain ash sticks and burned. Nevertheless, the *buber* can escape from the mouth of the body in the form of a butterfly which subsequently becomes a *buber* bird. A stone from the craw of a chicken put in the mouth of a corpse at the time of burial will prevent the *buber* from coming out. One of the means of protection against a *buber* is a spell which brings the *buber* near enough so that a person can beat it and kill it. Sometimes, however, when it is beaten, it turns to ashes only to become active later. Sometimes people shoot at it. Another way of protecting oneself is by tearing off the wristband of one's shirt or the band of one's bast shoes or by splitting a wooden pitchfork. A horseshoe in the threshhold prevents a *buber,* as well as other evil spirits, from entering the house.

A *buber* sucks milk from the cattle; the milk of a cow which has been visited by a *buber* contains blood or dirt. Vampire-like, it also sucks blood from both cattle and humans. A *buber* may suck blood by kissing a person on the mouth; such a person will die within a few weeks. There is also an account of a *buber kuba,* 'buber woman,' which became a man's lover, upset him so emotionally that he went into a decline, and it finally killed him. A *buber* may cause internal disorders by entering the stomach; it may enter the womb of a pregnant woman or animal and kill the fetus. It also "eats" eyes. The eyes of a cow which have been turned white by a *buber* can be cured by applying chewed mountain ash bark to them. If the *buber* attacks a man's eyes, there is a spell to cure them. A *buber* may also cause sores on the fingers. Sometimes it spoils food and water. The lunar eclipse is believed to be caused by a *buber's* having eaten the moon.

A meteorite, which is considered by some to be a dragon, is called *baraš buber.*

(B, 7–8, 96; Be, 44–50; Bu, 34; G, 17, 31 [102, 118]; H[1926], 13, 69; H[1927], 10; J; P, 80; S, 206; Sz, 290; Uj[FB], 12; Us[FB], 1; Usj[FB], 1, 49; T, 4.)

For *buča ümbal šukča,* see A.84.; *tamək buj,* A.90.; *buj jumə,* A.26.6.; *buj šukča,* A.84.; *oš buj vaňuška,* A.97.; *büt aba,* A.1.1.; *büt bodəz,* A.9.1.; *büt ia,* A.16.1.; *büt ian üdəržə,* A.96.2.; *büt imňə,* A.16.1.; *büt jumə,* A.26.7.; *büt kuba,* A.1.1. and A.16.1.; *büt kuguza,* A.16.1.; *büt on,* A.52.2.; *büt on jumə,* A.26.29.1.; *büt oza,* A.16.1.; *büt ört,* A.58.2.; *büt pujəršə,* A.70.3.; *büt uškəž,* A.16.1.; *büt ümbal šukča,* A.84.4.

A.11. *čatkən*

This evil spirit, the ghost of a person who perished in the forest, haunts the place where he died. Its main desire is to cause the death of someone else so that it may go free. For that reason, it frightens people and tries to make them lose their way in the forest. At night it scatters their fires and makes it appear as if all the trees were being uprooted. *Čatkən* may appear either in human form or as a bird. In a folktale (for type and motif analysis, see Sebeok, 1952, p. 20), it eats, gets drunk, can be shot, and has a cloak which makes it invisible. This spirit is also called *l'eši*.

For other forest spirits, see A.20., A.43., A.51., and A.86.

(Bk, 46; R, 182, 206.)

A.12. *čembulat*

There is a legend that *čembulat* was a Cheremis prince who ruled over his people in dangerous and warlike times. His subjects had to work for him and pay taxes. As long as he ruled the people, they remained united.

Čembulat, sometimes called *kugə jeŋ* 'great man' (A.21.2.), or *kurək kuguza* 'mountain old man' (A.21.2.1.), is a *keremet* (A.31.) to whom a black horse is sacrificed. The worship of this *keremet* was at one time connected with a huge stone which was located along the Nemda River near the town of Chembulatova. The stone, also called *čembulat,* was about thirty-five feet high and one hundred and ten feet wide. It was broken up by Russian missionaries in 1830 in order to destroy the Cheremis beliefs in pagan spirits. The name *čembulat* is rarely used in prayers but it is frequently used as a term of insult meaning "devil."

H[1926], 168–70, 172; H[1927], 155; Häm.[1936–37], 73; S, 154, 157–58.)

For *čerlak üdəržə,* see A.96.1.

A.13. *čes* 'provisions'

A duck is sacrificed to *čes* during the sacrifice dedicated to *buj ümbal jumə* (A.26.6.) at the time when a young man reaches the age of assuming his adult responsibilities (B.34.).

(Häm.[1908a], 9.)

For *čəbə jumə,* see A.26.8.; *čodra kuguza* and *kuba,* A.38.5.; *čodra on,* A.52.3.; *čon pujərsə,* A.70.4.

A.14. *čopakin*

A calf is sacrificed to this *keremet* (A.31.).

(S, 155.)

A.15. *čort* or *šart* 'devil'

This term may mean either 'devil' or 'water spirit' in much the same way as *ia* (A.16.). As a water spirit, the time when it is most likely to appear is at midnight, noon, and about six o'clock in the morning and evening. At these times, it is especially likely to catch a person who has gone to the water to swim or to fish. In a folktale (for type and motif analysis, see Sebeok, 1952, pp. 20–21) *čort* is distinguished from mortals by the fact that it has no eyebrows. Sometimes *šərt* is the helper of a *keremet* (A.31.) to whom sacrifices are made.

For other devils, see A.7., A.18., A.30., A.75., A.81., and A.93.

(Be, 63, 65; Bk, 47–48; J; R, 189, 203.)

A.15.1. *čurpan šərt* 'stump devil'

A hare is sacrificed to this *keremet* (A.31.).
(S, 155.)

A.15.2. *keremet šərt*

A sacrifice of a hare is made to this spirit.
For *keremet,* see A.31.
(S, 155.)

A.15.3. *kurək šərt* 'mountain devil'

A sacrifice of a ram is made to this *keremet* (A.31.).
For other mountain spirits, see A.9.9., A.16.2., A.21.2.1., A.26.21., and A.38.14.
(S, 154.)

A.15.4. *məlandə šərt* 'earth devil'

An offering of pancakes and beer is made to this spirit at *aga pajram* (B.2.).
For other earth spirits, see A.1.5., A.1.10.5., A.9.10., A.26.25., A.52.10., A.58.5., A.65.2., A.67.11., A.68.8., A.70.12., A.76.6., A.79.2., A.82.7., and A.84.14.
(H[1926], 73; P, 203.)

A.15.5. *mоča šərt* 'bathhouse devil'

A sacrifice of a bull is made to this *keremet* (A.31.).
For other spirits connected with the bathhouse, see A.2., A.38.16., and A.85.
(S, 155.)

A.15.6. *mükš šərt* 'bee devil'

A hare, a ram, and a ewe are sacrificed to this *keremet* (A.31.).
(S, 155.)

A.15.7. *pajberda šərt*

A calf is sacrificed to this *keremet* (A.31.).
(S, 149, 155.)

A.15.8. *rok šərt*

A goose is sacrificed to this *keremet* (A.31.).
(S, 155.)

A.15.9. *šerdəš šərt*

A bull is sacrificed to this *keremet* (A.31.).
(S, 155.)

A.15.10.   *undur šərt*

A ewe is sacrificed to this *keremet* (A.31.).

(S, 155.)

For *emšener,* see A.19.; *eŋer bodəž,* A.9.2.; *eprem kuguza,* A.38.6.; *er bolgastər,* A.26.10.; *er orolək,* A.55.1.; *er šukčə,* A.84.5.; *er tütra,* A.92.; *jüštə ergə,* A.38.11.; *ergə pujəršə,* A.70.4.; *ergə pujəršə jumə,* A.26.31.1.; *ergə šočən,* A.82.3.; *jüštə ərbezə,* A.38.11.; *pokšəm ərbezə,* A.38.22.; *ərləgan kuguza* and *kuba,* A.38.7.

A.16.   *ia* 'devil'

This term may mean either a spirit of a specified locality or devil in contrast to angel. According to some accounts, each person has both an angel and a devil, the former on his right shoulder and the latter on his left. These two compete for his soul, the angel writing down his good deeds and thoughts, the devil writing down the bad. The one who has a longer list takes the person's soul. The devil notes those who misbehave in church by looking back, looking at members of the opposite sex, or whispering. The devil laughs when men weep and weeps when they laugh; the devil also weeps when the angel gets a soul.

An *ia* has long hair which, according to one report, blazes like fire. It can travel about in a whirlwind. An *ia* may originate from the spittle of men, especially evil men and sorcerers; therefore, when a person spits on the floor, the spittle should be stepped on. A sinful priest may also become an *ia* after his death. It is also reported that the soul of a woman killed by *sotona kuba* (A.75.) became an *ia.*

Drunkards are taken by *ia* and so also are those who die in water. They are changed into horses, and in tales, when a smith lifts up such a horse's hoof to shoe it, the hoof becomes a human foot.

Lightning is the enemy of *ia* and comes to earth seeking to destroy it. If the devil is in a house, lightning may burn the house down; if the devil is with people, lightning may strike the people in an attempt to kill the devil. In order to keep the devil away and thus prevent lightning from striking, people make an 'iron fence,' *kərtńa pečə,* i.e., they draw a circle around them with an iron object (H.4.4.). If there is an empty tobacco pouch, the devil may get into it; for this reason the pouch is thrown away so that the devil will not be near.

If a baby is left alone, the devil can keep the child from growing, cause it to become sick, and make it cry; this can be prevented by leaving an iron object near the child's head. If a person looks through the hole of a big branch with his left eye, he may see the devil.

The devil causes all sorts of trouble and may appear in almost any form. It may tempt people in the form of a child; it may come to a woman as a lover. An *ia* also causes people to lose their way in the forest; it makes the familiar forest unrecognizable or makes one path look like another.

An *ia* sometimes lives in the barn. If it likes a horse, it takes care of it so that it becomes sleek and fat. If it doesn't like an animal, it will torment it and keep it from eating so that the horse becomes thin. The *ia* may even take the fodder from one horse and give it to another. Sometimes it rides a horse all night so that, in the morning, the horse is covered with sweat (cf. A.51.). According to tales, a farmer may stop this by putting tar on the horse's back so that the devil cannot get off. When the devil finally succeeds in dismounting, it never comes back.

An *ia* may also be helpful. In some accounts, people become rich by putting out food for an *ia* who leaves money in exchange. This devil usually lives under the house. If a cross is made over the food, the *ia* cannot eat it.

As a spirit of a specific place, *ia* is also called *oza,* 'master,' (A.54.). During prayers, the terms *ia* and *oza* are rarely used; the terms *kuguza* 'old man' and *kuba* 'old woman' are preferred, thus splitting the concept of a single spirit into two, male and female. In some regions the term *ia* is used in a more restricted sense to mean water spirit only (A.16.1.).

For other devils, see A.7., A.15., A.18., A.75., and A.81.

(B, 9–12, 67–68; Be, 377–78; Bj, 161–67; Bk, 49–50; Bu, 20, 39–41, 41–47, 66–86; L, 56 [64]; S, 163; Uj[FB], 11, 61–64, 94; T, 37; Up[FB], 25–26; Wu, 29.)

For *bakš ia,* see A.38.2.; *biča ia,* A.38.4.

A.16.1.   *büt ia* 'water devil'

A water spirit of this category, in some regions simply called *ia,* is most often thought to be an old man, sometimes with horns, which lives at the bottom of a river or lake. It is occasionally seen wandering along the bank, sunning itself, or combing its long hair. It may be dressed in rags or in rich clothes with silver coins on its chest; sometimes it is naked. Under the water it has a house, family and possessions; the wealth of a *büt ia* is in proportion to the size of the body of water in which it lives. In some regions, *büt ia* is believed to be female, but usually a female water spirit of human shape is called *büt ian üdərža* 'water devil's daughter' (A.96.2.). The water spirit can also appear as a horse, *büt imńə,* an ox, *büt uškəz,* or a fish. A fish which is a *büt ia* can be distinguished from other fish not only by its extraordinary size but also by the fact that it sleeps facing the current. *Büt ia* is also called *büt oza;* in prayers it is called *büt kuguza* and *büt kuba.* In some places it is believed that a person who drowns becomes a water spirit until someone else drowns and takes his place. As soon as *büt ia* is seen, it jumps back into the water or disappears. The appearance of the water spirit forebodes death or some other misfortune.

Sacrifices to the water spirit usually consist of money, pancakes, vodka, or a small animal such as a lamb, goose, or duck. Nevertheless, there is one account of large animals such as horses, cows, oxen, and sheep being sacrificed as well. In exchange for these sacrifices the *ia* allows fish to be caught and does not drown people, which it might do if enraged. In some places, after the first fish is caught in the spring, the fishermen cook and eat it without breaking any of the bones, which are thrown back into the water as a sacrifice to *büt ia.* A prayer is said asking that more fish may be caught.

For other water spirits, see A.1.1., A.9.1., A.26.7., A.38.8., A.52.2., A.58.2., A.70.3., A. 84.4., and A.96.2.

(G, 2–3 [82–84]; H[1913], 114–120, 127, 130; H[1926], 58–61; H[1927], 199–200; P[1948], 21; PG, 13 [74]; S, 169; Uj[T], 23; Usj[FB], 3.)

For *kožla ia,* see A.51.

A.16.2.   *kurək ia* 'mountain devil'

In the mountains live communities of these spirits which are about three feet tall. These flat-nosed dwarfs have grinning mouths and long hair. If a person lies down to sleep where they are, his feet begin to hurt so he cannot use them.

(H[1926], 56–57.)

For *moča ia*, see A.38.16.

A.16.3.   *paravoj ia* 'ship devil'

Spirits human in shape inhabit ships. They are heard moving about in the holds of ships in the winter and on summer nights.

(H[1926], 53.)

For *pört ia*, see A.38.23.; *surt ia*, A.38.23.; *ia kuguza* and *kuba*, A.38.8.; *ia saltak*, A.74.; *büt ian üdəržə*, A.96.2.

A.17.   *ibaška*

A cock is sacrificed to this *keremet* (A.31.).

(S, 155.)

For *idəm kuguza* and *kuba*, see A.38.9.; *idəm ört*, A.58.3.; *idəm perke*, A.67.3.; *idəm pujəršə*, A.70.5.; *idəm šukčə*, A.84.6.; *ikša keremet*, A.31.2.; *ikšəbə pujəršə*, A.70.4.; *ikšəbə šočən*, A.82.4.; *il'a jumə*, A.26.9.; *imńe targəldəš*, A.86.1.; *inləkan kuguza* and *kuba*, A.38.7.; *izə nur keremet*, A.31.6.; *ižera jumə*, A.26.10.

A.18.   *jabol* 'devil'

For other devils, see A.7., A.15., A.16., A.75., and A.81.

(Sz, 30, 49.)

For *jal ümbač koštšə keremet*, see A.31.5.; *jal(x)ter bodəž*, A.9.3.

A.19.   *jamšener* or *emsener* or *jomšeŋer*

This *keremet* (A.31.), which lives in the springs, sends disease to those whose hair or a piece of whose clothing has been thrown into the spring. Such a disease can be cured by sacrificing a fish or a woodpecker to *jamšener*. The meaning of the name of this spirit is not certain but may come from *jomš eŋer* 'jomš river,' or *jomšo eŋer* 'master of the well.'

(H[1913], 125; H[1926], 168; S, 153, 155; V, 307.)

For *jarčik*, see A.38.16.; *jauš keremet*, A.31.3.

A.20.   *jekšuk*

This forest spirit comes in the wind and scatters the fire of people who spend the night in the forest. To keep this spirit from entering, branches of rowan are put on top of the gate to a field and on bridges.

For other forest spirits, see A.11., A.43., A.51., and A.86.

(Beke[1949], 120; Bk, 45.)

A.21. *jeŋ* 'man'

A.21.1. *kož jeŋ* 'pine man'

A hare is sacrificed to this *keremet* (A.31.).
(S, 155.)

A.21.1.1. *toštə kož jeŋ* 'old pine man'

A cock is sacrificed to this *keremet* (A.31.).
(S, 155.)

A.21.2. *kugə jeŋ* 'great man'

This legendary hero, riding on a white horse, fought enemies of the Cheremis people. When he finally established peace on earth, he buried himself on a mountain peak. Before doing this, however, he promised to help the Cheremis if a new war should arise on earth. To awaken him, a man on a white horse should ride around the mountain three times and shout, "Arise, *kugə jeŋ*, there is war on earth." One time a Cheremis did this out of mere curiosity. When *kugə jeŋ* found that there was no war, he angrily made all the Cheremis his slaves, exacting a yearly sacrifice of a horse. Sacrifices are also made to the following, which are considered to be helpers of this spirit: *užedəš* (A.95.), *aš* (A.5.), *azren* (A.6.), *paškərče* (A.63.), *marče* (A.45.), *bitnəzə* (A.8.), and *bodəž* (A.9.). The sacrifice ceremony dedicated to *kugə jeŋ*, held about a week after Pentecost, resembles the *küsə* sacrifices (B.9.). In the fall, those present at the spring ceremony sacrifice a hen and a rooster.

Though sometimes *kugə jeŋ* is a *keremet* (A.31.) identified with *nemdə kurək kugə jeŋ* (A.21.2.1.) and *čembulat* (A.12.), elsewhere it is not considered to be a *keremet*, although even so it is a very important evil spirit. Sacrifices are made to it in the fall and in case of sicknesses or epidemic. The Cheremis are very reluctant to talk about this spirit and consequently not much is known. They do say, however, that they consider their sacrificing to this spirit as comparable to the way in which others go to a physician.
(Be, 63–65; H[1926], 170–71; P, 124; S, 155.)

A.21.2.1. *nemdə kurək kugə jeŋ* 'Nemda Mountain great man'

This widely known *keremet* (A.31.) is also called *nende kurək kugə, mendə kurək kuguza, lemdə kurək kuguza, kurək kugə jeŋ, kurək kuguza* 'mountain old man,' and *kugərak* 'prince.' This *keremet* was once a great leader of the people who buried himself on the top of Nemda Mountain. He told the people to awaken him only in case of war. A curious Cheremis aroused him, telling him there was a great war; the hero came forth to defend his people. However, when he found that there was no war, he became angry and decreed that the people make a yearly sacrifice of a brown horse (cf. A.12. and A.64.2.). This is the origin of the annual sacrifice made after Pentecost by the people near Nemda Mountain.

This *keremet* is sometimes also called the "northern czar." It is said to have an invisible city on a mountain and an invisible army; sometimes passers-by can hear the soldiers' shooting on the mountain. When there is an epidemic among the cattle, people say that the "northern czar" has sent its soldiers to kill and eat the cattle. Sometimes this *keremet* is worshipped in time of war. During the Russo-Japanese War, some

Cheremis soldiers made a vow to sacrifice a horse to it; this vow was fulfilled when they returned home. During the empire, it was believed that this *keremet* fought on the side of the Russian czar who prayed to it so that it would not go over to the enemy. This *keremet* is also worshipped in case of great drought and bad harvest. The primary reason for sacrifices, however, is to cure diseases which a seer says that it has caused. Usually a horse is sacrificed to it in a rite similar to that used at the *küsə* ceremony (B.9.). Even a small uprooted tree (F.15.1.) is bound with linden bark, as in the *küšə* sacrifice; however, sacrifice insignia are not fastened to it. At the end of the ceremony, the tree is thrown into the fire.

Nemdə kurək kugə jeη, traveling back and forth between Vyatka and Kazan, still watches over the Cheremis. Wearing a green cloak and a red cap, it rides a white horse or travels about in a silver wagon. A person who does not make way for it, but touches the horse or the wheels of the wagon, will become sick and must sacrifice to *nemdə kurək kugə jeη.*

Among those spirits which form the retinue of this *keremet* and are worshipped with it are *aba* 'mother' (A.1.) ; *tiak* 'scribe' (A.89.) ; *telmač* 'interpreter' (A.88.) ; *kapka orol* 'gate guard' (A.55.2.) ; *üstel orol* 'table guard' (A.55.3.) ; *aš* (A.5.) ; *kübar kuguza* 'bridge old man' (A.38.15.), also called *kübar jumal kuguza* 'old man under the bridge,' *ümbač koštšə* 'one who walks over,' *ümbal keremet* 'over keremet,' *osər pamaš* 'osər spring,' and *šüč pundəš* 'burnt stump' (A.71.) ; *bitnəzə* 'reporter' (A.8.) ; *šərt* 'devil' (A.15.) ; *bodəž* 'spirit' (A.9.) ; *azren* 'angel of death' (A.6.) ; *uzedəš* 'disease' (A.95.) ; and *piambar* 'prophet' (A.68.). One source reports a steer, two sheep, a goat, two geese, a rooster, a hen, a duck, two grouse, and a fish being sacrificed to these helping spirits at one ceremony. The number of the servants is believed to be nine and therefore nine loaves of bread are put before the sacrifice tree. If a man is sick but does not have the means to sacrifice at once, he may make a vow. Three times he strews meal in the fire promising *nemdə kurək kugə jeη* a foal and praying *tul bodež* (A.9.14.) to act as intermediary. He washes and heats a chisel or other iron implement and, striking it three times, puts it in the corner of the building where it is left until the vow is fulfilled. He promises a duck to the *bitnəzə* (A.8.) and a hen to the *šərt* (A.15.) ; then he makes three sacrifices: a hen to the *bodəž,* a cock to the *azren* (A.6.), and a hen to the *uzedəs* (A.89.).

According to an eighteenth century report, the Cheremis made pilgrimages to the Nemda River to sacrifice there. There was the belief that if a Cheremis went there but made no offering, he would die. A devil was also supposed to live in a brook near the Nemda; the brook was not deep and never froze in the winter. The belief existed that if a Cheremis came to that brook, he would die; however, it would not harm a Russian.

(Be, 62–65; H[1926], 167–72; H[1927], 155; Müller, 346–47; S, 149, 155; Uj[FB], 8; V, 148, 157, 234, 235, 281.)

A.21.3.   *nol' jeη*

A ram, a chicken, and a pig are sacrificed to this *keremet* (A.31.).
(S, 155.)

A.21.4.   *toštot jeŋ*

A hare is sacrificed to this *keremet* (A.31.).

(S, 155.)

For *jeŋ šočən aba,* see A.1.10.2.

A.22.   *kusnəšə jer* 'wandering lake'

A lake which does not remain in its bed but which moves from one place to another is personified. It becomes angry when it is defiled and consequently moves to another place. When such a lake intends to move, *pujəršə* (A.70.) appears to warn the people to make room for it.

For one such lake, see A.96.1.

(H[1926], 77.)

For *šišer jer jumə,* see A.26.11.; *jer bodəž,* A.9.4.; *jer kuguza,* A.38.10.; *jer oza,* A.38.10., A.51.; *ješ on,* A.52.4.; *ješ perke,* A.67.4.; *ješ pujəršə,* A.70.6.; *ješ šukčə,* A.84.7.

A.23.   *pasu jər* 'field offering'

A ram is sometimes sacrificed to this spirit during *aga kurman,* 'plow sacrifice,' (B.1.).

(H[1926], 183.)

For *jomšeŋer,* see A.19.

A.24.   *kugə jomšə* 'great *jomšə*'

The meaning of the name of this *keremet* (A.31.) is not known, although possibly it is borrowed from the Chuvash *jomža* 'sorcerer.'

(H[1926], 168.)

For *joškar ser,* see A.77.1.

A.25.   *jučuzo*

A grouse is sacrificed to this *keremet* (A.31.).

(S, 155.)

For *jul ser kugərak,* see A.37.

A.26.   *jumə* 'god,' 'sky'

The supreme god is called *kugə jumə,* 'great god,' to distinguish it from other gods. When *jumə* is used to designate a nature god, it is preceded by a word for the aspect of nature personified. In the polytheistic religion of the Cheremis it is very easy for the term *jumə* to be combined with other concepts. This has sometimes resulted in considering each attribute of this god as being a separate god. As a consequence, it is, at times, difficult to ascertain whether two names refer to the same or different deities. Furthermore, the term *jumə* is also used for the Christian God. Usually *kugə jumə* is not described as having specific characteristics. However, when such a description is made, *jumə* resembles a wealthy landowner. It is human both in appearance and emotions. It has a family, including a wife and children. It shoots with the rainbow and the wind is its breath. It lives in the sky where it cultivates land and raises extensive herds. It has a large retinue consisting of its *aba* 'mother' (A.1.) ; *bitnəzə* 'reporter' (A.8.) ; *šukčə* 'angel' (A.84.) ; *piambar* 'prophet' (A.68.) ; *kaznači* 'treasurer' (A.29.) ; *aš* (A.5.) ; *serlagəš* 'mercy' (A.78.) ; and *šerməčkəl kučən pušə* 'the one who holds the reins' (A.72.). Any deity called *jumə* may have a similar group of servants.

Kugə jumə is prayed to for all possible blessings. The sacrifice of a brown or a white horse is made to it at every *küsə* cermony. In the sacred grove the tree dedicated to *kugə jumə* is either the easternmost tree or the second one from the east. An offering is made annually at *aga pajram* (B.2.). Those who form the retinue of *jumə* also receive sacrifices when *jumə* is worshipped; sometimes they are said to intercede for man who does not always dare ask the help of *kugə jumə*. *Kugə jumə* is also called *pəl ümbal jumə* 'god above the clouds,' *mir jumə* 'world god,' and *tüńća jumə* 'world god.'

(G, 55 [148]; H[1926], 63–67, 120; H[1927], 265; P, 186, 189, 204; S, 166; Up[FB], 6.)

A.26.1.1.   *kində aba jumə* 'grain mother god'

For other grain spirits, see A.1.8.2., A.26.1.3.1., A.26.16., A.26.34., A.29.2., A.52.7., A.52.12.1., A.70.18., A.82.6., and A.84.13.

A.26.1.2.   *mükš aba jumə* 'bee mother god'

For other bee spirits, see A.1.6., A.1.10.6., A.15.6., A.26.1.2., A.26.28., A.26.38.2., A.27.1., A.28.3., A.29.3., A.52.11., A.58.6., A.65.3., A.67.13., A.68.9., A.70.13., A.76.7., A.78.3., A.79.1.2., A.82.8., and A.84.15.; see also A.67.12.

(B, 23; Up[FB], 9.)

A.26.1.3.   *perke aba jumə* 'blessing mother god'

Prayers are said to this deity both when the Cheremis begin to sow and when the first bread from the harvest is eaten.

For *perke aba*, see A.1.8.; for *perke*, A.67.

(B, 22; Uj[FB], 27.)

A.26.1.3.1.   *kində perke aba jumə* 'grain blessing mother god'

For *kinde perke aba*, see A.1.8.2.

(B, 24.)

A.26.1.4.   *šočən aba juməšaməč* 'fructifier mother gods'

For *šočən aba*, see A.1.10.

(B, 23.)

A.26.2.   *aga pajram jumə* 'plowing ceremony god'

An offering is thrown into the fire for this deity at *aga pajram* (B.2.) (cf. A.41.).

(Be, 709; H[1926], 177; Wu, 27.)

A.26.3.   *alak jumə* 'slanderer god'

This deity reports to god the evil deeds of men but defends good men who come up for judgment before god.

(B[1926], 66, 111; S, 163.)

A.26.4. *bolgeńčə jumə* 'lightning god'

This deity is usually worshipped together with the thunder god. The Cheremis pray to it not to cause any damage. On the other hand, they believe that if there is a great deal of lightning at the time when the grain is ripening, the harvest will be bountiful. The lightning god is also compared to the *saus* who keeps discipline at a wedding (B.17.3.).

(H[1926], 67–68; S, 163, 169.)

A.26.5. *bol'ək jumə* 'livestock god'

For other livestock spirits, see A.10.1., A.26.38.1., A.38.1., A.52.1., A.67.2., A.68.1., A.70.2., A.76.2., A.78.1., A.79.1.1., A.82.2., and A.84.3.

(Uj[T], 54.)

A.26.6. *buj jumə* 'head god'; *buj ümbal jumə* 'god over the head'

The 'head god' determines the age and fate of an individual. A sacrifice is made to this deity when a man reaches adulthood (B.34.); at that time eleven animals in all are sacrificed: a horse to *buj jumə* and smaller animals to each of its ten helpers.

(H[1926], 66, 156; Häm.[1908a], 2–3, 8–9.)

A.26.7. *büt jumə* 'water god'

For other water spirits, see A.1.1., A.9.1., A.16.1., A.26.29.1., A.52.2., A.58.2., A.70.3., A.84.4., and A.96.2.

(H[1913], 119; S, 163.)

A.26.8. *čəbe jumə* 'chicken god'

A candle is sometimes lit and a prayer said to this deity for the protection of the chickens.

For another spirit which protects fowl, see A.1.10.4.

(B, 23; Uj[FB], 23.)

A.26.9. *il'a jumə* 'Elijah god'

The Prophet Elijah has become a pagan god for certain Cheremis. This is probably a result of the fact that Russian missionary priests emphasized this Old Testament prophet, drawing parallels between him and the pagan gods. St. Elijah's Day (July 29) is a holiday for both pagan and Christian Cheremis. July thunderstorms are attributed to Elijah, thunder being the rumble of his wagon wheels as he rides through the heavens.

(H[1926], 68; S, 191; Zykov, 12–13, 31.)

A.26.10. *ižera jumə* 'dawn god'

The deity of dawn is also called *er bolgastər* 'morning brightening'; a libation is made to it at the *küsə* ceremony (B.9.).

(H[1926], 70; S, 163.)

A.26.11. *šišer jer jumə* 'milk lake god'

(S, 163.)

A.26.12. *jür jumə* 'rain god'

For other rain-producing spirits, see A.1.1., A.26.22., A.56.1., and A.96.1.

(H[1926], 70.)

A.26.13.   *kaba jumə* 'fate god'

On *kaba jumə* depends a person's fortune. It also protects the sown fields. A horse is sometimes sacrificed to it at the *küsə* ceremony (B.9.) and an offering is made at *aga pajram* (B.2.). Some Cheremis who have been in contact with Christianity identify *kaba jumə* with St. Nicholas.

For *kaba,* see A.27.

(Be, 705; H[1926], 66–67; S, 167, 169, 191.)

A.26.14.   *kajək jumə* 'bird god'; *kajək usa jumə* 'game god'

Prayers are said to this deity both for an increase in the poultry and for luck while hunting.

(B, 23; H[1926], 66; S, 163; Uj[FB], 22; Up[FB], 7.)

A.26.15.   *kečə jumə* 'sun god'

For other sun spirits, see A.1.3., A.10.3.1., A.26.31.2., and A.52.6.

(Wu, 27.)

A.26.15.1.   *oš kečə jumə* 'white sun god'

This deity causes plants to grow well.

(Häm.[1936–37], 71; S, 169.)

A.26.16.   *kində juməšaməč* 'grain gods'

For other grain spirits, see A.1.8.2., A.26.1.1., A.26.3.1., A.26.34., A.29.2., A.52.7., A.52.12.1., A.70.18., A.82.6., and A.84.13.

A.26.17.   *kugarňa jumə* 'Friday god'

This deity sees to it that Friday, which is the weekly sabbath of the Cheremis, is properly observed (cf. A.26.32.)

(H[1926], 66; S, 165.)

A.26.18.   *kugečə jumə* 'Easter god'

The Easter ceremonies (B.8.) are dedicated to this god. Among its helpers are *aš* (A.5.), *šočənžə* 'fructifier' (A.82.), *pujəršə* 'creator' (A.70.), and *aba* 'mother' (A.1.). (H[1926], 66, 191; S, 165; V, 82.)

A.26.19.1.   *piambar kuguza jumə* 'prophet old man god'

A sick person sometimes prays to this deity. At times a ram is sacrificed to it.

For *piambar,* see A.68.; for *kuguza,* A.38.

(Uj[FB], 6.)

A.26.20.   *kugužan jumə* 'ruler's god'

(H[1926], 66; S, 165.)

A.26.21.   *kurək jumə* 'mountain god'

Deities called *jumə* are usually considered to be "upper" deities, i.e., having their residence above the world. *Kurək jumə,* however, is a "lower" deity which resides under the earth. Private sacrifices are made to *kurək jumə* every three years by families. Additional sacrifices are made by individuals in case of illness.

For other "lower" spirits, see A.31.
(Häm.[1908a], 2; S, 163.)

A.26.22.   *küdərčə jumə* 'thunder god'

The thunder god, one of the most widely worshipped nature deities, is usually worshipped together with the lightning god (A.26.4.). It protects the crops from drought and hail, and blesses them; it also protects men and cattle. Sometimes people pray to this god for rain. It has its own tree in sacred groves where horses are sacrificed to it. Offerings are also made at *aga pajram* (B.2.). If this deity does not receive the proper sacrifice it may cause extensive destruction by hail. The thunder god is the enemy of the devil, *ia* (A.16.) or *šajtan* (A.81.), and tries to kill it with thunderbolts.

(H[1913], 122; H[1926], 67–68, 119; P, 72, 187, 203; S, 163, 169; Wu, 27.)

A.26.23.   *küllö jumə* 'küllö god'

For other *küllö* spirits, see A.67.10., A.68.7., A.70.7.2., and A.70.11.
(Be, 709; H[1926], 111.)

A.26.24.   *mardəž jumə* 'wind god'

This deity blesses and protects the grain.
For other wind spirits, see A.1.4., A.26.43., and A.52.9.
(B, 23; S, 163; Uj[FB], 25.)

A.26.25.   *məlandə jumə* 'earth god'

For other earth spirits, see A.1.5., A.1.10.5., A.9.10., A.15.4., A.52.10., A.58.5., A.65.2., A.67.11., A.68.8., A.70.12., A.76.6., A.79.2., A.82.7., and A.84.14.
(B, 22; S, 163; Wu, 27.)

A.26.26.   *mikola jumə* 'Nicholas god'

St. Nicholas is worshipped as a god by some Cheremis. A libation is made to it at the *küsə* ceremony (B.9.). Sometimes a cow is offered to this deity.
(H[1926], 141; V, 137; Zykov, 13, 31.)

A.26.27.   *mir jumə* 'world god'

This term is used for *kugə jumə* (A.26.); it is also used sometimes for Jesus Christ. *Mir* is used to designate a district in which the people hold joint sacrifice ceremonies (B.9.1.).
(G, 55 [148]; H[1926], 64, 112; S, 191; Wu, 27.)

A.26.28.   *mükš jumə* 'bee god'

For other bee spirits, see A.10.6., A.15.6., A.26.1.2., A.26.38.2., A.27.1., A.28.3., A.29.3., A.52.11., A.58.6., A.65.3., A.67.13., A.68.9., A.70.13., A.76.7., A.78.3., A.79.1.2., A.82.8., and A.84.15.; see also A.67.12.
(B, 23, 91; S, 101; Uj[FB], 24, [T], 54; Up[FB], 8.)

A.26.29.1.   *büt on jumə* 'water lord god'

For *büt on*, see A.52.2.
(H[1913], 119.)

A.26.29.2. *teŋəz on jumə* 'sea lord god'

For *teŋəz on,* see A.52.16.

(H[1913], 119.)

A.26.29.3. *tul on jumə* 'fire lord god'

For *tul on,* see A.52.18.

(Häm.[1936–37], 71.)

A.26.30. *perke jumə* 'blessing god'

For *perke,* see A.67.

(H[1926], 119; Uj[FB], 31; Up[FB], 10.)

For *pəl ümbal jumə,* see A.26.

A.26.31. *pujəršə jumə* 'creator god'

A horse is sacrificed to this deity at the *küsə* ceremony (B.9.), and beer and pancakes at *aga pajram* (B.2.).

For *pujəršə,* see A.70.

(G, 55 [148]; H[1926], 119; P, 72, 187, 203.)

A.26.31.1. *ergə pujəršə jumə* 'son creator god'

A stallion is sacrificed to this deity at the *küsə* ceremony (B.9.); beer and pancakes are offered at *aga pajram* (B.2.).

For *ergə pujəršə,* see A.70.4.

(G, 55 [148]; P, 187, 189, 203.)

A.26.31.2. *kečə pujəršə jumə* 'sun creator god'

For other sun spirits, see A.1.3., A.10.3.1., A.26.15., A.26.15.1., and A.52.6.

(Häm.[1936–37], 71.)

A.26.31.3. *tüñča ümbal pujəršə jumə* 'creator god over the world'

An offering is made to this deity at *aga pajram* (B.2.) and a foal is sacrificed at *küsə* (B.9.).

(H[1926], 112; P, 203.)

A.26.32. *rušarña jumə* 'Sunday god'

This deity sees to it that Sunday is properly sanctified (cf. A.26.17.).

(H[1926], 66; S, 165.)

A.26.33. *sakčə jumə* 'guardian god'

A ram is sacrificed to this deity at the *küsə* ceremony (B.9.); an offering of beer and pancakes is made at *aga pajram* (B.2.).

For *sakčə,* see A.84.

(P, 187, 203.)

A.26.34. *saska jumə* or *xirxa jumə* 'blossom god'

This deity is most often worshipped by beekeepers.

For another blossom spirit, see A.70.14.

(B, 22; H[1926], 66; S, 163; Uj[T], 54.)

A.26.34.1. *kində saska jumə* 'grain blossom god'

(B, 22; Uj[FB], 21.)

A.26.35. *spaš jumə* 'spaš god'

The Russian word *spas,* meaning both 'savior' and a religious holiday, is used to designate this Cheremis deity. In August two white sheep are sacrificed to it.

(V, 193, 311.)

A.26.36. *surt jumə* 'house god'

For other house spirits, see A.9.2., A.38.23., A.58.9., A.67.15., A.70.17., and A.84.18.

(S, 163.)

A.26.37. *sürem jumə*

During the *sürem* ceremony (B.18.), prayers are said to this deity and a sacrifice is promised; on the following day the vow is fulfilled.

(Wu, 29–30.)

A.26.38.1. *bol'ək šočən jumə* 'livestock fructifier god'

About five days after the birth of a calf, a ceremony is dedicated to this god (B.28.). Water is sprinkled on the oven and prayers are said to this god that the calf may grow as big as the oven.

For *bol'ək šočən,* see A.82.2.

(H[1927], 259.)

A.26.38.2. *mükš šočən jumə* 'bee fructifier god'

For *mükš šočən,* see A.82.8.

(S, 163.)

A.26.39. *šüdər jumə* 'star god'

For other star spirits, see A.1.12. and A.52.15.

(S, 163; Wu, 27.)

A.26.40. *teŋəz jumə* 'sea god'

For other sea spirits, see A.1.13., A.26.29.2., A.52.16., A.70.19.

(H[1913], 119; S, 163.)

A.26.41. *tələzə jumə* 'moon god'

For other moon spirits, see A.1.4. and A.52.17.

(S, 163; Wu, 27.)

A.26.42. *tul jumə* 'fire god'

A sacrifice is made to this deity at sacrifice ceremonies in *küs otə* (E.2.1.). If sacrifices are not made to *tul jumə* it may cause a conflagration.

For other fire spirits, see A.1.10.8., A.1.15., A.9.14., A.26.29.3., A.52.18., A.58.10., A.70.20., A.84.20., and A.88.1.

(S, 163, 169; Uj[T], 54.)

A.26.43.   *tul'a jumə* or *tul jumə*

This deity keeps the wind in chains. If angered, it frees the wind, which destroys everything in its path.

(H[1926], 71; S, 163, 169.)

For *tüńča jumə*, see A.26.

A.26.44.1.   *sot tüńča jumə* 'sot world god'

The god of the clear sky, because *sot* is identified with Russian *sotnya* 'hundred,' by folk etymology, is believed to be the god over one hundred gods. Some Cheremis who have been in contact with Christianity identify this deity with St. Nicholas.

(S, 168, 191.)

A.26.45.   *tütra jumə* 'mist god'

For another mist spirit, see A.92.

(H[1926], 70.)

A.26.46.   *umər jumə* 'good weather god'

(H[1926], 70.)

For *jumən aba*, see A.1.2.; *kaba jumən onən abažə*, A.1.7.1.1.; *kaba jumən onžə*, A.52.5.1.; *kaba jumən pujəršə*, A.26.13.; *jumən bitnəzə*, A.8.; *jumən kaznači*, A.29.1.; *jumən on*, A.52.5.; *jumən piambar*, A.68.2.; *jumən perke*, A.67.5.; *kaba jumən pujəršə*, A.70.7.1.; *küllö jumən pujəršəblak*, A.70.7.2.; *jumən salauz*, A.73.; *jumən serlagəš*, A.78.2.; *jumən šerməčkəl kučan pušə*, A.72.; *jumən šočən*, A.82.5.; *kaba jumən šočən*, A.82.5.1.; *jumən šukčə*, A.84.8.; *jür jumə*, A.26.12.; *jür oržə*, A.56.1.; *jüštə ergə*, A.38.11.; *jüštə ərbezə*, A.38.11.; *jüštə kuguza* and *kuba*, A.38.11.; *jüštə mužə*, A.46.1.; *jüštə muže üdər*, A.96.3.; *jüt bodəž*, A.9.5.

A.27.   *kaba* 'fate,' 'heaven'

The meaning of *kaba* is not entirely clear. Because it apparently comes from the Chuvash *kebe* 'fate,' it is translated by some as meaning 'fate.' Others say that it means the sky or all that is not on earth, including sun, stars, weather, gods, etc. A horse is sacrificed to *kaba* at the *küsə* ceremony (B.9.). An offering is also made to this deity at *aga pajram* (B.2.).

There are dictionary entries *kaba bitnəzə* 'heaven reporter'; *kaba kazna* 'heaven treasure' (A.28.2.); *kaba kugə jumə* 'great heaven god' (A.26.13.); *kaba kugə jumən šočənžə* 'great heaven god's fructifier' (A.82.5.1.); *kaba kugə jumən pujəršə* 'great heaven god's creator' (A.70.7.1.); *kaba kugə jumən onən abažə* 'great heaven god's lord's mother' (A.1.7.1.1.); *kaba kugə jumən onžə* 'great heaven god's lord' (A.52.5.1.); *kaba kugə jumən ašəžə* 'great heaven god's aš' (A.5.); *kaba kugə jumən perk(e) abažə* 'great heaven god's blessing mother' (A.1.8.1.1.); *kaba piambar* 'heaven prophet' (A.68.3.); *kaba pujəršə* 'heaven creator' (A.70.8.); *kaba perke* 'heaven blessing' (A.67.6); *kaba saus* 'heaven overseer' (A.76.3.); and *kaba šukčə* 'heaven angel' (A.84.9.). Nothing more is known about most of these spirits.

(G, 55, 58, 59, 148, 153, 154; J; P, 187, 189, 203; Sz, 61; V, 57.)

A.27.1.   *mükš kaba* 'bee fate'

An offering is made to *mükš kaba* at *aga pajram* (B.2.). A ram is sacrificed at *mükš jər* (B.11.), a ceremony dedicated to the bee gods.

For other bee spirits, see A.1.6., A.1.10.6., A.15.6., A.26.1.2., A.26.28., A.26.38.2, A.28.3., A.29.3., A.52.11., A.58.6., A.65.3., A.67.13., A.68.9., A.70.13., A.76.7., A.78.3., A.79.1.2., A.82.8., and A.84.15.; see also A.67.12.

(H[1926], 67; P, 203, 207.)

A.27.2.   *šurnə kaba* 'grain fate'

An offering of pancakes and beer is made to *šurnə kaba* at *aga pajram* (B.2.). A goose is sacrificed at *šurnə jər* (B.22.), a sacrifice dedicated to the grain deities.

For other grain spirits, see A.1.8.2., A.26.1.3.1., A.26.16., A.26.34.1., A.28.4., A.29.2., A.52.7., A.52.12.1., A.52.14., A.67.9., A.67.17., A.68.10., A.70.18., A.79.1.3., A.82.6., A.82.11., A.84.13., and A.84.19.

(H[1926], 66; P,203, 207.)

For *kaba jumə*, see A.26.13.; *kaba jumən onən abažə*, A.1.7.1.1.; *kaba jumən onžə*, A.52.5.1.; *kaba jumən pujəršə*, A.70.7.1.; *kaba jumən šočən*, A.82.5.1.; *kaba perke*, A.67.6.; *kaba piambar*, A.68.3.; *kaba pujəršə*, A.70.8.; *kaba saus*, A.76.3.; *kaba šukčə*, A.84.9.; *kajək jumə*, A.26.14.; *kajək keremet*, A.31.4.; *kajək šočən aba*, A.1.10.4.; *kajək usa jumə*, A.26.14.; *kapka orol*, A.55.2.; *kapka šukčə*, A.84.11.; *karman kurək kuguza*, A.38.14.; *kas peresta*, A.65.1.; *kas šukčə*, A.84.12.

A.28.   *kazna* 'treasure'

A.28.1.   *bol'ək kazna* 'livestock treasure'

For other spirits, see A.1.10.1., A.26.5., A.26.38.1., A.52.1., A.67.2., A.68.1., A.70.2., A.76.2., A.78.1., A.79.1.1., A.82.2., and A.84.3.

A.28.2.   *kaba kazna* 'heaven treasure'

For *kaba*, see A.27.

(V, 57.)

A.28.3.   *mükš kazna* 'bee treasure'

(G, 55 [148].)

A.28.4.   *šurnə kazna* 'grain treasure'

(G, 55 [148].)

For *kazna perke*, see A.67.7.; *kazna peri*, A.66.1.; *kazna piambar*, A.68.4.; *kazna pujəršə*, A.70.8.; *kazna saus*, A.76.4.; *kazna sərabočəš*, A.79.1.; *bol'ək kazna sərabočəš*, A.79.1.1.; *mükš kazna sərabočəš*, A.79.1.2.; *surt kazna sərabočəš*, A.79.1.3.; *šurnə kazna sərabočəš*, A.79.1.3.; *kazna šukčə*, A.84.10.

A.29.   *kaznači* 'treasurer'

The term *kaznači* is used to designate one of the members of the retinue of a god. The exact function of the *kaznači* is not clear but sacrifices are made to it at the same ceremony in which the god is worshipped. It often has its own priest and its own tree in the sacred grove. The animal sacrificed varies but it is always smaller than that sacrificed to the god; usually it is a goose, a duck, or a ram.

(H[1926], 66–67; Häm.[1908a], 9.)

A.29.1. *jumən kaznači* 'god's treasurer'

When a sacrifice is made to *kugə jumə* (A.26.) at the *küsə* ceremony (B.9.), an animal is also slaughtered to its treasurer. Animals commonly sacrificed are sheep, ducks, or geese. An offering is also made to this deity at *aga pajram* (B.2.).

(H[1926], 64–65; Häm.[1908a], 8; P, 188, 203.)

A.29.2. *kində kaznači* 'grain treasurer'

For other grain spirits, see A.1.8.2., A.26.1.3.1., A.26.16., A.26.34.1., A.27.2., A.28.4., A.29.2., A.52.7., A.52.12.1., A.52.14., A.67.9., A.67.17., A.68.10., A.70.18., A.79.1.3., A.82.6., A.82.11., A.84.13., and A.84.19.

(Uj[FB], 30.)

A.29.3. *mükš kaznači* 'bee treasurer'

An offering is made to this deity at *aga pajram* (B.2.); a goose is sacrificed at *mükš jər* (B.11.), a ceremony dedicated to the bee spirits.

For other bee spirits, see A.1.6., A.1.10.6., A.15.6., A.26.1.2., A.26.28., A.26.38.2., A.27.1., A.28.3., A.52.11., A.58.6., A.65.3., A.67.13., A.68.9., A.70.13., A.76.7., A.78.3., A.79.1.2., A.82.8., and A.84.15. See also A.67.12.

A.29.4. *oksa kaznači* 'money treasurer'

(Uj[FB], 30.)

For *kečə aba*, see A.1.3.; *kečə jumə*, A.26.15.; *oš kečə jumə*, A.26.15.1.; *kečə on*, A.52.6.; *kečə pujəršə jumə*, A.26.31.2.; *os kečə aba*, A.1.3.; *oš kečə šočən aba*, A.1.10.3.1.

A.30. *keltəmaš*

This evil spirit leads astray people who are in the woods late at night. It can also make things appear different from the way they really are. According to one story, it appeared to a man in the bathhouse in the form of his wife and caused the man to think that the ground outside was covered with snow. When the man recovered his senses, he was a long way from his home. At times *keltəmaš* travels about in the company of *čort* (A.15.) and *xuda sila* 'evil strength.' They go about at noon, at midnight, and at about six o'clock in the morning and evening. As a protection against *keltəmaš*, the Cheremis hang mirrors in the house; the devil sees itself in the mirror and is frightened away (H.4.8.). Lightning tries to kill *keltəmaš*.

For other evil spirits, see A.7., A.11., A.15., A.16., A.18., A.43., A.51., A.81., A.85., and A.86.

(Bk, 47–49; R, 196, 202, 205.)

A.31. *keremet*

A *keremet* is an evil spirit whose sole activity seems to be to cause man trouble. A *keremet* is the most powerful of evil beings and, as such, influences the lives of the

Cheremis to a far greater extent than the gods. A *keremet* is held in such awe that the Cheremis do not willingly speak of it, especially to strangers. Occasionally a *keremet* is reported to have caused someone to become rich or to have given luck to a fisherman, but this is extremely rare. A *keremet* is better known for the evil, misfortune, and disease that it causes men. A *keremet* may also be called *kuguza* 'old man,' *kugə jeŋ* 'great man,' *kugərak* 'prince,' or *bodəž* 'spirit.' A *keremet* is often known by the name of the place where its grove is located.

Keremet spirits originate in the dead. There are several legendary heroes which have become *keremet*s. In other instances, wicked persons after death have been able to continue their evil activities as *keremet*s. There are also accounts of people creating *keremet*s by winding a band of bast around a tree and sacrificing there. A *keremet* may also originate from spittle. According to some legends, *keremet* is the eternal rival, sometimes the brother, of *jumə* (A.26.), against which it is continually striving. There is also a story according to which *keremet* was originally a Tatar whom, when it started causing trouble, the people tried to kill. A Cheremis hid it from other Tatars, and after that the *keremet* itself became a Cheremis. The Tatar origin of *keremet* is further reflected by the fact that it is dressed in Tatar clothes, a blue shirt and a Moslem cap.

The Cheremis makes sacrifices to the *keremet*s both as a group and individually. They say that these sacrifices are made "downward" in contrast to those to the gods, which are made "upward." Periodic sacrifices are usually held annually by large groups of people (B.7.). A special sacrifice may be made by an individual to cure himself of a disease which a *keremet* has sent. The ritual is similar to that used to sacrifice to the gods (B.9.). *Keremet* spirits are not worshipped in the same grove as the gods but have a special grove, also called *keremet* (E.22.). A public sacrifice is performed by a priest, but a private sacrifice can be made by the person concerned or by some relative who knows the ritual. The most acceptable sacrifice is a horse but other animals are also sacrificed. As in the case of the gods, a *keremet* may also have helpers which receive sacrifices. Some *keremet*s are worshipped by large numbers of people. However, there are a great many called *ške keremet* 'own *keremet*' or *škenan onĉəmə keremet* '*keremet* which we take care of ourselves' (A.31.7.), which are worshipped only by a family. A family with a *keremet* never sacrifices in the grove of a *keremet* of another family. Nevertheless, a person may be related to two families with different *keremet*s and thus sacrifice to both. Sorcerers can bewitch a person by buying a bit of that person's clothing or a lock of his hair under a *keremet* tree; the *keremet* causes the person to become ill and eventually die.

For specific *keremet* spirits, see A.6., A.8., A.9., A.9.3., A.9.6., A.9.11., A.9.13., A.12., A.15., A.15.1., A.15.2., A.15.3., A.15.5., A.15.6., A.15.7., A.15.8., A.15.9., A.15.10., A.17., A.19., A.21.1., A.21.1.1., A.21.2., A.21.2.1., A.21.3., A.21.4., A.24., A.25., A.26.21., A.31.1., A.31.2., A.31.3., A.31.4., A.31.5., A.31.6., A.31.7., A.31.8., A.31.9., A.33., A.36., A.37., A.38.6., A.38.14., A.38.15., A.38.28., A.39., A.40., A.44., A.45., A.50., A.55.2., A.55.3., A.61., A.62., A.63., A.64.1., A.64.2., A.68., A.68.6., A.69., A.71., A.75., A.77.1., A.80., A.87., A.88., A.88.1., A.89., A.95., and A.97.

(Be, 376–80; H[1913], 125; H[1926], 159–76; H[1927], 151–57; Häm. [1930b], 43–51; P, 68, 212–214; R, 207; S, 149–56; Uj[FB], 2, [T], 48; Up[FB], 14.)

A.31.1.   *kugə aga keremet* 'great plowing *keremet*'

A bull and a ram are animals sacrificed to this *keremet*.
(S, 154.)

A.31.2.   *ikśa keremet* 'spring *keremet*'

This *keremet* was originally a robber. It destroys men and cattle which drink from the spring in which it dwells.
(H[1913], 125; S, 150.)

A.31.3.   *jauš keremet*
(S, 149.)

A.31.4.   *kajək keremet* 'game *keremet*'

Kajək is usually translated 'bird,' but in the name of this *keremet* it includes four-footed animals as well as birds. This *keremet* is worshipped jointly by two villages and receives a sacrifice of a ram or a duck at least every three years in its own grove.
(P, 213.)

A.31.5.   *jal ümbač koštśə keremet* '*keremet* passing through the village'
(S, 149.)

A.31.6.   *izə nur keremet* 'little field *keremet*'

A horse is sacrificed to this *keremet*.
(S, 155.)

A.31.7.   *škenan ońčəmə keremet* '*keremet* which we take care of ourselves'; *śke keremet* 'own *keremet*'

These terms are applied to a *keremet* which is worshipped only by one family; a family, however, may consist of many households. The sacrifice of a white ram or duck usually takes place in June before the *küsə* ceremony (B.9.).
(P, 204, 209, 213.)

A.31.8.   *serekan keremet*

A sacrifice of a hare or a ram is made to this *keremet*.
(S, 154.)

A.31.9.   *tumə dün keremet* '*keremet* under the oak'

When a person is ill, a prayer may be said to this *keremet* to restore that person to good health. A vow is usually made first and, in the winter, a hare is sacrificed.
(Be, 379–80.)

For *ümbal kermet*, see A.21.2.1.; *keremet śərt*, A.15.2.; *kəńe perke*, A.67.8.; *kərtńə bodəž*, A.9.6.; *kəzər piambar*, A.68.5.; *kiamat saus*, A.76.5.; *kiamat töra*, A.90.; *kiebak ümbal kugə*, A.36.; *kində juməšaməč*, A.26.16.; *kində kaznači*, A.29.2.; *kində on*, A.52.7.; *kində perke*, A.67.9.; *kində perke aba*, A.1.8.2.; *kində perke aba jumə*, A.26.1.3.1.; *kində perke xan*, A.52.12.1.; *kində pujərśə*, A.70.18.; *kində saska jumə*, A.26.34.1.; *kində šočən*, A.82.6.; *kində šukčə*, A.84.13.; *klem xan*, A.52.8.; *pokšəm koča*, A.38.22.; *kokša kuguza* and *kuba*, A.38.12.

A.32. *pelə kolšə* 'half dead'

This supernatural appears floating on the surface of the water, face down, resembling the corpse of a drowned man. A person who tries to save it is pulled under the water and drowned.

(H[1926], 61; H[1927], 208.)

For *utə kolšə*, see A.94.

A.33. *koltəšə* 'sender'

An offering of a piece of bread is made to this *keremet* (A.31.).

(S, 155.)

For *kornə bodəž*, see A.9.7.; *šište kornə palastarše*, A.60.; *kornə pujəršə*, A.70.10.; *ümbač koštšə*, A.21.2.1.; *jal ümbač koštšə keremet*, A.31.5.; *kož jeη*, A.21.1.; *toštə kož jeη*, A.21.1.1.; *kožla ia*, A.51.; *kožla kuguza* and *kuba*, A.38.13.; *kožla oza*, A.51.; *kožla peri*, A.51.

A.34. *pasu körgə* 'field center'

This field spirit is worshipped in the summer. Its helpers are *šurnə šočən* 'grain fructifier,' (A.82.11.); *šurnə pujəršə* 'grain creator' (A.70.18.); *šurnə perke* 'grain blessing' (A.67.17.); and *šurnə saus* 'grain overseer' (A.76.8.). Rams and sheep are considered to be suitable sacrifices for this spirit and its helpers.

(V, 154.)

A.35. *kuba* 'old woman'

A spirit called *kuba* appears in female form. This spirit may be helpful but more often than not causes trouble for humans. It is the female counterpart of *kuguza* 'old man,' and both of them are identified rather closely with a place or disease, together representing its supernatural elements. For *kuba*, see *kuguza* (A.38.).

For *jumən šerməčkəl kučən pušə*, see A.72.; *kudə bodəž*, A.9.8.; *kudə ört*, A.58.4.; *kudə ört kuguza* and *kuba*, A.38.20.; *kugarña jumə*, A.26.17.; *kugečə jumə*, A.26.18.

A.36. *kiebak ümbal kugə* 'great one on Kiyabak'

An *ülüsan patər* 'lower hero' (A.64.2.), who fought on horseback and shot arrows from one mountain peak to another, buried himself and his horse on the top of Kiyabak Mountain. In spite of his warning the people not to awaken him unless there was war, a man did so. Angered at being disturbed without cause, he decreed that the people near Kiyabak Mountain should sacrifice a brown horse to him. This sacrifice is now performed at Kiyabak River.

A disease called *kiebak ümbal čer*, which may be diagnosed by a soothsayer (D.7.), is fatal unless a sacrifice is made to this *keremet* (A.31.). First a vow is made to *kiebak ümbal kugə* promising to sacrifice a horse. In the evening, after the sun has gone down, and after the person has bathed and put on clean clothes, meal is sprinkled into the fire from the end of a spoon and *tul bodəž* (A.9.1.4.) is asked to act as intermediary. An iron tool is heated, struck three times, and put in the corner as a pledge that the vow will be fulfilled. The tool may not be used again until the promised animal has been sacrificed. A prayer is said to this spirit's *bitnəzə* (A.8.), meal is sprinkled into the fire, hens are promised to its *bodəž* (A.9.), *aš* (A.5.), *užedəš* (A.95), and *šərt* (A.15.); a cock is promised to its *azren* (A.6.).

(Be, 65–68.)

For *kugə jeη*, see A.21.2.; *nemdə kurək kugə jeη*, A.21.2.1.; *kugərak*, A.21.2.1.

A.37.   *jul ser kugərak* 'Volga bank prince'

This is a local *keremet* (A.31.).

(H[1926], 173.)

A.38.   *kuguza* 'old man'

A spirit which appears as a man is called *kuguza*. Such a spirit is usually given the name of the place it inhabits. Certain diseases are also characterized as being man-like spirits. In some places the term *kuguza* is used to designate a *keremet* spirit (A.31.).

A.38.1.   *agun kuguza* 'drying house old man'

Under the building used for drying grain are buried the remains of a small animal sacrificed in the fall to *agun kuguza*.

(H[1926], 53.)

For *azren kuguza* and *kuba,* see A.6.

A.38.2.   *bakš kuguza* and *kuba* 'mill old man' and 'old woman'

Mill spirits are most often called *bakš ia* 'mill devil' or *bakš oza* 'mill master' but are addressed in prayers as *kuguza* and *kuba*. The breast of *bakš kuba*'s dress is decorated with many silver coins. Sometimes a mill spirit lives under the floor of a mill, at other times behind the water wheel. It helps the miller who has a pact with it. When *bakš kuguza* is angry, the grinding does not go as well as it should. To placate the mill spirit, the miller must put under the floor or in some other suitable place a bowl of porridge in which there is a dab of butter and a spoon.

(H[1926], 53; H[1927], 16.)

A.38.3.   *basli kuguza* and *kuba* 'Vasili old man' and 'old woman'

This term is used primarily to designate those who masquerade during the *šorək jol* festivities (B.19.); however, there is a reference to an offering of pancakes made to these spirits and a prayer said for the blessing of the crops, cattle, and family.

(Uj[FB], 56.)

A.38.4.   *biča kuguza* and *kuba* 'pen old man' and 'old woman'

The spirits which inhabit the livestock pens are also called *biča ia* 'pen devil' and *biča oza* 'pen master,' but in prayers they are addressed as *kuguza* and *kuba*. They often appear to the inhabitants of the farm in human form; the *biča kuba* is seen as an old woman in white clothes who goes about among the cattle in the evening. The livestock are under the protection of this pair. If they do not like an animal, however, they will torment it and keep it from eating. Sometimes they ride a horse all night so that in the morning the horse is exhausted and covered with sweat (cf. A.38.20.). In order to gain the favor of *biča kuguza* and *kuba* a hen is sometimes sacrificed. A drink offering is also made to them in the sacrificial grove (E.2.1.).

(H[1926], 52; H[1927], 166; S, 162.)

For *buber kuguza* and *kuba,* see A.10.; *büt kuguza* and *kuba,* A.1.1. and A.16.1.

A.38.5. *čodra kuguza* and *kuba* 'forest old man' and 'old woman'

These forest spirits may either help or hinder the hunter. If a hunter makes an offering of porridge, he will have good luck; if, however, he neglects this, he will return empty-handed. *Čodra kuguza* may even cause him to be lost in the forest for days. When *čodra kuguza* is angry because it has not received an offering, the whole forest shakes and howls; needles and leaves drop from the trees. Sometimes it signals its desire for an offering by knocking on a tree. *Čodra kuba* is gentler than its male counterpart. Female forest spirits spend a good part of the time playing cards with each other. The stakes are the wild life in the forest so that when one loses, all the animals and birds go to the winner's part of the forest. A hunter cannot kill the animals while they are being moved from one part of the forest to the other to pay off such a gambling debt. In one account, forest spirits rewarded a man who sacrificed to them by giving him three handfuls of money. Forest spirits have a vocabulary slightly different from that of humans: for example, they call handfuls *tərtəka* 'circles.'

For other forest spirits, see A.38.13.

(B, 12–14; Uj[FB], 72.)

A.38.6. *eprem kuguza* 'Efraim old man'

A bull is sacrificed to this *keremet* (A.31.). Cheremis who have been in contact with Christianity identify it with St. Cassian.

(S, 149, 155.)

A.38.7. *ərləgan kuguza* and *kuba,* or *inləkan kuguza* and *kuba* 'measles old man' and 'old woman'

These spirits carry baskets from which *kuguza* passes out peas and *kuba* hemp seeds. Whoever receives these peas and hemp seeds comes down with the measles. However, a person who has previously prayed to these spirits does not become ill. The parents of a sick child make an offering of porridge and pray that the child will recover with no serious aftereffects. While the child is ill, it does not go into the bathhouse because *ərləgan kuguza* and *kuba* do not like the heat of the bathhouse; they say that *ərləgan kuba* burns its nose there.

For similar disease spirits, see A.38.12. and A.38.25.

(B, 16; Uj[FB], 59; Up[FB], 17.)

A.38.8. *ia kuguza* and *kuba* 'devil old man' and 'old woman'

Ia kuguza and *kuba* are seen along the banks of rivers, especially at noon and at night. They are sometimes observed combing their long hair. They may seize a person and carry him off into the water; this can be prevented by mentioning god or saying a magic formula. If a man knows a strong enough spell, they will entertain him at their home. These spirits may be found in a meadow as well as near the water. They can confuse a person so that he wanders about all night in a daze.

For *ia,* see A.16.

(Uj[FB], 65–67.)

A.38.9.   *idəm kuguza* and *kuba* 'threshing-floor old man' and 'old woman'

The spirit of the threshing floor, which appears both as an old man and an old woman, is most likely to be seen very early in the morning. When a person approaches, it disappears. At times, a drink offering is made in the sacrifice grove (E.2.1.) and sometimes *idəm kuguza* and *kuba* are worshipped during field ceremonies (B.2.).

(H[1926], 53; H[1927], 167.)

For *inləkan kuguza* and *kuba,* see A.38.7.

A.38.10.   *jer kuguza* and *kuba* 'lake old man' and 'old woman'

The spirit of a lake, also referred to as *jer oza,* can be offended by such things as washing dirty diapers in the lake or throwing in a dead dog. When offended, this spirit may move the whole lake to another place, flood a town, or cause a person whose clothes have been washed in the lake to become sick. Unless a fisherman makes an offering of porridge to *jer kuguza,* he will not have an abundant haul of fish from the lake. The lake spirit sometimes appears as an ox, sometimes as a cow; its bellowing is frequently heard from the lake.

For similar water spirits, see A.9.1., A.9.4., A.16.1., A.22., and A.96.1.

(Bj, 149–50; H[1926], 58, 60.)

A.38.11.   *jüštə kuguza* and *kuba* 'cold old man' and 'old woman'

Jüštə kuguza usually comes at night. It beats on fences, trees, and the walls of houses, keeping people awake; it calls children out to play; it tries to freeze people and pinches their feet, faces, and noses; it even kills people at times. According to one account, it hits people over the head with a wooden mallet. In another account, it becomes angry at the singing of a drunk and pushes him about in the snow. *Jüštə kuba* also comes at night; people can hear the sound of its needle as it sews up the door (i.e., as the door freezes shut). *Jüštə ergə* or *ərbezə* 'cold boy' or 'child' also comes on winter nights. It plays with a wooden ball, beats on the door, and tries to get the children to come out to play. The noise made by the rafters on a cold night is attributed to *jüštə ergə*. It pinches people's noses and freezes their hands.

(B, 14–15; J; Uj[FB], 77; Up[FB], 2, 29; Us[FB], 2; Usj[FB], 4.)

A.38.12.   *kokša kuguza* and *kuba* 'scabies old man' and 'old woman'

These spirits go about with baskets from which *kuguza* gives out beans and *kuba* flax seeds; a recipient of these beans or flax seeds gets a skin disease. If these spirits pinch a person, he will also get the disease. To cure such a skin disease, a porridge (C.6.) is prepared and prayers are said to *kokša kuguza* and *kuba.*

(B, 17; Uj[FB], 9; Up[FB], 5.)

A.38.13.   *kožla kuguza* and *kuba* 'forest old man' and 'old woman'

Some Cheremis believe that people who die in the forest become forest ghosts and haunt the place where they died. If such a ghost can succeed in causing someone's death at the place of its own demise, it can go free and the newly dead must take its place. Some believe that people who die in the forest become the servants of *kožla kuguza* and *kuba*. At times, 'forest old man' and 'old woman' cause a person to get lost in the forest. Those who have to stay in the forest overnight usually ask their protection. A hunter camping out in the forest cuts a little notch in a tree for them and puts a piece of bread there as an offering so that they will cause game to cross his path. Sometimes libations are made to these spirits in the sacrifice grove.

For other forest spirits, see A.11., A.20., A.38.5., A.43., A.51., and A.86.

(H[1926], 57; H[1927], 184.)

For *kudə ört kuguza* and *kuba,* see A.38.20.; *kurək kuguza,* see A.21.2.1.

A.38.14.   *karman kurək kuguza* 'castle mountain old man'

This is a *keremet* (A.31.).

(H[1926], 173; H[1927], 156.)

A.38.15.   *kübar kuguza* 'bridge old man'

This spirit, also called *kübar jumal kuguza* 'old man under the bridge,' is one of the retinue of *nemdə kurək kugə jeη* (A.21.2.1.) but is also sometimes worshipped in its own right. Sometimes a sacrifice of a steer, goose, or duck is made to it. Prayers are said to this spirit to cure illness.

(H[1926], 169; S, 149, 155; Uj[FB], 7.)

A.38.16.   *moča kuguza* and *kuba* 'bathhouse old man' and 'old woman'

A spirit which inhabits the bathhouse is also called *moča ia* 'bathhouse devil,' *moča oza* 'bathhouse master,' or, in some regions, *jarčik.* It is especially bothersome at night. Sometimes it is heard late at night crying like a little child; other times it is heard beating itself with the bath switch which is left on the sweatbench for it. *Moča kuba* is described as having long hair. When a person goes in to take a bath, he usually asks *moča kuguza* and *kuba* to make the bath good. If he has a cold, he may ask them to chase away *run kuguza* and *kuba* 'mucus old man' and 'old woman' (A.38.24.) which accompany the cold. When a new bathhouse is heated for the first time, butter is put on the bench for the bathhouse spirits to eat so that the steam will be good.

(B, 12; H[1926], 52–53; H[1927], 167; Uj[FB], 68; Up[FB], 18.)

A.38.17.   *nerge kuguza* and *kuba* 'cold old man' and 'old woman'

When a person catches a cold, it is said that *nerge kuguza* and *kuba* have come to him. A person with a cold should not take a bath in the bathhouse because they get angry. One way to get rid of them is to smear the body with radishes.

(Uj[FB], 57; Up[FB], 27.)

A.38.18.   *nur kuguza* and *kuba* 'field old man' and 'old woman'

These spirits protect the cattle while they are out to pasture. For this reason the Cheremis pray to them in the spring when the cattle are turned out to the meadows.

(H[1926], 58.)

A.38.19. *oksa kuguza* and *kuba* 'money old man' and 'old woman'

There is an account of a man who built over the threshing floor a special house which no one was allowed to enter. The man left food there for *oksa kuguza* and *kuba* who, when they had eaten, left money in exchange (cf. A.16.).

(B, 9.)

A.38.20. *kudə ört kuguza* and *kuba* 'hut soul old man' and 'old woman'

These spirits live in cattle pens and watch over the animals. If they like an animal, it thrives and grows sleek and fat. If, on the other hand, they take a dislike to an animal, they torment it and keep it from eating. Sometimes they take food away from an animal they dislike and give it to one which pleases them (cf. A.38.4.).

(B, 12; Us[FB], 3; Usj[FB], 5.)

A.38.21. *pasu kuguza* and *kuba* 'field old man' and 'old woman'

In some places these spirits of the cultivated fields are worshipped both in the fields and in the sacred grove.

(H[1926], 58.)

A.38.22. *pokšəm kuguza* and *kuba* 'frost old man' and 'old woman'

These spirits, also called *pokšəm obəška,* cause frost damage. Sometimes there is a whole family of frost spirits including *koča* 'grandfather,' *ača* 'father,' *ərbezə* 'child,' and *üdər* 'daughter.' They all come, one after another, pinching plants and taking them away. Cucumbers are perhaps the most vulnerable of all, since they are mentioned in most accounts. Of the whole family, the grandfather is considered to be the most destructive. According to one account, *pokšəm kuguza* and *kuba* are not considered to be manlike spirits; *kuguza* is the morning frost and *kuba* is the evening frost. People sometimes pray to these spirits to protect the crops from frost. Animal sacrifices, when made, are a grey or white ram for *kuguza,* and a grey or white sheep for *kuba.* Sacrifices may be made at such regular ceremonies as *aga kurman* (B.1.), *aga pajram* (B.2.), and *küsə* (B.9.), or on special occasions, such as when spring and summer frosts damage the crops. At one special ceremony (B.30.) dedicated to *pokšəm kuguza* and *kuba* an offering of porridge was made. An indication that *pokšəm kuguza* and *kuba* were not considered very important is that the participants in the ceremony did not put on their holiday clothes but just wore their everyday clothes.

(B, 15; G, 55 [148]; H[1926], 97, 111; P, 203–5; S, 162; Uj[FB], 50–52; Up[FB], 4.)

A.38.23. *pört kuguza* and *kuba* 'house old man' and 'old woman'

The house spirits are also called *surt kuguza* and *kuba; pört* is the word used specifically for the dwelling; *surt* is the word which means the house including all the farm buildings and pens. The terms *pört ia* 'house devil' and *pört oza* 'house master' are also used in referring to these spirits, but not in prayers. These spirits, in human form and dressed in Cheremis clothes, sometimes appear to members of the household. Their appearance usually forebodes some unusual event.

Pört kuguza and *kuba* are usually helpful and protective spirits. They guard the home against robbers, conflagrations, and sickness; they grant the family happiness and prosperity. Each night at bedtime the Cheremis mother prays to *pört kuguza* and *kuba* for blessings upon the family. If the house spirits are neglected or become angry for any reason, they can make trouble for the family, even to the extent of causing the whole family to die and the homestead to be deserted.

It is customary, when moving into a new house, to make an offering of cakes and bread to the house spirits. Often a blessing is also asked when the first log of a new house is laid. At times, a drink offering may be made in the sacrifice grove. If the harvest is good, a thank offering of porridge, beer, and pancakes may be made. In some places, offerings of beer, pancakes, and bread are made every fall in the cellar room under the floor of the house. In places where blood sacrifices are made, the most common animal sacrificed is a black sheep, although others are also used.

For other house spirits, see A.9.2., A.26.36., A.58.9., A.67.15., A.70.17., and A.84.18.

(H[1926], 50–52; H[1927], 165–66; S, 189; V, 195.)

A.38.24. *run kuguza* and *kuba* 'mucus old man' and 'old woman'

When *run kuguza* and *kuba* come, a person gets a cold. If the person takes a bath in the bathhouse, they leave and go elsewhere to avoid burning their noses in the bathhouse (cf. A.38.16. and A.38.17.).

(B, 16; Uj[FB], 58.)

For *sotona kuguza* and *kuba,* see A.75.; *surt kuguza* and *kuba,* A.38.23.

A.38.25. *šedra kuguza kuba* 'smallpox old man' and 'old woman'

These spirits go around with baskets from which *kuguza* distributes peas and *kuba* hemp seeds. If *šedra kuguza* and *kuba* go upstream, the cases will be very severe, but if they go downstream, the cases will be light. According to some, the severity of the illness depends on whether the child is given peas or hempseeds, the former causing severe cases, the latter milder ones. When a child has smallpox, the parents make offerings of pancakes, porridge (C.6.), unleavened bread, and sometimes fish. They pray to the smallpox spirits not to take the child away from them or to harm its face or eyes. The offerings are then left for a while. If, when the parents come back, the food appears to have diminished, it means that the sacrifice has been accepted and the case will be a mild one. The sick child's eyes should not be opened or the child will go blind; neither is the child taken to the bathhouse lest *šedra kuguza* and *kuba* become angry and take the child.

For similar disease spirits, see A.38.7. and A.38.12.

(B, 15–16; Be, 383; S, 189; Uj[FB], 53–54; Up[FB], 16; Wu, 72–73.)

A.38.26. *šokšə kuguza* and *kuba* 'warmth old man' and 'old woman'

Šokšə kuba warms old women; *šokšə kuguza* contends with *jüštə kuguza* 'cold old man' (A.38.11.).

(B, 14.)

A.38.27. *šurem kuguza* and *kuba*

When these spirits come, they cause a person to be ill with a headache and a runny nose. People drink tea which burns the noses of these spirits and causes them to go away.

(B, 16.)

A.38.28. *turek kuguza* 'Turek old man'

This *keremet* (A.31.) is named after Mari Turek, the town in which it is worshipped.
(H[1926], 172.)
For *piambar kuguza jumə*, see A.26.19.1.; *kugužan jumə*, A.26.20.

A.39. *kuplaŋgaš*

Instead of sacrificing a whole animal to this *keremet* (A.31.), just the nose, feet, and ears are offered.

(S, 177.)

A.40. *kugə kurək* 'great mountain'

This is a *keremet* (A.31.).
(H[1926], 170.)
For *kurək bodəž*, see A.9.9.; *kurək ia*, A.16.2.; *kurək jumə*, A.26.21.; *kurək kugə jeŋ*, A.21.2.1.; *nemdə kurək kugə jeŋ*, A.21.2.1.; *kurək kuguza*, A.21.2.1.; *karman kurək kuguza*, A.38.14.; *kurək piambar*, A.68.6.; *kurək šərt*, A.15.3.

A.41. *aga kurman* 'plowing kurman'

This deity is considered to be the recipient of the sacrifices of a white ram made at a ceremony also called *aga kurman* (B.1.).
(H[1926], 183–85.)
For *kusnəšə jer*, see A.22.

A.42. *kugə kübar* 'great bridge'

This is a *keremet* (A.31.).
(H[1926], 170.)
For *kübar kuguza*, see A.38.15.; *küdərčə jumə*, A.26.22.; *küllö jumə*, A.26.23.; *küllö jumən pujəršəblak*, A.70.7.1.; *küllö perke*, A.67.10.; *küllö piambar*, A.68.7.; *küllö pujəršə*, A.70.11.; *xan*, A.52.; *klem xan*, A.52.8.; *kində perke xan*, A.52.12.1.; *sirga perke xan*, A.52.12.2.; *xirxa jumə*, A.66.; *labasta*, A.2.; *lemdə kurək kuguza*, A.21.2.1.

A.43. *l'esak*

L'esak is a forest spirit of gigantic proportions. Its body is as big as a stack, its head as large as a barrel, its eyes as big as dishes, its hair as bristly as a hay stack, and its mouth as large as the opening in the oven. It has a liking for strong drink and sometimes becomes intoxicated. It can howl like a dog or make a noise like a raven. If a person hears the cry of this forest spirit, it means death either for himself, his wife, or his cattle. A *l'esak* can make things seem what they are not—for example, it can make pine cones seem to be a hare, dung to be bread, and a twig to be a gun. A *l'esak* is frightened away by a cross, and thus it is possible to capture one by putting crosses on all the doors and windows of a house so that it cannot escape (H.4.6.). A dog howls when the *l'esak* comes. Some Cheremis call *l'esak* an *ia* 'devil' (A.16.). A *l'esak* sometimes has the power to kill people.

For other forest spirits, see A.11., A.20., A.38.5., A.38.13., A.51., and A.86.

(B, 11, 61; Bj, 11, 186, 188–89, 191–92; Bu, 36–39.)

For *l'esi*, see A.11.

A.44.   *makar*

Makar was a man who wanted to appropriate some of his neighbor's fields. When the neighbor protested, Makar suggested that they ask the earth itself to whom they belonged. The neighbor agreed and they did so. Makar's son, who was hidden in a hole, said the land belonged to Makar and the neighbor was forced to yield to him. However, Makar's son suffocated in the hole and Makar himself died of grief shortly after. His spirit became a *keremet* (A.31.) and still haunts the field that he took.

(Häm.[1930b], 47; S, 149–50.)

A.45.   *marče*

A ram is sacrificed to this helper of *kugə jeŋ* (A.21.2.).

(H[1926], 170.)

For *mardəž aba*, see A.1.4.; *mardəž jumə*, A.26.24.; *mardəž on*, A.52.9.; *mendə kurək kuguza*, A.21.2.1.; *məlandə aba*, A.1.5.; *taškəm məlandə aba*, A.1.5.1.; *məlandə hodaž*, A.9.10.; *surt(lə) məlandə bodəž*, A.9.10.1.; *məlandə jumə*, A.26.25.; *məlandə on*, A.52.10.; *məlandə ört*, A.58.5.; *məlandə peresta*, A.65.2.; *məlandə perke*, A.67.11.; *məlandə piambar*, A.68.8.; *məlandə pujərša*, A.70.12.; *məlandə saus*, A.76.6.; *məlandə sərabočəš*, A.79.2.; *məlandə šərt*, A.15.4.; *məlandə šočən*, A.82.7.; *məlandə šočən aba*, A.1.10.5.; *məlandə šukčə*, A.84.14.; *mikola jumə*, A.26.26.; *mir jumə*, A.26.27.; *moča kuguza* and *kuba*, A.38.16.; *moča šərt*, A.15.5.

A.46.   *mužə* 'illness'

Mužə is a term for illness and the personified cause of illness. It also means an evil spirit; *mužəgožo* may be used as a collective name for all "lower" spirits (see A.31.).

(P[1948], 74, 115–16; Sz, 131; V, 124, 128.)

A.46.1.   *jüštə mužə* 'cold illness'

This spirit causes people to have chills. See also A.96.3.

(Be, 384–85.)

A.46.2.   *sürem mužə* 'sürem spirit'

These evil spirits are driven out of town at night. For *sürem*, see B.18.

(P[1948], 115–16; V, 196.)

For *jüštə mužə üdər*, see A.96.3.; *mü perke*, A.67.12.; *mükš aba*, A.1.6.; *mükš aba jumə*, A.26.1.2.; *mükš jumə*, A.26.28.; *mükš kaba*, A.27.1.; *mükš kazna*, A.28.3.; *mükš kazna sərabočəš*, A.79.1.2.;*mükš kaznači*, A.29.3.; *mükš on*, A.52.11.; *mükš ört*, A.58.6.; *mükš peresta*, A.65.3.; *mükš perke*, A.67.13.; *mükš piambar*, A.68.9.; *mükš pujəršə*, A.70.13.; *mükš saus*, A.76.7.; *mükš serlagəš*, A.78.3.; *mükš sərabočəš*, A.79.1.2.; *mükš šert*, A.15.6.; *mükš šočən*, A.82.8.; *mükš šočən aba*, A.1.10.6.; *mükš šočən jumə*, A.26.38.2.; *mükš šukčə*, A.84.15.

A.47. *nedək* 'toothache'

A toothache may be personified as an evil spirit.
(R, 86, 208.)

A.47.1. *kož nedək* 'pine *nedək*'

This spirit can enter a person's ear and cause it to ache.
(B, 71.)
For *nemdə* or *nendə kurək kugə jeη*, see A.21.2.1.

A.48. *pəl ner* 'cloud nose'

A libation is offered to *pəl ner* to protect the fields from downpours and destructive weather.
(H[1926], 70.)

A.49. *pi nereskə* 'dog nose'

These creatures are human in form but have dog noses. Usually they have only one foot and one hand and must consequently operate in pairs. They live in forests and in Siberia where they track down men by their smell, overtake them, and eat them.
(B, 8; Uj[FB], 14; Usj[FB], 7.)

A.50 *nerge*

A turkey cock is sacrificed to this *keremet*.
(S, 155.)
For *nerge kuguza* and *kuba*, see A.38.17.; *nol' jeη*, A.21.3.; *nur bodəž*, A.9.11.; *izə nur keremet*, A.31.6.; *nur kuguza and kuba*, A.38.18.

A.51. *obda*

This spirit, also called *kožla ia, kožla oza, kožla peri* and *suräli* in different regions, dwells in the forest. It is more or less human in appearance and may be either male or female. It is usually naked and its body is hairy. It has long hair which it frequently combs sitting up in a tree. It has long breasts which it throws over its shoulders while running. Its feet are backwards and, when it rides, it sits on the horse backwards; some say that a horse ridden by an *obda* runs backwards. In winter, an *obda* goes about on a single ski. There are holes in the armpits of an *obda* and a person who has fallen into the grasp of one may overcome its power by putting his hands into its armpits. After depriving an *obda* of its power, a person should go away stepping in the tracks of the *obda* so that it cannot follow. A person who is fighting an *obda* should be very careful not to spill any of its blood since from each drop of blood another *obda* comes forth.

Some Cheremis have the belief that an *obda* comes from an unbaptized child, born out of wedlock, which was killed or left to die by its parents. An *obda* is usually found in the forest where it may be heard clapping and laughing. It often comes to the edge of the forest to sun itself and comb its hair. Sometimes an *obda* lives in a lake or even a haystack.

An *obda* is afraid of the old Cheremis belt; therefore, those who wish to be undisturbed by an *obda* wear one when they go into the forest. An *obda* also fears dogs, so that if a man takes a dog into the forest with him, an *obda* will not bother him.

The most common way in which an *obda* troubles men is by causing them to get lost in the forest. An *obda* calls a man by name and leads him into the part of the forest he does not know. There it begins to wrestle with the man and tickles him to death. Sometimes it causes him to dance until he dies from exhaustion. An *obda* frequently torments a horse by riding it all night without stopping so that in the morning it is tired and covered with sweat (cf. A.38.4.). Usually a person seeing an *obda* is frightened. In one case, a person was so afraid that he lost the power of speech for several days. On the other hand, in another instance, the father of a little girl frightened by an *obda* secured a plant from the *obda* to make the girl more courageous. Sometimes an *obda* is frightened by a person and disappears as soon as it is seen. In one such case, the *obda* dropped its comb. The man who took the comb was then bothered in his sleep by the *obda* until the comb was returned. When people spend the night in the woods, the *obda* disturbs their sleep by shrieking, howling like a dog, and croaking like a raven.

An *obda* which lives in a lake is also called *jer oza* 'lake master.' It pulls men, but not women, into the lake. Although there are many fish in the lake, it does not permit them to be caught.

An *obda* which lived in a haystack became angry when the stack was taken away and cursed the whole village so that it would never increase.

The *obda*s often celebrate weddings. If a person knows which way the wedding party will pass and puts food and drink out for them, they will leave money in exchange. On the other hand, a person who knows but does not leave anything for them is cursed.

(B, 7, 95–96; Be, 40–44; Bu, 5–7, 18, 582–86; H[1926], 55–56; H[1927], 183–84; J; L, 34, 49 [37–8, 56]; P[1948], 80; Uj[FB], 60; Up[FB], 20–23.)

For *pokšəm obəška*, see A.38.22.; *oksa kaznači*, A.29.4.; *oksa kuguza* and *kuba*, A.38.19.; *oksa orola*, A.74.; *oksa saltak*, A.74.; *okna šukčə*, A.84.16.

A.52. *on* or *xan* 'lord'

This term is used for a nature deity which is of lesser importance than *jumə* (A.26.) but which may have a similar retinue of helpers.

(H[1927], 95; S, 167.)

A.52.1. *bol'ək on* 'livestock lord'

For other livestock spirits, see A.1.10.1., A.26.5., A.26.38.1., A.28.1., A.67.2., A.68.1., A.70.2., A.76.2., A.78.1., A.79.1.1., A.82.2., and A.84.3.

A.52.2. *büt on* 'water lord'

For other water spirits, see A.9.1., A.16.1., A.26.7., A.26.29.1., A.58.2., A.70.3., A.84.4., and A.96.2.

(H[1926], 95; S, 163; Uj[FB], 45.)

A.52.3.   *čodra on* 'forest lord'

(H[1926], 95; Uj[FB], 42.)

A.52.4.   *ješ on* 'family lord'

(H[1926], 95.)

A.52.5.   *jumən on* 'god's lord'

For *jumə*, see A.26.

(H[1926], 95; S, 163; Sz, 61.)

A.52.5.1.   *kaba jumən onžə* 'heaven god's lord'

For *kaba jumə*, see A.26.13.

(V, 57.)

A.52.6.   *keča on* 'sun lord'

For other sun spirits, see A.1.3., A.1.10.3.1., A.26.15., A.26.15.1., and A.26.31.2.

(H[1926], 95; Häm.[1936–37], 71; S, 163.)

A.52.7.   *kində on* 'grain lord'

This deity is responsible for the productivity of the grainfield. If a man takes the *kində on* from another's field, he becomes prosperous while the other becomes poor. In order to steal the *kində on,* a person must go to another man's fields early on *semək* (B.13.) with small bagpipes and a drum. He breaks off ears of rye either once or three times. He then puts the ears of grain in the bagpipes and goes off beating the drum.

For other grain spirits, see A.1.8.2., A.26.1.3.1., A.26.16., A.26.34.1., A.27.2., A.28.4., A.29.2., A.52.12.1., A.52.14., A.67.9., A.67.17., A.68.10., A.70.18., A.79.1.3., A.82.6., A.82.11., A.84.13., and A.84.19.; see also A.67.14.

(Uj[FB], 16, 44.)

A.52.8.   *klem xan*

The name of this spirit is borrowed from the Chuvash epithet *kelem khan* 'powerful lord'; by folk etymology, however, *klem* has been identified with Russian *kl'ej* 'glue' and this spirit is said to be the one which 'glued' the earth together.

(S, 168.)

A.52.9.   *mardəž on* 'wind lord'

For other wind spirits, see A.1.4., A.26.24., and A.26.43.

(H[1926], 95; S, 163.)

A.52.10.   *məlandə on* 'earth lord'

A black animal is sacrificed to this deity and the remains are buried in the earth.

For other earth spirits, see A.1.5., A.1.10.5., A.9.10., A.15.4., A.26.25., A.58.5., A.65.2., A.67.11., A.68.8., A.70.12., A.76.6., A.79.2., A.82.7., and A.84.14.

(H[1926], 95, 96; S, 163; Uj[FB], 43.)

A.52.11.   *mükš on* 'bee lord'

A duck is sacrificed to this deity at the *mükš jer* (B. 11.), a ceremony dedicated to the bee deities. An offering of pancakes and beer are made at *aga pajram* (B.2.).

For other bee spirits, see A.1.6., A.1.10.6., A.15.6., A.26.1.2., A.26.28., A.26.38.2., A.27.1., A.28.3., A.29.3., A.58.6., A.65.3., A.67.13., A.68.9., A.70.13., A.76.7., A.78.3., A.79.1.2., A.82.8., and A.84.15.; see also A.67.12.

(H[1926], 95; Häm.[1936–37], 64; P, 203, 207; S, 163; Uj[FB], 48.)

A.52.12.1.   *kində perke xan* 'grain blessing lord'

For *kində perke,* see A.67.9.

(H[1926], 95; S, 163.)

A.52.12.2.   *sirga perke xan* '*sirga* blessing lord'

(S, 163.)

A.52.13.   *pu on* or *pušeŋgə on* 'tree lord'

(B, 23; H[1926], 95; S, 163.)

A.52.14.   *šurnə on* 'grain lord'

For other grain spirits, see A.1.8.2., A.26.1.3.1., A.26.16., A.26.34.1., A.27.2., A.28.4., A.29.2., A.52.7., A.52.12.1., A.67.9., A.67.17., A.68.10., A.70.18., A.79.1.3., A.82.6., A.82.11., A.84.13., and A.84.19.

(H[1926], 95.)

A.52.15.   *šüdər on* 'star lord'

For other star spirits, see A.1.12. and A.26.39.

(H[1926], 95; S, 163.)

A.52.16.   *teŋəz on* 'sea lord'

For other sea spirits, see A.26.40., A.26.29.2., and A.70.19.

(H[1926], 95; S, 163.)

A.52.17.   *tələzə on* 'moon lord'

For other moon spirits, see A.1.4. and A.26.41.

(H[1926], 95; S, 163; Uj[FB], 46.)

A.52.18.   *tul on* 'fire lord'

For other fire spirits, see A.1.10.8., A.1.15., A.9.14., A.26.29.3., A.26.42., A.58.10., A.70.20., A.84.20., and A.88.1.

(H[1926], 95; S, 163; Uj[FB], 17.)

For *kaba jumən onən abaže,* see A.1.7.1.1.; *büt on jumə,* A.26.29.1.; *teŋəz on jumə,* A.26.29.2.; *tul on jumə,* A.26.29.3.; *škenan ončəmə keremet,* A.31.7.

A.53.   *opkən*

A large, fat water spirit which swallows boats and their occupants is designated by this term. In other dialects *büt opkən* means 'whirlpool' and *mələndə opkən* 'precipice.'

(Beke[1951b], 250.)

For *pešmän orbəška,* see A.70.

A.54.   *aga orman* 'plowing *orman*'

An offering of beer and pancakes is made to *aga orman* at *aga pajram* (B.2.).
(P, 203.)

A.55.   *orol* 'guard'

A.55.1.   *er orolək* 'morning guard'
This spirit is one of the helpers of *kugərak* 'prince' (A.21.2.1.) who receives an offering of oatmeal porridge.
(V, 298.)

A.55.2.   *kapka orol* 'gate guard'
Among the helping spirits of *čembulat* (A.12.) and *nemdə kurək kugə jeŋ* (A.21.2.1.) is this gatekeeper.
(H[1926], 169, 171.)
For *oksa orola*, see A.74.

A.55.3.   *üstel orol* 'table guard'
This spirit, a helper of *kugərak* (A.21.2.1.), receives an offering of bread.
(V, 235.)

A.56.   *orža* 'comb'

A.56.1.   *jür orža* 'rain comb'
During long dry spells the Cheremis sometimes pray to *jür orža* for rain.
(H[1926], 70.)

A.56.2.   *pəl orža* 'cloud comb'
Some Cheremis offer a libation to *pəl orža* in order to secure protection for the fields from downpours and destructive weather.
(H[1926], 70.)
For *osər pamaš*, see A.21.2.1.; *oš buj vańuška*, A.97.; *oš kečə aba*, A.1.3.; *oš kečə jumə*, A.26.15.1.; *oš kečə šočən aba*, A.1.10.3.1.

A.57.   *oza* 'master'

Some spirits are commonly referred to as *oza* but are addressed as *kuguza* (A.38.) and *kuba* (A.35.) in prayers.
For *bakš oza*, see A.38.2.; *biča oza*, A.38.4.; *büt oza*, A.16.1.; *jer oza*, A.38.10., A.51.; *kožla oza*, A.51.; *moča oza*, A.38.16.

A.57.1.   *pamaš oza* 'spring master'
This spirit, which lives in a spring, becomes angry if anyone fetching water uses a dirty pail, shouts, quarrels, uses improper language, or splatters water on his clothes. As punishment, it may send the guilty person boils or a rash. The offender must cook porridge at the spring and beg for forgiveness.
(H[1926], 61–62; H[1927], 215.)
For *pört oza*, see A.38.23.; *surt oza*, A.38.23.

A.58. *ört* 'soul'

Animals, trees, buildings, and the elements may have souls. Where the *ört* is content, there is prosperity and abundance. For the human souls, see J.1.

(B, 97; H[1926], 88–89; H[1927], 13.)

A.58.1. *biča ört* 'pen soul'

When the *biča ört* is content, the livestock thrive. A drink offering is made to it at the *küsə* ceremony (B.9.).

For other pen spirits, see A.38.4., A.67.1., A.70.1., and A.84.2.

(B, 97; H[1926], 88; H[1927], 14.)

A.58.2. *büt ört* 'water soul'

When the water *ört* goes away, the water becomes muddy and bad tasting. If a person drinks this water, he becomes sick. Libations are occasionally made to *büt ört* in the sacrifice grove (E.2.1.).

For other water spirits, see A.1.1., A.16.1., A.26.7., A.26.29.1., A.58.2., A.70.3., A.84.4., and A.96.2.

(H[1926], 87.)

A.58.3. *idəm ört* 'threshing-floor soul'

When the *ört* is content on the threshing floor, the yield is great. However, when there is no grain on the threshing floor, *idəm ört* does not stay there. At *aga pajram* (B.2.) and in the sacrifice grove (E.2.1.) offerings are made to *idəm ört*.

(H[1926], 88; H[1927], 14.)

A.58.4. *kudə ört* 'hut soul'

In the places where the summer hut is still used, the *kudə ört*, which is also sometimes called *kudə jumə* 'hut god,' is prayed to in case of illness, theft, or fire.

For other hut spirits, see A.9.8. and A.38.20.

(B, 97; H[1926], 88; S, 169.)

A.58.5. *məlandə ört* 'earth soul'

When *məlandə ört* is in the earth, the land is fertile and produces good crops. At the same time a sacrifice is made to *məlandə aba* (A.1.5.), a black animal, either a steer or a sheep, is sacrificed to *məlandə ört* in the *küsə* grove (E.2.1.). Offerings are also made at *aga pajram* (B.2.).

For other earth spirits, see A.1.5., A.1.10.5., A.9.10., A.15.4., A.26.25., A.52.10., A.65.2., A.67.11., A.68.8., A.70.12., A.76.6., A.79.2., A.82.7., and A.84.14.

(H[1926], 86, 97; P, 203.)

A.58.6. *mükš ört* 'bee soul'

For other bee spirits, see A.1.6., A.1.10.6., A.15.6., A.26.1.2., A.26.28., A.26.38.2., A.27.1., A.28.3., A.29.3., A.52.11., A.58.6., A.65.3., A.67.13., A.68.9., A.70.13., A.76.7., A.78.3., A.79.1.2., A.82.8., and 84.15.; see also A.67.12.

(H[1927], 169.)

A.58.7. *pasu ört* 'field soul'

This 'field soul' is similar to *məlandə ört* 'earth soul' (A.58.6.) in that on it depends the fertility of the soil. If the *pasu ört* leaves the fields, in order to bring it back, a white ram may be sacrificed at the place where the *aga kurman* ceremonies (B.1.) are held.

For other field spirits, see A.38.21., A.67.14., A.70.14., and A.84.17.

(H[1926], 86; H[1927], 240.)

A.58.8. *pu ört* or *pušengə ört* 'tree soul'

When the tree *ört* is happy, the tree is green and sends forth new leaves; when the *ört* goes away, the tree dries up. Sometimes beekeepers pray to this 'soul' when they hang hives on trees. At times, a duck is sacrificed to secure its blessing. Offerings are also made to *pu ört* at *aga pajram* (B.2.).

(H[1926], 85–86; H[1927], 188; P, 203, 207.)

A.58.9. *surt ört/pört ört* or *pörtšär* 'house soul'

Life in a house without an *ört* is unhappy and the house goes to ruin. The *pört ört* may leave the house if the inhabitants quarrel, shout, smoke too much, or dirty the house. When the building creaks at night, the Cheremis say that the *ört* is moving about. When some Cheremis move out to the summer hut, they take a bowl of porridge in their hands and pray that the *pört ört* move out with them. The *surt* and *pört ört* are mentioned in the long list of gods in the sacrifice prayers. In some places there is a *surt* and *pört jumə* 'god' instead of a 'soul.' All food offered to *surt jumə* is thrown into the hearth fire.

For other house spirits, see A.9.2., A.26.36., A.38.23., A.67.15., A.70.17., and A.84.18.

(B, 97; H[1926], 87–88; H[1927], 13–14, 168–69; P[1909], 17; R, 205.)

A.58.10. *tul ört* 'fire soul'

The *ört* of fire disappears if water is poured over fire. This means of extinguishing fire is considered unfitting; the normal procedure for putting it out is to draw the pieces of wood apart so that the fire dies out of its own accord.

(H[1926], 87; H[1927], 236.)

For *kudə ört kuguza* and *kuba*, see A.38.20.

A.59. *pailpak*

This dwarflike evil spirit lives in the house and disturbs sleepers with nightmares. It eats unborn children in their mother's wombs, and children's hearts.

(H[1926], 51.)

For *pajberda šərt*, see A.15.7.; *aga pajram jumə*, A. 26.2.

A.60. *šište kornə palastaršə* 'wax road expert'

An offering is made to this spirit at *aga pajram* (B.2.) and a goose is sacrificed at *mükš jər* (B.11.), a ceremony dedicated to the bee deities.

(H[1926], 186; P, 203, 207.)

A.61. *paltəkan*

This *keremet* (A.31.) is sometimes seen near its grove wearing a red cloak and traveling along the river in a golden boat.

(H[1926], 173; S, 150.)

For *osər pamaš*, see A.21.2.1.; *pamaš oza*, A.57.1.; *paravoj ia*, A.16.3.; *pasu jər*, A.23.; *pasu körgə*, A.34.; *pasu kuguza* and *kuba*, A.38.21.; *pasu ört*, A.58.7.; *pasu perke*, A.67.14.; *pasu pujəršə*, A.70.14.; *pasu šukťə*, A.84.17.

A.62. *paškan*

Paškan fought on the side of the Russians during the seige of Kazan and was killed by the Tatars. Since his death he has been worshipped as a *keremet* (A.31.).

(S, 204–5.)

A.63. *paškərče* 'Bashkir'

A ram is sacrificed to this helper of *kugə jen* (A.21.2.).

(H[1926], 70.)

A.64. *patər* 'hero'

A.64.1. *aren patər* 'Arino hero'

This *keremet* (A.31.) is worshipped near the town of Arino. It was a hero who fought against the Tatars and died at a gate called *patər kapka* 'hero gate.' It told the people to remember it, to give it a good horse to take to its grave, and to carry on the battle with slingshots. The Cheremis did as their leader commanded and the stones, making an unusual sound during their flight through the air, routed the enemy. At the place where the hero fell, there is a grove in which the Cheremis sacrifice a horse to this *keremet* in case of sickness. A stone is thrown into the air, and, if it makes a whirring sound, the sick person will recover.

(H[1926], 173; H[1927], 155.)

A.64.2. *ülüšan patər* 'lower hero'

This name is given to the three legendary heroes who fought on horseback and shot at each other with arrows from the three mountain peaks: Nemda, Kiyabak, and *jək*. Eventually, each buried himself on the top of his mountain promising the people to come to their aid in case of war. Both the hero on Nemda Mountain (A.21.2.1.) and the one on Kiyabak Mountain (A.36.) were awakened unnecessarily. Angrily they ordered that sacrifices be made to them. They both are worshipped as *keremet* (A.31.) spirits.

(Be, 61–65; H[1926], 170; H[1927], 155–56.)

For *pelə kolšə*, see A.32.

A.65. *perešta* 'angel'

A.65.1. *kas perešta* 'evening angel'

For another evening angel, see A.84.12.

(P, 70.)

A.65.2. *məlandə perešta* 'earth angel'

An offering is made to the 'earth angel' at *aga pajram* (B.2.).

For other earth spirits, see A.1.5., A.1.10.5., A.9.10., A.15.4., A.26.25., A.52.10., A.58.5., A.67.11., A.68.8., A.70.12., A.76.6., A.79.2., A.82.7., and A.84.14.

(P, 203.)

A.65.3. *mükš perešta* 'bee angel'

A duck is sacrificed to *mükš perešta* at *mükš jər* (B.11.), a ceremony dedicated to the bee deities. An offering is also made at *aga pajram* (B.2.).

For other bee spirits, see A.16., A.1.10.6., A.15.6., A.26.1.2., A.26.28., A.26.38.2., A.27.1., A.28.3., A.29.3., A.52.11., A.58.6., A.67.13., A.68.9., A.70.13., A.76.7., A.78.3., A.79.1.2., A.82.8., and A.84.15.; see also A.67.12.

(P, 203, 207.)

A.66. *peri* 'devil'

This evil spirit originates from the blood of a person who has been murdered or committed suicide, and usually haunts the place where it died. A *peri* can take almost any form: that of a man, a calf, a pig, a bear, a rolling cask. Sometimes it dazes people so that they cannot see things as they really are; other times it chases them. A *peri* loses its power when a person calls on god (A.26.) to help him.

(Be, 51–54.)

A.66.1. *kazna peri* 'treasure devil'

This spirit guards buried treasure which, from Pentecost to Midsummer's Day, it cooks over a blue flame. Whoever sees the fire, can find buried treasure underneath it.

For another guard of buried treasure, see A.74.

(H[1926], 56.)

For *kožla peri,* see A.51.

A.67. *perke* 'blessing'

The term *perke* involves concepts of blessing, prosperity, luck, benefit, and usefulness. To *kugə perke* 'great blessing' offerings are made at *aga pajram* (B.2.) and a mare is sacrificed at the *küsə* ceremony (B.9.). There are also specific spirits for each type of blessing desired by the Cheremis.

(H[1926], 88–89, 120; P, 187, 189, 203.)

A.67.1. *biča perke* 'pen blessing'

A libation is offered to *biča perke* at the sacrifice ceremony (B.9.).

For other pen spirits, see A.38.4., A.58.1., A.70.1., and A.84.2.

(H[1926], 89.)

A.67.2. *bol'ək perke* 'livestock blessing'

A libation is offered to this deity at the *küsə* ceremony (B.9.).

For other livestock spirits, see A.1.10.1., A.26.5., A.26.38.1., A.28.1., A.52.1., A.68.1., A.70.2., A.76.2., A.78.1., A.79.1.1., A.82.2., and A.84.3.

(G, 55 [148]; H[1926], 89; Häm.[1908a], 15.)

A.67.3. *idəm perke* 'threshing-floor blessing'

A drink offering is made to this deity at the *küsə* ceremony (B.9.).
For other threshing-floor spirits, see A.38.9., A.58.3., A.70.5., and A.84.6.
(H[1926], 89.)

A.67.4. *jeř perke* 'family blessing'

A libation is offered to this deity at the *küsə* ceremony (B.9.).
(G, 55 [148]; H[1926], 89; Häm.[1908a], 15.

A.67.5. *jumən perke* 'god's blessing'

For *jumə*, see A.26.
(H[1926], 89; P, 72.)

A.67.6. *kaba perke* 'heaven blessing'

For *kaba*, see A.27.
(V, 57.)

A.67.7. *kazna perke* 'treasure blessing'

For *kazna*, see A.28.
(V, 59.)

A.67.8. *kəńe perke* 'hemp blessing'

A libation is offered to this deity at the *küsə* ceremony (B.9.).
(H[1926], 89.)

A.67.9. *kində perke* 'grain blessing'

A drink offering is made to this deity at the *küsə* ceremony (D.9.).
For other grain spirits, see A.1.8.2., A.26.1.3.1., A.26.16., A.26.34.1., A.27.2.,
A.28.4., A.29.2., A.52.7., A.52.12.1., A.52.14., A.67.17., A.68.10., A.70.18., A.79.1.3.,
A.82.6., A.82.11., A.84.13., and A.84.19.
(H[1926], 89; Häm.[1908a], 15.)

A.67.10. *küllö perke*

For other *küllö* spirits, see A.26.23., A.68.7., A.70.7.2., and A.70.11.
(H[1926], 89, 120.)

A.67.11. *məlandə perke* 'earth blessing'

An animal sacrificed to *məlandə perke* is always black in color and its remains are
buried in the earth. An offering of pancakes and beer is made at *aga pajram* (B.2.).
For other earth spirits, see A.1.5., A.1.10.5., A.9.10., A.15.4., A.26.25., A.52.10.,
A.58.5., A.65.2., A.68.8., A.70.12., A.76.6., A.79.2., A.82.7., and A.84.14.
(H[1926], 97; P, 203.)

A.67.12. *mü perke* 'honey blessing'

A libation is offered to *mü perke* at the *küsə* ceremony (B.9.).
(H[1926], 89.)

A.67.13.   *mükš perke* 'bee blessing'

A ram or a sheep is sacrificed to this deity at *mükš jər* (B.11.), a ceremony dedicated to the bee gods. An offering is made at *aga pajram* (B.2.) and a libation is offered at the *küsə* ceremony (B.9.).

For other bee spirits, see A.1.6., A.1.10.6., A.15.6., A.26.1.2., A.26.28., A.26.38.2., A.27.1., A.28.3., A.29.3., A.52.11., A.58.6., A.65.3., A.68.9., A.70.13., A.76.7., A.78.3., A.79.1.2., A.82.8., and A.84.15., see also A.67.12.

(G, 55 [148]; H[1926], 89, 186; Häm.[1908a], 15; P, 203, 207.)

A.67.14.   *pasu perke* 'field blessing'

When the *pasu perke* is in the field, crops grow well. If, however, a field produces poor crops for two or three years, it means to the Cheremis that the 'field blessing' has been stolen. In order to get it back, the owner of the field goes to a soothsayer (D.7., D.10.) to find out who has taken it. The soothsayer learns whose fields were previously poor but have been better lately and names him as the culprit. The owner of the field from which the *perke* has been stolen must then go to the field where the *perke* is and, without anyone's knowing about it, he must put a little of the dirt in a bast shoe and drag it by a shoelace to his own field. Then he prays the *pasu perke* to stay in his field and not to respond when others try to steal it.

For other field spirits, see A.38.21., A.58.7., A.70.14., and A.84.17.

(H[1926], 89; H[1927], 240.)

A.67.15.   *surt perke* 'house blessing'

A libation is offered to this deity at the *küsə* ceremony (B.9.).

For other house spirits, see A.9.2., A.26.36., A.38.23., A.58.9., A.70.17., and A.84.18.

(H[1926], 89.)

A.67.16.   *šibundə perke* 'money blessing'

A libation is offered to this deity at the *küsə* ceremony (B.9.).

(H[1926], 89; Häm.[1908a], 15.)

A.67.17.   *šurnə perke* 'grain blessing'

A sheep is sacrificed to this deity at *šurnə jər* (B.22.), a ceremony dedicated to the grain deities. An offering is also made at *aga pajram* (B.2.) and the *küsə* ceremony (B.9.).

For other grain spirits, see A.1.8.2., A.26.1.3.1., A.26.1.6., A.26.34.1., A.27.2., A.28.4., A.29.2., A.52.7., A.52.12.1., A.52.14., A.67.9., A.68.10., A.70.18., A.79.1.3., A.82.6., A.82.11., A.84.13., and A.84.19.

(G, 55 [148]; H[1926], 89; P, 203, 207.)

A.67.18.   *ü perke* 'butter blessing'

A libation is offered to this deity at the *küsə* ceremony (B.9.).

(H[1926], 89.)

For *perke aba*, see A.1.8.; *kaba jumən perke aba*, A.1.8.1.1.; *kində perke aba*, A.1.8.2.; *perke aba jumə*, A.26.1.3.; *kində perke aba jumə*, A.26.1.3.1.; *perke jumə*, A.26.30.; *kində perke xan*, A.52.12.1.; *sirga perke xan*, A.52.12.2.; *pešmän orbəška*,

A.70.; *pəl aba,* A.1.9.; *pəl ümbal jumə,* A.26.; *pəl orža,* A.56.2.; *pəl ner,* A.48.; *taмək pi,* A.90. *pi nereškə,* A.49.; *pi targəldəš,* A.86.2.

A.68. *piambar* 'prophet'

Although this term is usually translated 'prophet,' it is really a term for a supernatural which has none of the functions of a prophet. Sometimes a *piambar* is the helper of a god (A.26.) or a *keremet* (A.31.); at other times it is a deity in its own right.
(G, 55 [148]; H[1926], 94.)

A.68.1. *bol'ək piambar* 'livestock prophet'

For other livestock spirits, see A.1.10.1., A.26.5., A.26.38.1., A.28.1., A.52.1., A.67.2., A.70.2., A.76.2., A.78.1., A.79.1.1., A.82.2., and A.84.3.
(H[1926], 94.)

A.68.2. *jumən piambar* 'god's prophet'

This spirit is one of the helpers of *kugə jumə* (A.26.); it has its own tree in the sacrifice grove (E.2.1.) and its own priest. An ox is usually sacrificed to it. An offering is also made to this deity at *aga pajram* (B.2.).
(G, 55 [148]; H[1926], 64–65; Häm.[1908a], 8–10; P, 72, 187, 203, 206.)

A.68.3. *kaba piambar* 'fate prophet'

This spirit is a helper of *kaba jumə* (A.26.13.). A steer is sacrificed to it at the *küsə* ceremony (B.9.) and an offering is made at *aga pajram* (B.2.).
(H[1926], 66; P, 187, 203.)

A.68.4. *kazna piambar* 'treasure prophet'

For *kazna,* see A.28.
(V, 59.)

A.68.5. *kəzər piambar*

A steer is sacrificed to this deity every third year at the *küsə* ceremony (B.9.) and an offering made at *aga pajram* (B.2.).
(H[1926], 94; P, 188, 203; Räsänen[1928], 214–16.)

A.68.6. *kurək piambar* 'mountain prophet'

A sacrifice of a brown bull is made to this *keremet* (A.31.).
(H[1926], 165; S, 154.)

A.68.7. *küllö piambar*

The meaning of *küllö* is uncertain. Some priests say that it means 'different' and that *küllö piambar* means 'different prophets.' A steer is sacrificed to this spirit at the *küsə* ceremony (B.9.) every third year. At *aga pajram* (B.2.) an offering is also made.
For other *küllö* spirits, see A.26.23.; A.67.10.; A.70.7.1., and A.70.11.

A.68.8. *məlandə piambar* 'earth prophet'

A steer is offered to *məlandə piambar* at the *küsə* ceremony (B.9.) every third year and a ram at *məlandə jər* (B.10.), a ceremony dedicated to the earth deities. Offerings are also made at *aga pajram* (B.2.).

For other earth spirits, see A.1.5., A.1.10.5., A.9.10., A.15.4., A.26.25., A.52.10., A.58.5., A.65.2., A.67.11., A.70.12., A.76.6., A.79.2., A.82.7., and A.84.14.

(H[1926], 94; P, 189, 203, 207.)

A.68.9. *mükš piambar* 'bee prophet'

A ram is sacrificed to this spirit at *mükš jər* 'bee offering' (B.11.). An offering is also made at *aga pajram.* (B.2.).

For other bee spirits, see A.1.6., A.1.10.6., A.15.6., A.26.1.2., A.26.28., A.26.38.2., A.27.1., A.28.3., A.29.3., A.52.11., A.58.6., A.65.3., A.67.13., A.70.13., A.76.7., A.78.3., A.79.1.2., A.82.8., and A.84.15.; see also A.67.12.

(H[1926], 94, 186; P, 203, 207.)

A.68.10. *šurnə piambar* 'grain prophet'

A ram is sacrificed to this spirit at *šurnə jər* (B.22.), a ceremony dedicated to the grain deities. An offering is also made at *aga pajram* (B.2.).

For other grain spirits, see A.1.8.2., A.26.1.3.1., A.26.16., A.26.34.1., A.27.2., A.28.4., A.29.2., A.52.7., A.52.12.1., A.52.14., A.67.9., A.67.17., A.70.18., A.79.1.3., A.82.6., A.82.11., A.84.13., and A.84.19.

(H[1926], 94; P, 203, 207.)

For *piambar kuguza jumə,* see A.26.19.1.; *pokšəm ača,* A.38.22. *pokšəm ərbezə,* A.38.22.; *pokšəm koča,* A.38.22.; *pokšəm kuguza* and *kuba,* A.38.22.; *pokšəm obəškə,* A.38.22.; *pokšəm üdər,* A.38.22.

A.69. *toktal poškudə* 'toktal neighbor'

This is a *keremet* (A.31.).

(H[1926], 172–73.)

For *pört bodəž,* see A.9.12.; *pört kuguza* and *kuba,* A.38.23.; *pört oza,* A.38.23.; *pört ört,* A.58.9.; *pörtšär,* A.58.9.; *pu on* or *pušengə on,* A.52.13.; *pu ört* or *pušengə ört,* A.58.8.

A.70. *pujəršə* 'creator'

Although the term *pujəršə* may be translated 'creator,' it is closely linked with the concepts of fertility, birth, and growth. In some places, a white lamb is sacrificed to this deity at the birth of a child. In legends, it wanders on the earth, sometimes accompanied by *piambar* 'prophet' (A.68.), as a poor pilgrim, performing miracles and teaching people. As protector of the fields, *pujəršə* walks along the edge of a field dressed in a white or green kaftan with a staff in its hand. Where the *pujəršə* is seen praying on the field, grain grows well. The strip along the edge of the field must be wide so that this deity does not get the hem of its kaftan wet with the dew; where it gets wet, the grain dries up. A person is not to sit or lie on the border of a field; if he does, he will get sick. It is also bad to go into the field on a Friday. According to one account, *pujəršə* travels along the edge of the field in a boat drawn by horses. In some places, the keeper of the border is called *pešmän orbəška. Pujəršə* also warns people to make room for a lake which is about to move. The second of the four sacrifices required of each man during his life is dedicated to *kugə pujəršə* 'great creator.' A foal is sacrificed to this deity and six or eight smaller animals to its retinue of helping spirits. The term *pujəršə* is also used to designate deities which have jurisdiction over specific phases of nature.

(H[1926], 77, 156, 191–93; PG, 20 [83]; S, 163.)

A.70.1.　*biča pujəršə* 'pen creator'

For other pen spirits, see A.38.4., A.58.1., A.67.1., and A.84.2.

(H[1926], 93.)

A.70.2.　*bol'ək pujəršə* 'livestock creator'

For other livestock spirits, see A.1.10.1., A.26.5., A.26.38.1., A.28.1., A.52.1., A.67.2., A.68.1., A.76.2., A.78.1., A.79.1.1., A.82.2., and A.84.3.

(G, 55 [148]; H[1926], 93.)

A.70.3.　*büt pujəršə* 'water creator'

For other water spirits, see A.1.1., A.16.1., A.26.7., A.26.29.1., A.52.2., A.58.2., A.84.4., and A.96.2.

(H[1913], 118; H[1926], 93.)

For *čon pujəršə*, see A.70.4.

A.70.4.　*ergə pujəršə* 'son creator'

This deity of fertility is also called *ikšəbə pujəršə* 'child creator' and *čon pujəršə* 'life (or "soul") creator' (for *čon*, see J.1.). The fourth of the sacrifices required of every man (B.34.) is dedicated to this deity. Seven animals are sacrificed at the ceremony; a foal to *ergə pujəršə* and six smaller animals to deities. In some places it is believed that only Russian Christians can pray to this deity and thus, when a Cheremis is childless, he asks a Russian priest to intercede for him. The term *ergə pujəršə* is used by some for Christ.

(H[1926], 91, 93, 119, 156; Häm.[1908a], 9–10.

A.70.5.　*idəm pujəršə* 'threshing-floor creator'

For other threshing-floor spirits, see A.38.9., A.58.3., A.67.3., and A.84.6.

(H[1926], 93.)

For *ikšəbə pujəršə*, see A.70.4.

A.70.6.　*ješ pujəršə* 'family creator'

(H[1926], 93.)

A.70.7.　*kaba jumən pujəršə* 'heaven god's creator'

For *kaba*, see A.27.; *kaba jumə*, A.26.13.

(V, 57.)

A.70.7.1.　*küllö jumən pujəršəblak* 'küllö god's creators'

For *küllö jumə*, see A.26.23.

(Be, 705.)

A.70.8.　*kaba pujəršə* 'fate creator'

For *kaba*, see A.27.

(H[1926], 119.)

A.70.9. *kazna pujəršə* 'treasure creator'

For *kazna,* see A.28.

(V, 59.)

For *kində pujəršə* see A.70.18.

A.70.10. *kornə pujəršə* 'road creator'

(H[1926], 93.)

A.70.11. *küllö pujəršə*

For other *küllö* spirits, see A.26.23., A.67.10., A.68.7., and A.70.7.1.

(H[1926], 93.)

A.70.12. *məlandə pujəršə* 'earth creator'

An offering is made to this deity at *aga pajram* (B.2.).

For other earth spirits, see A.1.5., A.1.10.5., A.9.10., A.15.4., A.26.25., A.52.10., A.58.5., A.65.2., A.67.11., A.68.8., A.76.6., A.79.2., A.82.7., and A.84.14.

(H[1926], 93; P, 203.)

A.70.13. *mükš pujəršə* 'bee creator'

A sacrifice of a ram or sheep is made to this deity at special ceremonies dedicated to the bee gods. An offering is also made at *aga pajram* (B.2.).

For other bee spirits, see A.1.6., A.1.10.6., A.15.6., A.26.1.2., A.26.28., A.26.38.2., A.27.1., A.28.3., A.29.3., A.52.11., A.58.6., A.65.3., A.67.13., A.68.9., A.76.7., A.78.3., A.79.1.2., A.82.8., and A.84.15.; see also A.67.12.

(G, 55 [148]; H[1926], 93, 186; Häm.[1909], 5; P, 203, 207.)

A.70.14. *pasu pujəršə* 'field creator'

(H[1926], 93.)

A.70.15. *pundə pujəršə* 'money creator'

(H[1926], 93.)

A.70.16. *saska pujəršə* 'blossom creator'

A duck is sacrificed to this deity at *mükš jər* (B.11.), a ceremony dedicated to the bee gods. An offering is also made at *aga pajram* (B.2.).

For blossom god, see A.26.34.

(H[1926], 93; P, 203, 207.)

A.70.17. *surt pujəršə* 'house creator'

For other house spirits, see A.9.2., A.26.36., A.38.23., A.58.9., A.67.15., and A.84.18.

(H[1926], 93.)

A.70.18. *šurnə pujəršə* or *kində pujəršə* 'grain creator'

A ram is sacrificed to this deity at *šurnə jər* (B.22.), a ceremony dedicated to the grain gods. An offering is also made at *aga pajram* (B.2.).

For other grain spirits, see A.1.8.2., A.26.1.3.1., A.26.16., A.26.34.1., A.27.2.,

A.28.4., A.29.2., A.52.7., A.52.12.1., A.52.14., A.67.9., A.67.17., A.68.10., A.76.8., A.79.1.3., A.82.6., A.82.11., A.84.13., and A.84.19.

(G, 55 [148]; H[1926], 93; P, 203, 207.)

A.70.19. *tenəz pujərśə* 'sea creator'

For other sea spirits, see A.1.13., A.26.29.2., A.26.40., and A.52.16.

(H[1913], 119.)

A.70.20. *tul pujərśə* 'fire creator'

For other fire spirits, see A.1.10.8., A.1.15., A.9.14., A.26.29.3., A.26.42., A.52.18., A.58.10., A.84.20., and A.88.1.

(H[1926], 93; Häm.[1936–37], 71.)

A.70.21. *tüńća pujərśə* or *tüńća ümbal pujərśə* 'world creator'

A horse is sacrificed to this deity at the *küsə* ceremony (B.9.).

(H[1926], 93, 119; P, 187.)

A.70.22. *tütra pujərśə* 'mist creator'

(H[1926], 70.)

For *pujərśə jumə*, see A.26.31.; *ergə pujərśə jume*, A.26.31.1.; *kećə pujərśə jumə*, A.26.31.2.; *tüńća ümbal pujərśə jumə*, A.26.31.3.; *pundə pujərśə*, A.70.15.; *pundə serlagəš*, A.78.4.; *pundə śoćən*, A.82.9.

A.71. *šüć pundəš* 'burnt stump'

This spirit is a helper of *kugərak* (A.21.2.1.) and as such receives an offering of bread.

(V, 281.)

A.72. *jumən šerməčkəl kučən puśə* 'one who gives holding reins'

This spirit leads the sacrificed horse to god (A.26.). As an intermediary between god and man, it has its own tree and priest, and receives a sacrifice of a sheep, duck, or goose.

(H[1926], 64–65; Häm.[1908a], 9.)

For *rok śərt*, see A.15.8.; *run kuguza* and *kuba*, A.38.24.; *rušarńa jumə*, A.26.32.; *sakćə*, A.84.; *sakćə jumə*, A.26.33.

A.73. *jumən salauz*

An offering is made to this deity at *aga pajram* (B.2.).

(P, 203.)

A.74. *ia saltak* 'devil soldier'

This spirit, also called *oksa saltak* 'money soldier' or *oksa orola* 'money guard,' guards buried treasure. It is usually seen between Easter and Pentecost; around Easter it hangs the money up to dry. Both the soldier and the money seem to be burning, sometimes with a green flame. When people see the fire, they try to get the money; the soldier defends it with a sword and a gun, and also calls on other evil spirits to help him. If a person is not frightened, he can succeed in taking the money.

For another guard of buried treasure, see A.66.1.

(B, 8–9; Bk, 50–51; Uj[FB], 1; Up[FB], 1.)

For *saska jumə*, see A.26.34.; *kində saska jumə*, A.26.34.1.; *saska pujəršə*, A.70.16.

A.75.   *satana* or *sotoña* or *sotña* 'Satan'

Satan is a horned, bearded, fiery devil, according to some the grandfather of *ia* (A.16.). Drunkards and practitioners of black magic fall into its power after death, are thrown into chains and beaten. This devil also can change those in its power into horses and thus use them to pull its wagon. An intoxicated man who is killed by *sotona kuguza* 'Satan old man' may become a *sotona* himself and thus not join other dead people in the afterworld. *Sotona kuba* 'Satan old woman' provokes Cheremis women to quarrel with their daughters-in-law and their sons. Once the discord has been sown, *sotona kuba* torments the woman until she commits suicide. The soul of the dead woman becomes an *ia* (A.16) which accompanies *sotona kuba*. According to one informant who was reminiscing about former times when his people worshipped *keremet*s (A.31.), *sotña* was the most important god of his people. When a horse was sick, it was dedicated to this god; when it recovered, it was never beaten. Later the horse was taken to the grove and burned.

For other devils, see A.7., A.15., A.16., A.18., A.20., A.81., and A.93.

(B, 9, 10; R, 207; Uj[FB], 70.)

A.76.   *saus* 'overseer'

(G, 55 [148]; H[1926], 94.)

A.76.1.   *aga saus* 'plowing overseer'

An offering is made to this deity at *aga pajram* (B.2.) and *aga kurman* (B.1.).
(P, 203.)

A.76.2.   *bol'ək saus* 'livestock overseer'

For other livestock spirits, see A.1.10.1., A.26.5., A.26.38.1., A.28.1., A.52.1., A.67.2., A.68.1., A.70.2., A.76.2., A.78.1., A.79.1.1., A.82.2., and A.84.3.
(G, 55 [148].)

A.76.3.   *kaba saus* 'heaven overseer'

For *kaba*, see A.27.
(V, 57.)

A.76.4.   *kazna saus* 'treasure overseer'

For *kazna*, see A.28.
(V, 59.)

A.76.5.   *kiamat saus* 'kiamat overseer'

This spirit is the helper of *kiamat töra* (A.90.), ruler of the underworld. Offerings are sometimes made to it at funerals and memorial feasts for the dead (B.23.).
(Be, 338, 704; H[1926], 15; Häm.[1936–37], 46; P, 208; Wu, 48; Wt, 60.)

A.76.6. *məlandə saus* 'earth overseer'

An offering is made to this deity at *aga pajram* (B.2.).

For other earth spirits, see A.1.5., A.1.10.5., A.9.10., A.15.4., A.26.25., A.52.10., A.58.5., A.65.2., A.67.11., A.68.8., A.70.12., A.79.2., A.82.7., and A.84.14.

(H[1926], 94; P, 203.)

A.76.7. *mükš saus* 'bee overseer'

A goose is sacrificed to this deity at *mükš jər* (B.11.), a ceremony dedicated to the bee gods. An offering is also made at *aga pajram* (B.2.).

For other bee spirits, see A.1.6., A.1.10.6., A.15.6., A.26.1.2., A.26.28., A.26.38.2., A.27.1., A.28.3., A.29.3., A.52.11., A.58.6., A.65.3., A.67.13., A.68.9., A.70.13., A.78.3., A.79.1.2., A.82.8., and A.84.15.; see also A.67.12.

(G, 55 [148]; H[1926], 94, 186; P, 203, 207.)

A.76.8. *šurnə saus* 'grain overseer'

A duck is sacrificed to this deity at a special ceremony dedicated to the grain gods. An offering is also made at *aga pajram* (B.2.).

For other grain spirits, see A.1.8.2., A.26.1.3.1., A.26.16., A.26.34.1., A.27.2., A.28.4., A.29.2., A.52.7., A.52.12.1., A.52.14., A.67.9., A.67.17., A.68.10., A.70.18., A.79.1.3., A.82.6., A.82.11., A.84.13., and A.84.19.

(G, 55 [148]; H[1926], 94; P, 203, 207.)

A.76.9. *tüńča saus* 'world overseer'

(V, 216.)

A.77.1. *joškar ser* 'red bank'

This is a *keremet* (A.31.).

(H[1926], 170.)

For *jul ser kugərak*, see A.37.; *serekan keremet*, see A.31.8.

A.78. *serlagəš* 'mercy'

(H[1926], 94.)

A.78.1. *bol'ək serlagəš* 'livestock mercy'

For other livestock spirits, see A.1.10.1., A.26.5., A.26.38.1., A.28.1., A.52.1., A.67.2., A.68.1., A.70.2., A.76.2., A.79.1.1., A.82.2., and A.84.3.

(H[1926], 94.)

A.78.2. *jumən serlagəš* 'god's mercy'

An intermediary between god (A.26.) and man is 'god's mercy.' When a sacrifice is made to god, one also is made to this deity which has its own tree and priest. The sacrifice animal may be a sheep, goose, or duck.

(H[1926], 64–65; Häm.[1908a], 9, 10.)

A.78.3. *mükš serlagəš* 'bee mercy'

For other bee spirits, see A.1.6., A.1.10.6., A.15.6., A.26.1.2., A.26.28., A.26.38.2., A.27.1., A.28.3., A.29.3., A.52.11., A.58.6., A.65.3., A.67.13., A.68.9., A.70.13., A.76.7., A.79.1.2., A.82.8., and A.84.15.; see also A.67.12.

(H[1926], 94.)

A.78.4.   *pundə serlagəš* 'money mercy'
(H[1926], 94.)

A.79.   *sərabočəš* 'key'

A.79.1.   *kazna sərabočəš* 'treasure key'
For *kazna,* see A.28.
(V, 59.)

A.79.1.1.   *bol'ək kazna sərabočəš* 'livestock treasure key'
For other livestock spirits, see A.1.10.1., A.26.5., A.26.38.1., A.28.1., A.52.1., A.67.2., A.68.1., A.70.2., A.76.2., A.78.1., A.82.2., and A.84.3.
(G, 55 [148].)

A.79.1.2.   *mükš (kazna) sərabočəš* 'bee (treasure) key'
A goose is sacrificed to this deity at *mükš jər* 'bee offering' (B.11.).
For other bee spirits, see A.1.6., A.1.10.6., A.15.6., A.26.1.2., A.26.28., A.26.38.2., A.27.1., A.28.3., A.29.3., A.52.11., A.58.6., A.65.3., A.67.13., A.68.9., A.70.13., A.76.7., A.78.3., A.82.8., and A.84.15.; see also A.67.12.
(G, 55 [148]; H[1926], 186; P, 207.)

A.79.1.3.   *šurnə kazna sərabočəš* 'grain treasure key'
For other grain spirits, see A.1.8.2., A.26.1.3.1., A.26.16., A.26.34.1., A.27.2., A.28.4., A.29.2., A.52.7., A.52.12.1., A.52.14., A.67.9., A.67.17., A.68.10., A.70.18., A.76.8., A.82.6., A.82.11., A.84.13., and A.84.19.
(G, 55 [148].)

A.79.2.   *məlandə sərabočəš* 'earth key'
An offering is made to this deity at *aga pajram.*
For other earth spirits, see A.1.5., A.1.10.5., A.9.10., A.15.4., A.26.25., A.52.10., A.58.5., A.65.2., A.67.11., A.68.8., A.70.12., A.76.6., A.82.7., and A.84.14.
(P, 203.)
For *sirga perke xan,* see A.52.12.2.; *sot tüńča jumə,* A.26.44.1.; *sotńa,* A.75.; *spaš jumə,* A.26.35.; stones, A.98.

A.80.   *sultan*

A red steer is sacrificed yearly in July after the *küsə* ceremony (B.9.) to *sultan,* a *keremet* (A.31.) of Tatar origin. It has its own special grove because it is not considered proper to worship a foreign *keremet* in the same grove as a Cheremis one.
(H[1926], 175; H[1927], 157; P, 213.)
For *suräli,* see A.51.; *surt ia,* A.38.23.; *surt jumə,* A.26.36.; *surt kuguza* and *kuba,* A.38.23.; *surt(lə) məlandə bodəž,* A.9.10.1.; *surt oza,* A.38.23.; *surt ört,* A.58.9.; *surt perke,* A.67.15.; *surt pujəršə,* A.70.17.; *surt šukčə,* A.84.18.; *sürem jumə,* A.26.37.; *sürem mužə,* A. 46.2.; *šačəktšə,* A.82.

A.81.   *šajtan*

A *šajtan* is a devil and the enemy of thunder and lightning. According to a legend, *šajtans* originated when *keremet* (A.31.) tried to imitate god (A.26.), who, by striking sparks from a stone, created angels. When the thunder god (A.26.22.) tries to kill a *šajtan,* it seeks protection among human beings, sometimes in the shape of a boy or girl. People can keep this devil from coming to them by carrying a metal object or by drawing a circle around them with a piece of iron (H.4.4.). The Cheremis exorcise *šajtan* from the village during the *sürem* ceremony (B.18.). At that time they also drive away wolves because they believe that this devil can go about in the form of a wolf.

In some places it is believed that *šajtan* brings cold from the north and thus, when *šajtan* is driven away, cold weather is also driven away.

For other devils, see A.7., A.15., A.16., A.18., A.30., A.75., and A.93.

(H[1926], 40, 69, 179; Häm.[1928], 29–34; S, 186–88, 200.)

For *šedra kuguza* and *kuba,* see A.38.35.; *juman šermačkal kučan puša,* A.72.; *šerdaš šart,* A.15.9.; *šart,* A.15.; *čurpan šert,* A.15.1.; *keremet šert,* A.15.2.; *kurak šert,* A.15.3.; *malanda šart,* A.15.4.; *moča šart,* A.15.5.; *mükš šart,* A.15.6.; *pajberda šart,* A.15.7.; *rok šart,* A.15.8.; *šerdaš šart,* A.15.9.; *undur šart,* A.15.10.; *šart bodaž,* A.9.13.; *šart terkan,* A.87.; *šibunda perke,* A.67.14.; *šišer jer juma,* A.26.11.; *šište korna palastarše,* A.60.; *ške keremet* or *škenan ončama keremet,* A.31.7.

A.82. *šočan* 'fructifier'; *šačaktša* 'begetter'

Šočan, which means literally 'giving birth,' is the spirit of fertility. In some places, the term *šačaktša* is used for this same spirit. *Kuga šočan* 'great fructifier' receives a sacrifice of a cow at the *küsa* ceremony (B.9.). Everything which can reproduce may have its own *šočan* spirit.

(H[1926], 90, 110; H[1927], 258–59; P, 187.)

A.82.1.1. *šočan aban šočanža* 'fructifier mother's fructifier'

A sheep is sacrificed to this deity at a ceremony dedicated to *šočan aba* (A.1.10.), to which a cow is sacrificed.

(Häm.[1908a], 9.)

A.82.2. *bol'ak šočan* 'livestock fructifier'; *bol'ak šačaktša* 'livestock begetter'

Prayers are said to this deity to help the livestock bring forth their young easily. A few days after a calf has been born, its owner invites his friends and relatives to his house. He pours water over the oven and prays that this spirit make the calf as big as the oven; he sprinkles water on those present expressing the hope that the cow will give much milk; he makes an offering to this deity and prays that the herd will be greatly increased (see B.28.).

For other livestock spirits, see A.1.10.1., A.26.5., A.26.38.1., A.28.1., A.52.1., A.67.2., A.68.1., A.70.2., A.76.2., A.78.1., A.79.1.1., and A.84.3.

(B, 24; G, 55 [148]; H[1926], 90–91; H[1927], 259.)

A.82.3. *erga šočan* 'son fructifier'

For other son spirits, see A.26.31.1. and A.70.4.

(H[1926], 90.)

A.82.4. *ikšaba šočan* 'child fructifier'

(H[1926], 90.)

A.82.5.   *jumən šočən* 'god's fructifier'

A cow is sacrificed to spirit at the *küsə* ceremony (B.9.) and an offering is made at *aga pajram* (B.2.).

For *jumə*, see A.26.

(H[1926], 90, 110, 112; P, 187, 189, 203.)

A.82.5.1.   *kaba jumən šočən* 'heaven god's fructifier'

For *kaba jumə*, see A.26.13.

(V, 57.)

A.82.6.   *kində šočən* 'grain fructifier'

At the end of the harvest, bread made from the newly harvested grain is offered to this spirit.

For other grain spirits, see A.1.8.2., A.26.1.3.1., A.26.16., A.26.34.1., A.27.2., A.28.4., A.29.2., A.52.7., A.52.12.1., A.52.14., A.67.9., A.67.17., A.68.10., A.70.18., A.76.8., A.79.1.3., A.82.11., A.84.13., and A.84.19.

(H[1926], 90–91.)

A.82.7.   *məlandə šočən* 'earth fructifier'

An offering is made to this spirit at *aga pajram* (B.2.).

For other earth spirits, see A.1.5., A.1.10.5., A.9.10., A.15.4., A.26.25., A.52.10., A.58.5., A.65.2., A.67.11., A.68.8., A.70.12., A.76.6., A.79.2., and A.84.14.

(H[1927], 259; P, 203.)

A.82.8.   *mükš šočən* 'bee fructifier'

An offering is made to this spirit at *aga pajram* (B.2.). A sheep is sacrificed at *mükš jər* (B.11.), a ceremony dedicated to the bee spirits.

For other bee spirits, see A.1.6., A.1.10.6., A.15.6., A.26.1.2., A.26.28., A.26.38.2., A.27.1., A.28.3., A.29.3., A.52.11., A.58.6., A.65.3., A.67.13., A.68.9., A.70.13., A.76.7., A.78.3., A.79.1.2., and A.84.15.; see also A.67.12.

(G, 55 [148]; H[1926], 90, 186; P, 203, 207.)

A.82.9.   *pundə šočən* 'money fructifier'

(H[1926], 90.)

A.82.10.   *šorək šočən* 'sheep fructifier'

(B, 24; H[1926], 188.)

A.82.11.   *šurnə šočən* 'grain fructifier'; *šurnə šočəktšə* 'grain begetter'

An offering is made to this spirit at *aga pajram* (B.2.) and a sheep is sacrificed at *šurnə jər* (B.22.), a ceremony dedicated to the grain spirits.

(G, 55 [148]; H[1926], 90; P, 203, 207.)

For *šočən aba*, see A.1.10.; *bol'ək šočən aba*, A.1.10.1.; *jeŋ šočən aba*, A.1.10.2.; *kajək šočən aba*, A.1.10.4.; *oš kečə šočən aba*, A.1.10.3.1.; *məlandə šočən aba*, A.1.10.5.; *mükš šočən aba*, A.1.10.6.; *šorək šočən aba*, A.1.10.7.; *tul šočən aba*, A.1.10.8.; *tüñča ümbal šočən aba*, A.1.10.9.; *uškal šočən aba*, A.1.10.10.; *šočən aba juməšaməč*, A.26.1.4.; *bol'ək šočən jumə*, A.26.38.1.; *mükš šočən jumə*, A.26.38.2.; *šokšə aba*, A.1.11.; *šokšə kuguza* and *kuba*, A.38.26.

A.83. šordan

Occasionally sacrifices are made to this spirit which protects the Cheremis in times of war.

(H[1926], 173–74.)

For šorǝk šoťǝn, see A.82.10.; šorǝk šoťǝn aba, A.1.10.7.

A.84. šukčǝ or sakčǝ 'angel'

A šukčǝ may be a personal guardian angel, a helper of god, or the guardian of some phase of nature. In the last case, the term šukčǝ is preceded by a word designating the province of nature over which it has jurisdiction. According to a legend, god struck sparks from a stone and they became angels.

Each person has his own guardian angel which is sometimes called buj šukčǝ 'head angel' or bučǝ ümbal šukčǝ 'angel on the shoulder.' The latter name comes from the belief that an angel sits on a person's right shoulder and an ia 'devil' (A.16.) on the left. The angel tries to influence the person to do good while the devil tempts him to do the opposite. Each writes down everything the person says or does which is in its favor; the one with the longer list takes the person's soul when he dies. Sometimes an angel chases devils away with a broom of fire. A solar eclipse is said to occur when angels screen the sun from sinful mankind with their wings.

For another angel, see A.65.

(B, 11; Bj, 161–2; G, 55 [148]; H[1926], 69, 93, 94; S, 200; Uj[FB], 10–11; Up[FB], 15.)

A.84.1. arňagočon šukčǝ 'Friday's angel'

See also Friday god, A.26.17.

(G, 55 [148].)

A.84.2. biča šukčǝ 'pen angel'

A libation is made to this angel at the küsǝ ceremony (B.9.).

For other spirits of the livestock pens, see A.38.4., A.58.1., A.67.1., and A.70.1.

(H[1926], 94.)

A.84.3. bol'ǝk šukčǝ 'livestock angel'

A libation is made to this deity at the küsǝ ceremony.

For other livestock spirits, see A.1.10.1., A.26.5., A.26.38.1., A.28.1., A.52.1., A.67.2., A.68.1., A.70.2., A.76.2., A.78.1., A.79.1.1., and A.82.2.

(H[1926], 94.)

A.84.4. büt ümbal šukčǝ 'angel on the water'

A libation is made to this angel at the küsǝ ceremony (B.9.).

For other water spirits, see A.1.1., A.16.1., A.26.7., A.26.29.1., A.52.2., A.58.2., A.70.3., and A.96.2.

(H[1926], 94.)

A.84.5.   *er šukčə* 'morning angel'

A libation is made to this deity at the *küsə* ceremony (B.9.) and an offering at *aga pajram* (B.2.).

(H[1926], 94; P,203.)

A.84.6.   *idəm šukčə* 'threshing-floor angel'

A libation is made to this deity at the *küsə* ceremony (B.9.).

For other threshing-floor spirits, see A.38.9., A.58.3., A.67.3., and A.70.5.

(H[1926], 94.)

A.84.7.   *jes šukčə* 'family angel'

A libation is made to this deity at the *küsə* ceremony (B.9.).

For other family spirits, see A.52.4., A.67.4., and A.70.6.

(H[1926], 94.)

A.84.8.   *jumən šukčə* 'god's angel'

This angel is one of god's helpers which receives sacrifices when an animal is sacrificed to god (A.26.). A sheep, goose, or duck is sacrificed by a special priest under the tree dedicated to this angel. In some places, the tree dedicated to *jumən šukčə* is the easternmost tree in the grove, the only one further to the east than the tree dedicated to *jumə* 'god' (A.26.).

(H[1926], 64–65, 94; Häm.[1908a], 9–10; P, 72, 187, 189, 203, 206.)

A.84.9.   *kaba šukčə* 'fate angel'

This angel is a helper of *kaba jumə* (A.26.13.). A ram is sacrificed to it at the *küsə* ceremony (B.9.) and an offering is made at *aga pajram* (B.2.).

For *kaba*, see A.27.

(H[1926], 66; P, 187, 189, 203.)

A.84.10.   *kazna šukčə* 'treasure angel'

For *kazna*, see A.28.

(V, 59.)

A.84.11.   *kapka šukčə* 'gate angel'

A libation is made to this angel at the *küsə* ceremony (B.9.).

(H[1926], 94.)

A.84.12.   *kas šukčə* 'evening angel'

An offering is made to this angel at *aga pajram* (B.2.) and a libation at the *küsə* ceremony (B.9.).

For another evening angel, see A.65.1.

(P, 70, 203.)

A.84.13.   *kində šukčə* 'grain angel'

A libation is made to this angel at the *küsə* ceremony (B.9.).

For other grain spirits, see A.1.8.2., A.26.1.3.1., A.26.16., A.26.34.1., A.27.2., A.28.4., A.29.2., A.52.7., A.52.12.1., A.52.14., A.67.9., A.67.17., A.68.10., A.70.18., A.76.8., A.79.1.3., A.82.6., A.82.11., and A.84.19.

(B, 22; H[1926], 94; Uj[FB], 29; Up[FB], 13.)

A.84.14.   *məlandə šukčə* 'earth angel'

Animals sacrificed to earth spirits are black and their remains are buried in the ground. A ram is sacrificed to the 'earth angel' at the *küsə* ceremony (B.9.) every third year; a duck is sacrificed at *məландə jər* (B.10.), a ceremony dedicated to the earth spirits.

For other earth spirits, see A.1.5., A.1.10.5., A.9.10., A.15.4., A.26.25., A.52.10., A.58.5., A.65.2., A.67.11., A.68.8., A.70.12., A.76.6., A.79.2., and A.82.7.

(H[1926], 94, 97; P, 189, 203, 207.)

A.84.15.   *mükš šukčə* 'bee angel'

A goose or duck is sacrificed at *mükš jər* (B.11.), a ceremony dedicated to the bee gods. An offering is also made at *aga pajram* (B.2.) and a libation at the *küsə* ceremony (B.9.).

For other bee spirits, see A.1.6., A.1.10.6., A.15.6., A.26.1.2., A.26.28., A.26.38.2., A.27.1., A.28.3., A.29.3., A.52.11., A.58.6., A.65.3., A.67.13., A.68.9., A.70.13., A.76.7., A.78.3., A.79.1.2., and A.82.8.; see also A.67.12.

(H[1926], 94, 186; Häm.[1909], 5; P, 203, 207.)

A.84.16.   *okna šukčə* 'window angel'

A libation is made to this angel at the *küsə* ceremony (B.9.).

(H[1926], 94.)

A.84.17.   *pasu šukčə* 'field angel'

A libation is made to this angel at the *küsə* ceremony (B.9.).

For other house spirits, see A.38.21., A.58.7., A.67.14., and A.70.14.

(H[1926], 94.)

A.84.18.   *šurt šukčə* 'house angel'

A libation is made to this angel at the *küsə* ceremony (B.9.).

For other house spirits, see A.9.2., A.26.36., A.38.23., A.58.9., A.67.15., and A.70.17.

(H[1926], 94.)

A.84.19.   *šurnə šukčə* 'grain angel'

A duck is sacrificed to this angel at *šurnə jər* 'grain offering' (B.22.). An offering is also made at *aga pajram* (B.2.) and a libation at the *küsə* ceremony (B.9.).

For other grain spirits, see A.1.8.2., A.26.1.3.1., A.26.16., A.26.34.1., A.27.2., A.28.4., A.29.2., A.52.7., A.52.12.1., A.52.14., A.67.9., A.67.17., A.68.10., A.70.18., A.76.8., A.79.1.3., A.82.6., A.82.11., and A.84.13.

(H[1926], 94; P, 203, 207.)

A.84.20.   *tul šukčə* 'fire angel'

A libation is made to this angel at the *küsə* ceremony (B.9.).

(H[1926], 94.)

A.84.21.   *tünča ümbal šukčə* 'angel over the world'

A ram is offered to this angel every third year at the *küsə* ceremony (B.9.) and an offering is made at *aga pajram* (B.2.).

(P, 188, 189, 203.)

For *šurem kuguza* and *kuba,* see A.38.27.; *šurnə kaba,* A.27.2.; *šurnə kazna,* A.28.4.; *šurnə kazna sərabočəš,* A.79.1.3.; *šurnə on,* A.52.14.; *šurnə perke,* A.67.17.; *šurnə piambar,* A.68.10.; *šurnə pujəršə,* A.70.18.; *šurnə saus,* A.76.8.; *šurnə šočən,* A.82.11.; *šurnə šukčə,* A.84.19.; *šüč pundəš,* A.71.; *šüdər aba,* A.1.12.; *šüdər jumə,* A.26.39.; *šüdər on,* A.52.15.

A.85.   *šükšəndal*

A *šükšəndal* is a spirit which may be found on mountains, under stones, and under the mill, but it most frequently inhabits the homestead, particularly the bathhouse. It may appear either as a handsome man or as a pretty girl with blond hair. It is about three feet tall and its hair is long. A *šükšəndal* tries to harm people, especially those who go into the bathhouse alone at night; it may even kill a person there. It also steals babies left alone in the house. To prevent this, a Cheremis mother puts scissors or some other iron object in the cradle to ward it off (H.4.4.). *Šükšəndal* also makes noise in the house at night and causes people to have nightmares. Sometimes it has sexual intercourse with people in their dreams. A stomachache may be caused by the bite of a *šükšəndal* from another homestead. Although a *šükšəndal* is usually evil, a tale is told of a helpful one which took a soldier to be an invisible guest at his brother's wedding many miles away. When a Cheremis thinks of it, he asks the *šükšəndal* to protect his home and keep out evil.

(Be, 55–61; H[1926], 51; H[1927], 166; J; P, 80; P[1948], 132.)

For *tamək buj,* see A.90.; *tamək pi,* A.90.

A.86.   *targəldəš* or *tarbəltəš*

This forest spirit, also called *ajməldəš* 'misleader' or *arəmdəš* in some regions, is believed to be of human origin. It is sometimes called *ademe targəldəš* to distinguish it from a forest spirit of animal origin. A man who dies in the forest, especially if his blood is shed, may become a *targəldəš.* Some say that a *targəldəš* may come from a man with a *buber* soul (A.10.). Others believe that a stillborn child or one which dies without a name becomes a forest spirit (cf. A.51.); to prevent this, it is the custom to give a name to a baby which died nameless. A *targəldəš* is primarily a forest spirit but it also roves the meadows and fields, and occasionally comes to town. It has a human form and may be of gigantic proportions (cf. A.43.). In some places it is said to have one eye in the middle of its forehead. Although it is normally human in shape, it has the ability to take the form of an animal, a bird, a log, a haystack, or almost anything else. In the forest it shrieks and laughs so much that it frightens the cattle. It attempts to lure people off into unknown parts of the forest by calling out to them. When a person gets lost as a result of following a *targəldəš,* he must change his shoes from one foot to the other in order to be able to find his way back. If a person falls into the power of the *targəldəš,* he is tickled to death. If the *targəldəš* is in a friendly mood, it may appear at a camper's fire to warm itself; if, however, it is angry, it will put out the fire. For this reason, hunters, when they kindle a fire, pray to *tul aba* 'fire mother' (A.1.15.) to protect them. Sometimes a *targəldəš* frightens mushroom gatherers and berry pickers by riding at them at full gallop. At times a *targəldəš* comes to a village where it mingles with the townspeople. A *targəldəš* itself occasionally prepares feasts and celebrates weddings in the forest where it has a family, servants, extensive property, and cattle. Will-o'-the-wisp, called *targəldəš tul* 'targəldəš fire,' is considered an unlucky omen.

For other forest spirits, see A.11., A.20., A.43., and A.51.

(B, 8; Beke[1951b], 250; H[1926], 54–55; H[1927], 186; P[1948], 139; Uj[FB], 12; V, 17, 26.)

A.86.1. *imńə targəldəš* 'horse *targəldəš*'

A horse which dies in the forest and is not properly buried may become a horse phantom which harasses those who spend the night in the forest. It has large eyes, neighs shrilly, and seems to be on fire.

(H[1926], 57; H[1927], 186; Uj[FB], 13.)

A.86.2. *pi targəldəš* 'dog *targəldəš*'

A dog which dies in the forest or in the field may become a spirit.

(V, 158.)

For *taškəm məlandə aba*, see A.1.5.1.; *teŋəz aba*, A.1.13.; *teŋəz jumə*, A.26.40.; *teŋəz on jumə*, A.26.29.2.; *teŋəz on*, A.52.16.; *teŋəz pujəršə*, A.70.19.

A.87. *šərt terkan*

A bull is sacrificed to this *keremet* (A.31.).

(S, 155.)

For *teləzə aba*, see A.1.4.; *teləzə jumə*, A.26.41.; *teləzə on*, A.52.17.

A.88. *təlməč* 'interpreter'

Among the helping spirits of *nemdə kurək kugə jeŋ* (A.21.2.1.) is its interpreter.

(H[1926], 169.)

A.88.1. *tul bodəž təlmaze* 'fire spirit *təlmaze*'

A piece of bread is sacrificed to this *keremet* (A.31.).

For *tul bodəž*, see A.9.14.

(S, 155.)

A.89. *tiak* 'scribe'

Tiak is one of the helping spirits of *nemdə kurək kugə jeŋ* (A.21.2.1.).

(H[1926], 169.)

For *toktal poškudə*, see A.69.; *toštə kož jeŋ*, A.21.1.1.; *toštot jeŋ*, A.21.4.

A.90. *kiamat töra*

This spirit, which is also known in some regions as *tamək buj*, is the ruler of life after death. In some places, this spirit is believed to be the first person buried in a cemetery. It judges each person after his death and decides whether or not his soul will live a happy, comfortable life in the light. For this reason, the Cheremis make intercessions to *kiamat töra* on behalf of the dead, light a candle to it, and make food offerings during funerals and memorial ceremonies (B.23.). The helper of this spirit, *kiamat saus* 'kiamat overseer' (A.76.5.), is also worshipped at these times. In some places a hen is killed during the funeral ceremonies to gather the finger- and toenails lost by the dead person during his lifetime because he may not appear before *kiamat töra* without them. The ruler of the underworld has a little dog (*tamək pi*) which attacks the dead on their way to the underworld; for this reason, sticks are placed in the hands of the corpse to chase it away.

(B, 17; Be, 389, 703; H[1926], 15, 19–20; H[1927], 75; J; P, 208; Wu, 48; Wt, 60.)

For *tul aba*, see A.1.15.; *tul bodəž*, A.9.14.; *tul bodəž təlmaze*, A.88.1.; *tul jumə*, A.26.42.; *tul on*, A.52.18.; *tul on jumə*, A.26.29.3.; *tul ört*, A.58.10.; *tul pujəršə*, A.70.20.; *tul šočən aba*, A.1.10.8.; *tul šukčə*, A.84.20.; *tul'a jumə*, A.26.43.; *tumə düŋ keremet*, A.31.9.; *turek kuguza*, A.38.28.

A.91.   *tüñča* 'world'

An offering is made to this spirit at *aga pajram* (B.2.).
(P, 203; S, 167.)
For *tüñča jumə*, see A.26.; *sot tüñča jumə*, A.26.44.1.; *tüñča (ümbal) pujəršə*, A.70.21.; *tüñča ümbal pujəršə jumə*, A.26.31.3.; *tüñča saus*, A.76.9.; *tüñča ümbal šočən aba*, A.1.10.9.; *tüñča ümbal šukčə*, A.84.21.

A.92.   *er tütra* 'morning mist'

Libations are offered to this spirit but no blood sacrifices are made. It is believed that the mist by rising and falling can make grass and crops grow well.
(H[1926], 70.)
For *tütra jumə*, see A.26.45.; *tütra pujəršə*, A.70.22.; *uber*, A.10.

A.93.   *uda* 'devil'

People put iron over the door to prevent this spirit from entering the house. An "iron fence" (H.4.4.) keeps it from entering the field.
For other devils, see A.7., A.15., A.16., A.18., A.30., A.75., and A.81.
(B, 67, 68.)
For *umər jumə*, see A.26.46.; *undur šərt*, A.15.10.; *kajək usa jumə*, A.26.13.; *uškal šočən aba*, A.1.10.10.

A.94.   *utəmə* 'left over'; *utə kolšə* 'uneven dead'

The dead which have not been properly buried or which have no family alive to hold memorial feasts for them are sometimes the recipients of special sacrifices. The appearance of destructive insects and worms in the fields is considered to be a sign that the *utəmə* wish a sacrifice. In some towns a periodic sacrifice is made every three years, either in May or in September. The black steer which is sacrificed at such a ceremony is usually bought with money collected from all the townspeople; in many towns the animal is stolen. The remains of the animal are buried in the earth.
(Be, 396–98; H[1926], 41–43; H[1927], 68–69.)

A.95. *užedəš*

This term is translated in one source as 'disease' and in the other as 'informer.' During a vow to a *keremet* (A.31.) a hen may be sacrificed to its *užedəš*.

(Be, 63; H[1926], 70; S, 155.)

For *ü perke,* see A.67.18.

A.96. *üdər* 'daughter'

A.96.1. *čerlak üdəržə* 'Cherlak daughter'

When people in the town of Cherlak need rain, they make sacrifices to the lake, which they call *čerlak üdəržə*. Before and after such a sacrifice, they also throw water on each other, and on black sheep and hens, with much merrymaking. Lake *čerlak* has two older sisters, Lake Kandry-Kul and Lake Asli-kul, which it sometimes visits. When the lake goes on a visit, it takes all its water, fish and water fowl (cf. A.22.). One time the lake dried up so much that the cattle could graze on the bottom. The inhabitants, disturbed by the lack of water, made a sacrifice of a black heifer to *čerlak üdəržə* and prayed that it return. The people put the bones, hide, and other remains in a pool of water that was left. Although the water came back, at first it was muddy and ill-tasting; therefore, the townspeople made a sacrifice of a black lamb. After that the lake became normal. Sometimes its older sisters come to visit *čerlak üdəržə* causing a flood.

(H[1926], 74, 77–79; H[1927], 210–11.)

A.96.2. *büt ian üdəržə* 'water devil's daughter'

A female water spirit of human shape is usually called *büt ian üdəržə*. Sometimes, in the early morning, it is seen on a river bank combing its long hair, which may be white, golden yellow, or black, with a silver or gold comb. Sometimes this spirit is dressed in fine clothes; at other times it is naked. If a human succeeds in touching it with iron or in grabbing it, it cannot escape. Sometimes a man may marry a water spirit, who will bear him children; if, however, he reveals the true identity of his wife, it dies.

For other water spirits, see A.1.1., A.16.1., A.26.7., A.26.29.1., A.52.2., A.58.2., A.70.3., and A.84.4.

(H[1913], 116 ,130; H[1926], 59; H[1927], 199–200; PG, 12 [72].)

A.96.3. *jüštə mužə üdər* 'cold illness daughter'

Ague is personified as a pretty girl which causes a person to have chills and fever. People say that this spirit is sleeping with the man who has the ague.

For *jüštə mužə,* see A.46.1.

(Up[FB], 28.)

For *pokšəm üdər,* see A.38.22.; *ülüšan patər,* A.64.2.; *ümbač koštšə,* A.21.2.1.; *ümbal keremet,* A.21.2.1.; *üstel orol,* A.55.3.

A.97. *vańuška*

A.97.1. *oš buj vańuška* 'white head (i.e., blond) *Vańuška*'

A sick calf was sacrificed to this *keremet* (A.31.).

(S, 149, 155.)

A.98. stones

Stones have been objects of worship for some Cheremis. Near Koz'modem'yansk the "white stone of Astrakhan" is venerated. A legend tells that a soldier who fell ill at Astrakhan took in his hand a little white stone and said, "You are my god. If you cure me, I will pray to you all my life." The soldier was cured and stone became an object of worship.

In a village in Yaransk sacrifices are made to a stone which is believed to be in Koz'modem'yansk.

See also *čembulat* (A.12.).

(S, 158.)

B. CEREMONIES

For *büt abalan pumaš* see B.6.

B.1.   *aga kurman* 'plowing sacrifice'

During the part of the summer when flies and other insects are especially numerous, some Cheremis hold an agricultural ceremony in a birch grove; at this time a ram or wether and a ewe are sacrificed either to *aga kurman* (A.41.) and *aga saus* 'plowing overseer' (A.76.1.) or to *pasu jər* 'field offering' (A.23.) and *šurnə šočəktšə* 'grain progenitor' (A.82.11.). The ewe is sometimes dedicated to the *bitnəzə* 'reporter' (A.8.).

The ceremony is similar to that of *küsə* (B.9.). The priest, his assistant, and a few other men go to the grove on the morning of the sacrifice, taking with them the animals and all the necessary implements. Under an old birch tree where sacrifices have previously been made, the assistant makes a fire. The priest digs up copper coins which have lain buried there since the last ceremony. Sacrifice loaves are placed on a white cloth under the tree. The others kneel while the priest says a prayer, holding a firebrand in his left hand and a knife in his right. After the prayer he strikes the knife against an ax which is lying before him on the ground. The priest then touches with the firebrand the forehead and chest of the ram and ewe which have been tied to a post near the fire. Water is poured on the ram as the priest prays that it will be acceptable to *aga kurman*. The ram is then killed and as it is being skinned, water is poured onto the ewe in preparation for the other sacrifice. According to the report of one ceremony, blood from the ram is poured into the fire for *aga kurman* and *tul bodəž* 'fire spirit' (A.9.14.) ; blood from the ewe is offered in the fire to *bitnəzə* and *tul bodəž*. While the meat is being cooked, the townspeople, dressed in their holiday clothes, assemble at the grove to partake of the feast. The *šübə šəl*, pieces of meat from certain parts of the sacrifice animals (C.12.2.), and pieces of the sacrifice bread on which there is a *ner* 'nose' design (C.2.1.) are put into two bowls as offerings. Money is given by individuals to the priest who says a special intercessory prayer for them. Following a long prayer said by the priest requesting all manner of blessings, especially for the grain, and protection from all evil, the people feast on the meat of the sacrificed animals.

In some villages, *aga kurman* is the name given to the ceremony described under B.2.

(H[1926], 183–85; J.)

B.2.   *aga pajram* 'plowing holiday'

In the spring a ceremony is held to insure the blessings of the gods on the crops. Outside of town a field which is used neither for cultivation nor for pasturing serves as a place of worship; occasionally the ceremony is held in a grove. There is no fixed day for *aga pajram* but it is usually before the grain is planted in the spring, each village deciding on the days for its own holidays; sometimes it is held on Whitsunday. *Aga pajram* may be held more than once a year, sometimes more than once during the spring. According to one source, a 'little *aga pajram*' is held in the home after sowing. At times a special ceremony is held in the summer if the grain is not growing well. In some places, a thanksgiving ceremony held after the harvest is called *aga pajram;* offerings of bread, pancakes and beer are made from the newly harvested grain.

Aga pajram usually lasts three days. In some places the annual exorcism of the devil (B.18.) takes place on the eve of *aga pajram*. The religious activities are held on the first day, at which time offerings of grain products are made to a great number of deities and spirits. After the ceremony and continuing for two more days the people celebrate the holidays with feasting, drinking, visiting, and merrymaking; there are races, wrestling matches, plays and other amusements. All young men contribute the money offered as prizes for the contests but a newly-wed is expected to contribute an additional prize.

According to one source, the ceremonial aspects of the holiday are as follows: Early in the morning on the appointed day, representatives from each household gather in the place of worship forming long lines to the north and south of the main fire; those who arrive first take positions nearer the fire. About nine o'clock the rest of the townsfolk go to the field bringing beer, baked goods, and omelets made from the eggs given to the young men who drove out evil spirits the night before. Two fires are lit and, to the east of the principal fire, a long linen cloth is spread out on which are put the baked goods, omelets, and beer. The chief priest and his assistant tell others, who are to act as priests, to which deity each is to make a sacrifice. If there are two chief priests, they alternate in saying the prayers. The chief priest stands in front of the principal fire and the others take their positions on both sides of him. To his right are those who sacrifice to the following gods: *jumən piambar* 'god's prophet' (A.68.2.), *pujərša juma* 'creator god' (A.26.31.), *küdərča juma* 'thunder god' (A.26.22.), *ergə pujərša juma* 'son creator god' (A.26.31.1.), *sakča juma* 'guardian god' (A.26.33.), *kuga perke* 'great blessing' (A.67.), *jumən šočən* 'god's fructifier' (A.82.5.), *jumən aba* 'god's mother' (A.1.2.), *kuga šočən aba* 'great fructifier mother' (A.1.10.), *keča aba* 'sun mother' (A.1.3.), *mardəž aba* 'wind mother' (A.1.4.), *kuga kaba* 'great fate' (A.27.), *kaba piambar* 'fate prophet' (A.68.3.), *kaba šukča* 'fate angel' (A.84.9.), *küllö piambar* (A.68.7.), *kəzər piambar* (A.68.5.), *tüñča ümbal kuga šukča* 'great angel over the world' (A.84.21.), *tüñča ümbal pujərša juma* 'creator god over the world' (A.26.31.3.), *jumən aš* (A.5.), *jumən kaznači* 'god's treasurer' (A.29.1.), *jumən salauz* (A.73.), *tüñča* (A.91.), *er šukča* 'morning angel' (A.84.5.), *kas šukča* 'evening angel' (A.84.12.). To the left of the priest are those who sacrifice to the following gods: *jumən šukča* 'god's angel' (A.84.8.), *šurna šočən* 'grain fructifier' (A.84.11.), *šurna pujərša* 'grain creator' (A.70.18.), *šurna perke* 'grain blessing' (A.67.17.), *šurna piambar* 'grain prophet'

(A.68.10.), *šurnə kaba* 'grain fate' (A.27.2.), *šurnə šukčə* 'grain angel' (A.84.19.), *šurnə saus* 'grain overseer' (A.76.8.), *mükš šočən* 'bee fructifier' (A.82.8.), *mükš pujəršə* 'bee creator' (A.70.13.), *mükš perke* 'bee blessing' (A.67.13.), *mükš piambar* 'bee prophet' (A.68.9.), *mükš kaba* 'bee fate' (A.27.1.), *mükš šukčə* 'bee angel' (A.84.15.), *mükš saus* 'bee overseer' (A.76.7.), *šište kornə palastarše* 'wax road expert' (A.60.), *mükš kaznači* 'bee treasurer' (A.29.3.), *saska pujəršə* 'blossom creator' (A.70.16.), *pu ört* 'tree soul' (A.58.8.), *mükš peresta* (A.65.3.), *mükš on* 'bee lord' (A.52.11.), *mələndə bodəž* 'earth spirit' (A.9.10.), *mələndə aba* 'earth mother' (A.1.5.), *mələndə šočən* 'earth fructifier' (A.82.7.), *mələndə pujəršə* 'earth creator' (A.70.12.), *mələndə perke* 'earth blessing' (A.67.11.), *mələndə šərt* 'earth devil' (A.15.4.), *mələndə piambar* 'earth prophet' (A.68.8.), *mələndə šukčə* 'earth angel' (A.84.14.), *mələndə saus* 'earth overseer' (A.76.6.), *mələndə sərabočəš* 'earth key' (A.79.2.), *mələndə ört* 'earth soul' (A.58.5.), *mələndə peresta* 'earth angel' (A.65.2.), *pokšəm kuguza* 'frost old man' (A.38.22.), *pokšəm kuba* 'frost old woman' (A.38.22.), *aga orman* (A.54.) and *aga saus* 'plowing overseer' (A.76.1.). Other worshippers remain behind those who are to make sacrifices, many grouped around the other fire which is west of the main fire.

The ceremony begins as the chief priest walks back and forth before the kneeling worshippers swinging a burning brand. Offerings of candles and coins are received by the assistants and placed on the linen cloth spread out before the fire. The candles, after being made into small bundles, are fastened to three logs near the fire and lit. During the prayer which follows, those who are to make offerings stand in a row with their heads covered; the others kneel bareheaded behind them. At the end of the prayer the priest leads those who are to make a saccrifice to the fire to the west. There he throws a few pieces of pancake and a few drops of beer into the fire as a sacrifice to *kugə jumə* 'great god' (A.26.) and calls on god's *bitnəzə* 'reporter' (A.8.) to take it to god. Each person in order, following his example, throws food and drink into the fire for a different deity and requests *tul bodəž* 'fire spirit' (A.9.14.) to take it to the deity. A similar sacrifice is made to the family *keremet, škenən oňčəmə keremet* (A.31.7.).

Other accounts report variations in this ceremony. For example, neither the number nor names of the gods are fixed but vary from place to place. According to one report the chief priest sacrifices to *aga pajram jumə* (A.26.2.), and *tul bodəž* 'fire spirit' (A.9.14.) is called on to act as intermediary.

All sorts of food are prepared for this ceremony. Animal sacrifice does not usually form part of this ceremony although one source mentions it. Another source reports a duck pie being made at home and brought to the ceremony; the bones, head, and feet of the duck are thrown into the fire as an offering. Colored eggs sometimes play an important role. They are given to the priest and exchanged with other worshippers after the ceremony. The egg of a young woman is thrown over a tree three times; if it is caught, she will have good fortune; if not, she will be unlucky. Sometimes eggs are thrown up into the air to express the wish that the grain grow as big as eggs. In some regions, on the way back from the ceremony, people bury in their fields an egg and a spoonful of porridge as food for the earth.

The ceremony may vary in other details too. Instead of having a linen cloth before the fire for the food there may be mats of pine needles or straw. The candles may be fastened to the edge of the beer buckets instead of a special holder. At the beginning of the ceremony, the priest, as he walks up and down consecrating the food which has been set out, may be followed by an assistant who strikes a knife against an ax.

Sometimes at the end of the ceremony, the priest throws grains of oats into the crowd of worshippers who hold out their shirts and coats to catch them. Whoever gets many grains will have a good harvest in the fall. Another custom is that of sprinkling the people with water so that there will be enough rain in the summer. In some places there is also a ceremony for newly-weds at which time they receive the blessing of the gods. There is also an account of a race from the place of worship to the town; the winners are awarded eggs and napkins by the priest.

Aga pajram is also celebrated by the Christian Cheremis in much the same way; in addition, however, it is a time for baptizing children.

(H[1926], 40, 176–79, 187; J; S, 106–7, 176–77, 185; Us[FB], 4; V, 16, 270; Wu, 27–28.)

B.3.   *agul kumaltəš* 'town prayer'

This ceremony, in which all the people from a town participate, lasts for two or three days in the summer. It usually takes place before the *küsə* ceremony (B.9.), but in some places it is held after or even on the last day of the *küsə* itself. A stallion is sacrificed to *kugə jumə* 'great god' (A.26.), a steer to *jumən piambar* 'god's prophet' (A.68.2.), a ram to *jumən šukčə* 'god's angel' (A.84.8.) and a goose to *jumən bitnəzə* 'god's reporter' (A.8.). The sacrifices are performed in a large grove in which each of the gods has its own tree.

(P, 206.)

For *ajar kon kečə*, see B.8.2.; *jumən ajar kon kečə*, B.8.4.; *ü arńa*, B.26.; *tubər čimə bodə*, B.8.1.

B.4.   *bučəktəmə* 'letting wait'

If it is decided that a sacrifice must be made to a deity, but an individual does not wish to, or cannot, do it at the time, he can make a vow to sacrifice later. An individual making such a vow takes a bath in the bathhouse late in the evening. After the rest of the family has gone to bed, he makes a little sack or bundle of clean linen into which he puts a silver coin, wax, and a handful of malt. These symbolize the offerings to be made: the money stands for the animal, the wax for the candles, and the malt for beer. This little bag is hung on a nail in the storehouse and the person promises to make the sacrifice. If he dies before fulfilling the vow, his children are under obligation to make the promised sacrifice. A vow is not made on Wednesday.

(Be, 66; H[1926], 157; Häm.[1908a], 4; S, 189; V, 42.)

B.5.   *buj kočmə pajram* 'head eating holiday'

In the autumn, in October, November, or even as late as December, falls the 'head eating holiday,' a day of feasting at slaughter time. There is no fixed date for this ceremony; each family decides on a different day, so that friends may be invited. On the appointed day, a feast is prepared. A man who knows the prayers, acting as the priest, kills an animal: a horse, cow, sheep, or goat, depending on the wealth of the family. The head, intestines, heart, liver, lungs, and other internal organs are cooked for the banquet. In the evening, when all the guests have assembled, the priest, standing next to the head which is in a large wooden bowl on the table, prays for prosperity and good fortune in cattle raising. Following the prayer, the priest eats three pieces of the head and then the owner of the house and his wife, relatives, and friends do likewise. After the guests have partaken of the head, they wish the people of the house prosperity and, particularly, abundant herds. After this, the rest of the food is served and the banquet lasts well into the night. Any meat left on the head after the ceremony is used by the family on subsequent days. The rest of the meat is kept for the family to eat during the winter.

In some places *buj kočmə pajram* is held on Easter Monday at which time guests are invited to eat the salted heads of animals which were slaughtered the previous autumn.

(H[1926], 187–88; J.)

For *buingorkə*, see B.23.8.; *sorta burgečə*, B.13.

B.6.   *büt abalan pumaš* 'offering to the water mother'

Rain is under the supervision of *büt aba* 'water mother' (A.1.1.) and, consequently, when rain is desired, an offering may be made to this deity. If there is a lake or river nearby, people gather at the edge of the water to pray and make the sacrifice. The most typical activity of the day is that of throwing water on people and animals with a great deal of merrymaking; this is done even in regions where rain-making is not a religious ceremony. In some places the offering consists of porridge; elsewhere a black sheep or ox is sacrificed. Some of the offering is thrown into the water and the rest is eaten by the worshippers.

The term *büt abalan pumaš* is also applied to a prayer said to *büt aba* if there is so much rain that work is hampered.

(H[1926], 73–74; J; V, 42.)

B.6.1.   *jür pučəməšdene kumalmaš* 'praying with rain porridge'

If there is no rain, a public prayer by this name is sometimes held to end the drought. (V, 314.)

For *čaza korka kušəmə*, see B.17.4.; *čaza küčaš*, B.17.3.; *sorta čiktəš*, B.8.3.2.; *tubər čimə bodə*, B.8.1.; *kogəl'ə čokləmə kečə*, B.8.5.; *sorta izarńa*, B.8.3.3.; *mələndə jər*, B.10.; *mükš jər*, B.11.; *šurnə jər*, B.22.; *šorək jol* or *šort jol*, B.19.; *jumə užatəmə kečə*, B.8.6.; *jumən ajar kon kečə*, B.8.4.; *üdər jümə*, B.17.1.; *jür pučəməšdene kumalmaš*, B.6.1.

B.7.   *keremet*

A sacrifice to a keremet spirit (A.31.) resembles the *küsə* ceremony (B.9.) at which sacrifices are made to the gods and 'upper spirits.' In some regions there is an annual *keremet* sacrifice in the summer or in the fall; in other places sacrifices are held only every three years. A special sacrifice may also be made to a *keremet* when there is sickness, a crop failure, epidemic among the cattle, or other misfortune which a seer traces back to a *keremet* spirit.

On the day of a *keremet* sacrifice all the men of the town gather under the sacrifice tree in the *keremet* grove. To the north of the sacrificers is a fir tree under which there is a fire, and a stand made of fir wood for the cauldrons. As in the *küsə* ceremony, there is sometimes a small uprooted tree (F.15.1.) encircled with bast which is burned after the ceremony. The ceremony is dedicated not only to the *keremet* but also to those in its retinue; consequently, if the *keremet* is believed to have nine helpers, nine loaves of sacrifice bread are put under the tree. In the middle and on the edge of these loaves are designs (C.2.1.). Other loaves brought by individuals are stacked up under the tree on a layer of pine needles. A pot of *ñemar* 'porridge' (C.6.) is placed under the tree. Animals are sacrificed to some, but not necessarily to all, helpers of a *keremet;* for example, during a sacrifice of a foal to *kurək kuguza* (A.21.2.1.), a white lamb may be sacrificed to its mother (A.1.), a brown steer to its prophet (A.68.6.), and a duck to its reporter (A.8.). All sacrifices are made under the same tree but each animal is sacrificed by a different priest. The priests stand in a row, each holding a fir branch; the high priest says the prayer. A candle fastened to the edge of a bowl burns during the ceremony. Before an animal is slaughtered, it is touched on the forehead with a burning brand and water is poured over its back through a fir branch. After the prayer the priest's helper strikes a knife against an ax. Five small pieces of wood are cut and the position in which they have fallen to the ground is studied; after that the pieces of wood are thrown into the fire. The animals are slaughtered one at a time and cooked. From the meat of the foal pieces are cut into two bowls. In the same bowls are also put the designs from the sacrifice bread and the loaves which the worshippers brought. The contents of one bowl are offered to the *keremet* and the other to the fire mother (A.1.15.) by throwing them into the fire. Meat from the other animals is also put into two bowls and offered in the fire, one to the spirit to whom the sacrifice is made and the other to the fire mother. Intercessions are made for all those who give an offering of money. The sacrifice meal is then eaten and afterwards the bones, hide, and other leftovers are thrown into the fire.

Some Cheremis do not actually sacrifice an animal, but, instead, baked goods in the form of an animal are offered.

(H[1926], 162, 164–67, 171.)

B.7.1.

A private sacrifice to a *keremet* may be made after an individual, in time of difficulty, has made a vow to the *keremet* (B.7.2.). At this time an individual may act as his own priest. The sacrifice, which follows the general pattern of the public ceremony, is performed late in the evening. The man making the sacrifice goes to the *keremet* grove (E.2.2.) accompanied only by his son; he may not receive guests or go visiting after such a sacrifice. A large loaf is put under the tree to the *keremet* and a small one for its prophet (A.68.) and its reporter (A.8.). The man reminds the *keremet* of the vow and then slaughters the animal. The meat is taken home as food for the family; however, it may not be served to guests.

(H[1926], 166–67.)

B.7.2.

A person who is not able to fulfill his vow to a *keremet* immediately sometimes makes a substitute sacrifice of a duck, goose, or hare instead of a horse. The priest and three assistants, after having bathed and put on clean clothes, go into the grove alone. A fire is started from burning coals brought from the village. Sacrifice bread on which there are three-fingered designs (C.2.1.) is baked in the grove by holding it over the fire on a wooden fork; when finished, it is placed under the sacrifice tree. A candle is placed in a hollow in the bark of the tree. The sacrifice animal with its feet bound is put under the tree. The priest takes a burning brand in his hand and one of his assistants takes a knife and ax. Both stand before the tree facing south and pray while waving the fire-brand and striking the knife against the ax. At this time, the other two assistants slit the throat of the duck. The priest pours the blood into the fire praying the *keremet* to mitigate the evil which it is causing and promising to sacrifice a horse in the fall. The animal is cooked and a little piece of the heart, liver, windpipe, neck, breast, back, wings, and feet are put into the bowls; the designs from the bread are also put into the bowls. The contents of one bowl are thrown into the fire as an offering to the *keremet,* the contents of the other are an offering to the fire mother (A.1.15.). The priest and his assistants eat the rest of the meat; that which is not eaten is thrown into the fire.

(H[1926], 163–64.)

For *u kində pajram,* see B.24.; *buj kočmə pajram,* B.5.; *kogəl'ə čokləmə kečə,* B.8.5.; *kolšə kon kečə,* B.8.2.; *kolšə pajram,* B.8.3.4.; *kolšən kuməčə,* B.23.1.; *kolšən nəlləžə,* B.23.3.; *kolšən šəməčə,* B.23.2.; *kon kečə* or *konom kečə,* B.8.2.; *jumən ajar kon kečə,* B.8.4.; *pel kon kečə,* B.8.1.; *čaza korka kučəmə,* B.17.4.

B.8.   *kuečə* or *kugečə* 'great day'

One of the most important holidays of the Cheremis is *kuečə* which coincides with the Christian Easter. Preparations begin on the Tuesday before Easter and the celebrations continue until the following Monday. During this time there is an important ceremony dedicated to the dead. There is at least one day on which work is taboo.

(Be, 703–6; H[1926], 191; J; P, 208–9; S, 145–46; V, 81; Wu, 52–56.)

B.8.1.   *pel kon kečə* 'half *kon* day'; *tubər čimə bodə* 'shirt donning evening'

The Tuesday before Easter is spent in preparing for the offering to the dead to follow. Beer is brewed and food is prepared, a long pie of peas and grain cooked in cream is made, and people bathe in the bathhouse. In some places a food offering is also placed in the bathhouse for the dead who come to bathe. This day and the next are sometimes called *kečəla kečə.*

(Be, 703; H[1926], 38; V, 82; Wu, 52.)

B.8.2.   *kon kečə* or *konom kečə; kolšə kon kečə* '*kon* day of the dead'; *ajar kon kečə* 'evil *kon* day'

No work may be performed on *kon kečə,* the Wednesday before Easter. People may not use their hands to feed cattle but they can kick fodder to them with their feet. The oven may not be lit; if a person lights a piece of linden wood, the oat crop will become rusty. Nothing may be taken from the house. In some places, young people are warned not to take a stick or spindle in their hands on this day lest a snake bite them in the summer. If a person combs his hair, chickens will scratch up his garden.

On this night a spoon for each member of the family is put at the window. Who-ever's spoon falls will die within a year.

It is believed that the dead wander on the earth on this day. In the night if a person puts on his clothes inside out or puts a horse collar around his neck and sits on the roof, he can see the dead. Precautions are taken so that the dead cannot harm the living. In some areas, on this day, the bathhouse is heated for the dead to bathe.

(B, 70; Be, 703; Häm.[1936–37], 46; H[1926], 37–39; J; P, 208–9; S, 145; Uj[FB], 15; V, 144.)

B.8.3.

An important part of the *kueča* holidays is the offering to the dead. In some regions it takes place on Wednesday, in others on Thursday. Sometimes both Wednesday and Thursday night are spent praying in the fields and ravines.

(S, 145–46.)

B.8.3.1.

On the Wednesday before Easter, in each household food and drink are put out for the dead, for *kiamat töra* (A.90.), the ruler of the dead, and for *kiamat saus* (A.76.5.), its helper. The offerings, placed on a bench near the table, consists of pancakes, bread, pies, and eggs; spoons are also put out for the dead to use. Candles are placed on the bench too, one for *kiamat töra,* one for *kiamat saus,* and one for each dead relative remembered. The head of the house puts a little of the food into a sieve or bowl on the bench for *kiamat töra* and *kiamat saus.* At the same time another member of the family pours a few drops of beer and vodka into another bowl. As the offering is being made, the head of the house prays the spirits of the underworld to gather his dead relatives together and to treat them well. They then make offerings to the dead relatives mentioning each by name and praying that they will bless and protect the living. After this the offerings are either thrown out the door or taken out into the yard and thrown onto the ground. The eggs are later picked up but the rest of the food is left there and is usually consumed by dogs. This ceremony may be performed in each household just for those who live there or members of a whole family may get together; in the latter case they often go from house to house performing the ceremony in each home.

(H[1926], 38–39; P, 208–9; Uj[FB], 15.)

B.8.3.2.   *sorta čiktəš* 'candle lighting'

On the Thursday morning before Easter, the Cheremis get up early. A silver coin is put in the wash basin; as each person washes his face, he says, "Grant me, god, a life as bright as this silver."

Someone goes to the forest and brings back a juniper tree. This is put in the middle of the floor and lit. All the members of the family jump over the fire three times saying, "Fire mother [A.1.15.], cleanse us from evil. Grant us, god, to live playing and laughing until next year."

Pancakes are made and a cock is killed and cooked; if there is no cock, fish soup is made. The pancakes, pie, cock or fish soup, sour milk, cooked cream, vodka, and beer are put on a bench near the door. The head of the house fastens candles on a piece of wood which is used to hold candles; seventeen candles in all are lit. The head of the house then makes the offering as the rest of the family kneel. He mentions all his dead relatives as he makes the sacrifice; he tastes the food and breaks off a little as an offering. Then each member of the household eats a bit and makes an offering; after this the other relatives do likewise. Four or five relatives take the food out, throw it down at the corner of the house and go back inside. Someone sits behind the table and asks, "How have the dead commanded us to live?" One of the men who has come in from outside replies that they are to become rich and live in peace.

After this, the people drink a great deal, sing and dance to the accompaniment of bagpipes. After a while they go on to another house where the ceremony is enacted in the same way.

(Häm.[1936–37], 48; Wu, 52–56.)

B.8.3.3. *sorta izarña* 'candle Thursday'

On Thursday the people bathe in the bathhouse and beat the bench with switches inviting the dead to bathe. Food is prepared, pancakes are made, a rooster and a hen are slaughtered, eggs are cooked. All this food is placed on a bench. Candles are lit for *kiamat töra* (A.90.) and *kiamat saus* (A.76.5.), the spirits of the underworld. Candles are also lit for each dead relative, who is mentioned by name. Food and drink are put in bowls as an offering. Then everyone begins to drink, sing and dance. On Friday the visiting and drinking continue.

(Be, 703–4; S, 135, 145–46.)

B.8.3.4. *kolša pajram* 'holiday of the dead'

On the Thursday before Easter the dead are invited to partake of a feast. Food is prepared, eggs are colored. On a bench near the door are put a bowl and a sieve, a bottle of vodka, three to five pancakes, and five to fifteen eggs, depending on the resources of the family. On the edge of the bowl are fastened candles, one for each dead relative remembered by the living; those for the grandfather and grandmother are lit first. Each person puts a little food into the sieve and a little vodka into the bowl. About noon the food is thrown on the ground outside; a little vodka is also poured out but the rest is drunk there. The dead are told not to come back until the next year. The eggs are put on the ground, then picked up and taken back in. The food may be left on the ground for the dogs to eat or it may be given to the cows, sheep and goats to eat. Back in the house people eat the eggs and drink. After this, they go on to someone else's house where the ceremony is repeated.

(J.)

B.8.4. *jumən ajar kon keča* 'god's evil *kon* day'

On Saturday no work may be done: the fire is not lit, the storehouse is not opened, the cow is not milked, a pitchfork may not be used to put out fodder for the animals, women do not comb their hair. In the evening the room is washed to get rid of the traces of the dead.

(Be, 704; P[1948], 2; V, 19.)

B.8.5.1. *kogəl'ə čokləmə keča* 'pie praying day'

On Easter Sunday, or on the Friday before Easter, the bathhouse is heated early in the morning; a woman bathes first and then prepares pancakes. Then men bathe and put on clean clothes, after which they make an offering of pancakes and eat. Cheese, a pie, an omelet, and hard-boiled eggs are prepared for the offering. All the people from a village may gather together to worship or there may be two groups. The men pray, make their offerings, and leave. Two young unmarried men remain behind and, following the instructions of the priest, give the women the *šočən* bowl (F.10.2.) full of beer from which to drink. Each woman gives the young men in return two eggs which are later cooked and given to children to eat.

(Be, 704–6; J; V, 82.)

B.8.5.2.   *kogəl'ə čokləmə kečə* 'pie praying day'

On Easter people go from house to house. In each house the priest prays and offerings of food and beer are thrown into the hearth. First the head of the house makes an offering to *kuečə*, then the priest makes an offering to *kugə jumə* 'great god' (A.26.). After that each person makes an offering to a different deity. A similar offering is also made to the family spirit *škenan ončəmə keremet* (A.31.7.). Sometimes a village is divided into sections (*kogəl'ə pölka*) of ten to fifteen households which worship together.

(H[1926], 191; P, 209.)

B.8.6.   *jumə užatəmə kečə* 'god escorting day'

Monday is the last day of *kuečə*. On this day people visit each other continuing their feasting and drinking. The priest is entertained in all the houses. There is no report of a religious ceremony held on this day.

(Be, 706; J; V, 203.)

For *jür pučəməšdene kumalmaš*, see B.6.1.; *tüńča ümbal kumalmə*, B.9.3.; *agul kumaltəš*, B.3.; *kolšən kuməčə*, B.23.1.; *kumət pajram*, B.23.1.; *aga kurman*, B.1.

B.9.   *küsə*

The most important sacrifice to the nature gods is held in the early summer just before the difficult work of haying and harvesting begins. In some places, a *küsə* ceremony is held annually or every two, three, or five years; in other places, it is only held on special occasions, such as when some great calamity indicates that the gods must be appeased or when a seer dreams that the gods have threatened to cause a disaster unless a sacrifice is made. A *küsə* ceremony may be held by each town separately or towns may traditionally worship together, in which case, the ceremony is usually called *kugə küsə* 'big *küsə*' or *mir küsə*, *mir* 'world' being the name given to a group of villages which sacrifice together. The number of towns thus worshipping together may be as many as twenty-five. In Urzhum the traditional districts are called *tištə* or *tištə körgə*, each one having its own name which is sometimes derived from the town near which the sacrifice grove is located: e.g., *kuprian mari tištə*. However, other names are also used: e.g., *molək mari tištə*, comprising villages which sacrifice in Aganur. Sacrifice customs within such a region are quite similar because of the frequent contacts. However, two districts which are close to each other may differ considerably. If both a village *küsə* and a *mir küsə* are held, either may take place first since there are no fixed dates for either. A sacrifice in which several districts take place is called *tüńča ümbal kumalmə* 'worldwide praying' (B.9.3.). Sometimes a great number of sacrifices are made; an unusual case was a ceremony at which three hundred animals were killed. Another time, worshippers intended to kill ninety-nine horses, ninety-nine cows, ninety-nine sheep, and ninety-nine fowls but were prevented from doing so by police intervention.

Each animal killed at a *küsə* ceremony is dedicated to a different deity. The Cheremis do not usually sacrifice every summer to all the gods which have trees in the grove; the number of sacrifices depends on the economic resources of the people.

The ceremony often lasts for a week or ten days; it does not begin on Tuesday, Wednesday or Saturday. In regions where Wednesday is considered to be an unlucky day, religious services are not held until afternoon on that day.

The tradition of making *küsə* sacrifices persisted in spite of attempted Christianization. There is a report that in 1913, after many years in which sacrifices had not been made in a certain community, a sacrifice ceremony was held at the order of a seer. The seer claimed that it had been revealed to him in a dream that if a ceremony were not held, a great disaster would occur. When the villagers heard this, although they were nominally Christian, they rebuilt the fence around the old *küsə* grove and made a sacrifice.

(Be, 734–36; H[1926], 7, 104–6, 108, 112, 146; H[1927], 262–63; Müller, 346; Roudenko; S, 95–96; Uj[T], 51.)

B.9.1.1. Preparation for *mir küsə*

When a *mir küsə* is to be held, a meeting of the priests is held to discuss the details. Sometimes they bathe and put on their holiday clothes for this meeting. At this time the date is set for the ceremony and it is decided as to which deities should receive sacrifices, what kind of animals should be sacrificed, and which priests should make the sacrifices. Another purpose is to discuss the sacrifice ritual and to agree on details—important because prayers and ceremonies, transmitted by oral tradition, differ from place to place. Those delegated to collect money for the expenses of the sacrifice are called *koštəšə* 'goer' (D.5.) ; they carry, as a symbol of their office, a linden stick on which is a carved sign.

The money to buy the sacrifice animals is contributed by the householders in the area whether they personally take part in the sacrifice or not. This money is all contributed voluntarily; the head of each household considers it his duty to set aside money for sacrifices. Sometimes the money is collected before, sometimes at the ceremony. If there isn't enough money to meet expenses, a second collection is made after the ceremony. Money for intercessions is also used to cover the expenses.

If an animal shivers during the selection of sacrifice animals, it is considered to be a good omen, signifying that the animal has been chosen by god. When an animal is selected, a band of cloth is tied around its neck as a sign that it is to be sacrificed. This cloth is removed before the sacrifice and hung on a branch of the sacrifice tree during the ceremony. Before taking the animal away, the priest prays in the owner's home that the animal be acceptable to god and that the household be blessed.

In some places, especially where the town *küsə* is not held at the time of the *mir küsə,* as the animal is being led to the *mir küsə* grove, the people from villages along the way go out to meet it and ask those who are leading it to go into the local grove and say a prayer.

The ingredients for bread and for mead are also collected from house to house. Mead is prepared by "pure" maidens and the bread is baked by the priests and their assistants.

In some areas it is customary to exorcise the evil spirits the night before the *küsə* ceremony (see B.18.).

(Be, 710, 734–35; H[1926], 108–9, 119; P, 186; S, 129; V, 131.)

B.9.1.2. *mir küsə* or *mer küsə* 'world (i.e., district) *küsə*'

The number of sacrifices at each sacrifice ceremony is different. According to one account, this schedule of sacrifices was followed: on the first day, a stallion to *kugə jumə* 'great god' (A.26.), a steer to *jumən piambar* 'god's prophet' (A.68.2.), and a wether to *jumən šukčə* 'god's angel' (A.84.8.); on the second day, a stallion to *pujəršə jumə* 'creator god' (A.26.31.) and a stallion to *küdərčə jumə* 'thunder god' (A.26.22.); on the third day, a stallion to *ergə pujəršə jumə* 'son creator god' (A.26.31.1.), a wether to *sakčə jumə* 'angel god' (A.26.33.), and a mare to *kugə perke* 'great blessing' (A.67.); on the fourth day, a cow to *jumən šočən* 'god's fructifier' (A.82.5.), a cow to *jumən aba* 'god's mother' (A.1.2.), and a cow to *kugə šočən* 'great fructifier' (A.82.); on the fifth day, a cow to *kečə aba* 'sun mother' (A.1.3.) and a cow to *mardəž aba* 'wind mother' (A.1.4.); on the sixth day, a stallion to *kugə kaba* (A.27.), a steer to *kaba piambar* 'fate prophet' (A.68.3.), and a wether to *kaba šukčə* 'fate angel' (A.84.9.); on the seventh day, a stallion to *tünča ümbal kugə pujəršə* 'great creator over the world' (A.70.21.), a wether to *jumən aš* (A.5.) and a wether to *jumən kaznači* 'god's treasurer' (A.29.1.); on the eighth day, a goose to *jumən bitnəzə* 'reporter' (A.8.). Every third year the number of sacrifices is greater. Then on the seventh day a steer is sacrificed to *küllö piambar* (A.68.7.), a steer to *kəzər piambar* (A.68.5.), and a wether to *tünča ümbal kugə šukčə* 'great angel over the world' (A.84.21.). The sacrifices which are usually performed on the seventh day are postponed until the eighth day and the sacrifice to the *bitnəzə* until the ninth. On the tenth day sacrifices to the earth spirits are made: a cow to *melandə bodəž* 'earth spirit' (A.9.10.), a cow to *məlandə aba* 'earth mother' (A.1.5.), a steer to *məlandə piambar* 'earth prophet' (A.68.8.), and a wether to *məlandə šukčə* 'earth angel' (A.84.14.).

Another account lists the following sacrifices: a brown foal to 'great god' (A.26.), a brown foal to 'slanderer god' (A.26.3.) and a brown foal to '*küllö* god' (A.26.23.), a brown steer to 'great blessing' (A.67.), a foal to 'creator god' (A.26.31.), a foal to 'world creator' (A.70.21.), a foal to 'son creator god' (A.26.31.1.), a foal to 'thunder god' (A.26.22.), a foal to 'blessing god' (A.26.30.), a foal to 'fate god' (A.26.13.), a brown steer to 'fate prophet' (A.68.3.), a white wether to 'god's angel' (A.84.8.), a white cow to 'god's mother' (A.1.2.), a brown steer to 'god's prophet' (A.68.2.), a brown steer to '*küllö* prophet' (A.68.7.), a white cow to 'sun mother' (A.1.2.), a brown cow to 'wind mother' (A.1.4.), a white wether to 'frost old man' and a white sheep to 'frost old woman' (A.38.22.).

At another ceremony the following sacrifices were made: a foal to each of the following: 'great god' (A.26.), 'creator god' (A.26.31.), 'son creator god' (A.26.31.1.), 'creator god over the world' (A.26.31.3.), 'world god' (A.26.27.), 'blessing god' (A.26.30.), 'fate god' (A.26.13.), and 'thunder god' (A.26.22.); a brown cow or a white sheep to 'god's mother' (A.1.2.); a brown steer to 'god's prophet' (A.68.2.); a brown steer to '*küllö* prophet' (A.68.7.); a white cow to 'sun mother' (A.1.3.); a white sheep to 'moon mother' (A.1.14.); a sheep to 'wind mother' (A.1.4.); a mare to 'god's fructifier' (A.82.5.); a black cow to 'earth mother' (A.1.5.) and a white lamb to 'grain creator' (A.70.18.). Under each tree where a horse is sacrificed, a sheep or goose is killed for the 'reporter' (A.8.).

All those who enter the sacred grove must first have bathed and put on clean white clothes and new bast shoes. In some places they bathe in the village; elsewhere they bathe outside the grove itself, either in a nearby brook or in warm water which is kept in big pots over a fire at the entrance to the grove. In some places it is also customary for worshippers to wash their clothes before entering the grove. Racks are sometimes provided for drying the clothes. Those who are waiting for their clothes to dry spend the time chatting and drinking tea.

Priests go to the grove on the morning of the first day about 9 A.M. and stay there until the end of the ceremony over a week later. In some areas they sleep overnight in a shed which has been built within the grove to protect them against inclement weather. In such a case a priest leaves the grove only to go into the village to bake the bread for the sacrifice which he is to perform. In other regions the priests return to the village for the night leaving assistants to keep the fire burning in the grove. Every morning the priests must bathe and wash their clothes before beginning the ceremonies. There is usually a different priest for each deity to whom sacrifices are made. The most important priest is the one who sacrifices to *kugə jumə* 'great god' (A.26.).

Outside the grove are kept whatever is to be used during the ceremony and the animals to be sacrificed. In a tent-like shelter outside the grove sits the *kaznači* 'treasurer' (D.3.) who counts the money collected during the ceremony.

After the priest and his helpers have bathed and put on clean clothes, they go into the grove taking with them the things needed to perform the sacrifice. Each of the assistants has a special task; one fetches water, another cuts up firewood, others braid linden bast into ropes, halters, and other articles to be used during the ceremony. A fire is built on the same spot on which fires have been made at previous ceremonies. The first fire is lit from burning coals which have been brought from the village in a pot; other fires are lit from the first fire. Over the fire is erected a frame from which a little pot of *ńemər* 'porridge' (C.6.) is hung. Since this is not strong enough to support the heavy meat cauldrons, a stand of stone or of logs is made for them. The first and last logs of this stand must be so placed that the root end of the logs is toward the sacrifice tree. The priest digs up money which is buried under the tree dedicated to the deity to whom the sacrifice is being made.

Under the sacrifice tree various objects are arranged which are to be used during the ceremony. To the left of the tree a short log is stood up on end; this is called *ši püken* 'silver stand' (F.17.), in a crack in the top is fastened a candle. In other areas a candle holder, *sandal* (F.18.), is made of three thin sticks to which the candle is fastened. On the right of the tree there is a stand on which is placed *kiš korka* 'resin bowl' (F.10.1.) for mead. In some places a bucket called *kugə jošman köraga* (F.5.; from the Chuvash 'pancake table') full of hydromel is also placed under the tree. A small tree which has been uprooted is tied to the sacrifice tree by a bast rope; this small tree is always of the same species as the large one (F.15.1.).

Under the tree are put fresh linden twigs on top of which is spread out a white linen cloth forming the altar (*üstel* 'table' [F.22.]). In some places a real table is used.

On the cloth are put the loaves of unleavened sacrifice bread (C.2.1., C.2.3.), usually eight small loaves and one large loaf to the right. Sometimes to the left is put a loaf of leavened bread brought by the former owner of the animal to be sacrificed. In front of the bread are placed nine wooden bowls which later in the ceremony are filled with mead. Usually the bread is placed in one row and the bowls in another; sometimes, however, the bread is placed in two rows and the bowls in two. A candle, in the candle holder, is lit from a piece of burning wood or directly from the fire. Sometimes a second candle, given to the priest by the seller of the sacrifice animal, is also lit.

The sacrifice animal is led into the grove wearing a bast halter made especially for the ceremony. It is tied to a long pole which has been driven into the ground about ten paces from the fire.

The priest, standing to the east of the fire, holds an ax blade horizontally over a bowl of water and prays the deity to whom the sacrifice is dedicated to signify its acceptance of the animal. His assistant pours melted pewter onto the ax blade from which it runs into the bowl. The priest observes the form the pewter takes as it solidifies in the water. If it in any way resembles the animal to be sacrificed, it is considered to be an indication that the deity is pleased with the animal. If it does not look like an animal, the pewter is thrown into the fire and more pewter is poured over the ax blade. When the likeness of the animal has finally been achieved, it is placed on the large loaf of sacrifice bread under the tree.

The priest, holding a firebrand, takes his position before the sacrifice tree. Sometimes the priest holds a knife in his right hand and strikes it against an ax which lies in front of him on the ground; other times the ax and knife are held by his assistant who, standing at the priest's left, strikes them at the appropriate times. The priest prays that the deity be present at the sacrifice and that the animal be acceptable to it. When there is an assistant, the priest walks to the right swinging the burning brand in his hand and the assistant follows him striking the knife against the ax three times. Sometimes the prayer is repeated twice.

The priest goes to the animal and touches it on the forehead and neck, or neck and back, once or three times with the firebrand. In some places a short prayer is said at the same time. Elsewhere the firebrand is thrown into the fire and a long prayer is said at which time all kneel bareheaded behind the priest who stands in front of the tree. At certain times during the prayer the priest takes off his cap and makes a deep bow while all the people touch their foreheads to the ground and say amen. In the middle of the prayer the priest pours a spoonful of hydromel into the fire for the fire mother (A.1.15.) which is asked to act as intermediary.

After this, the priest takes a knife and a green linden branch, circles the animal clockwise and stands to the east of the fire. He cuts a piece from the lower end of the branch, goes to the sacrifice tree and prays god to signify his acceptance of the people performing the sacrifice. As he prays, he cuts off a piece of the branch about six or seven inches long. The priest looks at the way in which it falls on the ground: if the thicker end is toward the tree or the east, it means that the deity is pleased. If the piece does not fall in the desired way, the priest goes around the fire in a clockwise direction and cuts another piece. When the cutting is favorable, the piece is placed in the porridge pot next to the 'silver spoon' (F.14.). A second and third piece are cut to find out if the objects used in the sacrifice and the animal are acceptable. These are also put in the porridge pot.

The assistant priest takes a bowl of water which sometimes has had the chill taken off it by heating it at the fire for a while. He takes linden branches in his other hand. Circling the fire clockwise, he goes to the animal which is held with its head toward the tree. As the priest prays the deity to accept the animal and shake from it the touch of human hand, the assistant pours the water through the linden branches onto the animal's back from head to tail. All the others present kneel with heads bared watching the animal to see if it shudders. If, after waiting a few minutes, the animal does not shake itself, more water is poured on and the prayer is repeated. Each time the animal fails to shake itself, the assistants check to see that nothing has been done wrong. They look to see that the fire has been built in exactly the same place as the previous fire, that the poles of the stand over the fire are placed so that the thinner ends are up, that the horizontal logs have the thicker ends toward the tree, that the things on the altar are placed correctly, that the halter is placed correctly on the animal's head, that the candle has not gone out. Different assistants try pouring the water on the animal. While waiting for the animal to shiver, the worshippers pray quietly. If, after the ninth (in some places, seventh) attempt, the animal has not shivered, it is taken away and another animal is procured. When the animal shivers, the people rise to their feet thanking god. Ducks and geese are not subjected to this sprinkling. Sometimes the pouring out of the pewter takes place at this time rather than at the beginning of the ceremony.

The feet of the animal are bound with a bast rope and the animal is laid on its left side with its head toward the tree. A little hole, dug next to the head of the animal is covered with linden branches so that the blood will not flow directly on the ground. If the sacrifice is dedicated to an earth deity, the hole is deep and not covered with branches. Sometimes the horse is dragged to a nearby hole which has been dug with an ax. The priest prays that the god accept the sacrifice as his helper slits the jugular vein of the animal with an old-fashioned knife used only at sacrifices. The blood flows through the linden branches into the hole. The priest catches the first few drops on a wooden spoon, goes around the fire to the tree, and says a prayer holding the spoon of blood. At the end of the prayer he throws the blood up into the tree or into the fire. He goes back to the animal a second time and catches another spoonful of blood. He goes to the fire and after asking the fire spirit to act as intermediary, throws the blood into the fire. After this the band which is to be bound to the sacrifice tree is drenched in blood by drawing it across the wound on both sides. The halter and rope used to tie the feet of the animal are taken off and hung on the post to which the animal was tied. The animal with its head toward the tree is skinned by four men. The candle under the tree is kept burning and, when it burns down, it is replaced.

The nose or part around the mouth of the animal is cut off as a special sacrifice and parched by roasting in the fire; similarly the head without the lower jaw is roasted as a special sacrifice. The meat is removed from the skeleton without breaking bones. Certain pieces of meat called *šübə šəl* (C.12.2.) are cooked in the cauldron which is nearest the sacrifice tree. The rest of the meat is cooked in two other cauldrons. The hide of the animal is stretched out on the ground next to the altar with the head toward the sacrifice tree so that it resembles an animal lying on its left side. The inedible parts of the animal are put in the hole into which the blood ran; later they are burned in a fire built over them.

During the three or four hours which it takes the meat to cook, the people wait outside the grove and newcomers arrive from nearby towns. The priest and his helpers remain in the grove tending the meat. During this time the blood-soaked band of bast is wrapped around the 'little sacrifice tree' (F.15.1.) encircling it three, five, seven, or nine times. Between the tree and the band are placed a bunch of green twigs, a tassel of bast and the pewter figure which was cast earlier in the ceremony.

In some places, the sacrifice to *bitnəzə* (A.8.)—a sheep, goose, or duck—is made at this time. The ritual is substantially the same as for the first animal except that the casting of the pewter, the striking of the knife and ax, and the cutting off of a piece of a branch are omitted. The sacrifice is made under the same tree and by the same priest as the first. If a sheep is killed, the skin is spread out next to the hide of the first animal with its head toward the tree, its back to the east. The meat is cooked in a fourth cauldron. In some places the sacrifice to *bitnəzə* is not made until the last day of the ceremony.

While the meat is cooking, the priest pours mead or beer into the bowls on the altar and cuts out of the bread the designs made on the loaves when they were baked, leaving them, however, in their places.

When the meat is cooked, the *šübə* meat is put in a special trough. From each part a piece is cut off and put in a round wooden dish which is then put under the tree. This meat is called *orolək* (C.12.3.). In addition, little pieces are cut from the *šübə* meat and put into two bowls, one of which is dedicated to the deity and the other to the fire spirit. The loosened pieces of bread are either put into the bowls or placed in three piles on the cloth. Sometimes pieces of meat are put into the holes in the bread and in the piles of bread. A little porridge is also placed in the bowls. The rest of the meat is put in troughs to the right of the tree.

On a thin pointed linden stick, *šopšar* (F.3.), are placed pieces of the following parts of the animal in this order: the large intestine, the right and left haunches, the kidneys, the middle of the chest, the heart, the aorta, the back of the neck, the throat, the tongue, the lips, and the liver. Aside from the liver, the pieces come in more or less the same order as they were in the animal. This stick is put in the band wound around the little sacrifice tree and a prayer is said. The meat remaining in the trough from the first cauldron, the left half of the big sacrifice loaf and five little loaves are cut up to be eaten; the right half of the big loaf and the remaining three loaves are put into the *orolək* dish. When the meat of the animal sacrificed to the 'reporter' is cooked, it is cut into two *šübə* bowls; however, no *orolək* meat or *šopšar* stick is prepared.

The priest, holding a burning brand in his left hand and a knife in his right, prays the deity to bless them in return for the sacrifice. After the prayer, he strikes the knife against the ax on the ground before him three times. He throws the firebrand into the fire and, taking up the linden branch from which he earlier cut the pieces, he goes around the fire clockwise. He stands before the tree and asks the god to signify its intention to bless the family by letting the piece fall in the desired position. He then cuts off a piece and examines its position on the ground. A fifth piece is cut off for the blessing of cattle, a sixth for the grain, the seventh for the bees, the eighth for money, and the ninth for all kinds of blessings. These pieces which are cut off are put bark upward in the porridge pot with the others.

Carrying the branch, the priest goes around the fire clockwise and stands to the east of it. With the knife in his hand, he looks into the fire and says a prayer. Then he cuts off the leaves of the branch so that they fall into the fire. He splits both ends of the forked branch and inserts the cutoff pieces in the order in which they were cut. This stick is called *šuldəš* (F.19.). It is smeared with porridge and put next to the meat stick on the sacrifice tree.

At this point the general public is called in from outside the grove where they have been conversing and drinking tea. At this time people make offerings of money and candles to have special intercessions said for them in which they are mentioned by name. As a person makes his offering, he tells the priest his name and his petition. Those who cannot come to the ceremony send money with those who do to have a prayer said for them. Sometimes the priest himself collects the money and says the prayers, other times his assistants do this. This contribution, *mama oksa* (C.9.1.), is used to cover the expenses of the ceremony and sometimes it is given to the priest and his helpers. A poor man gives only one candle and one coin. The priest prays for a greater blessing for a person depending on the size of his offering. The money is not touched by the hand of the giver or the receiver because it is believed that the bare hand defiles the coin. Sleeves are drawn over their hands or the end of their sashes cover their hands. Sometimes the money is let fall onto the cloth at the end of each prayer; other times the priest waits until his hand is full, then goes to the tree, raises the offering on high, falls on his knees and prays that it be acceptable to god, before putting it on the cloth.

After the intercessions have been made, the priest says the long sacrifice prayer which lasts about half an hour. During this prayer the priest asks for every possible blessing. The people kneel in long rows behind the priest and, after each petition, they bow their heads to the ground and say amen. After the prayer the priest kneels and, saying amen three times, touches his forehead to the ground. In some places the people lift their hands up three times. After the priest gets up, he speaks to the people exhorting them to live good lives. The people then arise and the older men thank the priest by shaking hands with him.

Soon after, the people kneel again. At this time sacrifices are thrown into the fire for the gods. Sometimes the priest takes the drinking bowl dedicated to the deity to whom the sacrifice was made and two assistants the *šübə* bowls. They walk to the fire one after the other, stand to the east of it and throw the contents of the bowls into the fire. The priest pours twice from his bowl, once for the god and the other for the fire spirit. Immediately afterwards an offering is made to the 'reporter' in the same way if an animal has been killed in its honor. From the large meat trough a helper takes a piece of meat to the fire built where the large animal was slaughtered and a piece of the smaller animal's meat to the place where it was slaughtered. He throws the meat into the fire and prays that the fire may burn up all the blood. Then the priest gives to eight helpers (*korka kondəštšə* 'bowl bearer' [D.4.]) each a bowl of mead telling him which god to offer the contents as a libation. Each goes around the fire in a clockwise direction and to the east of it pours in the mead. They go back to the priest who refills the bowls and indicates to which other gods to make an offering. In this way many Cheremis gods and spirits are honored at the sacrifice. After the drink offerings are made, the bowls are returned to their places under the trees. The priest prays with a bowl in his hand sprinkling mead on the tree three times. He does the same pouring meat broth onto the tree with a ladle. The assistant priest says the same prayer and sprinkles on mead and broth also.

In some places the priest begins to make the offerings right after the long prayer. He takes a spoonful of hydromel from *jošman köraga* (F.5.) and pours it onto the tree. His assistant takes a little broth in a ladle and puts in a little *šübə* meat (C.12.2.). Then the priest and the assistant go to the fire and pour in hydromel, broth, and meat, both saying the same prayer at the same time, asking that the offering be accepted. This is done three times, the third time the fire is asked to act as intermediary. The same is repeated at the smaller fire. The priest says a short prayer asking the deity to bless them and accept their gifts. He repeats it and his assistant also says it. It is repeated twice more by the priest and once by the assistant as they raise on high the bowl filled with *šübə* meat. The priest touches it to the tree and then the assistant holds out to him the bowl of hydromel. He sprinkles on the tree two spoonfuls of hydromel and the assistant one. Each time a prayer is said. Finally the priest falls on his knees and prays that the prayer may be acceptable. After the assistant has poured a little from each of the bowls and troughs before the tree, the offering comes to an end. Sometimes the priest gives a short sermon at this time.

When all these offerings have been made, the people sit on the ground and the helping priests circle the fire three times clockwise and shake all the objects used in the sacrifice: the troughs, the bowls, the dishes, the cloths, the little sacrifice tree, the skin, etc., saying to the deity, "This is yours."

By the time the sacrifice meal begins, it is late afternoon. First everyone tastes the porridge and the mead and all wish each other happiness and prosperity. After this the *šübə* meat and the bread in the *šübə* bowl (F.10.3.) are distributed. The remaining meat is distributed among the people. All the bones and leftovers are thrown into the fire, unless the ceremony is dedicated to an earth deity, in which case they are buried in the hole into which the blood ran. When the meat from the head has been eaten, the priest puts the bones back together and throws them into the fire. The little sacrifice tree is untied from the big tree and is burned in the fire together with all the objects tied to it. The hide of a horse is usually burned, held over the fire by four assistants by means of long poles fastened to head, tail, and feet. The priest circles the burning hide, a fire brand in his left hand and the 'resin bowl' (F.10.1.) in his right. He stands to the left of the fire and pours in the contents of the bowl. On the burning hide is put the halter of bast. The stand for the 'resin bowl' is also burned. Sometimes horse and cow hides are hung on a tree or on a stick. In some places the head, tail, and hoofs are removed from a hide before hanging it up. Sometimes a hide may be given to the priest, who receives no other remuneration for his services. A sheep skin is often returned to the one who sold the animal.

The *orolək* meat, the candlesticks, the other half of the large loaf, and the three small loaves are left under the tree overnight. The fire is kept burning all night. At sunrise the next morning, the *orolək* offering is made. From each piece of meat a bit is cut into two bowls; the rest is cut up in a large bowl. A bowl of mead is placed on the cloth under the tree together with the three small loaves and the coins which were dug up on the day before. A candle is lit. The priest takes a burning stick in his left hand

and a knife in his right. He strikes the ax three times and reminds the god of the sacrifice performed on the previous day. He circles the fire and throws in the burning stick and then says a long prayer. After the prayer everyone thanks the priest by shaking his hand. The priest makes a drink offering and his assistants throw the contents of the two bowls into the fire as on the previous day. The sacred objects are shaken as on the previous day and the *orolɔk* meat is eaten while all wish each other well. All the leftovers including the candlesticks are thrown into the fire. The coins, *ona pu oksa* (C.7.2.), dug up, plus some others, are buried again in the same place under the tree. In some places the uneaten meat is taken home. Sometimes the *orolɔk* sacrifice itself is made in the home.

This ritual is followed for each animal sacrifice but it is performed by a different priest under a different tree. The fire of a god previously worshipped is kept burning until the end of the *küsɔ* and a prayer is said there each morning by the priest.

Sometimes there is a sacrifice to *bitnɔzɔ* (A.8.) the last day of the ceremony. It may be for this reason that the last day of *küsɔ* is called *bitnena*. On the last day all the priests say a final prayer either all together or one after another.

When the fires are allowed to go out at the end of *küsɔ,* the priest stirs up the ashes and expresses the wish that whoever comes upon the ashes may be blessed.

Those who so desire may go to a special house in the village where pancakes, mead, and beer are served and the deities to whom sacrifices have been made are remembered.

For the duration of *küsɔ* people do not work. Those who wish to pray go to the grove. Sometimes they go to different trees, ask the assistant to which deity the tree is dedicated, make an offering of money and pray to the deity by name. People often stay at the grove for only a few days. Those who bring ingredients for the bread do not leave but stay for the whole ceremony. Worshippers usually sleep outside the fence of the grove; sometimes there is a building in which they can sleep in the grove.

(B, 29–30; Be, 709–37; Häm.[1908a], 1–17; H[1926], 7, 106, 111–13, 115–45, 150, 154–55; H[1927], 265–80; J; Müller, 355–361; P, 185–201; S, 95–96, 129–30, 175–76.)

B.9.2.

Many Cheremis villages have a grove in which there are a number of trees dedicated to the nature deities; here the *küsɔ* ceremony is held. Priests and the town elders decide on the date of the ceremony, the animals to be sacrificed, and the deities to whom the sacrifices will be made. The fact that all expenses must be paid by the inhabitants of the village limits the number of sacrifices. When a desired sacrifice cannot be made, a vow is made to sacrifice later; sometimes a promise is made to sacrifice to that deity first the following year.

(H[1926], 113.)

B.9.3.   *tüńʹa ümbal kumalmɔ* 'world-wide worship'

A ceremony in which people from many sacrifice regions take part is called *tüńʹa ümbal kumalmɔ*. One such ceremony was attended by approximately five thousand worshippers and about three hundred animals were sacrificed. These ceremonies are only held at the order of a seer in the face of a great calamity such as a very bad harvest or a war. The ritual is similar to that of *mir küsɔ* (B.9.1.2.).

(H[1926], 106.)

For *sürem küsə,* see B.18.; *melna lukmə,* B.17.4.; *mer küsə,* B.9.1.

B.10.   *məlandə jər* 'earth offering'

At this ceremony the following animals are sacrificed to the earth spirits: a sheep to *məlandə bodəž* 'earth spirit' (A.9.10.), a sheep to *məlandə aba* 'earth mother' (A.1.5.), a ram to *məlandə piambar* 'earth prophet' (A.68.8.), and a duck to *məlandə šukčə* 'earth angel' (A.84.14.).

A ceremony, not named in the source, is held in October or November in honor of the earth spirit. At this time a black bull is slain so that the crops will grow well the following year.

(P, 207; S, 186.)

For *mir küsə,* see B.9.1.; *u mü pajram,* B.25.

B.11.   *mükš jər* 'bee offering'

Mükš jər stands for *mükš jərgəč puena* 'we give concerning the bees.' About the end of June, when the young swarms of bees appear, there is a special sacrifice dedicated to the bee deities. The priests who officiate are beekeepers themselves; in some places only beekeepers participate in the ceremony. The sacrifices take place in a part of the sacred grove (E.2.) where trees are dedicated to the bee spirits, or in a special grove, *mükš otə* 'bee grove.' As at other sacrifices, the meat of the animals is cooked and eaten in the grove. During a *mükš jər* these sacrifices may be made: a sheep to *mükš šočən* 'bee fructifier' (A.82.8.), a sheep or ram to *mükš pujəršə* 'bee creator' (A.70.13.), a duck to *pujəršən bitnəzə* 'creator's reporter' (A.8.), a ram to *mükš piambar* 'bee prophet' (A.68.9.), a ram, sheep, or duck to *mükš perke* 'bee blessing' (A.67.13.), a sheep to *mükš šočən aba* 'bee fructifier mother' (A.1.10.6.), a duck to *mükš šočən aban bitnəzə* 'bee fructifier mother's reporter' (A.8.), a duck to *mükš šukčə* 'bee angel' (A.84.15.), a duck to *mükš saus* 'bee overseer' (A.76.7.), a goose to *mükš kaznaci* 'bee treasurer' (A.29.3.), a goose to *mükš sərabočəš* 'bee key' (A.79.1.2.), a goose to *šištə kornə palastaršə* 'wax road expert' (A.60.), a ram to *mükš kaba* 'bee fate' (A.27.1.), a duck to *saska pujəršə* 'blossom creator' (A.70.16.), a duck to *pu ört* 'tree soul' (A.58.8.), a duck to *mükš peresta* 'bee angel' (A.65.3.), and a duck to *mükš on* 'bee lord' (A.52.11.). Not all these sacrifices are made at any one ceremony.

(H[1926], 186; Häm.[1909], 5; P, 206–7.)

For *nəllə pajram,* see B.23.3.; *kolšən nълləžə,* B.23.3.; *orňalək,* B.34.; *aga pajram,* B.2.; *u kində pajram,* B.24.; *buj kočmə pajram,* B.2.; *kolšə pajram,* B.8.3.4.; *kumət pajram,* B.23.1.; *toštə mari pajram,* B.2.3.5.; *u mü pajram,* B.25.; *nəllə pajram,* B.23.3.; *u pučəməš pajram,* B.24.; *sorta pajram,* B.23.5.; *šəmət pajram,* B.23.2.; *šošəm pajram,* B.21.; *sürem pastramaš,* B.18.; *pel kon kečə,* B.8.1.; *puňčal puaš,* B.17.2.; *urlək pučəməš kečə,* B.13.; *u pučəməš pajram,* B.24.; *jür pučəməšdene kumalmaš,* B.6.1.; *sorla pukšaš,* B.15.; *büt abalan pumaš,* B.6.; *utəməlan pumaš,* B.23.7.; *puňčal puaš,* B.17.2.

B.12. *radińča*

On the Tuesday after Easter a feast is held for the dead. The evening before, the bathhouse is heated and, as the sweat bench is beaten the dead are invited to come and bathe. Pancakes, eggs colored red, cock or fish soup, pie, cheese cake, boiled milk, beer, mead and vodka are set out on the table in the morning and the dead are invited to partake of the food. The head of the house prays the dead to make the family prosperous. The family eats some of the food. After this, at noon, the people go to the cemetery and there pour vodka and beer and throw a little food onto the grave. The people eat and drink. As they begin to get drunk, they play the bagpipes, sing and dance. People also cry for their departed loved ones. After a few hours they go home. Sometimes the celebration lasts for three days during which time the people visit each other and the feasting continues.

For other memorial feasts for the dead, see B.8.3., B.13., and B.23.

(Wu, 56–58; S, 146; Uj, 69.)

B.13. *semək*

The days preceding Pentecost are a time for remembering the dead. The holidays last from Tuesday or Wednesday until Friday. During this time the Cheremis often visit the cemetery.

Tuesday is called *urlək pučəməš keča* 'seed porridge day.' The next day is *sorta bürgeča* 'candle Wednesday.' On this day or on Thursday there is usually a memorial feast for the dead. According to one account a boy goes about inviting friends and relatives to the feast. When the guests arrive, the head of the house brings into the house a piece of turf or snow on a spade. This is put on a bench and before it is spread out a piece of felt or a tablecloth on which are placed beer, honey, and food. On the cloth is also placed a thin birch stick to the end of which is fastened a candle. The 'candle distributer' (D.8.) puts two candles in the snow or sod and prays to *kiamat töra* (A.90.) and *kiamat saus* (A.76.5.), the rulers of the underworld. The head of the house approaches and whispers to him the names of the dead to whom candles are to be lit; for each one the 'candle distributer' places a candle and says a prayer. In other regions the number of candles lit is twenty-one. Sometimes the clothes of the dead are burned on this day.

Sometimes there is a public ceremony on Thursday in the sacrifice grove. The priest recites prayers, makes offerings of pancakes and beer to the dead into the fire.

(Häm.[1936–37], 46, 49; H[1926], 39; P, 209; S, 146; Sz, 197; V, 230; Wu, 55.)

B.14. *sorbalmə* 'praying for mercy'

An individual who prays to a god for help makes a vow to sacrifice. He and his family bathe in the bathhouse early in the morning and put on clean clothes. Pancakes and *tuara* 'cheese cake' are prepared. They go to the grove (sometimes the wife accompanies her husband). Each family has its own prayer tree in the sacred grove. The man takes off his hat under the tree. He fastens a candle to the bowl of pancakes he has brought and lights it. He puts the bowl under the tree and, kneeling, prays.

In some places, when such a vow is made, an article such as an ax, a pot, a towel, or a log, is put in the *kudə* (E.1.) or storehouse and may not be used again until the sacrifice is made. Such a vow is often fulfilled during the same year, usually in the fall. In some places porridge is offered first and later, at another time, the vow is renewed by the sacrifice of a small animal such as a fowl so that the god will wait for the larger animal. Sometimes when the family returns from making the vow in the grove, a candle is lit in the holy corner (E.7.) of the house and a prayer is said there.

When this vow is made to a *keremet* (A.31.) the person does not need to bathe or put on clean clothes.

(Häm.[1908a], 4–6; H[1926], 157–58.)

B.15.   *sorla pukšaš* 'sickle feeding'

When the Cheremis harvest the grain, they leave a few stalks standing in the field. These are called *sorla užaš* 'sickle share.' A day or two after harvesting, the family, dressed in holiday clothes, goes out to the field carrying sickles and food. The family kneels near the uncut stalks while the head of the house prays to the gods asking for a good harvest of grain. They eat the food which they have brought. They all kneel again; the head of the house takes all the sickles used in the harvest and wraps the blades in the stalks. When he picks up the sickles, the stalks are uprooted. In this way the sickles are believed to be fed and given strength to harvest the next year. The sickles, still wrapped in the stalks, are taken to the place where they are stored until the following summer.

(H[1926], 84–85; H[1927], 249; J.)

For *sorta bürgeča*, see B.13.; *sorta čiktəš*, B.8.3.2.; *sorta izarńa*, B.8.3.3.; *sorta keča*, B.23.5.; *sorta pajram*, B.23.5.

B.16.   *sukə* 'vow'

A person may make a promise to sacrifice by putting honey, barley, and money in a bag in the storehouse or he may make the vow in the sacrifice grove. If he promises to sacrifice a horse, he makes a bridle a little smaller than the actual size and goes to the grove late in the evening; he may also take a small bag with bread. He may hang the bridle up high on the tree by means of a stick or he may tie the stick with the bridle on the upper end to the tree trunk. He may also tie three logs together to make a little stand which is joined to the tree by another log extending from the top of the stand to the tree. On top of the stand he puts a coin and sometimes a candle.

Before a special sacrifice is made to a *keremet* by an individual, a vow is usually made. This is done late at night without anyone knowing about it; anyone who meets a person on his way to make a vow will become sick. Usually a little money, meal and honey, or a little loaf of bread baked for this purpose (*šokšə kində*, C.2.2.) are wrapped in a piece of cloth. A prayer is said to the *keremet* to alleviate the suffering it is causing and, at the same time, a vow is made to sacrifice an animal. This bundle of things symbolizing the future sacrifice is hung on the wall of the *kudə* (E.1.) or granary or on a *keremet* tree (F.15.). When the vow is fulfilled, the bundle is burned. Sometimes an offering is thrown into the fire during a vow and the fire is requested to act as intermediary. Sometimes, during the vow an article of clothing or an iron tool is hung on the wall of the *kudə,* where it is left until after the promised sacrifice. Sometimes, when a sheep or ox is promised, wool or hair of the animal is taken to the *keremet* grove (E.2.2.). If a horse is promised, a bridle of linden bast is hung in the grove. At the same time firewood is stacked under the sacrifice tree.

(Häm.[1908a], 7; H[1926], 162–63; V, 194.)

B.17.   *süan* 'wedding'

A Cheremis wedding is largely a social affair; the religious aspects play a minor role. Usually there are prayers asking that the couple be blessed; a few accounts mention an offering being made. By and large, however, a wedding is a secular ceremony. Even in nominally Christian communities, the church ceremony was not always considered to be the real wedding. It sometimes happened that a couple would have a church wedding and then return to their respective homes until the Cheremis wedding took place. In other places the Christian wedding was incorporated into the traditional Cheremis wedding so that the couple, on the way to the groom's home, stopped at a church along the way to have the ceremony performed.

Cheremis betrothal and wedding ceremonies vary greatly from region to region; the basic structure usually remains constant, however. The betrothal ceremony is quite simple. The suitor, his father, and a third man go to the house of a girl to ask formally permission for the couple to marry. Negotiations are carried on by the father, the friend of the suitor, and the parents of the girl; the young man and the girl usually play an almost passive role. The agreement is sealed by drinking vodka. At this time or sometime before the wedding, arrangements about the bride price and wedding gifts are made. On this underlying structure a great many elaborations may be worked.

Early summer is the most popular time for weddings. When the wedding day arrives, the groom's friends and relatives gather at his house where they eat, drink, sing and dance. They accompany the groom to the bride's home and continue their merry-making and revelry there. The bride and groom take part in a ritual eating and drinking after which they are blessed by the bride's parents. The groom takes the bride back to his own home; all the wedding guests follow. At the groom's home there is another ceremony of eating and drinking followed by a blessing from the groom's parents. The bride serves food and drink to her newly-acquired relatives; she also gives each a gift of a shirt, a towel, or a headscarf. They, in turn, give her money or promise to give an animal. The headdress of a married woman is put on her by one of the married women attendants. The celebration may continue for two or three days.

To this framework may be added an almost infinite number of local customs and the framework itself is occasionally modified. Many of the wedding customs have their origin in the two older forms of marriage of which earlier writers have given us accounts. The most approved marriage was one in which the groom paid a bride price to a girl's parents. If, however, the young man was unable or unwilling to do this he might take a bride without her parents' formal consent. If the girl was willing, it was a simple case of elopement. If, however, a young man wished to take a girl against her will, he organized a raiding party of his male friends and relatives and took her by force. Such marriages might or might not be made official later by the payment of a bride price and a celebration. In some areas the bride price was so high that it was impossible for most men to secure wives except by elopement or theft. One source describes a region in which, during a period of seventy years, only two brides were secured by the payment of the bride price.

(B, 35–52; Bk, 56–85; Häm.[1915], 100–140; Häm.[1930a], 65–105; J; Müller, 367–75; S, 119–25, 189–90; Uj[T], 24; Wu, 30–47.)

B.17.1.   *üdər jümə* 'girl drinking'; *üdər šörasaš* 'girl choosing'

When a young man wishes to get married, it is the custom in some regions for him to ask his parents' permission before making formal overtures. Before the betrothal, he and the girl, however, have often reached an agreement privately. Sometimes he enlists the aid of a neighbor woman who goes to the girl's parents and asks permission for the young man to marry their daughter. Then the young man and the woman go to the girl's home. If the young man likes the girl, he sets a date to 'drink' the betrothal.

On the day appointed for the betrothal ceremony, the young man, accompanied by his father and the *tular mari,* an older married man, goes to the girl's home. If the young man has no father, his elder brother goes with him. They usually take along with them a leather sack in which there is vodka, baked goods, cheese, and other food; this is called *kača kində* 'groom bread.'

When they arrive at the girl's house, the girl and the young man usually say little. The girl's parents invite them in, sometimes serving tea and engaging in small talk. The suitor's father and the *tular mari* begin to call the girl's parents *tular* and *tulačə,* terms of address used for affinal relatives.

The formal procedure for obtaining the permission of the parents and the consent of the young woman varies from region to region. According to one account the suitor indicates his intentions by giving vodka first to the girl's parents and then to the girl herself. If the girl accepts it, they all drink signifying their consent to the proposed match.

Another account states that the *tular mari* puts the *kača kində* out on the table. The father of the suitor puts the money he intends to give as a bride price on the food. The *tular mari* praises the suitor and asks for the girl. The parents never give their consent at once. If the money is sufficient, the girl's father refers him to his wife and daughter. When asked, the mother replies that the girl cannot marry because her dowry is not ready. After much persuasion the *tular mari* finally wins the parents' consent. He then addresses himself for the first time to the girl, asking her if she likes her suitor. When she answers affirmatively, the young man goes over to her. The girl's father brings out the dowry and vodka telling them to drink if it is satisfactory and, if not, to go home. If they are satisfied, they decide to drink. Before they do so, however, the girl goes to the storehouse and puts on her white holiday clothes. A neighbor woman acts as her attendant bringing to her in the storehouse a loaf of bread in a tablecloth. Then the girl and the woman return to the house bringing the bread. The woman takes the bread from the girl and puts it on the table. The young couple stand next to each other in the middle of the room. The girl's father lights a candle, a relative of his says a prayer and makes an offering. In the prayer he requests that the fathers of the two be blessed and then he prays for the young couple themselves. He then tells the couple to love each other all their lives. He tastes the *kača kində.* After this, each person tastes the food and calls on god to grant good fortune.

The parents of the bride are then seated at the table. The young man puts two or three rubles in the bosom of his fiancée's mother; this money is called *aba kumdar*. The *tular mari* gives the girl's parents and the young couple a cup of vodka each. As the young man and the girl drink, they touch their cups three times. After that, others also drink. Then the young man, his father, and the *tular mari* are seated at the table. The young girl and her attendant serve them vodka. The young girl gives each a towel or cloth; the money which they give in return is called *čaza korka oksa* 'čaza cup money' and her attendant *čaza korka kučəžə* 'čaza cup bearer.' Noodle soup is served to the suitor, his father, and *tular mari*. After this, they prepare to depart. They are accompanied out to the yard where the girl gives them a final drink of vodka and they give her money in return.

In another region the suitor, his father, and the *tular mari*, taking a leather bag of food, go to the prospective bride's village early in the morning before sunup. First they go to the house of an acquaintance, who is called *ońčəč košša* 'the one who goes before.' If the young man does not know the girl, he tries to have a look at her without her knowledge; this is often done as she goes out to milk the cow. If the young man is pleased with her, the *ońčəč košša* goes to her parents and declares the young man's intentions. Although the parents do not give a definite answer, the *ońčəč košša* reports to the young man how they received the proposal.

Then the suitor, his father, the *tular mari,* and the *ońčəč košša* go to the girl's home and place a *tuara* 'cheesecake' in the holy corner. As soon as the girl learns they have come, she hides herself in a neighbor's house or in another village. The go-betweens arrange for the wedding with her parents and then set out to find the girl. The *ońčəč košša* enlists the aid of the villagers to look for her. If she does not wish to be married, she may hide herself so well that she cannot be found. Usually, however, she is found and brought back to the house. Her parents ask her whether she wants to marry the suitor. If she doesn't, she frankly says so and the negotiations are broken off. If she consents, however, she merely says that the decision rests with her parents.

The *tular mari* offers the bride's parents vodka which he has brought. The parents decline, telling him to offer some to the girl. The girl takes a drink and then her parents drink. Pieces of the bread and cheesecake brought by the suitor are served to all. Before eating, they say that they have become relatives and pray to god to bless them.

The girl gives the suitor and his father each an embroidered cloth. As the suitor prepares to depart, the bride's family puts a loaf of bread and a cheesecake into the leather sack which he brought. If there is no bread or cheesecake, the sack is kept and returned filled the next time the groom comes.

In another region only one go-between is used; he is called *tular mari* or sometimes *kokla košša* 'go-between.' He places the young man's suit before the girl's parents before the betrothal ceremony.

As in previous accounts, when the young man and his father set out for this ceremony, they take vodka and bread in a leather sack. In the girl's village they go first to the home of *tular mari,* where they are given food and drink. After this the three go to the girl's house. As soon as she learns they have come, she hides in a storeroom or in a neighbor's house.

The *tular mari* takes the bread from the bag and puts it on the table; he tells why they have come and asks for their consent. The girl's parents do not give a definite answer. The suitor's father puts a sum of money (from ten to fifty rubles) on the bread as part of the bride price. The *tular mari* presses the suit again. The girl's father answers that he cannot speak for his daughter. The *tular mari* searches for her and brings her back. After this the matter of the bride price is discussed. The fathers argue back and forth and the *tular mari* tries to bring about a compromise. The amount of the bride price depends on the size of the girl's dowry. At this time they also discuss the presents which the bride must make to the groom's family.

When everything has been settled, the *tular mari* pours out vodka and seats the parents of the girl at the table. The girl and her suitor stand beside the table. The father asks his daughter if she wants to marry the young man and then asks the young man if he loves her. After answering affirmatively, the two young people drink the vodka, exchange glasses and drink again. Then both fathers drink and finally the amount of the bride price and dowry are mentioned.

The relatives of the bride are invited to celebrate the betrothal. At the end of the celebration the bride cooks noodle soup and serves it to the guests. Three loaves of bread are put into the leather sack brought by the suitor so that there is one more than he brought with him. The girl gives her suitor and his father each an embroidered cloth.

In another region the suitor and his father go on a Friday to the home of an acquaintance called *kokla kośśə, putləzə,* or *tular mari.* Both the man and his wife act as go-betweens. The man goes to the parents' house to discuss the matter with them. His wife follows the girl, who goes to a neighbor's house, and tries to win her consent. The betrothal itself is similar to the ceremonies described above.

Many other variations of the betrothal ceremony also exist. In some places an offering is made by throwing bits of food into the fire. Sometimes the suitor takes the initiative in asking for the girl and in settling the amount of the bride price and dowry. Sometimes the girl's consent is asked three times. Sometimes the girl's father tastes food first, then gives it to the suitor's parents after which it is served to the betrothed couple.

There are also variations in the way the pledge is drunk. Sometimes the young man and the girl take cups, exchange them, drink half, exchange again, and drink the rest. Another way in which the drinking may take place is for the suitor and his friend to offer the girl vodka. If she is willing to marry the young man, she takes the bottle of vodka and pours a glass for him. He drinks the vodka and refills the glass for her. After she has drunk, she pours out vodka for the *tular mari* and her parents. Further drinking occurs after the negotiations for the bride price are completed.

In some places, if the girl's parents refuse permission, the girl may step forward and take the glass of vodka offered to her father, indicating that she wants to marry the young man and that her parents are not responsible for her choice.

In some places, after the first formal drinking, friends and relatives are invited in to celebrate the betrothal. The relatives bring gifts and vodka. Sometimes the girl cooks porridge or noodle soup to serve to them. She also may choose at this time the girl who is to be her wedding attendant, *ońčəlnə šogəšə* (B.17.4.).

When the suitor leaves, his fiancée accompanies him into the yard. The usual custom is for the girl to serve him a drink and for him to give her a coin in return. There they may also exchange rings.

Sometimes the celebrating continues at the young man's home where they light candles and pray before continuing the feasting and drinking.

(B, 35–37; Bk, 56–60; Häm.[1915], 109–19; Häm.[1930], 67–69, 82–85, 95–96; S, 124–25; J. Wichmann, 33, 46, 72; Wu, 30–36.)

B.17.2.

One to four weeks usually elapse between a betrothal and a wedding. During this time preparations are made, the date for the wedding is set, and the bride price paid. If the bride price is very high, the groom may take six or seven months to pay it. In such a case there is a celebration when the last of it is paid.

Shortly after the betrothal, the groom's father usually calls on the bride's parents to make definite arrangements for the wedding; this is called *puńčal puaš* 'to set the date.' Sometimes before this the groom goes to see how the bride's family is progressing in the wedding preparations. Often the go-between goes with the groom's father to 'set the date.' If there is a go-between in the bride's village, the groom's father goes to his house first and gives him malt to be made into beer for the wedding. They go to the bride's home and discuss with her father not only the date of the wedding, but also the amount of the bride price, the dowry and number of gifts to be given to the groom's relatives if this has not already been settled at the betrothal. Often a part or all of the bride price is paid at this time. The groom's father puts this sum on top of a loaf of bread which he has brought. The bride-to-be sometimes gives the groom's father a present of linen and kneels to receive his blessing; in some places, as he is departing, she gives him a drink of vodka which he repays with money.

The wedding is held about two weeks from this time. In the meantime preparations for the wedding continue. Sometimes the bride's parents go to see where their daughter will live after her marriage. Sometimes the groom goes to the bride's home to be measured for a suit of clothes which will be his wedding present from the bride's parents. The bride and her family are kept busy sewing and embroidering gifts to be given to the groom's parents, his brothers and their wives, his sisters and their husbands, and his godparents. Neighbors and relatives often help with this work. Sometimes a couple of young girls related to the bride come to live at her house and help with the preparations. About a week before the wedding the groom takes the bride malt to make beer for the wedding. As he leaves, the bride gives him a drink of vodka and he gives her money. At both the groom's home and the bride's home food and beer are prepared and vodka is bought in anticipation of the wedding celebration.

(B, 36–37; Bk, 60; Häm.[1915], 120–21; Häm.[1930a], 69–70, 85–86; J; Wu, 35–36.)

B.17.3.

People living at a distance are invited to a wedding two or three days in advance; neighbors, however, are not invited until the day of the wedding. Sometimes the groom himself goes around on foot or on horseback inviting people on the morning before he fetches the bride from her house. In the afternoon, usually after consulting with his father, he chooses those who are to perform official functions at the wedding; the men are called *süan mari* and the women *süan batə*. The number of those who have a special role at a wedding varies from region to region. The chief person is called *süan buj* 'wedding head,' *süan kart* 'wedding priest' or *tün kart* 'chief priest'; he is either the *tular mari,* older male relative, or godfather of the groom. The function of *saus, sagus, sabus,* or *truška* is performed by a young man of the same age as the groom; he carries a whip as symbol of his authority and it is his duty to see to it that the wedding proceeds as it should. These two always form part of the official wedding party. In addition there may be a few other men who have special designations; these are not the same in all places. Sometimes when the head of the wedding is called *tün kart,* he has an assistant, *pel kart* 'half priest.' There may also be *izi truška* 'little *truška,*' a boy who helps serve the food. The term *kugə benə* 'big son-in-law' may be given to the groom's older brother-in-law or to the go-between, *tular mari.* Sometimes the groom's older brother or his father's younger brother is called *təklar mari.* There may be one or two young men, brothers or relatives of the groom, who are called *izi benə* or *ar binə.*

There is sometimes a person called *püraš* who is in charge of bringing the food; he is a relative, often the groom's sister's husband. In some regions the groom's older brother and his wife, his sister and her husband, or a rich man and his wife who give the groom money are designated *püraš mari* and *batə.* They precede the wedding party serving vodka. The woman attends the bride, helping her load her clothes on the sleigh or cart, riding with her on the way to the groom's house, and acting as a witness at the church ceremony along the way. In the groom's house she puts the headdress of a married woman on the bride. Another of the duties of this couple is to open a barrel of beer which has been brewed at the bride's house from malt supplied by the groom.

Buj pulčešə is not a relative but a friend who helps the groom, sometimes even helping to pay the bride price. *Burgəm šubuš kondəšə* is the man who brings the bride's possessions to the groom's house. There may also be a *modəš buj* 'head of playing.'

Women are also chosen to take an active role in the wedding. The most important woman is the one who puts the headdress of a married woman on the bride. She is often the wife of one of the men mentioned above, or a married sister or other relative of the groom, usually called *buj pütəršə batə* or *svaga batə.* *Püraš batə* may be a married sister of the groom or another relative; she and the *svaga batə* initiate the dancing. The wives of the *süan mari* are also considered to be *süan batə.* In addition, musicians are also chosen, usually a drummer and a bagpiper, although sometimes the music is supplied by an accordion player.

That same evening the musicians come to the groom's house and begin to play, thus signalling that the wedding has begun. Sometimes the young people and the musicians drive through town inviting everyone to the wedding. The horses and their harnesses are decorated with bells and ribbons.

The guests assemble at the home of the groom where there is much eating, drinking, singing, and dancing. The dancing is sometimes begun by *svaga batə* and *püraš batə* after which others join. In the yard there is a *šilək* (E.4.) with two tables in it. A ceremony of *čaza kücaš* 'cup bearing' may take place at this time. The *kugə truška* serves vodka and the *svaga batə* beer; the groom carries a wooden bowl in which there is bread. First the groom's father is served and he puts a coin on the bread. The groom's mother is served and then the other relatives and guests; each puts a coin in the bowl.

After this, food is eaten by the men at one table and by the women at the other.

Noodle soup is also served. After eating, the women dance again led by *svaga bata* and *püraš bata*. The young men jump, clap and sing. In other regions the men take part in the dancing, in which case the dancing is begun by the head of the wedding with the *buj pütarša bata* and the *kuga bena* with another woman.

When it is time to fetch the bride, the father blesses the groom; sometimes a girl takes the place of the bride and also receives the blessing. In some places the father holds a saint's picture while giving the blessing. When it is time to go, the official attendants hitch up the horses and load food and drink on the wagons. The official attendants at the wedding go in the first wagons and the other guests follow. Usually the *süan buj* leads the procession but he may be preceded by the musicians. The *sagus* sometimes rides on horseback so that he can move easily back and forth. Once they have left the village, the procession is halted so that the *sagus* can check to see that no one has been left behind. As many as forty or fifty persons may accompany the groom as he goes to fetch the bride. His father sometimes, but not always, goes with him. Sometimes the procession goes to the bride's house by one road and returns by another. In some regions they stop three times along the way.

(B, 38–39; Beke[1951b], 250–51; Bk, 62–65; Häm.[1915], 122–26; Häm. [1930a], 70–71, 86–88, 97–98.)

B.17.4.

On the day before the groom arrives to fetch her, the bride designates a close unmarried friend to be her wedding attendant. She is called *oṅčalna šogaša* or *oṅčač šogaša* 'the one who stands before.' Sometimes the bride also has a male attendant *üdar truška*, who serves as a mediator between the bride's and groom's families. A *čaza küčaš bata* '*čaza* bearing woman' is also chosen.

In one region it is the custom for the bride and the *oṅčač šogaša* to go to the house of the *oṅčač košša*, the go-between, in the afternoon. There they are seated at the table in the place of honor and served food and drink. The bride sings a song lamenting the fact that her parents are letting her go away like a stranger. After this the bride goes home to await the groom.

Before the wedding party arrives, everything has been made ready at the bride's home. The bride wears highly decorated white clothes and usually a green kaftan. On her head she wears both an embroidered cloth and a hat trimmed with fox fur. (For a detailed description of the bride's clothes see J. Wichmann.) The *oṅčalna šoraša* dresses like the bride and goes through much of the ceremony with her.

The groom and his friends usually arrive in the bride's village in the middle of the night or in the morning. As they near the village the women stand up in the wagons, swaying and holding up embroidered cloths. The men get out of the wagons and proceed on foot, dancing and singing.

If an intermediary living in the village helped arrange the marriage, they go to his house first. They wait at the gate while the *sagus* asks permission to enter. The man tells them to wait while the women finish their preparations. The *sagus* repeats his request and the third time permission is granted. In the yard there is a table laden with food and drink. The men eat at this table but the women take their food into the house to eat.

While the wedding guests are being entertained, the go-between and the *buj pulčešə* go to the bride's house. Any unpaid part of the bride price is paid and they ask if everything is ready for the arrival of guests. They return to the guests and all set out for the bride's house with the *süan buj* 'head of the wedding' and the wife of the go-between in the lead. The *sagus* enters the bride's house and asks permission for all to come in. This is not granted at once. The third time the *sagus* asks, permission is given and the guests enter the yard. They go around the *šelək*, a special building erected for the wedding celebration (E.4.), from right to left three times. The bride comes out and stamps in the tracks left by the groom's wagon.

Inside the *šelək* relatives of the bride are seated at tables. Those who came with the groom go in and *süan buj* assumes the duties of host. The wife of the go-between places beer that she has brought with her on the table. The last to get out of the wagon is the *püraš* who is escorted to the *šelək* in a procession and is served beer and vodka before the other guests.

In another place, while the wedding party is being entertained at the go-between's house, it is the custom for the go-between, *buj püteršə batə,* and her husband to go to the bride's house taking beer made from malt from the groom's home. The beer is placed on the table in the *šelək* and the go-between dips a ladleful and pours it back as he says a prayer. After this he serves beer to the bride's parents who are seated at the table. In the meantime the groom and his friends have arrived at the gate. The *sagus* goes in and asks the bride's parents if they can enter.

The bride and her helper *ončəč šogəšə* stand in the yard between the *šelək* and the gate. As the groom's guests enter they go around the bride three times. The bride stamps in the place where the groom has passed. The newcomers go into the *šelək* where the bride's parents give their places to *süan kart* and *kugə beŋə.* The latter gives the bride's mother the leather sacks of food brought from the groom's house.

In many regions the groom and his guests go directly to the bride's house when they arrive in the village. Usually only *tular mari, kugə beŋə,* or some other of the attendants is let into the house immediately. The others wait outside the house celebrating, eating and drinking provisions which they have brought with them. Inside the house, prayers are said for the wedding and there is some ritual drinking. In one place the go-between throws an offering of cake into the fire and *süan buj* later makes an offering of pieces of omelet. After a while the go-between comes out and the people are allowed to enter the yard and the house. Sometimes the groom waits in his wagon until the bride's father comes out to receive him. A felt mat is beaten twice with a whip and placed next to the groom's wagon. The groom steps out onto it and the bride's father gives him a pancake on which there is a coin.

In the yard there is a *šilək* in which there are two tables; the *süan buj* sits at one and the *kugə beŋə* at the other. From these tables drinks are dispensed to the wedding guests. Sometimes these tables are inside the house. The groom sits between the *kugə beŋə* and his wife.

When the bride's parents emerge from the house, the *süan buj* and the *kugə beŋə* serve them vodka. They say a prayer and then begin to eat the food which the groom and his friends have brought.

According to another account, when the wedding party arrives at the bride's house, the *truška* enters alone. He fills four bowls with beer and, bringing them out, gives them to the groom, his godfather, his godmother, and the *kugə benə*. The *truška* returns to the house and gives a bowl of beer to the bride, to her attendant *oṅčəlnə šogəšə* and to *šarbots,* the bride's wedding steward who performs functions similar to the groom's *truška.* The *truška* brings these people out, each carrying his bowl. The bride and the *oṅčəlnə* take their places facing the groom. The bride and groom take three steps toward each other and, exchanging bowls three times, drink the beer. After this they kiss holding each other's ears. Then the bride and groom go into the house. The *šarbots* asks the wedding guests if everyone is there; when they answer in the affirmative, the music and dancing begin.

Food and drink for celebrating are also supplied by the bride's parents. In some places the assisting girls must be bribed to open the *kudə* (E.1.) with the same number of kopeks as rubles were paid as a bride price. In other places the bride's mother must taste the food before serving it to the guests. The bride's relatives also contribute food and drink. The official attendants are usually served first.

At some time during the celebration the ritual of *čaza korka kučəmə* 'čaza cup holding' takes place. The bride, with the assistance of a helper serves a drink to each of those who have come from the groom's house and they, in return, put a coin in a bowl. The details for this ritual vary from region to region. In some places vodka is served, in others beer. In some places the bride, accompanied by *oṅčəč šogəšə,* serves the drinks and an older married woman collects the coins in a bowl in which there is bread; sometimes there is a silver coin in the crust of the bread. The bride and the *oṅčəč šogəšə* kneel to receive the blessing of those served after which they arise and the bride kisses them all. Sometimes the procedure is reversed so that the bride and her helper kneel before each person who in turn give money and are served a drink of vodka.

In some places permission to dance is asked from the bride's father. In doing so the *süan buj* sends the *ar bingə* into the house with a glass of vodka. The bride's father drinks, refills the glass, and, as he gives it back, tells them to sing and dance. The *ar bingə* takes the glass to the *süan buj* and communicates the message. After that the singing and dancing may begin.

In some places there is a special time for pancakes to be served called *melna lukmə* 'pancake bringing out.' In the house two wooden bowls are filled with pancakes. One is taken by the bride and the other by the *oṅčəč šogəšə* to the *šelək.* The bride puts her bowl on the men's and her helper puts her's on the women's table. At the first table the *sagus* cuts the pancakes into four pieces and the *buj pulčešə* does the same at the other. Each guest receives a piece of pancake. In some places one bowl has seven pancakes and the other five; the groom is given a piece from the bowl of seven pancakes and the bride from the bowl which contains five.

A barrel of beer made from malt brought by the groom is opened by the *püraš* and the *sagus.* In the house the bride serves the groom porridge which only he and his younger brother, or an unmarried friend sitting next to him, eat. The *oṅčəč šogəšə,* who is helping the bride, smears the spoon handle with porridge so that it will be difficult for him to pick up.

In one region, when the bride gets dressed, all the men from the groom's village leave the house. The bride sends the *oṅčəč šogəšə* to bring a young man whom she has already chosen the day before. He is called *čabən čišə mari* 'man wearing the kaftan.' When he comes in, he presents the bride with a new pair of shoes made from nine strips of bast. After he has had a drink, he goes out and invites other young men in the village. He brings them all to the house where they are served a drink. The bride gives *čabən čišə mari* her kaftan and wedding headcloth (see J. Wichmann) which he puts on. A bagpiper and drummer from the bride's village come in and play music for dancing. After a while they all go out to the *šelək* to drink and then return to the house. This is repeated until they have gone out to the *šelək* three times. The last time the wife of *buj pulčešə* takes the kaftan and cloth from the young man and puts them on the bride. On the bride's head a hat trimmed with fox fur is put over the cloth. The bride is taken out to the *šelək* and seated on a feather cushion on a bench.

The revelry continues at the bride's home, sometimes lasting until morning. In one place the bride goes around town saying good-by to everyone. In some places it is customary for the bride to make noodle soup for the guests before leaving. In one place it was formerly the custom for the bride's father to put a bowl of coins in front of her and let her take as many as she could grab in her hand.

The bride's dowry and other possessions are packed in a storehouse and shortly before the departure are loaded into a wagon. In one place it is the custom for the guests to hinder the removal of these things by putting the bride on them or blocking the doorway. The groom must give them money not to hinder him.

When the bride's possessions have been loaded onto the wagon, everyone makes ready to depart. The bride and groom are blessed by the bride's parents who take up an icon and give it to the bride or head of the wedding. The *kugə benə* takes a package of food prepared by the bride's mother. The bride kisses her parents and relatives and they all say good-by. In some places the bride, while going to the wagon, turns back three times and is struck with a whip by the *saus* or the groom. In other places she is pulled off her seat by *üdər truška,* her attendant, so that only on the third attempt is she able to take her seat. The bride and groom and sometimes the woman who is to put the headdress of a married woman on the bride ride in the first wagon; the rest follow behind. The parents of the bride do not usually accompany her; sometimes they send a couple called *kiamat ača* and *aba* to represent them and give their presents to the groom's parents in their name. These people become classificatory parents to the bride and marriage is then not possible between her children and theirs.

Sometimes a brother or sister of the bride stands at the gate and will not let them out until he has been given a coin. As the wedding party leaves, the *čabən čišə mari* tries to kiss the groom who struggles against it.

In some places the bride's father does not let the *burgəm šubuš kondešə* take the dowry until he has been paid twelve kopeks.

Sometimes a needle or nail is left on the gate post so that evil will be left behind. In one place the bride moves a needle three times from one gate post to the other making the 'iron gate' through which *keremet*s (A.31.) and other evil spirits cannot pass (H.4.4.).

Sometimes the wedding procession stops on the way in order to pray and make a bread offering. In one place the procession stops at the edge of the groom's village where they eat cheesecake and the groom's father comes out to meet them.

(B, 39–42; Bk, 65–72; Häm.[1915], 124–33; Häm.[1930], 71–78, 88–90, 99–100; J. Müller, 373–74; J. Wichmann, 24–27, 33–34, 50, 72, 73, 76; Wu, 40–44.)

B.17.5.

On arriving in the groom's village the wedding party may ride up and down the streets. In some places they first go to the home of *buj pulčešə* where they are served food and drink.

In one place it is the custom to fire a shot to announce arrival of the bride at the groom's house. In another place the bride and groom stop their wagon in the gate and eat a small piece from a loaf of bread and a pie which the bride has brought from her home.

There are different ways of receiving the bride. In some places, before the newly-weds get out of the wagon, the *sagus* goes to the groom's parents stating that there is a new addition to the family and asking what they promise the young couple. The groom's father specifies the things which they will receive; if the groom is his only son, he promises all his possessions. In one region this is not a completely serious matter. The father first promises a sick calf. This does not satisfy the couple so he promises a sick sheep, which is not satisfactory either. The third time he promises a sway-backed horse and they must be content with this. In another place an animal is promised to the bride.

In some places the bride and groom get out to the wagon hand in hand onto a felt mat which has been placed there for them and go into the house preceded by the *saus* who sweeps the way clear before them with a broom. According to another account the bride remains in the wagon until the groom's mother comes out to receive her; the bride steps out onto a mat which has been beaten by the *saus* and the groom's mother gives her a pancake on which there is a coin. In other regions, when the bride gets out of the wagon, she lets a coin fall to the earth, puts her heel on it and turns around three times. The coin is picked up by *izi truška* or *sagus* and thrown over the house. In some places the bride enters the groom's home with a cloth on her arm, perhaps symbolizing the bond with which captured brides were tied.

According to another account, when the bridal pair arrives at the groom's house, the *truška* comes out and lifts off the bride's veil. He returns to the house and gives the groom's father the holy image and his mother a loaf of bread. Then the three go out to welcome the bride and groom.

Food and drink are served either in a specially constructed shed, *šelək,* or in the house. There ritual eating and drinking take place and it is at this time that the bride and groom are usually considered to become man and wife. They kneel before the groom's parents to receive their blessing; prayers are said and a candle is lit before the holy image. In one place the icon brought from the bride's house is placed in the holy corner. In another place the bride and groom take a bite from the same cake at the same time; the rest of the cake is put in the holy corner and dedicated to the *kudə bodəž* (A.9.8.). In another place, the bride and groom exchange spoons three times before eating.

The bride's things are taken to a storehouse. In some places the groom gives money to those who have brought them. The bride is led off to the storehouse to the music of the bagpipe and drum. There the headdress of a married woman is put on her by a married woman chosen by the groom for this purpose. In some places the bride wears a highly decorated bridal cap which may be rented for the wedding. In another building the groom puts on the clothes which the bride has given him as a wedding present. In one place the bride and groom return to *šelǝk* where the bride is seated at the table with the groom's parents and serves beer to the guests. The *sagus* steals the bride's wedding cloth taking it from her head with a stick. He dances around the bride three times waving the cloth around his head and the bride must buy it back for a kopek.

In some places, after the bride has received the headdress of a married woman, she returns to the place where the groom's relatives are seated at a table eating. She places on the shoulder of each a gift of a shirt, towel, or headcloth; in return each promises her an animal. Presents are also given to the musicians who may make facetious gifts, such as "the rabbit that lives on the hill." The bride and groom also kneel on a felt mat spread out by *oń̌ǝlnǝ šogǝšǝ* to receive the blessings of these people. In one place an old man admonishes the bride to care for her husband and expresses the wish that "two may lie down but three get up from the bed." In the same place, after this, the *sagus* takes the cloth from the head of the bride and puts it in his belt.

The first time the bride goes to fetch water, either on the wedding day or shortly thereafter, the bride makes a sacrifice by throwing beads or coins into the spring. She is often accompanied by girls who are already known to the spring; sometimes she gives beads or a coin to these girls. The first occasion for fetching water is often the preparation of noodle soup for the wedding guests. According to one account, at the spring the bride and her helper each take a bucket of water and the bride throws a coin into the spring. Her helper carries the buckets a short distance and then leaves them for the bride who puts a coin for her at the end of the yoke.

In another region the bride draws the first bucket of water, pours it to the four points of the compass, refills the bucket, throws a coin into the spring, and returns to the house. In another place the bride throws a few beads and kopeks into the water and asks the water mother (A.1.1.) not to refuse her water. She pours the first bucketful she draws to the east, the second to the south, and the third to the west. She fills two buckets and carries them on a yoke. Three steps from the spring she gives her helper a coin which she put on the yoke at the spring.

In many regions the bride makes noodle soup for the wedding guests. This is often made from ingredients brought from her home. In one place, when it is finished, the guests go around the soup to the music of the bagpipes and drum. After this the bride sets the table with a tablecloth, bowls and spoons which she has brought. First she pours soup into her own bowl and then she serves the others. The bride and groom taste the soup first and then urge the others to eat it. In some places the *izi truška* takes from the bride's head the fox hat which she has been wearing. The bride buys it back for a kopek but does not put it on again.

Dancing is an important part of the celebration. In some places the *saus* dances alone first, then men dance with the *süan batǝ* in couples. After this the *oń̌ǝlnǝ šogǝšǝ* and the other girls dance alone. The eating, drinking, dancing, and singing continue for a long time. In some places, when the wedding guests leave, the bride and groom accompany them out into the yard and give them a final drink. The people then drive up and down the streets singing and sometimes go to the bride's parents' house where they are given another drink.

At many weddings, however, the guests do not leave until the bride and groom have been put to bed. In one place the bride and groom, accompanied by the guests, go in a procession around the out-buildings first. At the threshing place the bride may kneel while the others go around her three times. In the cattle pen the groom steps on the bride's foot three times and then she steps on his foot three times. The bride and groom are taken to bed by the *saus* to the accompaniment of music. The bed is usually prepared in a storehouse since the ordinary one- or two-room Cheremis house does not offer any privacy. In one region there is a coin for the *oñčət šogəšə* on the bed. In another region the *izi truška* lies on the bed and refuses to get up until he has been given a coin. The *saus* sees to it that the couple get into bed and sometimes presses their shoulders against the bed. He admonishes them to embrace each other and wishes them fertility. He strikes them with his whip and then the newly-weds are left alone.

In some regions the guests go home after this. In other regions, however, they wait until the bride and groom reappear dressed in their everyday clothes bringing out beer for the groom's parents. In some places they also serve beer to the other guests. At this time the bride distributes embroidered cloths to the wedding attendants. In some places food is placed on top of the drum and bagpipe in the *šelək* for the guests to eat before they go home.

(B, 43–45; Bk, 72–80; Häm.[1915], 134–39; Häm.[1930a], 78–80, 91–93, 101–4; H[1926], 75; J; Müller, 374–75; Wu, 44–47.)

B.17.6.

Shortly after the wedding, sometimes on the following day, the newly-weds invite everyone and especially the bride's parents to eat noodle soup or pancakes prepared by the bride. In some places the bride and groom eat from the same spoon. As the guests eat, they usually give money in return.

On another day the newly-weds may call on the bride's parents and other relatives with the wedding attendants and musicians. In one place, at the bride's home, her younger brother or sister steals the hats from the heads of the bride and groom as they are seated at the table. The groom must pay money to get them back.

The following is the most detailed account available of such festivities: On the second day of the wedding celebration, the bride makes pancakes to serve to the wedding guests. After eating, the guests go out and she washes the dishes. As she begins to sweep out the room, the guests throw coins into the dirt so that as the bride sweeps, she gathers money. The guests take the dirt and spread it around again putting more coins in it, thus forcing the bride to sweep again. The dirt is spread once more and someone puts a kopek in it behind her. The bride sweeps again and finds the last coin. After this there is more eating and drinking. The guests thank the family for the party and promise to take care of the newly-weds as long as they live. Just before the guests depart, the bride and groom serve the guests a final glass of vodka; each guest after he has drunk puts money into the glass.

On the third day the bride's younger brother comes to invite the newly-weds to a feast. The young couple serves the younger brother food and drink before he goes home. On the next day they prepare food and then set out for the home of the bride's parents together with the groom's parents and the matchmaker and his wife. There they eat and drink. Dancing is begun by the bride's father and mother, the groom's father and mother dance next, and then the matchmaker and his wife. They stop and give the newly-weds money to dance. After the young couple has danced, they all eat and dance again. Then the groom wraps three rubles in a cloth and puts them into his mother-in-law's bosom, saying, "This money is yours for the strength of your breast, for suckling your daughter." After this they continue eating and drinking until they go to sleep. In the morning, more food is prepared and they renew the feasting and dancing. At noon the guests go home after eating the food which the bride has brought. As they depart, the bride's father says, "Now go home well, brother-in-law, son-in-law. May my god accompany you half the way and may your god come out to meet you half way."

On the following day a feast is prepared at the groom's home and he invites his wife's parents. The next day the bride's parents, the matchmaker and his wife come. They eat and drink that day and the next morning. As they are about to depart, they are served vodka and they, in turn, leave money in the glass.

After two weeks the young wife goes home to her parents. Her mother asks her what kind of a husband she has and she answers that he is a good one. Then she spends two weeks knitting, spinning, sewing and making her husband a shirt. At the end of this time her husband comes, is entertained, and spends the night. The next day he takes his wife out to the barn and beats her. Then the couple spend the night together and the next morning they go home.

(B, 45–52; Bk, 80–85; Häm.[1915], 140; Häm.[1930a], 80, 93, 104–5; J; S, 115–16, 119–25, 189–90; Wu, 47.)

B.17.7.

In some regions those who are unwilling or unable to afford a wedding take a bride without going through the formalities described above. The young man desiring to take a bride in this fashion organizes a raiding party made up of friends and relatives. Some-times only two men called *tular mari* are chosen. In the girl's village there is a man called *ońćać košša* 'the one who goes before' or *kokla košša* 'go-between.' He advises the young man as to the best time to abduct the girl. If the girl wishes to elope with the young man, this person arranges a time and place for them to meet.

In some regions the groom has a protector called *buj pulćeša*. The groom takes his abducted bride to the home of this man and his wife and puts the headdress of a married woman on her. The *buj pulćeša* helps the groom with the wedding expenses and protects him from the bride's family which sometimes attempts to overtake them and recover the girl. If the bride's family succeeds in taking her back, the *buj pulćeša* tries to recon-cile the two families and reunite the young couple. The *buj pulćeša* and his wife become classificatory parents to the newly-weds. Although they are customarily called just *ača* 'father' and *aba* 'mother,' they are also called *kikunə ača* and *kakunə aba* to distinguish them from their real parents.

The wedding ceremony may take place either at the home of the *buj pulćeša* or the groom's parents. The bride and the wife of the *kokla košša* 'go-between' or a neighbor of the groom called *buj putərša batə*.

Friends and neighbors may be invited to the wedding celebration where there is feasting, drinking, dancing and singing. Sometimes parts of the regular wedding ceremony are performed during the celebration.

(Häm.[1915], 101–3; Häm.[1930a], 65–66, 81–82, 94.)

B.17.8.

There is little information about the way in which marriage vows are broken. The problem seems to be resolved by a simple separation of the individuals involved. According to one account, however, the couple who wish to be no longer married are tied together with a rope. The rope is then broken symbolizing the break in the marriage.

(S, 124.)

For *utam süan,* see B.23.7.

B.18.   *sürem* or *šürem; sürem küsə; sürem pastramaš* 'sürem driving out'

An exorcism of evil spirits usually takes place annually although not at the same time in all regions. In some places the exorcism is a separate holiday but often it is held on the eve of some other holiday such as *aga pajram* (B.2.), *kueča* (B.8.), or *küsə* (B.9.). In the eighteenth century it was held twice: first when the Cheremis family moved out to the summer hut in the spring and then again when it moved back into the house in the fall.

The exorcism is performed by the young men of the community who go about, usually at night or in the early morning, beating walls, fences, and steps with mountain ash switches. Women are also beaten so that the evil will not hide in their clothes. A greal deal of noise is made, horns (F.16.) blown, and sometimes shots fired. Horse racing is also sometimes connected with this holiday. In some places young men masquerade as bears, deer, etc., and one person, masquerading as *šajtan* (A.81.), is driven from house to house.

In one region the exorcism takes place on the evening before Palm Sunday. When it is believed that the devils have been driven out by the procedure described above, the switches are broken and thrown into a ravine outside the village as the men shout, "Evil spirit, go away to an evil place!" On the following morning, they drive away wolves with mountain ash twigs.

In another region, young men gather at the home of an assistant priest the night before *aga pajram.* After midnight, when the cock crows, the priest tells them that it is time to start. First they beat the ground three times with a switch; then they go around the village in a clockwise direction beating the houses. At each house they are given three eggs. After they finish, they burn the switches in the sacrifice place, gather under the *sürem* linden tree, and cook the eggs collected. They pray as they eat the eggs and one from their midst is chosen to make an egg sacrifice.

According to another account, on the eve of *aga pajram* young men and boys gather at the ceremonial place, cach with a rowan twig in his hand. One of them is selected as the egg collector (*munə pektaš*). The oldest, who acts as leader, stands in the middle of the ceremonial place and drives a knife straight into the earth. The others run around the ceremonial place three times while the leader prays god (A.26.) to drive out to the north the evil spirit (A.46.) which causes illness. After that they go in groups through the village driving out evil spirits. As they come to a house they beat the walls with their switches and shout for the evil spirit to go away. The head of the house gives them beer, cakes and a couple of eggs. When they have been to all the houses, they throw twigs into a river, saying, "Evil spirits, go flowing away." Then they return to the ceremonial place where they spend the night praying. The knife is not drawn from the ground until the *aga pajram* ceremony begins the next day. From the eggs collected cakes are made to be used as an offering at the *aga pajram* ceremony.

In another place, early on the morning of *aga pajram*, the young people dance around a fire on a hill. The young people holding a firebrand jump over the fire three times shaking their clothes. They drive the firebrand into the ground and cut the ground with knives. After this they go into town to drive out the devil in the usual manner. Outside of town the young people make another fire and jump over it.

Another account reports that people from ten to fifteen towns gather to exorcise evil. The young men ride around a grove on horseback as the old men kneel in the middle of the grove praying to *sürem jumə* (A.26.37.) to protect them from evil. They also promise to make a sacrifice the following day. The young men ride to their towns where they beat the walls, fences, and women, driving out the evil spirits. The next day many animals (horses, steers, heifers, sheep, ducks, and geese) are sacrificed in the grove in which they prayed the night before.

In some regions the exorcism takes place in the early summer. For a few weeks before *sürem*, while the rye is ripening, certain taboos must be observed lest the crop be damaged by hail and thunder. A person must not dig or even go into the rye fields, he must not make noise, dress in bright colors nor do anything which would cause a bad smell. The *sürem* festival occurs at the end of this time. Long horns are blown and later are carried around a tree. A priest, holding cakes in his right hand and beer in his left, says a prayer. If a horn breaks during this ceremony, it is regarded as a sign that there will be hail. Finally the horns are buried in the earth, hung on a tree, or broken.

In other places the driving out of the devil takes place in connection with the *küsə* ceremony. The young people from several towns gather in the evening at sundown. They go around the *sürem* oak tree three times, then go to the sacrifice place (*šelək olməš*, E.4.). They bring along cream, porridge, and pancakes which are eaten after the prayer. As the priest prays the young people kneel. Girls gather in the sacrifice place and the young men beat their clothes saying, "We are driving away your *šükšəndal* (A.85.)." They divide into two groups and go back to the towns on horseback or in wagons to the accompaniment of accordion music. After attending to the more serious business of driving out devils, the young people gather in a town and dance until the next day.

Sometimes in the spring the people go around the highest tree in the neighboring forest three times. They beat it with sticks and then throw the sticks into a nearby ravine. Each person throws an egg at the top of the tree three times. If he hits it, it means that the sacrifice will be accepted. Pieces of cake and beer are offered and the people have a joyous meal in honor of having chased *šajtan* away.

In some areas exorcism is held at the time of the new moon in March. It is believed that *šajtan*s bring cold from the north and that by exorcising them, the cold weather will also go.

In some places before *aga pajram* eggs are thrown in three directions: east, south, and north. An egg and a wheat dumpling are buried as a gift to *šajtan*.

Sometimes the term *sürem* is used to designate the *küsə* ceremony itself (B.9.).

(Be, 706, 734–35; Häm.[1925], 99–110; Häm.[1928], 29–34; H[1926], 39–40, 100, 178–79, 181–82; H[1927], 246ff.; J; P, 202; P[1948], 115–16; S, 96, 107–8, 159–60, 177–78, 186-88; V, 196; Wu, 29–30.)

For *kolšən šəməčə*, see B.23.2.; *šəmət pajram*, B.23.2.; *šorək šočən*, B.20.

B.19.   *šorək jol* or *šort jol* 'sheep foot'

In the winter, toward the end of December falls *šorək jol,* a holiday lasting from three days to a week. Merrymaking, masquerading, fortune telling, and magic rites are the principal activities of this holiday.

One of the most widespread customs, perhaps the one from which the holiday gets its name, is that of predicting the appearance of a future husband or wife by means of grabbing a sheep's foot. The young people go out to the sheep pen in the dark and grab either the foot of a sheep or some of its wool. If a white sheep is caught, the future mate will be a blond; if a black sheep, a brunet. From the size and age of the sheep it is also possible to predict the size and age of the future husband or wife.

There are also other ways for girls to learn about their future husbands. In some places girls pull a piece of wood from the woodpile. If the piece is short, she will marry a short man; if the piece is long she will marry a tall man. In some places each girl pulls a stalk from a stack. If there are many grains on the stalk, she will marry a rich man; if there are no grains on the stalk, she will marry a poor man.

The future can also be foretold from certain sounds which are heard at night. In some regions the girls go to a meadow to listen for these sounds. If a girl hears the sound of swipples, she will marry a rich man. If she hears a bell, she will be married with a wedding ceremony. If she hears no bell, she will either go to her husband without a ceremony or never marry. In some places people listen at the gate to the cattle pen before midnight. If threshing is heard, it means that a person will live but the sound of an ax means death. If the lowing of cattle is heard, the grain will grow well.

In some places there is the belief that if a person goes out to the crossroads on the eve of *šorək jol* and puts his ear to the ground, he will hear sounds which will indicate future events. If he hears bells, there will be many weddings in town. If he hears the sound of hewing boards and hammering, there will be many deaths. If he hears the sound of threshing, the grain will grow well. On the way home, he must not look back; if he does, the devil will follow him.

If a young man wishes to find out whether he will be conscripted, he sets fire to a little ball of flax. If, as it burns, it flies up, he will be taken into the army.

If there are many stars on *šorək jol* night, the livestock will increase. If it snows on *šorək jol* day, grain and nuts will grow well that year.

Sometimes cakes are baked or a porridge is made in which are hidden a piece of sheep's foot, a piece of a bridle, a coin, and other similar objects each representing a kind of wealth. The cakes or porridge is distributed and the object which each finds in his portion indicates the kind of good fortune which he will have.

Certain simple magical rites are performed to bring prosperity in the coming year. A heap of snow is built in the field or on the threshing floor to represent a stack of grain sheaves. In the evening people go out to the sheep pen and pull the legs of the sheep expressing the wish that the sheep have twins. If a person counts his money at this time, counting the copper kopeks as silver rubles, his money will increase in like proportion during the coming year. Some people shake the apple tree as if trying to shake down apples. Old women bake potatoes in the oven to cause the potatoes to grow large the next year. They feed the hens grain asking that the hens lay as many eggs as there are grains.

Masquerading also forms an important part of the *šorək jol* festivities. In some places boys do the masquerading, in other places, girls, and in others, both boys and girls. They pretend to be bears, wolves or old people called *basli kuba* and *kuguza* 'Valsili old woman' and 'old man' (A.38.3.). They go from house to house; when they pretend to be animals, they are led about on a leash. Before they arrive, the people in the house start spinning and making shoes to show their industriousness. When the masqueraders enter, the people in the house ask them for a good grain harvest the next year. In some places they scatter hemp seed indicating that the hemp will grow well. Sometimes they are taken out in the sheep pen to pull the sheep's feet and say that the sheep will have twin lambs.

This holiday is also characterized by drinking, feasting, dancing, and games. Sometimes the beer for the festivities is brewed in one house although all the villagers have contributed the ingredients; the festivities are then held in this house and continue until the beer is all consumed.

In some places there are prayers and offerings in connection with this holiday. On the first and last days of the festivities the head of the house places pancakes on the table and, addressing *šorək jol* day, prays for the family to be blessed; he throws some pancakes into the oven fire as an offering and asks *tul bodəž* 'fire spirit' (A.9.14.) to act as intermediary.

(B, 20, 69; Bk, 30; H[1926], 189–91; J; P, 210–11; S, 108; Uj[FB], 56; Uj[S], 61, 158, 205–13; Up[S], 42, 118, 171–72, 174–75; Wk, 79; Wt, 58–60; Wu, 14, 16.)

B.20.   *šorək šočən* 'sheep fructifying'

In late autumn a ceremony may be held to increase the fertility of the sheep if they have not been reproducing well. The sacrifice animal at such a ceremony is an owl or other wild bird, sometimes a hen. The head of the house carries the bird out to the sheep pen. His wife takes out objects to be used during the sacrifice. Children who have been asked to take part in the ceremony follow crawling on their hands and knees. They imitate the bleating of the sheep and the boys butt the girls as rams butt sheep. More girls than boys participate so that more ewes than rams will be born. The head of the house makes a fire in the sheep stall and the "sheep" crawl three times around it following the woman. After this they may stand up and the bird is cooked and eaten. A prayer is said to *šorək šočən* 'sheep fructifier' (A.82.10.) and *šočən aba* 'fructifier mother' (A.1.10.) for the increase of the sheep. The bones of the sacrificed bird are thrown onto the roof of the cattle shed.

(H[1926], 188–89; H[1927], 256–60.)

B.21.   *šošəm pajram* 'spring ceremony'

The spring ceremony is held at the time when the melting of the snow and the budding of maples announce the advent of spring. Villagers gather in a house and throw offerings to the protective deities into the fire. There is a ritual dance under the direction of the priest. A man and a woman other than his wife go to the center of the room. The man, wearing a cap, goes to the table and receives from the priest a jug of beer; the woman stands near the door. The man drinks a bit, then dancing and making beer splash out of the jug, goes over to the woman. The two drink until the jug is empty. Still dancing, the man gives the empty jug to the priest. The man and woman continue dancing and finally, when they finish, they each receive a jug of beer which they share with the musicians. Other couples dance in the same way until all have had the opportunity of dancing.

(S, 184–85.)

For *üdər šörasaš*, see B.17.1.

B.22.   *šurnə jər* 'grain offering'

A sacrifice ceremony for the grain spirits is held in order to secure an abundant crop. The following sacrifices are made: a sheep to *šurnə šočan* 'grain fructifier' (A.82.11.), a ram to *šurnə pujəršə* 'grain creator' (A.70.18.), a sheep to *šurnə perke* 'grain blessing' (A.67.17.), a ram to *šurnə piambar* 'grain prophet' (A.68.10.), a goose to *šurnə kaba* 'grain fate' (A.27.2.), a duck to *šurnə šukĉə* 'grain angel' (A.84.19.), and a duck to *šurnə saus* 'grain overseer' (A.76.8.).

(P, 297.)

For *šürem*, see B.18.

B.23.   *tojaš* or *tojmaš* 'burial'

Special preparations for death are made as a person is dying. In some places a moribund person is placed on a bed of straw because of the belief that, if a person dies on a feather bed, he must count the feathers in it in the next life, or, if he dies on a felt mat, he must count the hairs in the felt. Sometimes the dying person requests the clothing in which he will be buried. Each one present asks the dying person to forgive him for any wrong which he may have committed. The dying person gives his blessing to his children. Forgiveness for any possible unknown offense is often asked even after the person has died.

Relatives are called to the funeral, which is usually held on the same day the person dies. If death takes place late in the day, the burial is not held until the following day. In some places burial takes place on the third day. Relatives and neighbors are invited to the funeral by a person who knocks on the window because one from a house in which there is a corpse may not enter other houses. During the night relatives and neighbors keep vigil to see if by any chance the *ört* 'soul' (J.1.) returns to the corpse and the person revives. Those who thus spend the night must accompany the corpse to the grave. If there is a mirror in the room, it must be turned around or covered so that the dead person may not select a companion from among those present.

The corpse is prepared for burial by a person of the same sex. In Cheremis villages there are often special persons who perform this duty. The eyes and mouth of the corpse are closed and, in some places, little tufts of thread cover the eyes, ears, and nostrils. The body is washed with soap and dressed in clean white clothes.

In the meantime a coffin is made. As the coffinmaker begins his task, he asks the deceased not to become angry if he doesn't like the 'house,' i.e., coffin, which he is preparing. A small window is made in the coffin near the head of the corpse.

When the coffin is finished, leaves or pieces of felt and a pillow are put in the bottom for the corpse to lie on. When the corpse is laid in the coffin, the survivors wish the dead person a good life in the next world and ask him not to bother the living. The corpse is dressed as if he were about to set out on a journey. Extra clothes and tools and bast to make new shoes when the old ones wear out are put in the coffin. Things that a man uses such as tools, a wooden comb, and, if he smoked, his pipe, tinderbox, and tobacco are placed in a man's coffin. Household articles such as a broken pot, cup and spoon are also given to the deceased. Money is put in the coffin, too, for the dead person to buy a place to live in the other world. In some places a silver coin with a hole is tied to the middle finger of the right hand to "redeem his blood on the other side." Sometimes the money in the coffin is said to pay a person's debts and other coins are thrown into the grave to pay for land in the other world. Cloth, needles and thread are put in the coffins of women; toys are buried with children. Food is also placed in the coffin so that the dead person will not return hungry. Some people also put nuts in the pockets of the corpse's clothing for the little children in the next world. In the hands of the corpse are placed mountain ash sticks for the dead person to defend himself against dogs, serpents, and evil spirits in the next world. There may be some connection between this custom and the fact that burial is called *tojaš* and the word for 'stick' is *toja*.

Relatives and friends bring linen cloths to cover the face and body of the corpse. Over these cloths, running the whole length of the body, is laid a thread, sometimes three threads of different colors, by which the dead is supposed to be able to go up into heaven; some call this the 'swing' of the dead. Sometimes the thread placed on a dead child is as long as that of a grown man; in this way the Cheremis express their hope that the child will continue growing in the other world.

If an unmarried young man dies, the mourners express the wish that he find himself a suitable bride in the next life. If a single girl dies, in her coffin are put materials and ornaments for her to make her wedding clothes, especially a married woman's head-dress. An unmarried dead person is accompanied to the grave as if to his wedding. Wagons and horses are decorated with bells and ribbons; all his young friends accompany the deceased to the graveyard; sometimes even wedding attendants are chosen.

In some places, when the coffin is taken out into the yard, a bundle of threads is placed on top; each person takes a thread from the bundle and says, "Although you perhaps died an untimely death, do not take me with you. See, I have a long thread, grant me a long life, too." The thread is later tied at the neck of a shirt and protects the wearer from sorcery. In some other places, threads are drawn from the clothing on the corpse. Sometimes the mourners merely touch the coffin and ask the dead person not to take away the prosperity of the house. In some places children jump over the coffin of their dead parent "so that they do not become poor, but quickly become accustomed to the household chores."

In some places as the coffin is carried out the door, it is pulled back three times to keep it from taking away good fortune.

As the corpse is carried from the yard into the street, a hen is killed at the gate; if it dies in the yard, it means there will be another death within a short time, but if it runs headless out into the street, death will not visit the house again soon. It is believed that those who have previously died come to meet the recently deceased on the spot where the hen is slaughtered. Some say that in the other world the hen gathers all the nails which the dead person has lost during his life because a person may not appear before the ruler of the dead (A.90.) without all his nails. In other places, at the slaughter it is customary to say, "Loosen with this blood your own blood from death!" The first drops of the hen's blood are then smeared on the eyebrows of the corpse. In some regions the hen is left where it died to be eaten by dogs. In other places it is cooked and eaten. Sometimes a chicken (a cock for a dead man and a hen for a dead woman) is hung by the neck under the wagon to "free the blood" of the dead person. Sometimes the gate is not closed until the people return from the cemetery.

People accompanying the coffin to the grave must not look around. The townsfolk do not watch them but often close their windows "so that they do not follow the dead." Those who meet a funeral procession wish the dead person a good life in the other world. In one region, linen for a shirt is given to the first one who meets the procession.

The coffin is closed for the last time at the grave. Before this is done, the cloth is lifted from the face of the corpse "so that he can see daylight once more." The grave is dug either before or after the procession arrives. Ground is broken with an ax and a prayer is said to *məlandə on* 'earth lord' (A.52.10.) and *məlandə aba* 'earth mother' (A.1.5.). Money is given to the one who breaks the ground; if not, the hands of all those who help dig the grave become stiff. The bottom of the grave is sometimes strewn with fir needles and money may be thrown into the grave. As the coffin is lowered into the grave it is raised three times and the dead person is told not to be afraid. The pieces of linen used to lower the coffin are sometimes left at the grave. In some regions candles are put into the grave. In one place three candles, one for *kiamat töra* (A.90.), one for *kiamat saus* (A.76.5.) and one for the deceased, are put in the north end of the grave before the coffin is lowered. In some places mountain ash and ramble twigs are put into the grave; the mountain ash is said to drive away dogs and the bramble to drive away snakes. In some places a small animal is killed at the grave; the meat is taken home to be eaten, but the bones are thrown into the grave.

After the grave is covered, the people once more wish the dead person a happy life in the other world and ask him not to return to frighten his family but to protect his old home, the family, and the cattle. On the grave a three-branched candle is fastened in a lump of clay and lit; one branch is for the ruler of the dead (A.90.), one for his helper (A.76.5.), and one for the dead man himself. Sometimes five candles are lit, the two additional candles for those who have died previously. Dirt is swept onto the grave mound three times from each side and the mourners express the wish that the earth rest lightly on the deceased.

In some places young linden trees are planted at both ends of the grove; to these trees are fastened threads whereby the dead are believed to rise to heaven. In another region birch boughs are stuck into the ground at the head and the foot of the grave. On the grave of a young girl, cloths are fastened to the end of a stick. In some places the earth is packed down on the grave, turf replaced, and a linden twig moved up and down the grave. The mourners go three times around the grave, break a piece of wood and leave it on the grave.

In the meantime the house has been thoroughly cleaned. After the corpse is taken from the house, ashes are strewn on the place where the person died or a pot of glowing coals or a heated stone is placed there to purify the spot. The clothing in which the person died, the soap and linden bark used to wash the corpse and everything defiled by death are either buried in the cemetery or thrown away along the road or in the forest. The wagon or sleigh—in some places a coffin is carried on a sleigh even in the summer—in which the corpse is taken to be buried is either left at the cemetery or remains out on the street for three days and nights before it can be used again. The wood remaining after making the coffin is also left at the cemetery.

Sometimes the people returning from a burial, about half way between town and the cemetery, cut down a tree leaving a stump about three feet high. This is done so that if the deceased starts to return home, he will realize that the village is still far off and turn back.

People returning from a burial may only go to the house where the death took place so that they do not take death elsewhere. They bathe there or, at least, cleanse their hands by washing or rubbing them with ashes. Sometimes they change clothes, too. In some places the dead person is also invited to take a bath and the living beat the sweat bench.

Sometimes the funeral feast takes place while the corpse is still in the house. In such a case, two bowls are placed at the head of the corpse. To the edge of the bowl are fastened candles for the dead person and for the spirits of the underworld. Little pieces of food for the deceased are placed in one bowl; in the other bowl are poured vodka and mead. As the mourners do this they express the wish that the dead person have a great abundance in the other world.

In some regions the corpse is offered food in the yard after it has been placed in the coffin. On top of the coffin is placed a cup into which each mourner, beginning with the oldest, puts a piece of cake. In many places food and drink are taken out to the cemetery and put on the grave mound over the corpse's mouth.

The custom of having the funeral feast after the burial is widespread. After the mourners have returned from the cemetery and bathed, dishes and a spoon are put out for the deceased on a cloth-covered bench on which no one sits. Two candles burn next to the dishes; as these candles are lit, it is customary to tell the deceased not to burn his hands or feet. The *kiamat töra* (A.90.) is also asked to grant the deceased a happy life in the other world. The first servings of vodka, mead, and food are put in the dishes for the deceased. Each person, from oldest to youngest, takes a piece of cake and puts it in the plate for the dead person. Other dead relatives are also invited to take part in the feast.

Although it is no longer the custom to kill a large animal for the funeral, an eighteenth century account reports that a horse, usually the deceased's best or favorite horse, was killed at the funeral of a rich man and eaten by those attending the funeral.

In some places the survivors greet the dead person in the cemetery on the day after the funeral. They light candles and put bread at the foot of the grave. It is said that if no one greets the dead person before dawn, the *kiamat töra* puts out his eyes. The dead person is also told that if anyone caused his death, to take that person within the year.

In some regions an offering is put out for the deceased each day for forty days after his death.

(B, 31–33; Be, 387–92; Beke[1954]; Häm.[1930a], 133–35; Häm.[1936–37], 43–48; H[1926], 15–25; H[1927], 21–25; J; Müller, 378, 380; S, 133–48; Uj[FB], 81, [T] 47; Up[FB], 32, 33, 35; Wu, 47–48; Wt, 60–61.)

B.23.1. *kumət pajram* 'third holiday'; *kolšən kuməčə* 'the dead's third'

On the third day after a death a memorial ceremony is held. It is often announced at the funeral and only relatives who live nearby attend. They go to the cemetery and sometimes put pieces of pancake on the grave. Returning home they light one or three candles for the dead and the spirits of the realm of the dead (A.90. and A.76.5.), and express the hope that the deceased walk in light. A place is set for the deceased guest of honor and each person present puts a bit of food in the dish. Later the contents of the dish for the dead person are thrown out in the yard where dogs eat the food; the hunger of the dogs indicates the condition of the dead. Sometimes the food is given to the cows or the sheep to eat.

(Be, 392; Häm.[1930a], 135; Häm.[1936–37], 43, 45; H[1926], 26; S, 142; Wt, 63.)

B.23.2. *šəmət pajram* 'seventh holiday'; *kolšən šəmətə* 'the dead's seventh'

On the seventh day after his death, the deceased is guest of honor at a remembrance feast. In some places relatives go to the cemetery and offerings are made at the grave. Sometimes seven candles are lit on the edge of a bowl. In some places a relative drives a wagon to the cemetery and invites the dead person to come to a memorial feast at the house. A hen or a sheep is slaughtered and a bath is prepared for the dead person. All night long he is guest of honor at the celebration where food is put into a bowl for him. This food is later given to the dogs, cows, or sheep. In the morning he is driven back to the cemetery.

(B, 33; Be, 392–93; Häm.[1930a], 135; Häm.[1936–37], 43, 45; H[1926], 26–27; S, 142–43; Wt, 63–64.)

B.23.3. *nəllə pajram* 'fortieth holiday'; *kolšən nəlləžə* 'the dead's fortieth'

On the fortieth day after a death, a farewell memorial feast is held because it is believed that after forty days the dead person ceases to be in close contact with the living. In many places a dish, spoon, and food are put out for the deceased each day for forty days following his death.

In some places a sheep or larger animal is killed for the fortieth day feast and neighbors and relatives are invited. In some places a horse is killed for a man and cow for a woman. All the meat must be eaten during the feast; none can be kept until the next day.

In some regions on the fortieth day some of the relatives of the deceased drive out to the cemetery. The best horse and a wagon decorated with bells are used because the dead person is told that he is invited to a great wedding (*kugə süan*). The wagon is driven around the grave in a clockwise direction one to three times. Next to the grave on a linen cloth are put food and drink. The relatives kneel bareheaded and invite the dead to the celebration. Sometimes they also sprinkle food and drink on the grave. The dead person is also told to bring with him the other dead relatives; the spirits of the other world (A.90. and A.76.5.) are also invited. After those who have gone to the cemetery have tasted the food brought along, they invite the dead person to get into the wagon; the dead person is assured that everything is that which he already knows. A white cushion is placed as a seat for the dead person. Often on the journey to town they speak to the dead person who is believed to be sitting there. If more than one wagon has gone out to the cemetery, the one believed to be carrying the dead person goes far ahead of the others.

In some places a horse is offered to the dead man on the way to the house; the horse is slaughtered as soon as they arrive home from the cemetery. The meat is cooked and eaten; the hide is cut and put on the grave.

In the yard the widow waits to receive her husband; she and the children kneel weeping beside the steps. A person designated to be the leader of the ceremony stands bareheaded in front of her holding food and drink. This person speaks to the dead man in a friendly way, calls him by name, and invites him into the house. After the dead man is believed to have descended from the wagon, his cushion is taken into the house for him to sit on. Near it the clothing and shoes of the deceased are hung from a rafter so that he will see that all his things are still there. Food and drink are offered to the dead person. After a while, the men accompany him out to inspect the barns, cattle, and so on. They also take him to the bathhouse to bathe and then strike the bath switch three times against the platform. After sundown all the friends and relatives of the deceased come to the house bringing gifts of food and drink. Each guest also brings a candle to be fastened to a candle holder or bowl near the back wall. In some regions the guest buys the candles from his host for a few kopeks. Separate candles may be lit for *kiamat töra* (A.90.), *kiamat saus* (A.76.5.), and the deceased; or there may be in the middle a large candle made of three regular candles twisted together. On the right is a row of small candles, one for each dead relative remembered by the living; to the left of the large candle each guest places a candle. The big candle burns until daybreak; the small candles are replaced as they burn out.

Throughout the celebration the dead person is considered to be the guest of honor. All kinds of food and drink are served to him; each person kneeling puts a little food and drink into his dishes. If a sheep has been killed little pieces of most of the organs are put into the bowl. The old people kneel and exhort the dead to bless the family, cattle, and crops. The living also receive their share of food and drink. The extent to which the living enjoy themselves is an indication of the enjoyment of the dead.

By midnight everyone has eaten his fill and is drunk. Everyone is in high spirits and the guests dance wildly to the music of the bagpipes. As they tire, people fall asleep in corners. Sometimes the widow sleeps with the cushion on which her dead husband is believed to sit, saying that this is the last time they will sleep together.

In some places the food and drink in the bowls dedicated to the dead are poured out in the yard or the street and the bowls are broken. The people go singing around the food and broken bowls three times.

In many regions a person plays the role of the deceased. In some places a person— often the best friend of the deceased—puts on his clothes and receives all the attentions given to the dead. This person is called *burgem čiša* 'the one who puts on the clothes,' or *kolša olmeš šinčəš* 'the one who sits in the place of the dead.' The widow embraces him as if he were her husband. Men shake hands with him and call him by the name of the dead person. He is served food and drink and treated with the greatest courtesy. He tells about his experiences in the other world and admonishes his relatives to work and live in harmony. The inhabitants of the house ask him for his protection. (D.1.)

In some places several people play the role of the deceased instead of just one. They each put on one article of the deceased's clothing. In one region, when those wearing the clothing of the dead person enter, two people sit in the place of honor and ask them why they have come. They reply that they have come to their fortieth day festival and promise that the grain will grow well, the bees will increase, and life will be peaceful.

Just before daybreak the dead person returns to the grave. The people kneel facing him and tell him that it is time to go back. They wish him wealth and advise him to make friends among the dead Cheremis, *toštə mari*. They also ask him not to scatter the family or hide the cattle. One person takes the candle holder, another the bowl of food, the third the cup, and the widow and others each take part of the dead man's clothing. They all leave the house with the person acting the part of the dead man in the lead. The women weep loudly as the procession wends its way toward the cemetery. The procession stops at a grassy spot outside of town or at a crossroads. The candles, food, and drink are thrown away; a wooden spoon and cup are broken and left there for the dead person. They wish the dead person well in the next world and ask him not to return to the world of the living unless invited. The one who has been representing the dead person changes back into his own clothes. The clothes belonging to the dead person are later given away to the needy or sold among the Tatars.

In some regions the dead person is driven back to the cemetery in a wagon decorated with bells and to the accompaniment of bagpipe music. The grave is swept with a bath switch. Sometimes along the road there is a special place where the mourners put a little one-legged table called *kolšə üstel* 'table of the dead' on which a dish and three spoons are placed. In some places a long pole called *kolšə kübar* 'bridge of the dead' is put across a brook or gully so that the dead can pass over. Sometimes on the day after the ceremony, before going back to the cemetery, food and drink are put out for the hangover which the dead may have.

An eighteenth century account reports that a few weeks or months, or even a year, after death a memorial feast is held and a horse is killed. Two poles are put up in the farmyard and a heavy thread is stretched between them on which a ring is hung. All the young relatives shoot arrows at it from a distance of ten paces. The first to shoot an arrow through the ring takes the horse—if the deceased was a man, the one he usually rode—and races three times to the grave and back. The horse is then slaughtered, cooked and eaten.

Failure to observe a fortieth day properly may anger a dead person. It is related that once a man held a fortieth day ceremony with only sour buttermilk. The deceased took his revenge by knocking the man down as he tried to work so that he could not harvest any grain that day.

(B, 33–34; Be, 393–96, 398; Häm.[1930a], 136; Häm.[1936–37], 43, 48; H[1926], 27–36; H[1927], 49–55; J; Müller, 379–80; S, 135, 140, 143–44; Wt, 64–66; Wu, 49–52.)

B.23.4.

Sometimes a memorial feast is held a year after a person has died. All the clothes of the deceased are laid on the back of his favorite horse. The horse is taken to the cemetery and led three times around the grave. A three-branched candle is lit, food is offered, and the dead person is reminded that it is his anniversary and told that his horse will be slaughtered in his honor. On returning home the horse is killed and the meat cooked and eaten. As meat and cakes are offered to the dead person, he is told that the horse has not been used since his death and he is to take it to himself. At the end of the feast, the bones are taken to the cemetery and put on the grave, the skull is hung on a tree, and the hide is sold; the proceeds from this sale are given to orphans and needy people.

Sometimes memorial ceremonies are also held on the second, third, and fourth anniversaries of a person's death.

(B, 34; H[1926], 36–37; H[1927], 57.)

B.23.5. *sorta keča* 'candle day'; *sorta pajram* 'candle holiday'; *tošta mari pajram* 'dead Cheremis holiday'

Memorial ceremonies for all dead relatives may be held at various times during the year. Ceremonies of this type are usually held at Easter (B.8.) or Pentecost (B.13.). Occasionally in some districts such a ceremony is also held in the fall. There is no special day for the memorial feast in the fall; each family decides on the day and invites friends and relatives. Candles are not lit at the memorial feast in the fall.

(Häm.[1936–37], 44–49; H[1926], 37, 39; H[1927], 60–63; S, 146.)

B.23.6.

A special offering is made to a dead person if it is believed that he is molesting the living. If a horse or a cow is lost and the owner is convinced that one of his dead relatives had hidden it, he lights a candle and makes a food offering asking the deceased to return the lost animal. If a widow has a backache, she believes it is caused by her dead husband coming to sleep with her; she also makes an offering and prays her husband not to come to her. A memorial offering is made when a dead relative has appeared to a member of the family in a dream.

(H[1926], 40–41; H[1927], 58–59; S, 145.)

B.23.7. *utəməlan pumaš* 'offering to the left over (dead)'; *utəm süan* 'wedding of the left over (dead)'

A memorial ceremony is held for the dead who were not buried or who have no living relatives to give a feast in their honor (A.94.). A sacrifice to the *utəmə* may be made in the fall. Or the appearance of worms and destructive insects in the fields signals the need for making an offering to these dead. The townspeople put on their holiday clothes and the ceremony resembles a wedding (B.17.). The leader of the ceremony is called *süan buj* 'wedding head.' The women attendants, *süan batə,* dress up in their finery and there are *kuštəšə* 'dancers,' a *saus* to keep order with his whip, and musicians as at a wedding. A procession sets out from town carrying food and drink. In a field it circles in a clockwise direction three times. When the procession halts, a candle is lit, a food offering is made, and everyone eats. Wedding music is played and songs are sung.

Meanwhile the sacrifice priest slaughters and cooks a black steer to the *utəmə* (A.94.) at the edge of the cemetery, often outside the fence. After the procession has gone around all the fields of the village, it goes to the cemetery. There each person puts a candle on the fence in remembrance of the *utəmə* and asks the dead not to harm the crops. The meat of the steer is eaten; the bones and leftover meat are buried in the cemetery. The hide of the steer is cut into thin strips so that it can enclose the whole cemetery.

A sacrifice is not always performed; sometimes only a vow is made. To make a vow the oldest man in the village wraps a strip of linden bast around a tree dedicated to the *utəmə*. The number of times it is wrapped around indicates the number of years before the animal is to be sacrificed; it is always an uneven number. When the vow is fulfilled, the promise band is burned.

Sometimes an individual family is called on to make a sacrifice to the *utəmə* when mice get into the granary. Usually the head of the house finds a long strip of bast and wraps it around a tree in the cemetery nine times. The sacrifice is made at the end of the nine years. The procession goes around all the buildings on the farm and a black steer is sacrificed and eaten at the cemetery.

(H[1926], 41–43; H[1927], 68, 70; V, 231.)

B.23.8. *buingorka*

This is a memorial service for the dead.

(Sz, 288.)

For *toštə mari pajram*, see B.23.5.; *tubər čimə bodə*, B.8.1.; *tüńča ümbal kumalmə*, B.9.3.

B.24. *u kində pajram* 'new bread holiday'; *u pučeməš pajram* 'new porridge holiday'

A thanksgiving ceremony is held either at the end of the rye harvest or after all the grains have been harvested. At the end of the rye harvest, the head of each family prays over bread made from the new grain. When the ceremony takes place after all the work in the field is done, the head of the house, after having bathed, puts a little of each kind of grain and malt as well as cakes and beer made from them in a little bowl on the table; then bareheaded he carries the bowl into the yard. He holds it up to the sun and thanks the gods for the blessings he has received during the year.

(H[1926], 185–87; S, 186; V, 227.)

B.25. *u mü pajram* 'new honey holiday'

A yearly thanksgiving ceremony is performed in late summer after the honey is gathered. The worshipper lights a candle and prays to the bee god (A.26.28.) not to be angry if he has harmed the bees. He also prays that the bees be blessed. After the prayer he begins to eat the honey.

(B, 91; H[1926], 186.)

For *urlək pučeməš kečə*, see B.13.; *üdər uše*, B.27.; *utəm süan*, B.23.7.; *utəmələn pumaš*, B.23.7.; *jumə užatəmə*, B.8.6.

B.26. *ü arńa* 'butter week'

'Butter week' falls at Shrovetide. At this time the young people go sledding down hills scattering hempseeds and shouting, "May the hemp grow high." Boys also masquerade as *ü arńa kuba* and *kuguza* 'butter week old woman' and 'old man.' One wears men's clothes and a beard and blackens his face; the other wears women's clothes padding himself so as to protrude both in front and in back. The townspeople ask them if the grain will grow well in the coming year and they answer that it will. The older people spend the time eating, drinking, and telling stories. During this week they only work in the morning; on Thursday and Friday no work at all is done.

(B, 19; H, 191; J.)

For *üdər jumə*, see B.17.1.; *üdər šörasaš*, B.17.1.

B.27. *üdər uše* 'girl's holiday'

After work is finished in the fields in November, there is a holiday called *üdər uše*. Religious aspects of this holiday are minimized, generally being limited to songs asking for god's blessing. In some regions only women attend, but in others men also participate. The celebration is often a time when girls of marriageable age give a party for young men. Although all villagers are invited, the party is primarily an opportunity for young people to get better acquainted. The girls of a village organize a party, preparing beer, pancakes and other food; married women also contribute food. At the party the guests dance, play the gusle and bagpipes, improvise songs, play games, and tell stories. As is customary for most Cheremis celebrations the festivities last for two or three days. Reports of sexual license at this time have been refuted by Vasiljev.

This holiday has nationalistic overtones and its celebration is a manifestation of an attempt to preserve the old traditional way of life; as such, it is celebrated by Cheremis regardless of their religious beliefs. Some Russians living near Cheremis villages have taken over this holiday and celebrate it in much the same way as the Cheremis.

(Vasiljev[1915]; Zykov, 40–41.)

B.28. cow's milk feast

When a calf is born, friends and relatives of the owner are invited to participate in a ceremony in honor of *bol'ək šakčektšə* 'cattle fructifier' (A.82.2.). The head of the house pours water on the stove and prays that the calf grow to be the size of the stove. Those present are also sprinkled with water as a prayer is said that the cow give much milk. Standing next to a bowl of porridge mixed with butter, the host prays that the *bolək šačəktšə* give "as much cattle as there are hairs on the cow, so that one end of herd might be still on the road when the other has entered the cowshed."

(H[1926], 91; H[1927], 259; S, 188.)

B.29. fire ceremony

In the hottest part of the summer new fire is made to protect the people from the destruction of this time. On an appointed day all fires in a village are put out. A new fire is made by friction; the new fire is called *pu tul* 'wood fire' or *baštar tul* 'rubbing (?) fire.' People and livestock jump over the fire. To make it easier to drive the cattle over the fire, it is usually made at a gate; the gate is decorated with mountain ash boughs. From this fire, which often burns two or three days, the head of each house takes a firebrand with which he smokes out his cattle pens and lights the fire in his house. No prayer is said nor sacrifice made at this time.

(H[1926], 180–81; H[1927], 236–37.)

B.30.   frost spirits' ceremony

A ceremony dedicated to *pokšəm kuguza* and *kuba* 'frost old man' and 'old woman' (A.38.22.) is held in a meadow near town at the beginning of June. Most of the worshippers are young men. They wear their everyday clothes and do not put on new bast shoes as is customary for other religious ceremonies; they believe that their everyday clothes are good enough for the frost spirits. At the place of worship they make a fire and cook a large pot of porridge, the ingredients for which have been gathered in the village in the morning. Two priests stand next to each other and say the same prayer, one addressing *pokšəm kuguza* and the other *pokšəm kuba*. From time to time they lift up on high a bowl of porridge. At the end of the prayer the priests throw a few spoonfuls of porridge into the fire and pray the fire spirit (A.9.14.) to take the sacrifice to the frost spirits. The porridge is then poured out and the ceremony comes to an end.

(P, 204–6.)

B.31.   harvest

B.31.1.

When a man goes out to the field to reap, he cuts eight stalks and prays that his back will be as supple and flexible as the stalks. He fastens these in his belt; then his back will not hurt him no matter how hard he works.

At the beginning of the harvest, the first ears cut are put on the holy shelf in the *kudə* 'hut' (E.1.).

(B, 67; H[1926], 186; Uj[FB], 92.)

B.31.2.

At the end of the harvest the last stalks are either left standing or are cut on the same day of the week the harvest began. After the end of the harvest, the workers gather and throw the sickles back over their heads. Whoever's sickle falls away from the others will die soon.

(B, 67; H[1926], 186; J.)

B.32.   house building and dedication

As a house is being built coins are placed in three corners "so that the house will be wealthy." Copper coins are also struck against the ridgepole which is put into place quietly and carefully "so that noise and din do not come into the new house."

When a family moves into a new house, bread is taken from the old house to the new in the belief that the former good luck will come with it. Friends and relatives are invited to the dedication of the house. It is not clear whether the house itself or household spirits are being worshipped. When a Cheremis enters a new house, he prays for good health and good fortune for the inhabitants.

(H[1926], 52, 82.)

B.32.1.   new bathhouse ceremony

The first time a new bathhouse is heated, butter is put on the bench for *moča kuguza* 'bathhouse old man' (A.38.16.) so that the steam will be good.

(H[1926], 52.)

B.33.   naming ceremony

A Cheremis child is named twice. On the day of his birth a temporary name is given by the midwife. This is necessary lest the child die without and name and become an *obda* (A.51.). The child may be given a name similar to that of his parents or he may be named after the day on which he is born, especially if he is born on Thursday or Friday. There is no ceremony attached to this naming. Sometimes a child is named after the first person who comes to the house after the birth. It is considered to bring good luck if people come to visit after a child is born; the parents serve drinks to the visitors.

A second name is chosen later. Because a child's well-being may depend on the selection of the correct name, the aid of a priest (D.6.) or soothsayer (D.7.) is sometimes enlisted in choosing a name. He takes up the child while it is crying and, as he rocks it, says different names. The one at which the child stops crying is considered to be the proper name. In earlier times the soothsayer or priest said different names as he tried to strike a fire. The name that was said as the tinder caught fire was given to the child.

The midwife may be called on to select the name a few days after birth. If the child is a girl it is given a name similar to the mother's; if a boy, it is given a name similar to the father's. The midwife makes three loaves of rye bread and gives each a name. The loaves are baked in the oven and the name of the one which comes out best is given to the child.

Among Christian Cheremis the name is given by the godparent at baptism.
(H[1926], 194; Häm.[1945], 7–8; J; Müller, 365–66; Sebeok[1950c].)

B.34.   private sacrifices

In some places each adult man is expected to make a certain number of sacrifices during his life. This number varies from one to four according to the region. The first sacrifice is usually made when a boy reaches manhood. In one place the sacrifices are dedicated to *buj ümbal jumə* 'god over the head' (A.26.6.), *kugə pujəršə* 'great creator' (A.70.), *šočən aba* 'fructifier mother' (A.1.10.), and *ergə pujəršə* 'son creator' (A.70.4.). At each of these ceremonies not only must a large animal be sacrificed to the deity being worshipped but also additional animals to its helpers.

At the first one a horse is sacrificed to *buj ümbal jumə* 'head god' (A.26.6.), a cow to *jumən aba* 'god's mother' (A.1.2.), a heifer to *jumən piambar* 'god's prophet' (A.68.2.), a goose or duck to *jumən aš* (A.5.), a goose or duck to *jumən kaznači* 'god's treasurer' (A.29.1.), and a sheep to *jumən perke aba* 'god's blessing mother' (A.1.8.), a sheep to *jumən serlagəš* 'god's mercy' (A.78.2.), a duck to *jumən šerməčkəl kučən pušə* 'the one who gives holding god's reins' (A.72.), a duck to *jumən sakčə* 'god's angel' (A.84.8.), a goose to *jumən bitnəzə* 'god's reporter' (A.8.) and a duck to *jumən čes* 'god's provisions' (A.13.).

At the second sacrifice a foal is sacrificed to *kugə pujəršə* 'great creator' (A.70.), a heifer to *piambar* 'prophet' (A.68.), a sheep or duck to *perke aba* 'blessing mother' (A.1.8.), a goose or ram to *kaznači* 'treasurer' (A.29.), a duck to *sakčə* 'angel' (A.84.), a duck to *bitnəzə* 'reporter' (A.8.), and a duck to *serlagəš* 'mercy' (A.78.).

At the third ceremony a cow is sacrificed to *šočən aba* 'fructifier mother' (A.1.10.), a goose to *kečə aba* 'sun mother' (A.1.3.), a sheep to *perke aba* 'blessing mother' (A.1.8.), a sheep to *šočən aban šočənžə* 'fructifier mother's fructifier' (A.82.1.1.), a goose to *aš* (A.5.), a duck to *sakčə* 'angel' (A.84.), and a duck to *kaznači* 'treasurer' (A.29.).

At the fourth ceremony a foal is sacrificed to *ikšəbə* (or *ergə*) *pujəršə* 'child (or son) creator' (A.70.4.), a heifer to *piambar* 'prophet' (A.68.), a sheep to *perke aba* 'blessing mother' (A.1.8.), a ram to *serlagəš* 'mercy' (A.78.), a duck to *sakčə* 'angel' (A.84.), a goose to *aš* (A.5.), and a duck to *bitnəzə* 'reporter' (A.8.).

The priest who makes the sacrifices is chosen by the individual; he does not necessarily have the same priest for every sacrifice. If a person is a priest himself, he performs his own sacrifices. The first time a priest is asked to perform a ceremony he usually refuses and must be asked again. The *šinčan uššə* 'seer' (D.10.2.) may tell the person to get a new priest. In one region each man has a *tün kart* whom he greatly respects and calls *ača* 'father.' This man was the *buj pultəšəžə ača* at his wedding, the husband of the woman who placed the headdress of a married woman on his bride.

The sacrifice ceremony is similar to the *küsə* (B.9.). Lead is melted and cast over an ax blade or a frying pan; the resulting figure is hung on the sacrifice tree. All the animals are usually sacrificed under the same tree but the ceremony to *šočən aba* takes place under a different tree. The animal is tied to a tree and then slaughtered. A coin is put on the design in the middle of the sacrifice bread (C.2.1.). A horse's hide is burned, the other skins are kept for later use; formerly they were hung on trees. The meat is cooked and eaten in the grove; sometimes women help with the cooking. The meat left over is taken home and not used for a week. At the end of the week the *orńalək* feast is held. After that, leftover meat is eaten without ceremony, but the bones are burned.

Many poor people cannot afford these sacrifices and so make vows to sacrifice later. (Häm.[1908], 8–17; H[1926], 155–56.)

B.35.   purification of a spring

To purify a spring meal is gathered from all the villagers, cooked, and eaten at the edge of the spring. *Büt kuba* (A.1.1.) is pleased and gives good water.
(R, 206.)

B.36.   sowing

Before a man begins to sow he says a long prayer requesting that the crop be blessed.
(Up[FB], 36.)

C. SACRIFICES AND OTHER OFFERINGS

For *argamak*, see C.1.

C.1.   *purələk bol'ək* or *buj bol'ək* 'head live stock'

An animal sacrifice is the most important act of worship performed by the Cheremis. In addition to regular sacrifices (B.9., B.7.) made annually to gods and *keremets*, sacrifices may be required to avert a threatened misfortune or to abate some evil caused by a supernatural.

The more valuable the animal sacrificed, the greater the honor paid to the supernatural; consequently, a horse is the sacrifice most suitable for a god (A.26.) or a *keremet* (A.31.). A sacrifice horse is called *orgamak* (or *argamak*). As a rule, female animals are sacrificed to female spirits; the most common sacrifice to an *aba* 'mother' (A.1.) is a cow, although occasionally a mare is used. Bulls, oxen, sheep and rams are sacrificed to less important spirits such as a 'prophet' (A.68.) or a 'creator' (A.70.). Ducks and geese are sacrificed to minor spirits, usually those worshipped because of their association with a more important god or *keremet;* chickens are rarely sacrificed. Although a hare or grouse is sacrificed occasionally, wild animals and birds are not usually considered suitable. In a sheep fructifying ceremony (B.20.) an owl is killed. If nothing else is available a fish may also be sacrificed.

Ideally, only the finest animals may be used as sacrifices. Furthermore they must be just reaching maturity, never having been used for work or breeding purposes; sheep may not have been shorn. Horses and cattle are usually selected when not quite two years old. Fowl must have been hatched within the year and the females must not have begun to lay. Animals must be of just one color. Horses and cattle are usually brown, although occasionally white. Sheep and fowl are white. Black animals are sacrificed to earth spirits (A.1.5., A.9.10., A.67.11., A.68.8., A.84.14.).

Although certain types of animals are traditionally sacrificed, the selection of animals for a specific ceremony rests with the priests (D.6.) or seers (D.10.). Priests usually decide the sacrifices for the annual public ceremonies; seers are consulted when special sacrifices must be made. In the case of public ceremonies the choice of animals depends on the economic resources of the worshippers and the importance of the spirits to whom the sacrifices are made. Only one animal is sacrificed to each spirit; however, when a sacrifice is made to an important god or *keremet,* a number of smaller animals must also be sacrificed to the lesser spirits in its retinue. When many gods are worshipped at a *küsə* (B.9.), a great number of animal sacrifices are necessary.

Animals for public sacrifices are purchased only from Cheremis, not from Russians, Tatars, or people of other ethnic groups. Before a sacrifice money is collected from all the householders in the area. The head of each house considers it his duty to set aside and contribute willingly money for sacrifices. Money offered at the ceremony is also used to defray expenses. If this is not sufficient, a second collection may be taken up after the ceremony. The priest who selects the animal offers a fair price which the owner accepts without haggling.

The selection of a large animal is quite important and, only after several tests have been made, is it considered worthy to be sacrificed. An animal which shudders is believed to have been chosen by the god for which it is intended. If, during inspection, an animal shudders at sight or on being touched lightly, it is regarded as an especially good omen. A cloth is tied around the neck of the animal signifying that it has been chosen for a sacrifice. This cloth remains on the animal until it reaches the grove, where the cloth is removed and hung on a branch of the sacred tree. If, for some reason, the sacrifice does not take place, the animal is not slaughtered or sold. In some regions, as an animal is being led to a *mir* sacrifice (B.9.), people from villages along the way go out to meet the animal and ask the priest leading it to take it to the village grove and say a prayer there. In the grove where the sacrifice is to take place, three tests may be made to ascertain that the animal is acceptable to the god. Water is poured over the back of the animal; if the animal shudders, it is a sign that the god is pleased with the animal. It is also said that at this time the animal shakes off the impurity of human contact. If the animal does not shudder, the trial is repeated until it does. Failure of an animal to shudder is not always the fault of the animal; it may indicate that sacrifice utensils have not been placed properly or something else has been done wrong. If after seven or nine trials, depending on the region, the animal does not shudder, it is returned to its owner and another animal is sought. If there is no other animal immediately available, the ceremony may be delayed a day while another is found. An animal is not paid for until it has passed this test. Fowl are not usually subjected to this trial. Another way in which the supernatural's acceptance may be indicated is by the shape which molten pewter takes when poured into a pan or over an ax blade into a bowl of water. If the figure resembles an animal, it signifies the deity's acceptance. In the event of unfavorable results another figure is cast; however, the slightest resemblance to an animal is sufficient. When pieces are cut from a branch to make a *šuldəš* (F.19.) and to determine the acceptability of different parts of the sacrifice, one is also cut to see if the animal is acceptable. Only after the animal has passed these trials is it sacrificed. At less elaborate ceremonies the last two trials may be omitted.

In some places animals to be sacrificed are voluntarily given by individuals. Although they receive money offered by other worshippers in return, this is not regarded as a purchase since the donor selects the animal and the amount of money which he receives does not depend on the value of the animal.

In prayer the sacrifice animal is highly praised, being described as both silvery and shining. A horse is described as silver-tailed, silver-hoofed and having a shining coat and a shining mane. Bulls are called silver-horned and sheep silver-wooly.

All animal sacrifice rituals are similar although they vary in elaborateness. The most elaborate sacrifice ceremony is *küsə* (B.9.); others resemble this but are not usually as complete.

The language of the prayers seems to imply that the whole animal is offered; in reality, most of the meat is eaten by the worshippers. Only small pieces of meat, bones and inedible parts are offered to the supernatural, usually as a burnt offering, although offerings to earth spirits are buried. Uncooked meat is never offered. The soul (*čon*) of the animal is believed to go to the spirit world where it serves the supernatural for whom the sacrifice is made. The animal is butchered so that the bones are not broken.

The hide of a sacrificed horse is either burned or hung on the eastern part of a sacred tree. Cowhides and sheepskins are returned to the former owner or given to the priest. In some regions they are sold but in others this is not done lest they be defiled by foreigners.

Because worshippers are not always willing or able to make the prescribed sacrifice, substitutes are sometimes used. In some regions whole animals are not sacrificed but pieces of meat, heads, feet and organs purchased in a market are offered. In another place, gingerbread in the shape of animals is offered. The term *orgamak,* usually used for a sacrifice horse, is also applied to this substitute. Instead of a duck a small pike whose head resembles that of a duck may be used.

If an individuaul makes a vow to sacrifice an animal, hair or wool may be taken to the grove as an indication of his intentions. Other times a linden bast bridle, slightly smaller than the normal size, is hung on a sacrifice tree symbolizing the promised horse.

(Be, 735; Häm.[1908a], 7–10, 17; Häm.[1930a], 7; H[1926], 42, 46, 47, 50–51, 71–77, 90, 108–9, 120, 122, 125–28, 130–31, 150, 163, 167, 184–85, 188; H[1927], 263–64; J; Müller, 355–57, 361; P, 186, 194; S, 95–96, 174–78; Uj[FB], 8; V, 25, 36, 49, 147, 148, 157, 168, 193; Zykov, 27–28.)

For *tüp egərče,* see C.2.1.; *izə kində,* C.2.1.; *jošman pürə,* C.10.; *kača kində,* B.17.1.; *kap,* C.2.1.

C.2.   *kində* 'bread'

C.2.1.   *mamalək kində* or *mama kində* or *üjan šöran kində* 'buttery milky bread'; *šər kində* 'milk bread'

Bread is commonly used as an offering. It may be offered either alone or with other food. When an important animal sacrifice is made, bread is also offered. The number of loaves varies from region to region. Often nine loaves are made: one large loaf called *tüp egərče* 'root *egərče*' or simply *kugə kində* 'large bread,' and eight small loaves called *izə kində* 'small bread.' The bread is flat, round in shape and often unleavened. Ingredients for the bread are collected from all the households participating in the sacrifice. The bread is made in town by the priest who is to make the sacrifice or his assistant on the day before, or early on the morning of the sacrifice. Bread for different sacrifices is baked separately. Designs are made in the dough by the priest. These are made simply by pressing the tips of three fingers into the dough in the center and on the edge of each loaf; the design in the center is called *kap* 'body' and that on the edge *ner* 'nose.' In addition the large loaf has lines made by three fingers along the edge; the lines opposite the 'nose' are called *poč* 'tail' and those on the sides *šuldər* 'wing.' In this way the bread remotely resembles a bird. The bread is placed on the altar so that the 'nose' points toward the tree. The part of the bread in which the designs have been made is torn out and offered to the god; the rest is eaten by the worshippers. Five small loaves and the left half of the large loaf are used on the day of the sacrifice. The other three loaves and the right half of the large loaf are used when the *orolək* meat (C.12.3.) is eaten.

The term *mamalək kində* is used for bread brought to ceremonies by worshippers. The bread is placed on a table and later taken home at the close of the ceremony to be eaten.

(B, 43; Be, 710, 735; H[1926], 119, 134, 147, 165; Häm.[1908a], 17; J; P, 186, 190; V, 67, 235, 287.)

For *kača kində,* see B.17.1.

C.2.2.   *šokšə kində* 'warm bread'

This bread is used when a vow (B.16.) is made to a *keremet* (A.31.).

(H[1926], 162.)

C.2.3.   *ončəl tičmaš kində* 'unbroken bread before'

This term is used in prayers to designate bread brought to a ceremony by the worshippers. In some regions, the owner of the animal sacrificed at a *küsə* (A.9.) gives a loaf of bread to be placed on the altar. This bread, in contrast to the sacrifice bread (C.2.1.), is usually leavened.

(J; P, 190.)

C.3. *kogəl'ə* 'pie'

Pies are sometimes taken to religious ceremonies by the worshippers. Small pies are offered to supernaturals and eaten by the worshippers on Easter Day (B.8.5.). In some Christian communities, parents wishing to have their child baptized distribute small *kogəl'ə* in one of which there is a coin. The person who gets the tart with the coin becomes the child's godparent.

(Be, 704–6; H[1926], 191; J; P, 209; V, 82, 195.)

For *kugə kində*, see C.2.1.; *kugə ši sorta*, C.11.; *mamalək kində* or *mama kində*, C.2.1.

C.4. *melna* 'pancake'

Thin pancakes are commonly offered to supernaturals, especially at ceremonies such as *aga pajram* (B.2.) at which no animal sacrifice is made. Usually only a piece from each pancake is thrown into the fire as an offering, the rest is eaten by the worshippers.

(Häm.[1908a], 4; H[1926], 147–78; J.)

C.5. *munə* 'egg'

Eggs are closely associated with such spring ceremonies as *aga pajram* (B.2.), Easter (B.8.), and *sürem* (B.18.). At the *aga pajram* in one region eggs are given to the priest and exchanged by the worshippers. A young woman's egg is thrown over a tree three times; if it is caught, she will have good luck. An egg may be placed in a hole in a field for the earth to 'eat.' Eggs are boiled and colored at Easter. Eggs which have been offered to the dead at a memorial ceremony (B.8.3.4.) are later eaten by the living. Eggs are given to the young men who exorcise evil spirits.

(H[1926], 176; J; S, 106–7, 185; Wu, 28.)

C.6. *ńemer* 'porridge'

A porridge made of oat, rye, or wheat flour is often prepared as an offering. It may either be offered alone or with some other sacrifice. At an animal sacrifice *ńemer* is placed on the altar under the sacrifice tree and smeared on the stick (F.19.) which is bound to the tree. Some is also put into the bowl of food which is offered to the deity. Offerings of *ńemer* are also made by sick people to spirits which are believed to have caused the disease.

(H[1926], 118, 124, 133, 136, 165; J; V, 82.)

For *ner*, see C.2.1.

C.7. *oksa* 'money'

Money is often offered to a spirit. A coin is thrown into the spring for the 'water mother' (A.1.1.) the first time a Cheremis bride draws water at her husband's house. A washed coin is sometimes offered by an individual who is asking for something from a god. A silver coin representing the money to be spent in purchasing a sacrifice animal is put in a bag and hung in a storehouse when a vow (B.4., B.16.) is made. Sometimes a coin is put on the design on the bread (C.2.1.) at a sacrifice ceremony.

(Häm.[1908a], 4, 6, 17; H[1926], 162–63.)

C.7.1.   *mamalək oksa* or *mämäla oksa* or *mama oksa*

Money given by an individual to have a prayer said for him is designated by this term. This money is most often given at sacrifice ceremonies; those who do not attend the sacrifice may send their offering with one who does. A person offering money covers his hand with his sleeve or the end of his belt so that the coins are not defiled by human touch. The priest or his assistant also receives the money with his hand covered. The donor tells his name and the priest prays for him, mentioning him by name. Although there is no specified amount which must be contributed, the more coins a person gives, the greater blessing is asked for him. At the end of the prayer the priest lets the money fall onto a cloth spread out before the altar. The money is used to defray the costs of the ceremony.

(Be, 730, 731, 737; H[1926], 136–38; J; P, 196–97; V, 132.)

C.7.2.   *ona pu oksa* 'sacred tree money'

Copper coins lie buried under sacred trees. At the beginning of a sacrifice ceremony they are unearthed. A few coins are added and the money is reburied at the end of the ceremony.

(H[1926], 117, 144.)

For *ončəl tičmaš kində*, see C.2.3.; *orgamak*, C.1.; *orolək*, C.12.3.; *poč*, C.2.1.

C.7.3.   *nadər*

Money brought for a special intercession at a sacrifice to a *keremet* (A.31.) is called *nadər*.

(H[1926], 166.)

C.8.   *pučəməš* 'porridge'

A porridge of oatmeal or wheat meal is often used as an offering to supernaturals.

(H[1926], 73; J; V, 82, 314.)

C.9.   *pura* 'beer'

Libations of beer are often made to supernaturals. Sometimes when a vow to sacrifice an animal (B.4., B.16.) is made, malt is put in a bundle and hung in the storehouse or on the sacrifice tree. This represents the beer which will be offered at the promised sacrifice.

(Häm.[1908a], 4, 6; Häm.[1930a], 7; H[1926], 178.)

For *puralək bol'ək*, see C.1.

C.9.1.   *tašlama pura* 'tašlama beer'

Beer served to women after the Easter ceremony (B.8.5.1.) is called *tašlama pura*. *Tašlama* is said to mean a large round handleless wooden cup. The informant did not recognize this ceremony but says that *tašlama* is a Tatar word meaning 'don't throw it away'; this is said when beer is served to people indicating that they are to drink it all.

(Be, 706; J.)

C.10.   *jošman pürə* 'jošman mead'

Mead (*pürə*) or hydromel (*urba*) offered as a libation is called *jošman pürə* (*jošman* Chuvash 'pancake'). It is prepared by 'pure' village maidens. Bowls of mead are placed on the altar under the sacrifice tree. The number of bowls usually corresponds to the number of loaves of sacrifice bread (C.2.1.).

(H[1926], 118–19, 132, 148; P, 190; S, 101.)
For *pütün šəl,* see C.12.1.

C.11.   *sorta* 'candle'

Candles are burned at most Cheremis ceremonies. They are usually slender and about six or seven inches long; however, bundles of twenty to twenty-five candles are sometimes burned. Each worshipper brings one to three candles to a service.

All candles are handmade; at sacrifice ceremonies they are often made right in the grove itself. The worshipper uses a piece of wax which he has brought from home or buys from a beekeeper who sells it in little square pieces. He softens the wax in his hands or over the fire and then wraps it around flax or hemp fibers with his fingers. In prayer the candle is called *kugə ši sorta* 'great silver candle.'

Often there is a stand for candles but sometimes they are simply fastened to the edge of a bowl or sieve into which offerings are put.

When a vow to sacrifice (B.4.) is made, a little wax is put in a bag in a storehouse, symbolizing the candle to be burned when the vow is fulfilled.

(Bk, 58; Häm.[1908a], 4; Häm.[1936–37], 41–49; H[1926], 21, 117–18, 147; J; P, 195; Wu, 45.)

C.11.1.   *mama sorta* '*mama* candle'

Candles donated by individuals in order to have an intercessory prayer said for them are called *mama sorta.*

(P, 186, 196–97.)
For *šuldər,* see C.2.1.

C.12.   *šəl* 'meat'

C.12.1.   *pütün šəl* 'whole meat'

This term is used for meat from a sacrifice animal which is put on a piece of linden bark and hung on the firestand (F.8.) at the end of a sacrifice.

(V, 169.)

C.12.2.   *šübə šəl* '*šübə* meat'

This term is used for certain pieces of meat of a sacrificed animal which are cooked apart from the rest of the meat. All this meat is sometimes called *šübələk* and the term *šübə šəl* is reserved for smaller pieces of it which are offered to the supernatural. The pieces of meat which make up the *šübə šəl* are not the same in every region although they represent in general all parts of the animal's body. For example, the *šübə šəl* of a horse may consist of the part around the nose and mouth, the tongue, the brain, the throat, the back of the neck, the breastbone, the heart, the shoulders, five ribs from the right side and three from the left, the meat from both haunches, pieces from the hind knees, the stomach, the liver, the kidney and the intestine. The *šübə* meat of a duck may consist of pieces from the heart, liver, windpipe, neck, breast, back, wings and feet. Little pieces from each part are put into two bowls and thrown into the fire as an offering to the supernatural being worshipped and to the fire spirit (A.9.14.). A little slice of each is put on a stick and fastened to the sacred tree. Places from the *šübə* meat of a large animal are put aside to be offered later. The rest of the *šübə šel* is distributed to be eaten by the worshippers.

(Be, 727; H[1926], 130, 164, 185; P, 195–96.)

For *ši sorta*, see C.11.

C.12.3.   *orolək*

Sometimes pieces of the *šübə šəl* (C.12.2.) are set aside to be offered later. This may take place on the same day as the sacrifice, on the next day in the grove, or even later at home. Small pieces of the *orolək* meat are offered to the deity to whom the animal was sacrificed and the rest is eaten. In one place the meat is kept for a week at home before it is used. After that it may be eaten but care must be taken not to drop it and the bones must be burned. If the meat is from an animal sacrificed by an individual to a *keremet* (A.31.), the meat brought home must not be eaten by anyone except family members.

(H[1926], 132, 155, 166–67; Häm.[1908a], 17.)

For *šər kində*, see C.2.1.; *šokšə kində*, C.2.2.; *ońčəl tičmaš kində*, C.2.3.; *tüp egərče*, C.2.1.; *urba*, C.10.; *üjan šöran kində*, C.2.1.

D. RELIGIOUS FUNCTIONARIES

For *ar binə*, see B.17.3.; *agul töra*, D.6.; *izi beŋə*, B.17.3.; *kugə beŋə*, B.17.3.; *bošt ušə*, D.10.2.; *modəš buj*, B.17.3.; *süan buj*, B.17.3.; *buj pulčešə*, B.17.3. and B.17.7.; *burgəm šubuš kondešə*, B.17.3.; *čabən čišə mari*, B.17.4.; *čaza korka kučəzə*, B.17.1.; *čaza küčəš batə*, B.17.4.; *izi beŋə*, B.17.3.; *izi truška*, B.17.3.

D.1.   *burgem cišə jeŋ* 'person dressed in clothes'; *kolšə olmeš šińčəš* 'one who sits in the place of the dead'

At the memorial feast forty days after a person's death (B.23.3.), someone, often his best friend, plays the role of the dead person, putting on the shirt, coat, cap and shoes of the deceased. He is treated as if he were the dead person come back to life. He is shown every courtesy, seated in the place of honor, served food and drink, and called by the name of the deceased. Sometimes he is taken out to inspect the farm. In some places, he dances alone to the music of the bagpipe as others kneel holding candles. He tells the living about life in the other world and admonishes them to live in peace and harmony. At dawn, accompanied by the others, he sets out for the cemetery. Along the way he takes off the clothes of the dead person and resumes his own identity.

(H[1926], 32–34; Wt, 65–66; Wu, 50–52.)

For *koštšə jeŋ*, see D.5.; *jomze*, D.2.4.

D.2.   *juzə* or *jozə* 'sorcerer'

A person who can cause trouble by supernatural means is greatly feared by the Cheremis. Sorcerers, in contrast to seers (D.10.) and soothsayers (D.7.), bring about misfortune, illness, and death to men and cattle. Both men and women may be sorcerers.

(R, 297; Sz, 59; Wu, 67–68, 73.)

D.2.1. *loktəzə* or *loktəlšə* 'spoiler'; *tušman batə* 'enemy woman'; *koldun* 'sorcerer'

A sorcerer who spoils the health and well-being of others is called 'spoiler' or 'enemy'; sometimes the Russian term *koldun* is also used. It is said that "a destroyer is human, but his soul (*čon*) is a devil (A.16.)." A sorcerer can change himself into an animal at will. He also can travel about in the wind causing people harm.

In the spring a sorcerer can cast a spell so that people and cattle will waste away and die. On the Wednesday or Thursday before Easter he goes about secretly collecting bits of clothing and hair with which to work contagious magic. On the Wednesday before *semək* (B.13.) he goes alone or with another sorcerer to a fir tree in the forest where the spell is cast. The things which the sorcerer has collected are used in one of the following ways: they are buried under the tree, thrown into a spring, or carried between the sorcerer's teeth as he climbs to the top of the fir tree. If he has a companion, the companion remains below and asks, "What hurts?" The sorcerer climbs down the tree head first shouting that various parts of his body hurt. Each part that he mentions begins to bother those from whom he took something. They become sick and die within a few years. In a similar manner this spell affects cattle from whom hair has been taken. Some believe this spell is effective because the devil (A.16.) hears the sorcerer and causes the illness.

(B, 18; Bk, 122; G, 58 [149]; H[1926], 54, 195; Uj[FB], 3; Up[FB], 30; Wu, 67–68, 73.)

D.2.2. *pošarəšə* 'presser'

A sorcerer who 'presses' and causes people to have nightmares is called a 'presser.' Discomfort caused by supernaturals is sometimes called 'pressing,' as, for example, when the 'cold old man' (A.38.11.) attacks drunks on the street, or *šürem* 'old woman' (A.38.27.) causes a person to become sick. 'Pressing' may result in death.

(J; Wu, 73.)

D.2.3. *vedən* 'sorcerer'

This sorcerer who can assume the shape of an animal is feared by the Cheremis.

(H[1926], 195; V, 46.)

D.2.4. *jomze* 'sorcerer'

(Sz, 56.)

D.2.5. *köräza* 'sorcerer'

(Sz, 88.)

For *jüktulš*, see D.6.; *kakunə ača* and *aba*, B.17.7.; *kart*, D.6.; *pel kart*, B.17.3. and D.6.; *süan kart*, B.17.3.; *tün kart*, B.17.3.

D.3. *kaznači* 'treasurer'

A man is appointed to act as treasurer for a public sacrifice. During the ceremony he sits in a tent at the edge of the sacred grove and counts money collected from the worshippers. He is later called on to render an account of all the money collected.

(H[1926], 109, 115.)

For *kəɲər buj mužetšə*, see D.7.1.; *kit sär palašə*, D.7.2.; *koldun*, D.2.1.; *uššə kolšə* or *ulšə kolšə*, D.10.2.; *kolšə olmeš šiṅčəš*, D.1.; *burgəm šubuš kondəšə*, B.17.3.

D.4.   *korka kondəštšə* 'bowl bringer'

This name is given to eight men who, under the direction of the priest, make libations to nature gods and spirits at a *küsə* ceremony (B.9.).

(H[1926], 14.)

D.5.   *koštšə jeŋ* 'traveling person'; *koštošo* 'traveler'

Those designated to buy animals for a *mer küsə* ceremony (B.9.) are called *koštšə jeŋ*. Before they set out to select an animal they bathe and put on white holiday clothes.

Those sent to announce in all the villages that a large public sacrifice is to be held carry a linden stick on which is carved the mark of the dream seer (D.10.1.). This stick is a symbol that they are authentic *koštošo* and not impostors.

(H[1926], 108; S, 129.)

For *kokla koššə*, see B.17.1.; *čaza korka kučəžə*, B.17.1.; *kokla koššə*, B.17.1.; *oṅčəč koššə*, B.17.1.; *köräza*, D.2.5.; *čaza korka kučəžə*, B.17.1.; *kugə beŋə*, B.17.3.; *kuguza*, D.6.; *čaza küčəš batə*, B.17.4.; *loktəzə* or *loktəlšə*, D.2.1.; *modəš buj*, B.17.3.

D.6.   *molla; kart; kuguza* 'old man'; *jüktülš*

Public and sometimes private ceremonies are conducted by men called priests. Among the Eastern Cheremis the term *molla* is used; other Cheremis call the priest *kart* or *kuguza;* an eighteenth century account calls him *jüktülš*. Each village has at least one priest, but often there are several. A priest is not set apart from the other members of the community in any way and wears no symbol of his office. He is self-supporting, receiving little or no remuneration for his services as priest. On the death or retirement of a priest, the remaining priests or the older men of the village select a successor. If there is any disagreement, the majority rules. Sometimes a dream interpreter (D.10.1.) selects the new priest. Often an old priest grooms a successor by having him act as his assistant during ceremonies. A priest is usually chosen while still a young man in his twenties, and functions as such until he dies or gets too old to perform his duties. The qualifications for a priest are an upright life in the eyes of the community and a good memory for remembering long prayers. During the time when the influence of the Russian Church was strong, nominal Christianity was not necessarily a hindrance to becoming a priest.

Since there is no centralized authority nor written records, priests have the responsibility of maintaining unchanged the religious traditions. When more than one priest officiates at a ceremony, the priests hold a council beforehand to reach an agreement as to the ritual to be followed. Priests also set the date for ceremonies and decide which gods and spirits are to be worshipped and what kind of animals are to be sacrificed.

It is customary for each sacrifice at a ceremony to be performed by a different person; therefore, there must be as many priests as there are sacrifices. Priests are often ranked according to seniority; older and more experienced priests are usually considered to be better than younger men. The chief priest is usually the oldest or most capable of the priests; sometimes he is elected by the other priests. Terms for chief priest are *kugə kart* 'big priest,' *tüŋ kart* 'source priest,' *kugə molla* 'big priest,' and *agul töra* 'village chief'; other priests are called *izə kart* 'small priest' or *pel kart* 'half priest.' The chief priest conducts public ceremonies at which only one priest is necessary and at other public ceremonies he performs all sacrifices to the 'great god' (A.26.). If there are two chief priests, they alternate in performing their duties. The rank of other priests is reflected in the importance of the deity to which they sacrifice. In one place the lowest ranking priest is the one who sacrifices to *tüńća ümbal kugə šukćə* (A.82.21.). When a new priest is chosen, he does not take the rank of his predecessor but starts at the bottom and other priests each move up one place. A priest may have an assistant (D.11.) and other helpers who make articles to be used during the ceremony, bring wood and water, butcher the sacrifice animal, cook the meat, and attend to other such matters.

During a prayer the priest stands while others kneel behind him. Although he dresses no differently from other worshippers, he may wear his cap while praying whereas the others are all bareheaded.

An individual may enlist the services of a priest for a private sacrifice. When he asks the priest to perform a sacrifice, the priest usually declines at first and only consents after repeated requests. An individual does not always use the same priest; a seer (D.10.) may even advise him to use a different priest.

(Be, 735; Häm.[1908a], 10; Häm.[1930a], 7; H[1926], 113–14, 116, 150–51; H[1927], 264–65; J; Müller, 354; P, 183–85, 189, 193; P[1948], 145; S, 130, 182–83.)

D.7.   *mužetšə* or *mužedəšə* or *mužan marə* 'soothsayer'

A highly respected member of the Cheremis community is a man or woman who is believed to be able to foretell the future. A soothsayer usually predicts future events or learns information not available by natural means through the manipulation of certain objects. Some soothsayers use beans or nuts. According to one account a soothsayer puts forty-one beans on a table one by one. As he moves them about, he watches them closely. After quite a while he supplies information as to the time, place, and animal to sacrifice to an angry spirit which has been causing some misfortune. Another soothsayer may put a piece of bread and a coal at opposite ends of a board; from the movement of an object hanging above, the soothsayer can find out whatever information is desired. Some put a piece of bread on their finger tips, believing that it turns around as they attempt to find out something. Soothsayers may also look at cards, read palms, and look into people's eyes.

In regions where the health and well-being of a child are believed to depend on its name, a soothsayer selects an auspicious name. While the baby is crying, the soothsayer takes it in his lap and rocks it as he says different names. The name at which the child stops crying is believed to be propitious. In the past there was also another means of selecting a name; the soothsayer said different names as he tried to strike a fire. The name said when the fire caught was given to the child.

Simple predictions can be made by people without special training or ability. For example, a person can learn the answer to a question for which there are two alternatives by trying to make his forefingers meet without looking at them. If the fingers meet, the answer is favorable; if not, unfavorable.

(Bk, 122; Häm.[1908a], 3–4; H[1926], 193–94; J; Müller, 348–50; R, 207; Sz, 131; Uj[T], 49; Wu, 73.)

D.7.1.   *kəńər buj mužetšə* 'elbow soothsayer'

A soothsayer who diagnoses illnesses by measuring is called *kəńər buj mužetšə*. It is believed possible, by measuring certain parts of the body of a sick person, to determine whether his illness is increasing or decreasing. The circumference of the head or the distance between the elbow and the tip of the middle finger is measured three times. The measurements are compared and, depending on whether the distance seemed to get smaller or larger, the illness will increase or decrease. Anyone can do this type of measuring but some are more skilled than others.

(Häm.[1908a], 3–4; H[1926], 194–95; Müller, 350.)

D.7.2.   *kit šer paləšə* 'one who knows the pulse'

A soothsayer who takes the pulse of a sick person can tell whether the person will live or die. He also finds out in this way what kind of offering should be made for the patient's recovery. In one district a strong pulse beat means that the 'mountain old man' (A.21.2.1.) wishes a horse sacrificed.

(Bk, 55; H[1926], 194.)

For *oma uššə* or *omanče, see* D.10.1.; *ončač košša,* B.17.1.; *ončəlnə šogəšə* or *ončač šogəšə,* B.17.4.; *pel kart,* B.17.3., D.6.; *pošarəšə,* D.2.2.

D.8.   *sorta puedešə* 'candle distributer'

A 'candle distributer' functions as a priest at memorial services for the dead (B.8.3.2., B.23.). He lights a candle and says a prayer to the spirits of the other world (A. 90., A.76.5.) and to the dead. The head of the family stands beside him and supplies the name of each dead member of the family so that the 'candle distributer' can mention by name each person for whom a candle is lit.

(Häm.[1936–37], 46–49.)

For *buj pulčešəč,* see B.17.3. and B.17.7.; *puraš mari* and *batə,* B.17.3.; *putləzə,* B.17.1.; *püraš,* B.17.3.; *sabus,* B.17.3.; *sagus,* B.17.3.; *saus,* B.17.3.; *süan batə,* B.17.3.; *süan buj,* B.17.3.; *süan kart,* B.17.3.; *süan mari,* B.17.3.; *svaga batə,* B.17.3.; *šarbots,* B.17.4.; *šińča uššə* or *šińčan uššə,* D.10.2.; *kolšə olmeš šińčeš,* D.1.; *ončəlnə šogəše* or *ončač šogəšə,* B.17.4.; *burgəm šubuš kondəšə,* B.17.3.

D.9.   *šübedəšə* 'spitter'

A person who works magic by means of charms (cf. Part Two: "Charms") is called a 'spitter' because, as he says a charm, he sometimes spits or blows. He may also spit on butter or salt which is then used as medicine. Burns and scratches which do not heal readily are rubbed with the butter; the salt is taken internally. Water into which such a healer spits is used both internally and externally.

When a child's *ört* 'soul' leaves its body through fright, a charm is said over the child; at the same time tin is poured over the child's head. The *šübedəšə* foretells the child's future from the shape the tin takes as it hardens. This tin figure is later hung around the child's neck.

If a charm works the patient sleeps; if it doesn't, someone else may try to say a charm. (B, 18; H[1926], 195; J; Up[FB], 38; Wu, 73.)

For *taklar mari,* see B.17.3.; *truška,* B.17.3.; *üdər truška,* B.17.4.; *tular mari,* B.17.1.; *tušman batə,* D.2.1.; *agul töra,* D.6.; *tüṅ kart,* B.17.3. and D.6.

D.10.   *uššə* 'seer'

When a Cheremis has to deal with the supernatural, he often goes to a seer who tells him which spirit is the cause of his difficulty and advises him as to what offering should be made. In areas influenced by Christianity, seers are asked to decide whether an offering should be made to a pagan supernatural or to the Christian God and saints. Cheremis seers have also been consulted by Russians who believed that they could enlist the aid of spirits. A seer may be either male or female and is usually old. (H[1926], 47–48, 71, 76, 89, 193; Zykov, 9, 23–24.)

D.10.1.   *omə uššə* 'dream seer'; *omənčə* 'dreamer'

An old man or woman who interprets dreams is highly respected in a Cheremis community. In addition to interpreting the dreams of others, a dream seer receives special revelations himself; it is believed that his *ört* goes into the spirit world when he is in a trance. He may also convey the message of a deity who wishes a sacrifice. In some places he is called on to select someone to fill a vacancy in the priesthood. His help is sometimes enlisted to determine the cause of an illness which has no obvious explanation. To do this the seer sleeps with his head on an article that has been in contact with the sick person. The seer is also consulted when cattle are sick or lost, the crops are bad, or other misfortunes occur. He usually indicates the offerings which must be made and to which spirits; spirits most often requiring offerings are the *kudə* spirit (A.9.8.), *keremet*s (A.3.1.) and the dead. (Bk, 54; H[1926], 7, 113, 192–93; S, 129.)

D.10.2.   *šinča uššə* 'eye seer'; *šinčan uššə* 'eyed seer'; *bošt uššə* 'through seer'; *uššə kolšə* or *ulšə kolšə* 'seer hearer'

A seer of this type sees things 'with his eyes' rather than in dreams. He can tell everything about a person's past, present and future. He also has means of learning the disposition of gods and spirits. The way in which a seer receives this information is by looking at a highly polished coin, water, vodka, or a mirror (sometimes a candle is placed on top of the mirror). In addition to simply telling fortunes, a seer is consulted to find out who has stolen something or who is at fault in a dispute. A seer of this type is also consulted in case of illness; he tells which spirit has caused the illness and what kind of offering must be made to appease it. He may also tell a person to find a different priest to perform the sacrifice. If he knows that a person is to die, he tells the relatives not to bother sacrificing. Sometimes a seer is consulted in matters of public interest such as choosing a priest, setting a date for a sacrifice or selecting the deities to whom sacrifices should be made.

Gypsies who travel through the countryside are often skilled at fortunetelling.

(B, 18; Häm.[1908a], 3–4, 8, 10; H[1926], 193; J; Sz, 221; Uj[FB], 4, 78; Up[FB], 31; Usj[FB], 8.)

D.11.   *utšə* 'assistant'

Each priest may have an assistant who helps him during a sacrifice. His duties vary from region to region. When actively assisting a priest, he may stand and wear his cap during a prayer; at other times he kneels bareheaded during prayers as do the other worshippers.

(H[1926], 114, 165–66; P, 192; S, 183.)

For *ü arńa kuguza* and *kuba*, see B.26.; *üdər truška*, B.17.4.; *vedən*, D.2.3.

E. SACRED PLACES

For *aga pajram olmə*, see E.4.; *asaba*, E.2.2.; *sürem puč kudaltəmə ber*, E.3.; *izə kudə*, E.1.; *jal küs otə*, E.2.1.; *jumən pusak*, E.7.; *jumən otə*, E.2.1.; *keremet*, E.2.2.

E.1.   *kudə* 'hut'

A *kudə* is a rectangular, one-room, windowless log hut. Inside there is a fireplace in the center of the earthen floor and a smoke hole above in the roof. In earlier times this hut was the Cheremis dwelling and the term *kudə* is still often used to mean 'home.' The *kudə* has been supplanted by a different type of dwelling (*pört*), but in some regions it is still used as a storehouse and as a summer cookhouse (see Introduction).

The part of the *kudə* opposite the door has in the past been reserved for religious purposes. A possible present-day trace of this is the fact that the table, which is in a farther corner in the house, is near the door in the *kudə*. Another significant fact is that benches are built along both sides in the *kudə* but not along the back wall as they are in the house. Across the back wall there is sometimes a shelf on which tools and cooking utensils are stored. This shelf may also be used for religious purposes. In some places the shelf on which religious objects are placed is called *kudə bodəž toja* 'hut spirit stick.' A round or rectangular box (F.6.) may be placed in a corner. Sometimes there are only withered birch leaves near offerings placed in the corner. In one *kudə* in Birsk there was only a paperbag fastened with a birch twig. In most huts there is no longer a box, but the corner shelf continues to be considered sacred. Guests are not permitted to sit near it lest some misfortune overtake them. Children and women also avoid approaching it. In some regions a partition to protect this holy place is built around one corner or across the back of the hut. This closet is called *izə kudə* 'little hut.' Into this little room there is a small door through which only adult men may pass; furthermore they only enter when there is a valid reason for doing so. In olden times tools and equipment were kept in the 'little hut.' Vows were made in there and ceremonial objects to be used during the promised sacrifice were also kept there. Legends relate that the *izə kudə* had an outside exit so that if the hut were attacked, the family could escape by the rear door.

Offerings to *kudə bodəž* 'hut spirit' (A.9.8.) are placed on the holy shelf or in the box. The first ears of grain harvested, for example, are put on the holy shelf.

Even after leaving home members of a family may remain dependent to a certain degree on their childhood *kudə*. A newly married woman returns to make offerings to her parents' *kudə*. Grown sons who have established their own homes sometimes return to worship in the *kudə* of their parents.

In regions where the *kudə* is no longer used, the site of a former *kudə* is respected because the 'hut spirit' is believed to dwell there still. To defile such a spot would be to invite illness sent by this spirit. Some Cheremis who no longer have a *kudə* keep a sacred box in the storehouse or in the entrance to the bathhouse.

(Be, 43; Häm.[1908a], 4, 6; H[1926], 44–49, 186; Heikel, 8–18; J; Ränk[1949–51], 109–17; Ränk[1949], 87–97; S, 84, 122; Uj[FB], 5.)

For *küs otə* or *küs olmə* or *küšəl otə*, see E.2.1.; *mer küs otə*, E.2.1.; *nasəl otə*, E.2.1.; *aga pajram olmə* or *selək olmə*, E.4.; *omaš*, E.2.1.

E.2.   *otə* 'grove'

Sacrifice ceremonies are usually conducted in groves which have been set aside for this purpose. Groves vary in size from a few trees to a forest. Within the grove a tree is dedicated to each god or spirit to whom sacrifices are regularly made. A fence or an open space separates a grove from the surrounding fields; groves are frequently located on a rise of land. There is at least one grove near almost every Cheremis village. If a man sets up his household far away from any established village, he may start a new grove by planting a few trees and dedicating them to deities. Groves are held in great respect even by those who are religiously indifferent.

There are two kinds of groves: those in which trees are dedicated to gods and nature spirits, and those in which trees are dedicated to *keremet*s (A.31.). In some places, all supernaturals are worshipped in one large grove. In such a case fir trees dedicated to "lower" spirits are located in the northern or western part of the grove, and those to "upper" spirits in the eastern and southern parts. Some groves are used by the whole community; others are restricted to one family or clan.

If, by chance, a sacred grove has been defiled, an expiatory sacrifice must be made. A live goose or chicken is cut to death in the grove and thrown into the fire; at the same time the vengeance of god is called down, "may you find and punish with a similar death the sacrilegious person who cut the tree."

(Be, 735; H[1926], 100–104, 107, 115–16; J; P, 185, 189; S, 128, 181; V, 92, 148.)

E.2.1.   *küs otə* '*küs* grove'; *küs olmə* '*küs* place'; *küšel otə* 'upper grove'; *jumən otə* 'god's grove'

Although the term *küs otə* is used for any sacred grove in some regions, it is usually applied only to the groves in which sacrifices are made to 'upper' deities, i.e., gods and nature spirits which are believed to live above the earth. *Küsə* ceremonies (B.9.) are held in these groves—usually quite large and sometimes unfenced. If there is a fence it often has several gates. In one place there were gates on the east, west, and south sides; worshippers entered from the east, sacrifice animals from the west, and water was brought in from the south. Groves are often located near streams, the water of which is used for bathing and ceremonial purposes. There is a *küs otə* near almost every Cheremis village.

A *küs otə* is made up largely of deciduous trees of which only lindens, oaks and birches are sacred trees (F.15.). These trees are about fifty feet apart and form an arc from east to south. The easternmost tree is usually dedicated to 'great god' (A.26.); sometimes this god's tree is preceded by one dedicated to its angel (A.84.8.). Trees dedicated to other gods and spirits are in the order in which sacrifices are made at the *küsə* ceremony. Those dedicated to earth spirits are sometimes located in the northern part of the grove. In some groves each family in the community has one or more sacred trees for private sacrifices. In some regions there is a shelter (*omaš*) in case of rainy weather for priests who spend the night in the grove during *mer küsə* ceremony. In some places the building has been enlarged to accommodate up to fifty worshippers who have come from a distance and are unable to return home at night.

A *küs otə* is respected but not feared. When a ceremony is being held people do not enter a grove without having bathed and put on clean clothes. At other times, however, they may hunt, gather berries, and collect firewood. Nevertheless, trees are not felled nor branches broken within a grove.

A *küs otə* may serve a village, a sacrifice district, or several such districts; groves are designated accordingly *jal küs otə* 'village *küs* grove,' *mer küs otə* 'sacrifice district *küs otə*,' or *tüñča küs otə* 'world *küs* grove.' A grove belonging to a family is called *nasəl otə* or *tukəm otə;* such a grove is often named after its owner or founder, e.g., *pli otə* 'Pli's grove.'

(Be, 735; H[1926], 7, 18, 100–104, 107, 111, 113, 115–16; H[1927], 262; P, 185, 189; S, 128–30, 180–82; V, 92, 131, 148.)

For *šelək otə*, see E.4.

E.2.2.   *üləl tüle küs otə* '*küs* grove of the lower blessing'; *üləl otə* 'lower grove'; *ülkə kumalmə küs otə* 'downward praying *küs* grove'; *keremet; asaba*

Groves dedicated to *keremet* spirits (A.31.) are smaller than groves dedicated to gods and are almost always enclosed by a fence. Fir trees are preferred in a *keremet* grove in contrast to deciduous trees for an "upper" grove. A *keremet* grove is greatly feared by the Cheremis and never entered except for religious purposes. They even avoid speaking about it. Women may not enter it and avoid looking at it when passing by. Only Cheremis may be spoken in or near such a grove because *keremet* spirits dislike foreign tongues. A *keremet* grove is especially to be feared late in the evening.

Some Cheremis villages have no *keremet* groves, but others have several. Some groves are owned by families; such a grove may be named after its founder, e.g., *oskan kašak otə* 'Oskan family grove.' A family having its own grove does not worship in the grove of another family; nevertheless, an individual may belong to two such families and thus be entitled to worship in two such groves. Some *keremet* groves, although serving the whole community, may have a different tree for each family.

(H[1913], 125; H[1926], 100–103, 159–60, 174; Müller, 345; Sz, 152; V, 233.)

For *jumən pusak,* see E.7.

E.3.   *sürem puč kudaltəmə ber* '*sürem* horn discarding place'

After an exorcism ceremony (B.18.) prayers are said and horns are thrown away at this place where the *sürem* tree is located outside the village.

(Häm.[1925], 109; H[1926], 181–82.)

E.4. *šelək* or *šelək otə* 'šelək grove'; *selək olmə* 'selək place'; *aga pajram olmə* 'plowing ceremony place'

These terms are used for an uncultivated field on the edge of town where people meet to pray. Sometimes there are a few deciduous trees but often it is an open meadow. *aga pajram* (B.2.) and other religious ceremonies are held here. This area is not fenced as are sacrifice groves (E.2.). The *sürem* tree (B.18.) may be located here.

The term *šelək* or *šilek* is also used for a rough shelter erected for a wedding. It is a foursided structure of roughly hewn logs; one of the sides is open to permit people to enter and leave freely. Inside are benches and two tables from which food and drinks are served to the guests. A structure of this type may be erected not only at the groom's and the bride's home but also at any other place the wedding party is entertained.

(Be, 707, 734–35; Bk, 66; Häm.[1915], 124, 128; Häm.[1930], 74, 78, 87; H[1926], 99, 176; J; S, 120; V, 287.)

E.5. *šügarla* 'cemetery'

Most Cheremis villages have their own cemeteries but occasionally a cemetery may be shared by two or more villages. A cemetery is usually located in a fenced grove a short distance from town. A cemetery may be easily distinguished from a sacrifice grove (E.2.) by cloths and pieces of clothing which are hung on the trees. On the ground, often outside the enclosure, sleighs in which a corpse has been carried and pieces of wood left over from the boards used to make the coffin are left to rot. Some graves are marked by man-like figures; others are enclosed by a fence; at some graves a shelter is erected. In the eastern regions a cuckoo is put on a long pole near graves; some Cheremis believe that the bird entertains the dead.

(H[1926], 17, 21–22; J.)

For *kudə bodəž toja*, see E.1.; *tukəm otə*, E.2.1.; *tüñča küs otə*, E.2.1.; *üləl tüle küs otə, üləl otə, ülkə kumalmə küs otə*, E.2.2.

E.6. *t'ablo*

The shelf on which the holy image is kept is called *t'ablo*.
(S, 86.)

E.7. holy corner

As do many peoples of northeastern Europe, the Cheremis regard a rear corner of the house or *kudə* (E.1.) to be sacred. A corner of the *kudə* may be dedicated to the 'hut spirits' (A.9.8.) and offerings may be placed there. Women, children and unrelated men are not permitted to go near this corner. In some places a corner is partitioned off from the rest of the hut so that there will be no danger of breaking the taboo accidentally.

A back corner of the house has also become a sacred place. Offerings and candles are put there and vows are sometimes made there. Icons are also kept in the holy corner which is then called *jumən pusak* 'god's corner.'

The holy corner may be either on the left or the right. The informant says icons are not placed on the north side. This is significant considering the fact that the north has been traditionally associated with *keremet* (A.31.) and other spirits regarded as living in the earth.

(Häm.[1908a], 6; H[1926], 44–49; J; Heikel, 8–18; Ränk[1949–51], vol. 1, 109–17; Ränk[1949], 87–97; Sz, 86; Wu, 41.)

E.8.

There is sometimes a special place for holding the *aga kurman* ceremony (B.1.). One such place is an unfenced part of a birch grove.

(H[1926], 99.)

F. CEREMONIAL OBJECTS

In many regions ceremonial vessels are no different from those used for ordinary cooking purposes. In some places it is customary to burn all wooden objects at the end of a ceremony. Among the western Cheremis sacrifice utensils are often decorated. Sometimes bird-like designs are carved on the handles of sacrifice bowls and silver coins are fastened to the bottom. That ceremonial vessels were more valuable in earlier times is indicated by the fact that the Russian Church came into possession of a copper pot and a silver ladle formerly used in pagan Cheremis ceremonies.

(H[1926], 149.)

For *aba kumdar,* see B.17.1.; *baštar tul,* B.29.

F.1.   *bulnə* 'tin'

Before a horse or steer is sacrificed a tin or pewter figure is cast in an attempt to find out whether the animal is acceptable to the deity for whom it is intended. Frequently this figure is cast in the sacred grove (E.2.). Molten metal is poured into a frying pan, onto an ax blade, or over an ax blade into a bowl of water. At the same time a prayer is said asking the god to indicate its acceptance of the animal by causing the pewter figure to take the form of the animal as it solidifies. If the figure can in any way be construed to resemble the animal, it is accepted as proof that the deity is pleased with the sacrifice. If it does not look like an animal, another figure is cast. This metal figure may be cast either when the animal is taken from its owner or, more frequently, during the sacrifice ceremony. This animal-like figure is later tied to a sacred tree (F.15.); sometimes it is temporarily placed on the sacrifice bread on the altar before it is tied to the tree.

A tin figure is also cast as a means of telling whether a sick child will recover. The figure is later hung around the child's neck.

(B, 713; Häm.[1908a], 17; H[1926], 120–21, 150, 195; S, 175.)

For *čaza korka oksa,* see B.17.1.; *izə ona pu,* F.15.1.

F.2.   *šagalta djəm(ə)*

An icon brought by a bride to her husband's home is put in a shrine called *šagalta djəm(ə).*

(Bk, 73.)

F.3.   *jəpš* or *šopšar šəl* 'šopšar meat'

A stick on which are put small pieces of meat is fastened to the sacred tree during a
sacrifice ceremony. These slices of meat, called *jamša,* are cut from the *šübə šəl* (C.12.2.)
and represent different parts of the sacrifice animal. The number and order of pieces of
meat on the stick varies from region to region; there may be five, seven, nine, or twelve
such pieces. In one place the meat is put on the stick in the following order: a piece from
the intestines, right and left haunches, kidney, middle of the chest, heart, aorta, back of
the neck, throat, tongue, lips and liver. Except for the liver these pieces are more or less in
the same order as on the animal. Although the number and order of these pieces vary, the
lowermost is always a piece from the intestines and the uppermost a piece from the
liver. This stick is not always made for secondary sacrifices to a deity's helpers. Usually
no such meat stick is prepared when a fowl has been sacrificed, but in some places a
stick is made using the meat of a goose sacrificed to god's 'reporter' (A.8.). In regions
where this stick is fastened to the 'little sacrifice tree' (F.15.1.), the meat stick is burned
together with the tree. In places where it is fastened to the growing sacrifice tree it may
be taken off and burned or simply left there until the following year.

   (Häm.[1908a], 15; H[1926], 133–34, 152–53; H[1927], 273.)
   For *jumə,* see F.26.

F.4.   *jolba* or *šöša* 'tassel'

A tassel of linden bast is fastened to the sacred tree during a sacrifice ceremony.
   (Be, 713; H[1926], 150.)

F.5.   *jošman köraga*

A bucket for hydromel placed under the sacred tree during a sacrifice is called
jošman köraga (<Chuvash *jusman* 'pancake' *kərägä* 'table laden with food and drink').
   (P, 190.)

F.6.   *kudə bodəž kalta* 'hut spirit box'

A small sooty round or rectangular box of linden or birch bark with a lid is sometimes considered sacred. Perhaps in earlier times the box contained idols. The box is
usually placed on the holy shelf of the *kudə* (E.1.) and sacrifices to the *kudə* spirit
(A.9.8.) are put there. In regions where the *kudə* is no longer used, the box may be
kept in a storehouse or in the entrance to the bathhouse.

   (H[1926], 44; Ränk[1949], 93; V, 82.)

F.7.   *pot kaška* 'pot log'

A stand to hold the huge cauldrons used for cooking the meat of sacrificed animals
is made of birch logs stacked up horizontally so that the larger end of the first and last
logs is toward the sacred tree.

   (H[1926], 116–17, 185.)

F.8.   kašta 'pole'

F.8.1.   pot kašta 'pot pole'

At a sacrifice ceremony a light stand is erected to hold a pot for cooking ńemer (C.6.). The term pot kašta refers to a horizontal pole supported by pot meŋge 'pot post.' Pots are hung from this stand by wooden hooks. This stand is not sturdy enough to hold the large meat cauldrons which are placed on pot kaška (F.7.).

(H[1926], 116, 149; P, 190–91.)

F.8.2.   sorta kašta 'candle pole'

A log to which candles can be fastened is placed on the altar under a sacrifice tree.
(H[1926], 147.)

F.9.   kepšəl 'footband'

A bast rope is used to tie the forefeet of the sacrifice animal as it is slaughtered. This rope is braided especially for the sacrifice by the priest's helpers.

(H[1926], 120.)

For kolšə kübar, see B.2.3.3.; kolšə üstel, B.23.3.

F.10.   korka 'drinking bowl'

F.10.1.   kiš korka 'resin bowl'

A wooden bowl to hold mead (notwithstanding its being called 'resin bowl') is placed on a stand under the sacred tree at a ceremony in which a horse is sacrificed and its hide burned. This practice is not widespread among the Cheremis.

(H[1926], 118, 149.)

F.10.2.   šočən korka 'šočən bowl'

At Easter (B.8.5.1.) tašlama beer is served to women by boys after the men have left the service. The purpose of this ritual is not stated and can only be inferred from the name given to the bowls in which the beer is served—šočən korka. The term šočən has the meaning of 'fructifying,' 'giving birth,' and 'growing.'

(Be, 706.)

F.10.3.   šübə korka 'šübə bowl'

Two bowls called šübə korka are used during a sacrifice ceremony. Into these bowls is placed šübə meat (C.12.2.). The contents of one bowl are offered into the fire to the deity for whom the sacrifice is made; the contents of the other bowl are thrown into the fire for the intermediary, the fire spirit (A.9.14.).

(H[1926], 132–33, 140.)

For keremet pu, see F.15.; čaza korka oksa, B.17.1.; jošman köraga, F.5.; kudə bodəž kalta, F.6.; kudə bodəž toja, E.1.; kumaltəš pu, F.15.; aba kumdar, B.17.1.; kolšə kübar, B.23.3.

F.11.   küzə 'knife'

A sacrifice animal's throat is slit with an old knife that is used only at sacrifices.
(H[1926], 128; H[1927], 271.)

F.12.   *meŋgə* 'post'; *orgamak joləštəm meŋge* 'horse-tying post'

A long birch pole is set up about ten paces to the right of the fireplace near the sacred tree. The sacrifice animal is tied to this post until it is slaughtered. Failure to put this post in the proper place may displease the deity so that it does not let the animal shudder when water is poured on it.

(H[1926], 120; P, 194.)

For *ńi üštə,* see F.24.

F.13.   *ši nukta* 'silver bridle'

A bridle, called *ši nukta* in prayers, is made especially for a sacrifice horse. It is made of linden bast and braided so that the 'under part is up and the upper part down.' As the horse is killed, the bridle is smeared with blood and later burned in the fire.

(Be, 170; H[1926], 120.)

For *čaza korka oksa,* see B.17.1.; *olača üštə,* F.23.; *ona pu,* F.15.; *orgamak joləštəm meŋge,* F.12.

F.14.   *ši pańə* 'silver spoon'

A roughly carved piece of linden bark is placed in the pot of *ńemer* (C.6.) on the altar during a sacrifice ceremony. In ritual language it is called a 'silver spoon.'

(H[1926], 118.)

For *pot kaška,* see F.7.; *pot kašta,* F.8.1.

F.15.   *ona pu* 'ona tree' or *kumaltəš pu* 'prayer tree' or *keremet pu* 'keremet tree'

A tree dedicated to a god or spirit is called *ona pu.* Under this tree, sacrifices are made and prayers said to the deity. In some regions, each family has an *ona pu* in the sacred grove (E.2.) under which private sacrifices are made. Linden trees are the most suitable for gods and nature spirits, but oaks and birches are also used. Fir trees are dedicated to *keremet*s (A.31.). An oak or linden may be a *sürem* tree under which the young men who exorcise evil hold a ceremony (B.18.).

These trees may stand either in a grove or in a meadow. Even when prayers are no longer said beneath it, such a tree is respected; branches are not cut from it nor is it harmed in any way.

In regions where there is no sacred grove, a long branch is erected in place of a sacred tree.

(Be, 707, 734; H[1926], 102, 112, 164; Häm.[1908a], 5; P, 189; S, 160, 181; Uj[FB], 3; Up[FB], 30; V, 144; Wu, 67–68.)

F.15.1.   *izə ona pu* 'little ona tree'

In some regions, it is the custom to have a small sacred tree as well as a large one at a sacrifice. A young tree of the same species as the large sacred tree is uprooted and tied to the large tree with a bast rope. During the ceremony a *šuldəš* stick (F.19.), a *šopšar* stick (F.3.), a tassel (F.4.), a pewter figure (F.1.), and twigs are tied to the little tree. At the end of the ceremony the small tree is burned.

(H[1926], 118, 142, 146, 154.)

For *pu tul,* see B.29.

F.16.   *türet puč* or *treč puc* 'türet horn'; 'treč horn'

Horns are used in many regions during the exorcism ceremony (B.18.). Such a horn is about three feet long and made of linden bark around which strips of birch bark have been wrapped. In some regions there is the belief that if a horn is broken during the ceremony, there will be hail. In some places horns are thrown away at the end of the ceremony, in other places they are kept from year to year. Sometimes the horns are blown not only during the ceremony but for a month or two weeks before.

A horn is also used in the 'blessing of the cream,' a ceremony of apparently religious significance on which there is no information available.

Horns are also used for non-ceremonial purposes. In some places, horns are blown in the fall to announce to any interested young men that there is a girl of marriageable age in the house. In Urzhum, wedding guests try to steal the horn from the bride's parents when the bride leaves for her new home; if they succeed, it is believed that they take the prosperity of the fields' *pasu perke* (A.67.14.) to the groom's home.

Taboos surround the use of the horn. For example, if a horn is sounded for other than religious purposes while the grain is ripening, the winter will be extremely cold.

(H[1926], 181–82; H[1927], 246–47; Häm.[1925], 101, 105, 109; Häm.[1928], 29–34.)

F.17.   *ši püken* 'silver holder'

A short roughly carved log is stood on end under the sacred tree at a sacrifice. A candle is fastened in a crack in the top.

(H[1926], 117–18.)

F.18.   *sandal*

In some regions there is a little stand (*sandal*) made of three thin sticks used for holding candles at sacrifice ceremonies.

(P, 190.)

For *sorta kašta*, see F.8.2.; *šöša*, F.4.; *šagalta djəm*(*ə*), F.2.; *ši nukta*, F.13.; *ši paňə*, F.14.; *ši püken*, F.17.; *šočən korka*, F.10.2.; *šopšar šəl*, F.3.

F.19.   *šuldəš*

During an animal sacrifice ceremony, a twig is prepared to be fastened to the sacrifice tree. A priest making a sacrifice takes up a green linden branch and cuts from the lower end (i.e., the end by which it grew from the tree) pieces about six or seven inches long. The number of pieces cut varies from region to region but it is usually an uneven number. Sometimes three pieces are cut off first and then, later, six more are cut. In some places all the pieces are cut before the animal is sacrificed, whereas in others the last six are not cut until after the sacrifice. As each piece is cut, the position in which it falls to the ground is observed. In some regions if the piece falls so that the lower end points toward the sacrifice tree, this is regarded as a good omen. In other places, the priest looks to see whether the bark or inner side is up; if the inner side is up, it is a good omen. If a piece does not fall satisfactorily, another piece may be cut. In Urzhum, before making the cuttings, the priest touches with the tip of the branch the tree, the *ńemer* pot (C.6.), the candle, and other objects used during the ceremony. In some places, each of the first three cuttings is made to find out whether the deity is pleased with certain specific parts of the sacrifice such as the worshippers and the priests, the sacred objects, and the sacrifice animal. In some places, cuttings are made to find out whether the deity will grant the worshipper certain blessings. In one place, for example, the first cutting is made to see whether the deity will accept the offering, the second whether the god will give health and long life to the worshippers, the third whether they will be blessed with a family, the fourth whether they will be blessed with cattle, the fifth whether they will be blessed with grain; the sixth whether they will be blessed with bees; the seventh whether they will be blessed with money; the eighth whether they will receive all blessings, and the ninth whether they will receive all blessings and an abundance of everything. The pieces are sometimes placed temporarily in the pot of porridge under the sacrifice tree.

In some places the branch is trimmed so that only a forked stick remains; the leaves are allowed to fall into the fire as they are cut off. The branches of the fork are split and the cuttings inserted crosswise. Usually the porridge or broth is smeared on the sticks. In one place half of a design taken from the sacrifice bread (C.2.1.) is put on the stick. The *šuldəš* stick is then fastened to the sacred tree or the 'little sacred tree' (F.15.).

(Häm.[1908a], 15; H[1926], 124–25, 134–36, 151–52.)

For *šübə korka,* see F.10.3.

F.20.　*tobar* 'ax'

A knife is struck against an ax while prayers are said at *aga pajram* (B.2.), *küsə* (B.9.), and other ceremonies. The sound of metal is said to attract gods and at the same time drive away evil.

(G, 56 [149]; H[1926], 177.)

For *kudə bodəž toja,* see E.1.

F.21.　*tul* 'fire'

Most offerings to supernaturals are thrown into a fire. In the home they are thrown into the hearth, but elsewhere a fire is built for this purpose. Fire personified (A.1.15. and A.9.14.) is believed to transmit each offering to the spirit for whom it is intended. Meat, bread, pancakes, porridge and drink are all thrown into the fire. Leftovers, bones and other inedible parts are also burned and a fire is built in the hole into which the sacrifice animal's blood has run. In some regions the hide of the sacrificed animal is also burned. Even many of the ceremonial objects are often thrown into the fire. It has been suggested that the use of a 'little sacred tree' (F.15.1.) which could be burned came about as the result of such great emphasis on fire as an intermediary for taking things to spirits.

Offerings to earth spirits, water spirits and the dead, however, are not usually thrown into the fire.

(H[1926], 154–55; Häm.[1936–37], 72–75.)

F.21.1. *utšo tul* 'auxiliary fire'

In addition to the principal fire at a sacrifice, a secondary fire is built over the hole into which the sacrificed animal's blood has flowed. The inedible parts of the sacrifice are burned in this fire.

(H[1926], 140; P, 165.)

For *pu tul*, see B.29.; *baštar tul*, B.29.; *treč puč* or *türet puč*, F.17.

F.22.   *üstel* 'table'; *küs koltəmə üstel* 'table sending up'

Before a sacrifice begins a table is placed under the sacrifice tree for the offerings to the god. In many places fresh linden twigs are spread out on the ground under the sacrifice tree and a white linen cloth is placed on top of the twigs. This is also called a table and serves as an altar for offerings.

(H[1926], 119; P, 190; V, 92.)

For *kolšə üstel*, see B.23.3.

F.23.   *ńi üštə* 'bast belt'

During sacrifices and vows to sacrifice a band of linden bast is tied around the trunk of the sacred tree (F.15.). In some places it is called *olača üštə* 'variegated band' because it is ornamented. The band encircles the trunk from three to nine times—always an uneven number; at vows this signifies the number of years before the vow is to be fulfilled. When there is a 'little sacred tree' (F.15.1.), the band is wrapped around the small tree; another band may also be put on the large tree. Between the band and the tree are placed various objects such as a *šuldəš* (F.19.), a *šopšar šəl* (F.3.), a tassel (F.4.), and a pewter figure (F.1.). It is also the custom in some places to put pine, linden, and birch twigs between this band and the tree. In some places bundles of grass and pine needles are fastened to the tree by means of this band. According to one account the objects fastened to the tree have a symbolic meaning; the pewter figure signifies that the god has accepted the offering, the *šopšar šəl* proves that the sacrifice has been made and the *šuldəš* means that god is satisfied with the worshippers and will bless them.

(H[1926], 131, 146, 153–54; H[1927], 272.)

F.24.   bag

When a vow (B.4., B.16.) is taken a small linen bag is made to hold items representing pledged offerings. This bag is hung in a storehouse and burned when the vow is fulfilled.

(H[1908a], 4, 6; H[1926], 162.)

F.25.   idols

Visible representation of supernatural beings are extremely rare among the Cheremis. An eighteenth century observer mentions small clothed figures roughly carved from wood representing household gods in more or less human shape. They were six or seven inches tall and kept in a birch bark shrine in a corner of the house. They were placed on a table during a wedding and the priest prayed before them. Another observer from approximately the same period says that the Cheremis had idols made of twigs and cloth as *kudə* (E.1.) deities. Offerings were put on the shelf in the *kudə* or storehouse where they were kept.

There is also mention of a different type of image—a dummy to represent a dead person was made for a memorial ceremony. Although there is no information available as to how or of what material this dummy was made, the clothes of the deceased were probably used.

No description of any pagan idol or image has been given in more recent accounts and it is doubtful whether such representations still exist.

Under the influence of the Russian Church, icons were introduced into Cheremis homes. These may in turn be incorporated in the traditional ceremonies so that, for example, a bride may take an icon from her parent's home to be placed in the holy shrine in the groom's home.

In two twentieth century texts the term *jumə* 'god' (A.26.) is used for a holy image. At a wedding (B.17.) a *jumə* accompanies the groom as he goes to fetch the bride. It is brought forth when blessings are said and when the wedding party returns to the groom's house, a candle is lit before the *jumə*. Because the nature of this image is not revealed in the sources, it is impossible to determine definitely whether this is a pagan idol or a Christian icon. However, it is probably the latter since both sources show evidence of strong Christian influence.

(B, 39, 43; Bk, 71, 73; H[1926], 49; Häm.[1936–37], 127; Müller, 363; Wu, 39–40, 43, 45.)

F.26.   votary stand

During a *sukə* vow (B.16.) a little stand is attached to the sacred tree. Three short logs form a tripod, a fourth log connects the tree and the tripod. A coin, and sometimes also a candle, is put on top of the tripod.

(H[1926], 163; Häm.[1908a], 7.)

G. OMENS

Predictions of the future are common among the Cheremis. The designations for sayings containing signs and predictions vary, however, from region to region; the following terms have been recorded: *toštə jeŋən mutšə* 'old people's words,' *šanəmə* 'thinking,' *primetbəlä* or *primeta* or *oňčək palmə* 'knowing before.'

Certain natural and uncontrollable occurrences are considered to be omens from which the future can be foretold. In this section sayings are classified according to omens. The interpretations of such omens usually concern luck, crops, or the weather; these are listed in the Index.

Most omens occur regardless of the presence of a human observer. However, there is a special subclass of omens which involve active human participation. An individual can in no way control the future by means of such omens, but he creates a situation through which he may learn something which has not been revealed to him by other means. Such divinations are listed in this section as number G.34. See D.7. and D.10. for descriptions of the way in which soothsayers and seers predict.

(Departing from the practice in the preceding sections, source references here to B, Bk, and W refer not to the page but to the number of the saying within a collection. These sayings are found on the following pages: B, 53–71; Bk, 24–43, and W, 4–26.)

G.1.   *jeη* 'person'

G.1.1.1.   If you meet a lucky person, you will be able to buy something. (B, 119b.)

G.1.1.2.   If you do not meet a lucky person you will not be able to buy anything. (B, 119a.)

G.1.2.1.   If you meet a man, you will have luck. (Uj, 101a; Up, 94a; Wm, 187a; Wt, 139.)

G.1.2.2.   If on your way to work you meet a man, your work will be easy. (Bk, 38a; J.)

G.1.2.3.   If on your way to sow you meet a man with a beard, you will have good luck; the grain will grow well. (B, 122.)

G.1.2.4.   If the first person to enter your house on Easter morning is a man, life will be good. (Uj, 100; Wt, 123a.)

G.1.3.1.   If you meet a woman, you will not have luck. (Bk, 77; Uj, 101b; Up, 94b; Wm, 187b; Wt, 142.)

G.1.3.2.   If on your way to work you meet a woman, the work will be difficult. (Bk, 38b; J.)

G.1.3.3.   If on your way to sow you meet a woman, you will have no luck—the grain will not grow. (B, 120.)

G.1.3.4.   If the first person to enter your house on Easter is a woman, life will be hard. (Wt, 123b.)

G.1.3.5.   If when hunting you meet a woman with bare genitals, you will not have luck— you will not catch anything. (B, 123; J; Up, 95.)

G.1.3.6.   A woman who gives birth to a male child first is a lucky woman; if you meet her, you will have luck. (B, 115; Uj, 102; Up, 98.)

G.1.4.1.   If a child is born backwards at its birth, it will not live. (B, 117; Uj, 144; Up, 112.)

G.1.4.2.1.   If a child is born with ordinary soles, it will live. (Up, 110a.)

G.1.4.2.2.   If a child is born flat-footed, it will not live. (Up, 110b.)

G.1.4.2.3.   If a child is born horseshoe-footed, it will live. (Uj, 147a.)

G.1.4.2.4.   If a child is born unshod, it will die. (Uj, 147b.)

G.1.4.3.1.   If a woman gives birth to a child in a shirt, the child will be lucky. (B, 116.)

G.1.4.3.2.   If a child is born with a hat and a shirt on [with a caul?], it will be lucky— it will become rich. (Uj, 149; Up, 114.)

G.1.4.4.   If a child is born in soldier's clothing, it will become a soldier. (Bj, 152, 156; Bu, 74; Uj, 148; Up, 111.)

G.1.4.5.   If a newborn child is seen with a book and pencil, it will be a clerk. (Bj, 154, 157.)

G.1.4.6.   If a newborn child is seen with carpenter's tools, it will be a carpenter. (Bj, 152, 156.)

G.1.4.7.   If a newborn child looks like a dog, it will be a sorcerer (*juzə* D.2.). (Bj, 154, 156–57.)

G.1.4.8. If a newborn child is seen with a horse, basket, and loaf of bread, it will be a farmer. (Bj, 154, 157.)

G.1.4.9. If a newborn child is seen with a measure, thread, and needle, it will be a tailor. (Bj, 155, 158.)

G.1.4.10. If a child is born with a rope on its neck, it will be hanged. (Bu, 73.)

G.1.4.11. If a newborn child is seen with two sacks and old clothes, it will be a beggar. (Bj, 152, 156.)

G.1.4.12. If a newborn child is seen with scales and a purse, it will be a merchant. (Bj, 155, 157.)

G.1.4.13. If a newborn child is seen lying in water, in later life it will be drowned. (Bu, 75.)

G.1.4.14. If a newborn child is seen with a weapon and a game animal, it will be a hunter. (Bj, 153, 156.)

G.1.5.1. If a person has much hair in his armpits, he has luck. (B, 131.)

G.1.5.2.1. If a man has hair on his hands and chest, he has luck. (J; Uj, 108a; Up, 93a.)

G.1.5.2.2. If a man does not have hair on his chest and hands, he does not have luck. (J; Uj, 108b; Up, 93b.)

G.1.6.1.1. If your right ankle itches, your road will be good. (B, 127a.)

G.1.6.1.2. If your left ankle itches, your road will be difficult. (B, 127b.)

G.1.6.2. If your anus itches, a Tatar is coming. (Usj, 43e.)

G.1.6.3.1. If your right cheek itches, you will be ashamed. (Wm, 182a; Wu, 137a.)

G.1.6.3.2. If your left cheek itches, you will get a box on the ear. (Wm, 182b; Wt, 137b.)

G.1.6.4. If your ear itches, there will be rain. (B, 128; J; Uj, 184; Up, 16.)

G.1.6.5. If your eye itches, you will cry. (B, 125b; Uj, 186; Usj, 43b; Wm, 183.)

G.1.6.5.1. If your left eye itches, you will cry. (Up, 164b.)

G.1.6.5.2. If your right eye itches, you will laugh. (Up, 164a.)

G.1.6.6.1. If your left eyebrow itches, you will cry. (Wm, 179b.)

G.1.6.6.2. If your right eyebrow itches, you will see someone you know. (Wm, 179a.)

G.1.6.7. If your face itches, you will get a slap. (Uj, 187b; Up, 165a.)

G.1.6.8. If your forehead itches, you will be ashamed. (B, 125a; J; Uj, 185; Up, 163; Usj, 30.)

G.1.6.9.1. If your lip itches, you will eat food brought by a guest. (B, 125c; J; Uj, 187a; Up, 166; Usj, 43a; Wt, 131.)

G.1.6.9.2. If your lip itches, you will kiss someone. (Wm, 180.)

G.1.6.10.1. If the tip of your nose itches, you will drink vodka. (J; Up, 165b; Usj, 22; Wm, 181.)

G.1.6.10.2. If the tip of your nose itches, you will hear of a dead person. (Bk, 36; Usj, 22; Wt, 145.)

G.1.6.10.3. If the tip of your nose itches, there will be a rage against somebody. (Uj, 187c.)

G.1.6.11. If your palm itches, you will get money. (Bk, 33; Usj, 43c.)

G.1.6.11.1. If your right palm itches, money will come. (B, 126a; J; Uj, 183b; Wt, 132a.)

G.1.6.11.2.   If your left palm itches, money will go. (B, 126b; J; Uj, 183c; Wt, 132b.)

G.1.6.12.   If your sole itches, you must go far away. (Usj, 43d.)

G.1.7.1.   If the right side of your head pulsates, people praise you. (Wm, 184a; Wt, 136a.)

G.1.7.2.   If the left side of your head pulsates, people find fault with you. (Wm, 184b; Wt, 136b.)

G.1.8.   If your eyelid pulsates, you will see someone that you have not seen. (Wt, 135.)

G.1.9.   If the tip of your tongue prickles, you will speak with a good person or a person you have not seen. (Bk, 15.)

G.1.10.   If the larynx emits a sound, it will be possible to drink vodka somewhere. (Uj, 183a.)

G.1.11.   If a person's ear rings, he will hear of a death. (Uj, 188, 189.)

G.1.12.   A big-testicled man's testicles begin to ache before there is rain; his testicles descend; then the rain comes; the weather will be wet. (B, 129; Uj, 196; Up, 20.)

G.1.13.1.   If while going into the house, you catch your foot in the door, a guest will come. (B, 130; J; Uj, 259; Up, 141; Wm, 178; Wt, 134.)

G.1.13.2.1.   If in the winter it is going to get cold, one's feet are cold even if it is warm in the house. (Uj, 39a; Up, 35a.)

G.1.13.2.2.   If in the winter the weather will get warm, one's feet will sweat a lot. (Uj, 39b; Up, 35b.)

G.1.14.   If at a wedding the bride and groom fall out of the cart or sleigh, one of them will die. (Uj, 136.)

G.1.14.1.   If as the bride is being taken away she falls out of the sled, it is not good. (Up, 103.)

G.1.15.1.   If you hear a child's whimper when going somewhere at night, it is not good. (Up, 106.)

G.1.15.2.   If a child cries while people go somewhere at night, it is not good; there will be some trouble. (Uj, 119.)

G.1.16.   If a woman has to yawn, she will get a present. (Bk, 7.)

G.1.17.   If you sit down to eat without a belt, you won't get your fill. (Uj, 222; Up, 168.)

G.1.18.1.   If as you go somewhere you have to urinate, you will not have luck. (B, 124a; Uj, 113.)

G.1.18.2.   If on your way somewhere you must defecate, you will have luck. (B, 124b.)

G.1.19.   If people sleep without covers on St. Elijah's Day [July 20], the winter will be mild. (B, 201.)

G.1.20.   If Russians sing, there will soon be rain. (J.)

G.1.21.1.   If a sick person lies with his face to the wall, he will not recover, he will die. (Bk, 65a.)

G.1.21.2.   If a sick person lies facing the middle of the room, he will recover. (Bk, 65b.)

G.1.22.1.   If a man becomes ill on Wednesday, he will not recover. (B, 155; Up, 109.)

G.1.22.1.1.   If a man becomes sick on a Wednesday and lives until the following Wednesday, he will live for two more weeks before dying. (Uj, 142.)

G.1.22.2.   If a man becomes ill while wearing a shirt which he puts on clean on Wednesday, he will not recover. (Up, 108; Wm, 191; Wu, 99.)

G.1.22.2.1. If a man becomes sick on Wednesday after putting on a new shirt but survives for a week from that Wednesday, he will live; if not, he will die. (Uj, 141.)

G.1.23.1. If a child sleeps with its back to its mother, it will die. (Uj, 145.)

G.1.23.2.1. If a child sleeps with its head hanging off the pillow, it will not live. (Uj, 146a; Up, 113a.)

G.1.23.2.2.1. If a child falls off the pillow, it will not live. (Uj, 146b.)

G.1.23.2.2.2. If a child falls off, it will live. (Up, 113b.)

G.2. *bol'ək i jalnək* 'livestock and animals'

G.2.1.1. You will live like whatever kind of animal you see when you go into the field for the first time as the snow is melting. (J.)

G.2.2.1.1. If game come to meet the hunter in the forest, he will have luck. (B, 55a; Up, 100a.)

G.2.2.1.2. If game go with their back toward the hunter, he will have no luck. (B, 55b; Up, 100b.)

G.2.2.2.1. If the hunter meets female game first, he will have luck, he will shoot many. (B, 56a.)

G.2.2.2.2. If a hunter meets male game, he will have no luck. (B, 56b.)

G.2.3.1.1. If the bear lies in its den before the arrival of snow, the winter will be cold. (J; Uj, 45a.)

G.2.3.1.2. If the bear lies in his den after the arrival of snow, the winter will be mild. (J; Uj, 45b; Up, 39b.)

G.2.3.2.1. If the bear goes into its den to hibernate at *pokro* [October 1], the winter will be cold. (B, 57a; Up, 39a.)

G.2.3.2.2. If the bear goes about in the forest after *pokro* [October 1] its tracks are seen in the snow, the winter will be mild. (B, 57b.)

G.2.4.1.1. If the cat sits on the floor, the weather will be warm. (Wm, 156; Wt, 121.)

G.2.4.1.2.1. If the cat sits in front of the stove, the weather will be cold. (B, 74; J; Uj, 34; Up, 33.)

G.2.4.1.2.2. If the cat lies in the stove, the weather will be cold. (J.)

G.2.4.2. If the cat scratches with its claws, there will be a snowstorm. (Bk, 28, 76; J; Up, 31; Wu, 76.)

G.2.4.2.1. If the cat claws something in the house, there will be a snowstorm. (Wm, 152.)

G.2.4.2.2.1. If the cat claws the leg of a table, there will be a snowstorm. (B, 72; J; Uj, 27; Up, 30.)

G.2.4.2.2.2. If the cat claws the leg of the table, there will be a snowstorm in winter or rain in summer. (Wj, 53.)

G.2.4.2.3. If the cat claws the wall, there will be snow. (Wt, 110.)

G.2.4.3. If the cat washes its face, a visitor will come. (Wj, 70.)

G.2.4.3.1. If the cat washes its face from behind its ear, a guest will come. (J.)

G.2.4.3.2. If the cat washes its face or sits on a bench with its tail hanging down, a visitor will come. (Wt, 133.)

G.2.4.3.3.1. If the cat washes its face with its left paw, a Russian will come. (Wk, 49a.)

G.2.4.3.3.2.   If the cat washes its face with its right paw, a Cheremis will come. (Wk, 49b.)

G.2.4.4.   If a cat crosses your path, you will not have luck. (J; Usj, 11; Wm, 185; Wt, 140.)

G.2.4.5.   If the cat runs away from the house, life will be bad—someone will die. (Bk, 29.)

G.2.5.1.   If the first animal to come into the village from the meadow is a black cow, there will be rain. (Wt, 114.)

G.2.5.2.   If a domestic animal brings grass home in its mouth from the pasture, it will be a bad year for fodder; the fodder will not last until spring. (Bk, 63; Wm, 167.)

G.2.5.2.1.   If the cow coming in from the pasture brings grass in its mouth, there will not be enough fodder in the winter. (J.)

G.2.5.2.2.1.   If in the summer the cow brings in grass in its mouth, fodder will be expensive the next year. (B, 62; Wj, 67; Wk, 34.)

G.2.5.2.2.2.   If in the fall the cow brings grass to the village in its mouth, straw and hay will be expensive. (J; Uj, 93.)

G.2.5.3.1.   If a pregnant cow lies facing the north, it will calve at night. (B, 63a; Bk, 78b; J; Uj, 204c; Wk, 36a.)

G.2.5.3.1.1.   If a pregnant cow lies facing the northeast, it will calve at midnight. (Uj, 204d.)

G.2.5.3.2.   If a pregnant cow lies facing the south, it will calve in the middle of the day. (B, 63b; Bk, 78a; J; Uj, 204a; Wk, 36b.)

G.2.5.3.3.   If a pregnant cow lies facing the east, it will calve in the morning. (B, 63c; Bk, 78c; Uj, 204b.)

G.2.5.3.4.   If a pregnant cow lies facing the west, it will calve in the evening. (B, 63d; Bk, 78d; Uj, 204e.)

G.2.6.1.   If on your way to sow you meet a dog, you will have no luck—no grain will grow. (B, 70.)

G.2.6.2.1.   If the dog rolls about, there will be a storm. (Uj, 28; Up, 29; Usj, 27.)

G.2.6.2.2.   If the dog rolls about, there will be rain. (J.)

G.2.6.2.3.   If the dog rolls on the street, someone will die. (B, 71.)

G.2.6.3.1.1.   If the dog howls, there will be death in the village. (Up, 117.)

G.2.6.3.1.2.   If someone's dog howls, death will visit his house. (Wu, 98.)

G.2.6.3.2.   If the dog howls looking upward, it will not be good. (J.)

G.2.6.3.2.1.   If the dog howls looking upward, there will be a fire. (Usj, 28; Wm, 190b.)

G.2.6.3.2.2.   If the dog howls looking upward, there will be a death. (B, 72; Uj, 137.)

G.2.6.3.3.   If a dog howls in front of a house looking at the ground, there will be a death in that house. (Wm, 190a.)

G.2.6.4.   If the dog eats grass in the summer, it will rain. (B, 69.)

G.2.6.4.1.   If the dog eats green grass, it will be rainy. (Up, 13.)

G.2.6.4.2.   If the dog eats yellow grass, rain will come. (Uj, 15.)

G.2.7.1.   If while going to work a hare runs across the road in front of you, the work will go well. (J.)

G.2.7.2.1.1.1.   If in the fall the hare turns white early, snow will come early; the fall will be short; winter will come early. (Bk, 35, 101; J; Uj, 32b; Up, 24a; Wm, 159; Wu, 73a.)

G.2.7.2.1.1.2.   If the hare turns white early in the fall, winter will not come soon. (B, 75a.)

G.2.7.2.1.2.   If the hare turns white late in the fall, snow will come late; the fall will be long. (J; Uj, 32a; Up, 24b; Wu, 73b.)

G.2.7.2.2.   If the hare is grey in the fall, snow will come soon. (B, 75b.)

G.2.7.2.3.   If the hare becomes red soon in the spring, summer will come soon. (Bk, 50.)

G.2.8.1.   If the hair on a colt's head begins to fall out, it will become a fine horse. (B, 61; Uj, 151; Up, 82.)

G.2.8.2.1.1.   If a person's horse harnessed for a trip defecates in the yard, he will have luck. (Bk, 74a; J; Uj, 114; Up, 66.)

G.2.8.2.1.2.   If a person's horse harnessed for a trip urinates in the yard, he will not have luck. (Bk, 74b.)

G.2.8.2.2.1.   If, they are taking a horse to be sold, it defecates in the yard, they will not be able to sell it. (B, 60; Uj, 199a; Up, 157a.)

G.2.8.2.2.2.   If as a horse is being taken to be sold it does not defecate in the yard, it will be sold; it will not be brought back. (Uj, 199b; Up, 157b.)

G.2.8.2.3.   If you harness a guest's horse and the horse defecates, the guest will come back. (Usj, 45.)

G.2.8.3.   Before wet weather the horse lies in its stall. (B, 59.)

G.2.8.4.   If the horse snorts through its nose, rain will come. (Bk, 12.)

G.2.8.5.   If the horse becomes unharnessed on the road as it goes, you copulated with your wife that day. (Usj, 15.)

G.2.9.1.   The person in whose field a mole lives will be lucky. (Uj, 110; Up, 92.)

G.2.9.2.   If a mole throws earth up on the snow, the winter will be warm. (Bk, 13.)

G.2.10.1.   If there are many red mice the crop will not grow. (J; Uj, 67; Up, 43.)

G.2.10.1.1.   If there are many red-haired mice in the summer, the grain will not grow. (B, 77.)

G.2.10.1.2.   If there are many little mice in the winter, the next year the grain will not grow well. (J.)

G.2.10.2.1.1.   If many mice start to live in the stack, it won't be good for the family. (J; Up, 107.)

G.2.10.2.1.2.   If there are very many mice in the stack, the man to whom it belongs will be lost. (Uj, 132.)

G.2.10.2.2.1.   If the mouse does not eat of the stack, there will be grain to eat. (Uj, 73a.)

G.2.10.2.2.2.   If the mouse eats of the stack there will be little grain to eat. (Uj, 73b.)

G.2.10.3.1.1.1.   If the mouse eats the bread from the top, bread will be expensive; the price of bread will rise. (J; Wm, 165a.)

G.2.10.3.1.1.2.   If the mouse eats the bread from the top, grain will grow well, the price will fall, and it will be cheap. (B, 78b; J; Uj, 69c, 94b; Up, 78b, 79a; Wu, 90a.)

G.2.10.3.1.2.1.   If the mouse eats the bread from the bottom, the price of bread will go down. (J; Wm, 165b.)

G.2.10.3.1.2.2.   If the mouse eats the bread from the bottom, grain will not grow well, the price will rise, and it will be expensive. (B, 78a; J; Uj, 69a, 94a; Up, 78a, 79b; Wu, 90b.)

G.2.10.3.1.3.   If the mouse eats the bread from the side, grain will be medium-priced. (B, 78c; J; Uj, 69b.)

G.2.10.3.2.1.   If the mouse eats from the upper part of the stack, grain will be expensive. (Bk, 70a.)

G.2.10.3.2.2.   If the mouse eats from the lower part of the stack, grain will be cheap. (Bk, 70b.)

G.2.10.3.3.   If the mouse eats hay from the top of the stack, hay will be expensive. (Bk, 19.)

G.2.10.4.   If the small mouse makes its nest in the top of the grain, snow will be deep. (J.)

G.2.11.1.   If you meet a pig, you will have luck. (Wt, 138.)

G.2.11.1.1.   If you meet a pig as you go out the gate, you will have luck. (Wm, 186.)

G.2.11.1.2.   If you meet a pig on your way to plow, you will have good luck. (B, 66.)

G.2.11.2.   If the pig comes squealing from the field, there will be rain. (B, 67; Uj, 20; Up, 14.)

G.2.11.3.   If the pig brings straw in its mouth into the pen for a litter, the weather will be cold. (B, 68; Bk, 98; Uj, 35; Wt, 119.)

G.2.12.1.   If the sheep bleat, it will rain. (B, 64; Wm, 146; Wu, 75.)

G.2.12.2.   If the sheep butt one another, rain will come. (B, 65; Uj, 16; Up, 15.)

G.2.12.2.1.   If two black sheep butt each other, there will be rain. (Wt, 115a.)

G.2.12.2.2.   If two white sheep butt each other, the weather will be clear. (Wt, 115b.)

G.2.13.1.   If a squirrel comes into the village, the village will burn down. (Up, 136.)

G.2.13.2.1.   If in the fall the squirrel becomes white, the snow will not come soon. (B, 76a.)

G.2.13.2.2.1.   If in the fall the squirrel remains red, snow will come soon. (B, 76b.)

G.2.13.2.2.2.   If the squirrel turns red, it will be fall soon. (Uj, 33a.)

G.2.13.2.2.3.   If the squirrel turns red early in the fall, winter will come early. (Up, 37a.)

G.2.13.2.3.1.   If the squirrel does not turn red, the fall will not come for a long time. (Uj, 33b.)

G.2.13.2.3.2.   If the squirrel does not turn red early in the fall, winter will not come soon. (Up, 37b.)

G.2.14.   If a weasel lives in the stall, it is good for the household. (J; Uj, 112.)

G.2.15.1.1.1.   If a wolf eats a sheep at new moon, the sheep will be destroyed, they will not multiply. (J; Uj, 156a; Up, 86a.)

G.2.15.1.1.2.   If a wolf eats a sheep at the new moon, the sheep will increase. (J.)

G.2.15.1.2.1.   If a wolf eats a sheep when the moon is waning, the sheep will multiply. (J; Uj, 156b; Up, 86b.)

G.2.15.1.2.2.   If a wolf eats a sheep as the moon is waning, the sheep will not increase. (J.)

G.2.15.2.1.   If a she-wolf eats a sheep, the sheep will increase. (B, 58a.)

G.2.15.2.2.   If a male wolf eats a sheep, the sheep will not increase. (B, 58b.)

G.3.   *kajək* 'birds'

G.3.1.1.   If birds chirp, the weather will be mild. (Usj, 10.)

G.3.1.2.   If birds chirp, there will be rain. (Wt, 113.)

G.3.1.2.1.   If birds gather chirping on a tree, there will be rain. (B. 79.)

G.3.2.1.1.   If the cock crows a long crow in the spring, he will move your heart. (J; Uj, 215.)

G.3.2.1.2.   If the cock crows little in the fall, it will be cold. (Uj, 36.)

G.3.2.1.3.   If the cock crows after sundown, the weather will change the next day. (Bk, 61.)

G.3.2.1.4.   If the cock crows until midnight, it will be a lucky day. (Bk, 2.)

G.3.2.1.5.   If the cock crows at the entrance to the house, a guest will come. (B, 82; J; Uj, 261; Up, 138; Wu, 93.)

G.3.2.1.6.   If the cock comes to the head of the steps in front of the house and crows, a guest will come. (J; Usj, 1.)

G.3.2.1.7.   If the cock crows under the house, rain will come. (Bk, 59.)

G.3.2.1.8.   If the cock sits crowing on a post, rain will come. (Bk, 1.)

G.3.2.1.9.   If the cock crows out in the open, there will be clear weather. (Bk, 60.)

G.3.2.1.10.   If the cock sits on the fence and crows, no rain will come, the weather will be clear. (Bk, 3.)

G.3.2.2.1.   If the hen shakes its tail, there will be rain. (Wk, 7; Wu, 111.)

G.3.2.2.2.1.   If the hen lays large eggs, grain will be abundant. (Wm, 163; Wu, 85.)

G.3.2.2.2.2.   If the hen lays big eggs, the grain will be clean. (Up, 55.)

G.3.2.2.2.3.   If the hen lays large eggs, the grain (the rye) will grow well. (B, 83.)

G.3.2.2.2.4.   If the hen keeps laying large eggs in the spring, the rye or oats will grow well. (J; Uj, 68.)

G.3.2.2.2.5.   If the first egg laid in the spring is heavy, grain should be sown early. (J.)

G.3.2.2.2.6.   If the hen lays a large egg first in the spring, one should sow early. (J; Uj, 90a.)

G.3.2.2.2.7.   If in the spring when the hen first starts to lay it lays a big egg, oats must be sown early. (Up, 74a.)

G.3.2.2.2.8.   If the hen lays large eggs in the middle of the spring, then oats should be sown in the middle of the sowing time. (J; Uj, 91.)

G.3.2.2.2.9.   If the second egg which a hen lays in the spring is heavy, grain sown in the middle time will grow well. (J.)

G.3.2.2.2.10.   If the hen lays a big egg late, the oats sown last will be good. (Up, 59.)

G.3.2.2.2.11.   If the third egg the hen lays is heaviest, the grain sown later will grow well. (J.)

G.3.2.2.2.12.   If the hen lays a small egg first, it is not necessary to sow early. (J; Uj, 90b; Up, 74b.)

G.3.2.2.2.13.   If the hen lays little in the spring, the oats sown later will be small. (J; Uj, 92.)

G.3.2.2.3.   If the hen crows like a cock, it means nothing good. (Wm, 189; Wt, 144.)

G.3.2.2.3.1.   If a chicken crows like a cock, it is asking for the knife. (J.)

G.3.3.1.   If the cranes cry in the field, there will soon be rain. (J.)

G.3.3.2.1.   If the cranes fly straight southward in the fall, the fall will be short. (Uj, 30a.)

G.3.3.2.2.   If the cranes fly southward in the fall stretched out long, the fall will be long. (Uj, 29a, 30b.)

G.3.3.2.3.   If the cranes do not go stretched out behind, the fall will be short. (Uj, 29b.)

G.3.4.   If the crows caw much, there will be rain or something. (Up, 12.)

G.3.4.1.1.   If the crow caws sitting on the earth, there will be rain. (J.)

G.3.4.1.2.   If the crow caws on the top of the tree, there will be rain. (Uj, 14.)

G.3.4.1.3.   If the crow sits cawing on the fir tree, there will be wet weather. (B, 86.)

G.3.4.2.   If the crows fly in large flocks before sowing time, rye must be sown thick. (Wm, 172.)

G.3.4.3.   When the black crow has arrived the snow will go away soon. (Uj, 26.)

G.3.4.3.2.   When the black crow comes down on the road, spring will come soon; the snow will go away soon. (B, 87.)

G.3.4.3.3.   When the black crow [*Nycticorax n. naevius*] has come, it is time to sow rye. (Up, 68.)

G.3.5.1.1.   If the cuckoo comes into the village to cuckoo, it is not good; there will be some trouble in the village. (Uj, 140; Up, 123.)

G.3.5.1.2.   When a cuckoo comes singing into the village, it is not good; the village will burn down. (B, 90.)

G.3.5.2.   If in the spring you hear a cuckoo sing with your right ear, you will not be lucky. (J.)

G.3.5.3.   If the cuckoo calls out after St. Peter's Day [June 29] the fall will be long. (B, 89.)

G.3.5.4.   A sorrowing man cannot hear a cuckoo without crying; it is hard on the heart. (B, 91; Uj, 20.)

G.3.6.   If the dove bathes in water, rain will come. (B, 93.)

G.3.7.   If the duck bathes, there will be rain. (Wt, 106.)

G.3.8.1.   If there are many young geese, there will be few young bees. (B, 81.)

G.3.8.2.   If the goose stands on one foot, the weather will be cold. (Bk, 27.)

G.3.8.3.   If the goose makes a clicking sound with its mouth, the weather will be cold. (J.)

G.3.8.4.1.   If the goose begins to lay eggs on a meat day, there will be many goslings. (B, 163a.)

G.3.8.4.2.   If the goose begins to lay eggs on a fast day, there will not be many goslings. (B, 163b.)

G.3.8.5.   If wild geese fly honking, the weather in summer will be clear. (J.)

G.3.8.6.1.   If the wild goose goes away soon, the winter will come soon. (B, 80a.)

G.3.8.6.2.   If the wild goose does not go away soon, the winter will not come soon. (B, 80b.)

G.3.8.7.1.   If the wild geese go northward in the fall with their tails stretched out, the fall will be long. (Uj, 31a.)

G.3.8.7.2.   If the wild geese fly straight, the fall will be short, snow will soon come. (J; Uj, 31b.)

G.3.8.8.   If the wild goose flies southward in the fall, snow will soon come. (Uj, 25; Up, 25.)

G.3.8.9.   If in the fall the wild goose flies southward early, it will get cold early. (Wu, 74.)

G.3.8.10.   If the wild goose flies north in the fall, a cold winter is coming. (Wm, 158.)

G.3.8.11.1.   If the wild goose flies low, the fall will be long. (Wj, 55.)

G.3.8.11.2.   If the wild goose flies low, the winter will be warm. (Wk, 8.)

G.3.9.1.   If the nightingale sings sitting on top of the branch of a tree, there will be no rain. (Bk, 48a.)

G.3.9.2.   If the nightingale sings under the leaves, there will be rain. (Bk, 48b.)

G.3.10.1.   If the owl comes to the farm and hoots, it forebodes evil. (Wt, 143.)

G.3.10.2.   If at night an owl sits hooting on top of a house, something bad will happen to the owner of that house. (J.)

G.3.10.3.   If the owl sits on the roof and hoots, someone will die in the house in a year. (Bk, 54, 108.)

G.3.10.4.   If an owl hoots in the village in the spring, someone in the village will die. (B, 84.)

G.3.10.5.   If an owl lives in the village, it will be good for the village because the owl "cuts" evil and does not let it enter. (Uj, 246.)

G.3.11.1.   If the quail sings many times in a grainfield, the harvest will be great. (B, 92; Bk, 6, 75.)

G.3.11.2.   If the quail calls four times in a rye field, there will be twenty pood of rye in the barn; if it calls three times, there will be fifteen pood; if it calls six or seven times, there will be thirty or thirty-five pood. (Uj, 70.)

G.3.11.3.   If the quail calls three times in the grain field, three wagonfuls of grain will grow in one field; if it calls four or five times, four or five wagonfuls will grow; if it calls six or seven times, six or seven wagonfuls will grow. (J.)

G.3.12.1.1.   If the raven flies croaking over the village, someone in the village will die. (J.)

G.3.12.1.2.   If the raven comes croaking into the village, someone in the village will die. (B, 85.)

G.3.12.1.3.   If the raven comes into the birch grove to croak, there will be the death of a man or one of the livestock in the village. (Uj, 138.)

G.3.12.2.   If a raven flies croaking over a house, it forebodes evil for those in the house. (Wm, 188.)

G.3.12.2.1.   If a raven croaks on the roof of a house, someone in that house will die. (J; Uj, 139a; Up, 120a; Wu, 97.)

G.3.12.3.1.   If a raven sits croaking on top of the stall, some of the livestock will die. (J; Uj, 139b; Up, 120b.)

G.3.12.3.2.   If a raven sits croaking on top of the hayloft, some of the livestock will die. (Usj, 17.)

G.3.13.1.   If the skylark sings a long song, the weather will be wet. (Uj, 6a.)

G.3.13.2.   If the skylark sings a short song, there will not be rain. (Uj, 6b.)

G.3.14.1.   If the sparrows chirp, there will be rain. (Wj, 52; Wk, 6.)

G.3.14.2.   When in the fall sparrows come down on the yellow grass, it is time to sow. (J.)

G.3.15.1.1.   If the starling comes early in the spring, the spring will come early, the snow will go away soon. (B, 88; J; Up, 27; Wu, 71.)

G.3.15.1.2.   If the starling comes soon in the spring, the summer will come early. (Wm, 160.)

G.3.15.1.3.1.   If in the spring starlings come before March 17, then it will be cold in the spring. (J.)

G.3.15.1.3.2.   If in the spring starlings come late, after March 17, it will not be cold. (J.)

G.3.15.2.   When the starling leads its young out of the nest, it is time to sow buckwheat. (Up, 75; Wm, 176; Wt, 126.)

G.3.16.1.   If swallows fly very high, the day will be clear. (J.)

G.3.16.2.   When swallows fly, the time to sow has come. (B, 98.)

G.3.16.2.1.   If swallows pass over the field in a flock, it is time to sow rye. (B, 97; Uj, 86a, 87a.)

G.3.16.2.2.1.   If swallows pass over a field scattered, it is necessary to wait a bit before sowing. (Uj, 87b.)

G.3.16.2.2.2.   If only one, two, or three swallows fly over the field, it is necessary to wait a bit before sowing. (Uj, 86b.)

G.3.16.2.3.   When the swallows fly playing over a plowed field, the time has come to sow rye. (Wu, 80.)

G.3.17.1.   If the swan comes in the spring when there is still snow, the grain will grow poorly. (Uj, 56a; Up, 64.)

G.3.17.2.   If the swan arrives after the disappearance of the snow, the crop will grow well that year. (Uj, 56b.)

G.3.18.1.   Before rain comes, the titmouse bathes in the river. (B, 96; Uj, 13; Up, 11.)

G.3.18.2.1.   If you see a titmouse up high, the hemp will be long. (Wt, 129a.)

G.3.18.2.2.   If you see a titmouse down low, the hemp will be short. (Wt, 129b.)

G.3.19.   If the *t'ulik* bird comes and sings in the village at night, the village will burn. (Bk, 55.)

G.3.20.1.   If as you go hunting in the forest the woodpecker cries *kər-kər,* you will have luck. (B, 94.)

G.3.20.2.   If as you go hunting in the forest the woodpecker emits a shrieking sound, you will not have luck. (B, 95.)

G.4.   insects

G.4.1.1.   If black ants increase greatly in the yard, the sheep will increase. (Wk, 39.)

G.4.1.2.   When ants become winged, there will be rain. (J.)

G.4.1.3.1.   If the ant goes into the ground quickly, there will be snow. (Usj, 19.)

G.4.1.3.2.   If the ant enters its hill quickly, snow will come quickly in the fall. (B, 111; Up, 26.)

G.4.1.4.   If in the spring the ant climbs over the handle of the ax in the forest, oats will grow nicely. (Usj, 37.)

G.4.1.5.   If an ant urinates on your foot, your foot will be injured. (Uj, 193; Up, 129.)

G.4.2.1. The man around whom bees swarm will be lucky with bees. (Up, 115.)

G.4.2.2. If while a person is walking in the field bees come swarming on his head, he is said to be a lucky man. (Uj, 114.)

G.4.3.1. If there is a big cockroach in the house, it is a good sign. (Uj, 111.)

G.4.3.1.1. If there is a large cockroach in the house, it will be good for the family, and the livestock; the sheep will multiply. (Up, 84.)

G.4.3.2. If there are many cockroaches in the house, the livestock will increase. (J.)

G.4.3.2.1. If there are many cockroaches in the house, the sheep will multiply. (Uj, 154; Up, 83.)

G.4.3.2.2. If the cockroach comes into the house from someone else, the sheep will multiply. (Up, 85.)

G.4.3.2.2.1. If in the summer cockroaches come into a house where there have been no cockroaches, the sheep will multiply. (Uj, 157.)

G.4.3.2.3. If black cockroaches multiply in the house, the sheep will multiply. (B, 103.)

G.4.3.3.1.1. If cockroaches leave the house, the sheep will die. (Uj, 159.)

G.4.3.3.1.2. If the cockroaches leave the house, there will be a fire. (J.)

G.4.3.3.2.1. If the cockroaches escape from the village, the village will burn down. (J; Up, 137.)

G.4.3.3.2.2. If the cockroaches hide in summer, it is not good, the village will burn down. (B, 104.)

G.4.4. If snow fleas come down, the grain will grow well. (B, 109.)

G.4.5.1. If the flies are plentiful in the summer, the harvest will be plentiful. (B, 106.)

G.4.5.2. If the gnats keep flying back and forth and up and down, it is time to sow. (Uj, 83; Up, 67.)

G.4.5.3.1. If gnats, when they swarm in the spring, bite people on the upper part of the body, oats will grow nicely. (Usj, 38a.)

G.4.5.3.2. If the gnats bite on the lower part of the body, oats will be short. (Usj 38b.)

G.4.5.4. If in the spring long-legged gnats fly up and down in one place in a swarm grain will grow well. (B, 107.)

G.4.6.1.1. If there are many midges before St. Peter's Day [June 29], grain will grow well. (Uj, 54.)

G.4.6.1.2. If there are many midges at St. Peter's Day [June 29], grain will grow well. (Up, 56.)

G.4.6.2. If midges fly high, oats will grow well. (Wm, 170; Wt, 124.)

G.4.7.1.1. If after the harvest spiders spin many webs on the stubble in the field, the weather will be clear. (J.)

G.4.7.1.2. If the spider spins a web in the stubble in the fall, the grain will grow well the next year. (B, 112; Uj, 52; Up, 49.)

G.4.7.2.1. If the spider web falls from above, rye will grow well the next year. (Wk, 61.)

G.4.7.2.2. If the spider web falls from above, it is time to sow rye. (Wk, 20.)

G.4.8.1. If a tick fastens itself to the upper part of the body, hemp will grow tall. (Usj, 29.)

G.4.8.1.1. If in the spring a tick fastens itself to the neck or armpit, hemp will grow tall. (B, 108a.)

G.4.8.1.1.1.   If a tick sticks to one's neck in the spring, hemp will grow tall. (J; Uj, 76a.)

G.4.8.1.1.2.   If in the spring a tick fastens itself above the armpit, hemp will grow long. (Up, 61a.)

G.4.8.2.1.   If in the spring a tick fastens itself below the armpit, hemp will be short. (Up, 61b.)

G.4.8.2.2.   If a tick fastens itself to the small of one's back, hemp will be short. (B, 108b.)

G.4.8.2.3.   If a tick fastens itself at the height of the navel, hemp will be short. (J; Uj, 76b.)

G.5.   *rake* 'crabs'

G.5.1.   If there are many crabs in the river, life will be good for people. (B, 100b; Uj, 98.)

G.5.2.1.   If there aren't many crabs in the river, life will be hard for people. (B, 110a; Uj, 99.)

G.5.2.2.   If all the crabs disappear from the river, there will be war. (Uj, 128; Up, 117.)

G.6.   *kol* 'fish'

G.6.1.   If the fish breathe much in the lake, life will be hard for the livestock, they will begin to die. (Bk, 26.)

G.6.2.   In the spring the fisherman catches a pike. He inspects the heart and liver. If it is thick at the top, the grain must be sown early in the spring. If it is thick at the end, one should sow late. If it is thick in the middle, one should sow in the middle. (B, 99.)

G.6.3.1.   If the mudfish (*ñugə*) becomes red at its head, the early crop will be good. (Usj, 6a.)

G.6.3.2.   If the mudfish becomes red in the middle, the middle crop will grow well. (Usj, 6b.)

G.6.3.3.   If the mudfish becomes red on its tail, the later crop will be good. (Usj, 6c.)

G.7.   *žaba* 'frog'

G.7.1.   If there are drops of water on the frog in summer, there will be rain. (B, 102; Uj, 17; Up, 10.)

G.7.2.1.   In the spring when the frogs croak very much, it is time to sow oats. (J; Uj, 84; Up, 73; Usj, 36; Wu, 79.)

G.7.2.1.2.   If frogs in the swamp bark like a dog, one should sow early—the oats and the grain sown in the spring will grow very well then. (B, 101.)

G.7.2.2.   When the frog croaks in the spring, it is time to plant cabbage. (Wt, 128.)

G.7.2.3.   If the frog croaks, potatoes must be planted early. (Bk, 58.)

G.8.   *šinašal'ə* 'lizard'

G.8.   If a lizard urinates on your foot, it will be wounded. (Usj, 33.)

G.9. *šukš* 'worms'

G.9. If in the fall there are worms in the ground, the grain will be poor—the worms will eat the crop. (Uj, 74.)

G.10. *šurnə* 'grain'

G.10.1. If the grain stack bulges, the woman will become pregnant. (B, 137; J.)

G.10.1.1. If the front of the rye stack bulges, the woman will become pregnant. (J; Up, 158.)

G.10.1.2. If the oat stack bulges, the woman will become pregnant this year. (J; Uj, 150.)

G.10.2.1.1. If rye with two ears grows in someone's field, he will become rich. (J; Uj, 123.)

G.10.2.1.2. If someone finds two-eared rye in the field, he will become rich in grain. (Up, 102.)

G.10.2.2.1. When rye is in bloom, fish do not let themselves be caught; they do not go into the net. (B, 44.)

G.10.2.3.1.1. If rye begins to bloom at the bottom of the ear, rye must be sown early. (Up, 71.)

G.10.2.3.1.2. If the rye begins to bloom at the bottom of the ear, grain will be cheap. (B, 42a.)

G.10.2.3.2.1. If the rye begins to bloom in the middle of the ear, rye sown in the middle time will be better. (Up, 71b.)

G.10.2.3.2.2. If the rye begins to bloom in the middle of the ear, the grain will have a middle price. (B, 42c.)

G.10.2.3.3.1. If the rye begins to bloom at the tip of the ear, the rye sown late will be good. (Up, 71c.)

G.10.2.3.3.2. If the rye begins to bloom at the tip, grain will be expensive. (B, 42b.)

G.10.2.4. If a strip of ground in the middle of the rye field remains unsown, someone in the family will die. (B, 139; Uj, 134; Up, 119.)

G.10.3. If inside the grasshopper there is a grain of wheat in the spring, wheat will grow well. (B, 105.)

G.10.4. The time when peas bloom is difficult for children; they die then. (B, 45.)

G.11. *šudə* 'hay'

G.11.1. If hay and straw are expensive in the fall, they will be cheap in the spring. (Bk, 102.)

G.11.2.1. If during the mowing it is so damp that the hay rots, the grain planted in the spring will grow well. (B, 138.)

G.11.2.2. If during the mowing the hay rots on account of rain, rye and oats will be nice that year. (Uj, 65.)

G.12. *jeməš* 'fruits and vegetables'

G.12.1. If much fruit grows on the ground, then grain won't grow. (B, 47; J; Uj, 51; Up, 80; Usj, 31.)

G.12.2.1.1.   If the root of the cabbage has not dried up by spring, it can be planted in the garden. (Up, 77.)

G.12.2.1.2.   If the roots of the cabbage do not dry up by spring, the grain sown in the spring will grow well. (B, 46.)

G.12.2.2.   If the cabbage slips are expensive, the fodder is expensive. (Wk, 35.)

G.12.3.   If many potatoes grow in the ground, much grain will grow. (Uj, 49.)

G.12.4.1.   If much equisetum (*ur boč*) grows in the field, much grain will grow. (B, 54.)

G.12.4.2.1.   If much equisetum grows in the field, then not much grain will grow. (Uj, 50.)

G.12.4.2.2.   If much equisetum grows in the field, then the oats will be small (Up, 65.)

G.12.5.1.   If there are many hazelnuts, many girls will become pregnant. (Bk, 44.)

G.12.5.2.   If in the spring many 'earth hazelnuts' grow, much grain will grow. (B, 52.)

G.12.6.   If many mushrooms grow in the summer, grain will grow well next year. (B, 53; Uj, 66.)

G.12.7.1.   If there are many raspberries, the crop will grow well. (Uj, 64.)

G.12.7.2.1.   If the raspberries are large, the grain will grow well. (B, 50; Bk, 9a; Wu, 86.)

G.12.7.2.2.   If the raspberries are small, the grain will be small. (Bk, 9b.)

G.12.7.2.3.1.   If the raspberries are large at first, one should sow early. (B, 51a.)

G.12.7.2.3.2.   If the raspberries are large later, one should sow later. (B, 51b.)

G.12.7.2.3.3.   If the raspberries are large very late, then one should sow very late. (B, 51c.)

G.12.8.   If many cranberries, strawberries, and raspberries grow in the summer, the children will get smallpox in the winter. (D, 49.)

G.13.   *pušenge* 'trees'

G.13.1.   If many trees break under the pressure of snow, life will be hard for people. (Up, 134.)

G.13.2.1.1.   If leaves are thick on the trees in spring, grain will grow well. (J.)

G.13.2.1.2.   If in the spring leaves are sparse on the trees, grain will grow sparsely. (J.)

G.13.2.2.   When the birch sends forth leaves, it is time to sow oats. (Wm, 175.)

G.13.2.2.1.   If the leaves of the birch tree grow from the bottom of the tree, the early crop will be good. (Usj, 16a.)

G.13.2.2.2.   If leaves grow from the middle of the birch tree. the middle crop will be good. (Usj, 16b.)

G.13.2.2.3.   If leaves grow from the top of the birch, the late crop will be good. (Usj, 16c.)

G.13.2.3.   When the leaves on the tree turn yellow, it is time to sow. (B, 32.)

G.13.2.3.1.   When the leaves on the tree turn yellow, the time has come to sow rye. (Wm, 173.)

G.13.2.3.2.1.   If there are yellowing leaves on top of the birch tree, the time has come to sow rye. (Up, 69.)

G.13.2.3.2.2.   If in the fall leaves begin to get yellow at the top of the birch tree, it will be bad for the livestock. (J.)

G.13.2.3.2.3.   If birch leaves begin to turn red at the top of the birch tree, one must sow later. (Up, 70c.)

G.13.2.3.3.1.1.   If the birch tree has begun to turn yellow in the middle, one should sow early. (Uj, 88b.)

G.13.2.3.3.1.2.   If the birch tree doesn't turn yellow in the middle, the first sowing and the last sowing will be good. (Uj, 88c.)

G.13.2.3.3.2.   If birch leaves turn red in the middle, rye must be sown in the middle time. (Up, 70b.)

G.13.2.3.4.1.   If the birch tree has begun to turn yellow at the bottom, one must sow early. (Uj, 88a.)

G.13.2.3.4.2.   If the birch leaves begin to get yellow from the bottom, it will be good for livestock. (J.)

G.13.2.3.4.3.   If the bottom of the birch tree turns yellow, the early sowing will be good, the later will be sparse and short. (Uj, 72b.)

G.13.2.3.4.3.2.   If the bottom of the birch tree does not turn yellow, rye sown early will be sparse and short. (Uj, 72a.)

G.13.2.3.4.4.   If the birch leaves begin to turn red at the bottom of the tree, rye must be sown early. (Up, 70a.)

G.13.2.3.5.   If the top and middle of the birch tree turn yellow, or if the top and bottom of the birch tree turn yellow, then the rye will be uniform. (Uj, 71.)

G.13.2.3.6.   When the elm leaves begin to change color, it is time to sow rye. (Wk, 19.)

G.13.2.4.1.   If all the leaves fall from trees in the autumn, life will be easy. (J; Uj, 122b; Up, 133b.)

G.13.2.4.2.   If leaves do not fall from the trees in the autumn, life will be difficult. (Bk, 97; J; Uj, 122a; Up, 133a; Wm, 166.)

G.13.2.4.2.1.1.   If in the fall leaves stay green and unimpaired upon the trees, people will start dying. (Uj, 143.)

G.13.2.4.2.1.2.   If in the fall leaves do not fall from the trees, people will become ill and begin to die. (Wu, 100.)

G.13.2.4.2.2.1.   If all the oak leaves do not fall in the autumn, life will be difficult for people. (If frost comes early in the fall, the oak leaves fall late in the winter, in January or February.) (J; Wk, 18.)

G.13.2.4.2.2.2.   If oak leaves do not fall from the tree in the autumn, life will be difficult for men. (Bk, 49a.)

G.13.2.4.3.   If birch leaves do not fall, life will be difficult for women. (Bk, 49b.)

G.13.2.4.4.   If the leaves of the birch and oak do not fall quickly in the autumn, life will be difficult for people. (Wj, 68.)

G.13.2.4.4.1.   If the leaves of the trees fall on snow, life will be difficult for people. (B, 34.)

G.13.2.4.5.1.1.   If the leaf falls right side up in the autumn, the winter will be mild. (B, 33b; Uj, 44a; Up, 38a.)

G.13.2.4.5.1.1.1.1.   If the maple leaf falls rightside up, the winter will be warm. (Wk, 5a.)

G.13.2.4.5.1.1.1.2.   If maple leaves fall rightside up, the thief will be caught. (Wk, 48a.)

G.13.2.4.5.1.1.2.   If the birch leaves fall rightside up, the winter will be warm. (Wj, 54a.)

G.13.2.4.5.1.2.   If the leaves of the tree fall rightside up, the winter will be cold. (Bk, 8a.)

G.13.2.4.5.2.1.   If leaves fall upside down in the autumn, the winter will be cold. (B, 33a; Uj, 44b; Up, 38b.)

G.13.2.4.5.2.1.1.1.   If maple leaves fall upside down, the winter will be cold. (Wk, 5b.)

G.13.2.4.5.2.1.1.2.   If maple leaves fall upside down, the thief will not be caught. (Wk, 48b.)

G.13.2.4.5.2.1.2.   If the birch leaves fall upside down in the autumn, the winter will be cold. (Wj, 54b.)

G.13.2.4.5.2.2.   If the leaves of the tree fall upside down, the winter will be warm. (Bk, 8b.)

G.13.2.5.   If the leaves of the trees rustle when there is no wind, rain will come. (Bk, 41.)

G.13.3.   If there is much sap in the trees in spring, the summer will be spoiled by rain. (Bk, 51.)

G.13.4.1.1.   If the apple tree blooms in autumn, the autumn will be long; snow will not come soon. (Bk, 37.)

G.13.4.1.2.   If the apple blossoms fall off prematurely, there will be no apples; they will dry up. (Bk, 85.)

G.13.4.2.1.   When the mountain ash blooms, it is time to shear the lambs. (J; Uj, 160; Wt, 130.)

G.13.4.2.2.   When the mountain ash blooms, fish spawn; they can be caught then. (Uj, 160.)

G.13.4.2.2.1.   When the mountain ash blooms, the red eyes (*šerenge kol*) spawn; one can catch them then. (B, 40; Up, 89.)

G.13.4.2.3.   When the mountain ash blooms, it is good to sow wheat. (B, 39; Wj, 60.)

G.13.4.3.   When brier bushes bloom, tenches spawn; then the fisherman catches many tenches. (B, 41.)

G.13.5.   If there are many cones on the trees, much grain will grow. (B, 37; J; Uj, 46.)

G.13.5.1.   If there are many pine cones, oats will grow well. (J.)

G.13.6.1.   If the aspen has much ament, then much grain will grow. (J; Uj, 47.)

G.13.6.1.1.   If the aspen has much ament, barley will grow well. (Up, 53; Usj, 39; Wj, 62.)

G.13.6.2.   If birch trees have much ament in the spring, much grain will grow. (B, 36.)

G.13.6.3.   If elm trees have many seeds, much wheat will grow. (B, 38.)

G.13.6.4.   If many mountain ash berries grow, the crop will be meager in the coming year. (Usj, 20.)

G.13.6.5.   If in spring there are many small cones on the pine trees, oats will grow well. (Uj, 63; Up, 54; Wm, 169; Wu, 84.)

G.13.6.6.   If there are many rowanberries, the next year's grain will grow well. (J; Wk, 21.)

G.13.6.6.1.   When there are many rowanberries, the crop will grow well after only one plowing. (J; Uj, 78, 79, 80a; Up, 50, 51, 52; Wu, 87.)

G.13.6.6.2.   If not many rowanberries grow, it is necessary to plow twice before sowing. (J; Uj, 80b.)

G.13.6.7.   If cranberries and rowanberries grow large, one should sow late. (Bk, 45.)

G.13.6.8.   If there is ament on the sallow early, it will soon be warm. (Bk, 14.)

G.13.7.   If in the fall there are 'pine berries' on the pine trees, grain and flax will grow. (B, 48.)

G.14.   *keč̌ə, tələzə, i šüdər* 'sun, moon, and stars'

G.14.1.1.   If the sun comes up early, there will be rain that day. (Up, 4.)

G.14.1.2.1.   If the sun rises red, there will be rain. (J; Uj, 9; Up, 6.)

G.14.1.2.1.1.   If the sun rises very red, rain will come by noon. (J; Uj, 10.)

G.14.1.2.2.   If the sun rises red, snow will come. (B, 3.)

G.14.1.3.   If the sun rises "playing" on Easter Day, life will be easy for people. (J; Uj, 1, 121; Up, 132.)

G.14.1.3.1.   If the sun "plays" on Easter, the grain will grow well; life will be easy for people. (B, 166.)

G.14.1.4.1.   If there is a ring around the sun in the winter, the weather will be cold and dry. (J; Uj, 42.)

G.14.1.4.1.1.   If there is a ring around the sun in the winter, the weather will be cold for a long time. (J; Uj, 41; Up, 32; Wm, 155; Wt, 120.)

G.14.1.4.1.2.   If there is a ring around the sun, the weather will be clear. (Up, 1.)

G.14.1.4.2.   If there is a ring around the sun, the weather will be damp. (B, 4.)

G.14.1.5.   If the sun goes behind clouds, there will be rain or snow. (B, 2; Bk, 21; Wm, 147.)

G.14.1.5.1.   If the sun sets behind clouds in the summer, there will be rain. (Uj, 11; Up, 5; Wt, 109.)

G.14.2.1.1.   If the moon rises with its horns upward, life will be difficult for people in that month. (Bk, 34a, 107.)

G.14.2.1.2.   If the moon rises on a slant, life will be easy. (Bk, 34b.)

G.14.2.2.1.   If the new moon grows downwards, the weather will be rainy. (J.)

G.14.2.2.2.   If the new moon grows upwards, the weather will be clear throughout the month. (J.)

G.14.2.3.1.   If there is a ring around the moon, there will be rain. (Wt, 108.)

G.14.2.3.2.   If there is a ring around the moon, there will be snow. (Bk, 52; Wm, 151; Wt, 108.)

G.14.2.4.   If there are pillars of fire on both sides of the moon, the weather will be cold. (Bk, 53.)

G.14.2.5.1.   If a woman, cow, or mare gives birth at new moon, she will give birth to a male offspring the next year. (Wk, 37a.)

G.14.2.5.2.   If a woman, cow, or mare gives birth during the waning moon, she will give birth to a female offspring the next year. (Wk, 37b.)

G.14.3.1.1.1.   If there are few stars in the sky, the weather will be clear. (B, 7; Uj, 4.)

G.14.3.1.1.2.   If there are few stars in the sky at Christmas the smaller livestock will not multiply. (Uj, 158b.)

G.14.3.1.2.1.1.   If there are many stars in the sky, there will be rain. (Wt, 107.)

G.14.3.1.2.1.2.   If there are many stars in the sky, there will be sleet. (Wm, 150.)

G.14.3.1.2.1.3.   If there are many stars in the sky, there will be snow. (Uj, 23; Up, 23.)

G.14.3.1.2.2.1.   If the stars are thick on Christmas night, there will be much small livestock. (Uj, 158a; Up, 118.)

G.14.3.1.2.2.2.   If the stars are thick on Christmas night, there will be many goslings. (Wk, 42.)

G.14.3.1.2.2.3.   If there are many stars at Christmas time, the grain will grow well. (J.)

G.14.3.1.2.2.3.1.   If there are many stars on Christmas night, wheat will grow well. (Bk, 46.)

G.14.3.1.2.2.4.   If at Christmas there are many stars, different fruit will grow well. (J.)

G.14.3.1.2.2.5.   If at Christmas there are many stars in the sky and if they twinkle, nuts will grow well in the summer. (J.)

G.14.3.2.1.   If the morning star disappears, there will be war. (Bk, 68.)

G.14.3.2.2.   If the evening star disappears, there will be war. (B, 8; Uj, 129.)

G.14.3.3.   If a man sees a star falling from the sky, it means that somebody has died. (B, 6; J; Uj, 221; Up, 116.)

G.15.   *šokšə i jüštə* 'heat and cold'

G.15.1.1.   If it is warm in winter, it will be cool in summer. (J; Uj, 43.)

G.15.1.2.   If it is warm in summer, it will be cold in winter. (Bk, 20a.)

G.15.1.2.1.   If it is very warm in summer, it will be very cold at that time in winter. (J.)

G.15.1.3.   If it is warm at Christmas, life will be easy for women. (J.)

G.15.1.3.4.   If it is warm on the Friday before Easter, no grain will grow. (Bk, 39b.)

G.15.2.1.   If the winter is cold, the summer will be hot. (B, 1; Bk, 104a; J; Up, 40; Wm, 157; Wu, 72.)

G.15.2.1.1.   When it is cold in the winter, exactly half a year later it will be hot. (J.)

G.15.2.2.   If it is not warm in summer, the winter will be warm. (Bk, 20b.)

G.15.2.3.   If it is cold at Christmas, life will be lucky for men. (J.)

G.15.2.4.   If it is cold on Epiphany, the grain will be good. (Wk, 12.)

G.15.2.5.   If Palm Sunday night is clear or cold, grain sown early will grow well. (Wk, 13.)

G.15.2.6.1.   If it freezes on the Wednesday before Easter, no grain will grow. (B, 164.)

G.15.2.6.2.   If it freezes on the Wednesday before Easter, the barley sown early will grow well. (Bk, 39a.)

G.15.2.6.3.1.   If it freezes on the Wednesday before Easter, peas will grow well. (Bk, 95a.)

G.15.2.6.3.2.   If it is cold and clear on the Wednesday and Friday nights before Easter, the grain sown in the middle period will be good. (Wk, 14a.)

G.15.2.7.   If it freezes on the Friday before Easter, oats will grow well. (Bk, 95b.)

G.15.2.8.1.   If it freezes on the Saturday before Easter, barley will grow well. (Bk, 95c.)

G.15.2.8.2.   If it is cold and clear the night before Easter, grain sown late will grow well. (Wk, 14b.)

G.15.2.9.   If it freezes on Easter Day, the grain sown late will grow well. (Bk, 39c.)

G.15.2.10.   If it is cold during the plowing month, grain will increase. (V, 16.)

G.15.2.11.   If the night is cold at 'new bread' [July 20], rye must be sown early. (Wm, 174.)

G.15.2.12.1.   If the ground freezes hard in the fall, the crop will grow nicely. (Usj, 21.)

G.15.2.13.   If cold follows the snow, it is not good; grain will not grow well. (B, 21.)

G.15.2.14.   If the earth freezes deep, people begin to die. (B, 26.)

G.15.2.15.   If the Volga freezes on a meat day, the cows will give rich milk and there will be many fish. (Wk, 43.)

G.15.3.1.1.   If the surface of the ice has frozen rough, the grain will grow well. (Bk, 10a.)

G.15.3.1.2.   If the surface of the ice has frozen smooth, the grain will not grow well. (Bk, 10b.)

G.15.3.2.   If ice remains in the millpond in the spring, life will be hard for people. (Bk, 62.)

G.15.3.3.1.   If ice floes pile up high in the river in the spring, the water will rise high. (Bk, 5.)

G.15.3.3.2.   If the ice does not flow down the river in spring, life will be hard for people. (B, 24.)

G.15.3.3.3.   If ice does not go down the river with the water in the spring, life will be difficult for people; grain will not grow. (Wu, 91.)

G.15.3.3.4.1.   If the ice remains at the edge of the mountain in spring, people will have a hard time. (Uj, 208a.)

G.15.3.3.4.2.   If ice disappears down the river in the spring, life will be easy for people. (Uj, 208b.)

G.15.3.4.   If in the spring the road remains high (i.e., ice remains on the road), peas will grow well. (B, 19; J; Uj, 77; Up, 60; Wm, 171; Wt, 127.)

G.15.3.5.   If long icicles hang from the eaves in spring, the grain sown in the spring will grow well. (B, 23; Bk, 64.)

G.15.3.5.1.   If long icicles freeze on the eaves in the spring, oats will grow well. (Bk, 32; J; Uj, 55; Up, 58; Wm, 168; Wt, 125; Wu, 83.)

G.15.3.5.2.   If long icicles hang from the eaves in winter, barley will grow tall. (Wk, 24.)

G.15.4.1.   Before it turns cold in winter, the house is very warm. (B, 145a; J; Up, 36a.)

G.15.4.2.   Before it becomes warm in winter, the house cools off. (B, 145b; J; Up, 36b.)

G.16.   *jür i lum* 'rain and snow'

G.16.1.   If the winter is dry, the summer will also be dry. (B, 22b; Bk, 104b.)

G.16.1.1.   On whatever day is clear in 'butter week' [Shrovetide], on that day of the week wheat must be sown. (Wj, 59.)

G.16.1.2.1.   If it is clear on Easter day, wheat will grow well. (Wk, 15.)

G.16.1.2.2.   If the weather is clear on Easter Day, it will be clear throughout the summer. (Uj, 3; Up, 3.)

G.16.1.3.   If the weather is clear on *mokej* day [May 11], there will be many cucumbers. (Wj, 63.)

G.16.2.1.1.1.   If it begins to rain on a Wednesday, it will be wet for a long time. (B, 154; Uj, 8.)

G.16.2.1.1.2.   If it rains on a Wednesday, there will be rain for a week. (J; Up, 21.)

G.16.2.1.2.   If it rains on Friday, it will also rain on Sunday. (B, 156.)

G.16.2.2.1.   If it begins to rain in the morning, it will rain for a long time. (Bk, 83.)

G.16.2.2.2.   If it begins to rain in the evening, it will rain throughout the night. (J.)

G.16.2.3.   If the rain comes at midday with a great rush, then it will rain hard. (Bk, 22.)

G.16.2.4.1.   If there is rain on *kogo spas keča* [Aug. 15], then the fall will be rainy. (Wk, 3.)

G.16.2.4.2.   If there is rain on St. Nicholas' Day, the grain will grow well. (V, 119.)

G.16.2.5.   If the rain falling on water makes bubbles, there will be rain for a long time. (B, 17; Bk, 16; Uj, 21; Up, 9.)

G.16.3.1.1.1.   If it thunders for a long time, there will be rain for a long time. (B, 11; Bk, 69; J; Uj, 5a; Up, 7a.)

G.16.3.1.1.2.   If it thunders for a long time, life will be hard. (Usj, 7.)

G.16.3.1.2.   If it thunders briefly, the weather will be clear. (J; Uj, 5b; Up, 7b.)

G.16.3.2.1.   If thunder is heard first from the north, life will be difficult. (Bk, 23a.)

G.16.3.2.2.1.   If thunder is heard first from the south, life will be easy. (Bk, 23b.)

G.16.3.2.2.2.   If in the summer thunder is heard first from the south, the summer will be rainy. (Wj, 51.)

G.16.3.3.1.1.   If in spring you first hear thunder in front of you, life will be good. (B, 12b; Uj, 115a; Wu, 89a.)

G.16.3.3.1.2.   If you hear thunder in front of you, your stomach will be full. (Wt, 122.)

G.16.3.3.2.   If you hear thunder behind you, life will not be good. (Uj, 115b; Wu, 89b.)

G.16.3.4.1.   If you hear the first thunder of the spring on a full stomach, you will always have your fill. (B, 12a.)

G.16.3.4.2.   If you hear the first thunder of the spring on an empty stomach, you will live hungry. (B, 12c.)

G.16.3.5.1.   If it thunders for the first time in the spring on a meat day, the cow will give much rich milk. (B, 162; Uj, 153a; Up, 88a; Wu, 92a.)

G.16.3.5.2.   If it thunders for the first time in the spring on a fast day, many fish will be caught. (Uj, 153b; Up, 88b; Wu, 92a.)

G.16.4.1.   If the rainbow is high, the weather will be clear. (B, 9a; J; Uj, 7a; Up, 2a.)

G.16.4.2.   If the rainbow is low, there will be rain for a long time. (B, 9b; J; Uj, 7b; Up, 2b.)

G.16.5.1.1.   If there is much snow in winter, there will be much rain in summer. (B, 22a; J; Uj, 22; Up, 28.)

G.16.5.1.1.1.   When there is snow in winter, exactly six months later there will be rain. (J.)

G.16.5.1.2.   If there is much snow in winter, the grain will grow well. (B, 22a; Bk, 105; J.)

G.16.5.1.2.1.   If the snow is deep on the field in winter, grain will grow well in the summer. (Uj, 59; Up, 47; Wm, 161; Wu, 81.)

G.16.5.1.3.1.   If there is much snow in winter, the water will go away slowly in the spring. (B, 20a; J; Uj, 2a; Up, 41a.)

G.16.5.1.3.2.   If there is not much snow in the winter, the water will go away quickly in the spring. (B, 20b; J; Uj, 2b; Up, 41b.)

G.16.5.2.1.   If the first snow comes at night, it will remain the whole winter. (Wj, 56; Wk, 9.)

G.16.5.3.1.   If the first snow falls on a Friday or Wednesday, it will not melt. (Bk, 25a.)

G.16.5.3.2.   If the first snow falls on a day other than Wednesday or Friday, the snow will melt. (Bk, 25b.)

G.16.5.4.1.1.   If there is snow on Christmas Day, the grain will grow well. (Bk, 99; Uj, 61; Up, 42; Wu, 88.)

G.16.5.4.1.2.   If there is snow on Christmas Day, there will be many hazelnuts. (Wk, 32.)

G.16.5.4.2.   If it snows on New Year's Day, the grain will grow well. (Uj, 61, 62; Up, 42; Wu, 88.)

G.16.5.4.3.1.   If it snows on Epiphany, the grain will grow well. (Uj, 61; Up, 42; Wm, 164; Wu, 88.)

G.16.5.4.3.1.1.   If snow falls on the priest's head on Epiphany, much grain will grow. (B, 159.)

G.16.5.4.3.2.   If there is a snowstorm on Epiphany, there will be rain on St. Elijah's Day [July 20]. (Bk, 31.)

G.16.5.4.4.1.   If it snows during 'butter week' [Shrovetide], wheat and mushrooms will grow well. (B, 160.)

G.16.5.4.4.2.   If it snows on the first day of 'butter week,' buckwheat will grow well. (Uj, 75.)

G.16.5.4.4.3.   If it snows on 'butter week day' [the Sunday before Lent], it will be rainy during haymaking. (Wk, 1.)

G.16.5.4.5.   If there is snow on St. Nicholas' Day, grain will grow well. (Uj, 58.)

G.16.5.4.5.1.   If there is snow on St. Nicholas' Day, oats will grow well. (J; Up, 57.)

G.16.5.4.5.2.1.   If it snows in the morning on St. Nicholas' Day, the grain sown early will grow well. (B, 168a.)

G.16.5.4.5.2.2.   If it snows at noon on St. Nicholas' Day, the grain sown in the middle time will grow well. (B, 168c.)

G.16.5.4.5.2.3.   If it snows in the afternoon on St. Nicholas' Day, the grain sown late will grow well. (B, 168b.)

G.16.5.4.6.   As many weeks before *pokro* [October 1] as snow falls for the first time, that many weeks after *pokro* winter will come and the snow will not melt until spring. (Bk, 96; Wk, 10.)

G.16.5.5.   If in the spring an uneven hard crust of snow lies in the field, the grain sown in the spring will grow well. (Wk, 25.)

G.16.5.6.1.   If the snow is even in the field, the grain will grow well. (B, 18a.)

G.16.5.6.2.1.   If the snow is uneven in the field, the crop will grow nicely. (Uj, 60; Up, 48.)

G.16.5.6.2.2.   If the snow is uneven in the field, the grain will not grow evenly; it will be good in some places and sparse in others. (B, 18b.)

G.16.5.7.1.   If the snow on a tree stump is peaked, the crop will be nice. (Up, 44a.)

G.16.5.7.2.   If the snow on a tree stump is flat, the crop will be ugly. (Up, 44b.)

G.16.5.8.   If there are piles of snow on the tops of trees, there will be many swarms of bees in the following summer. (Wk, 44.)

G.16.5.9.   If the wind blows sand on top of the snow, grain will grow nicely. (B, 13; J; Uj, 53; Up, 43.)

G.16.6.   If there is rain or snow during a person's wedding, that person will be lucky. (J.)

G.16.6.1.   If it snows during a young man's wedding, he will be rich his whole life long. (B, 152.)

G.16.6.2.   If there is rain when the groom goes to fetch the bride, the bridegroom will be lucky. (J; Uj, 106a.)

G.16.6.3.1.   If there is rain when the bride is taken away, she will be lucky. (J; Uj, 106b.)

G.16.6.3.2.   If there is no rain when the bride leaves her house, she will not have luck. (J; Uj, 106c.)

G.16.7.   If there is much frost on the trees in winter, grain will grow well. (B, 27; Bk, 42, 106; J; Uj, 48; Up, 45, 46; Wu, 82.)

G.16.7.1.   If there is frost on the trees at Christmas, grain will grow well. (J.)

G.16.7.2.   If there is much frost on the trees on the eve of Candlemas, grain will grow well. (Wm, 162.)

G.16.7.3.   If there is frost on the trees during 'butter week' [Shrovetide], peas will grow well. (J.)

G.16.8.   If there is honeydew on the leaves of trees in summer, there will be much honey. (B, 35.)

G.17.   mardəž 'wind'

G.17.1.1.   If the wind blows from the south, there will be rain. (Up, 8; Wt, 112.)

G.17.1.2.   If the wind turns southward, rain will come soon. (B, 15; J; Uj, 19.)

G.17.2.1.1.   If the wind blows the snow on Candlemas, summer will not come soon and it will not be possible to turn the livestock out to graze early. (Bk, 57.)

G.17.2.1.2.   If drifts are formed on the road on Candlemas, the next year fodder will be expensive. (Wk, 33a.)

G.17.2.2.   If it is calm on Candlemas, fodder will be cheap and abundant. (Wk, 33b.)

G.17.3.1.   If the wind is from the east on Easter, one should sow grain early. (B, 165a.)

G.17.3.2.   If the wind is from the west on Easter, one should sow late. (B, 165b.)

G.17.3.3.   If the wind blows from the south on Easter, one should sow in the middle time. (B, 165c.)

G.17.4.1.   If the wind blows from the north on St. Elijah's Day [July 20], rye should be sown early. (B, 157a; Uj, 89a; Up, 72a; Wu, 77.)

G.17.4.2.   If the wind blows from the east on St. Elijah's Day, rye should be sown early. (B, 157a.)

G.17.4.3.   If the wind blows from the west on St. Elijah's Day, rye should be sown late. (B, 157b.)

G.17.4.4.   If the wind blows from the south on St. Elijah's Day, rye should be sown in the middle time. (B, 157c; Uj, 89b; Up, 72b.)

G.17.5.1.   If on *pokro* [October 1] the wind blows from the other side of the Volga [i.e., from the north], the winter will be cold. (Wk, 4a.)

G.17.5.2.   If on *pokro* the wind blows from the south, the winter will be warm. (Wk, 4b.)

G.17.6.   If in the spring or summer the wind breaks and uproots many trees, life will be difficult for people and there will be many deaths. (B, 14; Bk, 43, 103.)

G.17.7.   If a white cloud comes against the wind, there will be hail. (B, 10.)

G.18.   *oŋgər* 'bell'

G.18.   If the bell resounds long, there will be rain for a long time. (B, 150; Uj, 12; Up, 17.)

G.19.   *kində* 'bread'

G.19.1.   If a piece of bread goes into the windpipe while one is eating, someone will come. (B, 132; J; Uj, 262; Up, 104.)

G.19.2.   If bread falls out of your mouth while eating, you will not have anyone to give you food and drink when you are old. (Usj, 12.)

G.19.3.1.   If a piece of bread is left over, a guest will come. (Up, 140.)

G.19.3.2.   If a piece of bread is left over during a meal, your son, when he grows up, will seize you and beat you. (Uj, 198.)

G.19.3.3.   If a piece of bread is left over after a meal, there is someone in the family who is hungry. (B, 133.)

G.19.4.   If big cracks form on top of the bread as it bakes in the oven, someone in the family will die. (B, 134; Uj, 135; Up, 122.)

G.20.   *tarbaš* 'chip'

G.20.1.   If the first chip of wood cut when a house is being built falls upside down, life will be bad. (Bk, 40a.)

G.20.2.   If the first chip of wood cut when a house is being built falls right side up, life will be good. (Bk, 40b.)

G.21.   *ter kudatəmə kečə* 'sled putting away day'

G.21.1.   If the day for putting away the sled [Annunciation Day, March 25] falls on a meat day, the fisherman will catch many fish. (B, 161a.)

G.21.2.   If the day for putting away the sled falls on a fast day, the fisherman will not catch fish. (B, 161b.)

G.22.   *opsa* 'door'

G.22.   If the door creaks in winter, the weather will be cold. (B, 146.)

G.23.   *jara* 'empty'

G.23.1.1.   If as you are going somewhere you meet an empty cart, you will not have luck. (B, 118b; J; Uj, 105b; Up, 96b.)

G.23.1.2.   If as you are going somewhere you meet a cart full of grain, you will have luck. (B, 118a; J; Uj, 105a; Up, 96a.)

G.23.2.   If as you are going somewhere you meet someone with an empty pail, you will have bad luck. (B, 121; Bk, 84; J; Uj, 107; Up, 97; Wt, 141.)

G.23.2.1.   If as you set out you meet a woman with an empty pail, you will have no luck. (J; Usj, 14; Wu, 95.)

G.24.   *tul* 'fire'

G.24.1.1.   If the oven fire burns brightly, the weather will be cold. (B, 29a; Uj, 37a.)

G.24.1.2.1.   If the fire in the oven burns slowly, there will be snow. (Uj, 37b.)

G.24.1.2.2.   If the oven fire does not burn brightly, the weather will be mild. (B, 29b.)

G.24.2.   If the fire sings when the room is being heated, the weather will be cold. (Usj, 41.)

G.24.2.1.   If the fire sounds like a bell, the weather will be cold. (J; Uj, 38; Up, 34.)

G.24.3.1.   Before a snowstorm the fire crackles and is green. (B, 28.)

G.24.3.2.1.   If the pipe crackles, there will be rain. (Wt, 105.)

G.24.3.2.2.   If the pipe crackles, there will be sleet. (Wm, 148.)

G.24.4.1.1.   If the fire crackles and a glowing ember pops out onto the floor, a guest will come. (B, 148; Bk, 17, 71; J; Up, 142; Usj, 42; Wm, 177; Wu, 94.)

G.24.4.1.2.   If an ember pops out of the stove and falls onto the floor an angry man will come. (J; Uj, 263.)

G.24.4.2.   If wood burning in the stove leans forward, a guest will come. (J; Uj, 260.)

G.24.5.   If the soot on the bottom of the pot burns, there will be rainy weather. (B, 149; Bk, 94.)

G.24.6.1.1.   If the smoke from the chimney rises straight up, the weather will be clear. (J; Wm, 153; Wt, 117.)

G.24.6.1.2.   If the smoke from the chimney rises straight up, the weather will be cold. (Bk, 47a; Usj, 32a.)

G.24.6.2.1.   If the smoke from the chimney goes downward, the weather will be mild. (Bk, 47b; Usj, 32b.)

G.24.6.2.2.   If the smoke from the chimney goes downward, there will be rain. (B, 31; Wt, 116.)

G.24.6.2.3.   If the smoke from the chimney goes downward, there will be sleet. (Wm, 149.)

G.25.   *puč̌əməš̌* 'porridge'

G.25.1.   If while a Cheremis woman is cooking porridge the porridge keeps popping up very high, the woman will not have a good life. (Uj, 127.)

G.25.2.   If porridge boils over while cooking, there will be some loss in the family. (Up, 121.)

G.26.   *kəńə* 'hemp'

G.26.   If a bundle of hemp sinks to the bottom as hemp is being taken out of the water, some one in the family will die. (B, 142.)

G.27. *oksa* 'money'

G.27.1.   If someone gives you too much change and you don't return it, you will lose some of your own money. (B, 143; Uj, 118; Up, 186.)

G.27.2.   If you find money and take it, you will have trouble. (B, 144; Uj, 116, 117.)

G.27.2.1.   If you find money, you will lose money yourself. (Up, 184.)

G.28. *jondal* 'shoes'

G.28.1.   If your shoes squeak, it is not good. (Uj, 120; Up, 139.)

G.28.2.   If your shoe becomes untied while you are walking, your wife is having sexual intercourse with another man. (B, 135; J; Uj, 161; Up, 182.)

G.29. *muraš* 'singing'

G.29.1.1.   When a woman sings she is asking for the whip. (J; Uj, 264a; Up, 170a.)

G.29.1.2.   When a young girl sings, she is asking for a young man. (J; Uj, 264c; Up, 170c.)

G.29.1.3.   When a wife sings, she is asking for a brother-in-law. (J; Uj, 264e.)

G.29.2.1.   If a young man sings, he is asking for a girl. (Uj, 264b; Up, 170b.)

G.29.2.2.   If a handsome man sings, he is asking for a sister-in-law. (J; Up, 170d.)

G.29.2.3.   If a husband sings, he is asking for a sister-in-law. (J; Uj, 264d.)

G.29.3.   When a bird sings, it is asking for good weather. (J; Up, 170f.)

G.29.4.   When a crane sings, it is asking for peas. (J; Uj, 264h; Up, 170g.)

G.29.5.   When a pig squeals, it is asking for the knife. (J; Uj, 264f; Up, 170e.)

G.29.6.   When a wolf howls, it is asking for a dog. (J; Uj, 264g; Up, 170h.)

G.30. *sapando* 'swipples'

G.30.   If swipples touch while threshing, snow will come. (J; Uj, 24; Up, 22.)

G.31. *büt* 'water'

G.31.1.   Water warms up before rain. (B, 16; Uj, 197; Up, 18.)

G.31.2.   If the water rises high in the spring, flax will grow well. (B, 25.)

G.31.2.1.1.   If the Lemde [Nemda?] River stays flooded for twelve days equally high, much grain will grow. (Uj, 57a.)

G.31.2.1.2.   If the Lemde River does not stay flooded for twelve days, the grain will not grow well. (Uj, 57b.)

G.31.2.2.1.   If the water flows away evenly in the spring, one should sow early. (J; Uj, 85.)

G.31.2.2.2.   If the water goes away suddenly in the spring, oats must be sown early. (Up, 76a; Usj, 35b; Wu, 78a.)

G.31.2.2.3.   If the water goes away slowly in the spring, oats must be sown late. (Up, 76b; Usj, 35b; Wu, 78b.)

G.31.2.3.   On whatever day of the week the water rises high in the spring, on the same day in the summer one should sow flax in order that it grow well. (B, 151.)

G.32.   *kuaš* 'weaving'

G.32.1.   If a person comes when the weaving of linen is being finished, he will die. (B, 141a.)

G.32.2.   If a person comes as the web is being set up, he will have a long life. (B, 141b.)

G.33.   *törza* 'window'

G.33.   If the window becomes moist, there will be rain. (B, 147; J; Uj, 18; Up, 19.)

G.34.   divinations

G.34.1.1.   If one sticks an ax handle in an ant hill and the ants run along the ax handle, the grain sown in the spring will grow well. If they do not run along the handle the grain will not grow well. (B, 110.)

G.34.1.2.   If you place a stick into an ant hill and many ants climb up the stick, cucumbers will grow well that year; if they don't climb up, cucumbers will grow only here and there. (Uj, 82.)

G.34.2.1.   During 'half fast' little tarts are made; in each something is put: in one a coin, in another a goose feather, in a third rye, and in a fourth wheat. The person who finds money in the pastry he is eating will be lucky with money; the one who finds a feather will become lucky with geese and other fowl, the one who finds rye will have luck with grain. (B, 215.)

G.34.2.2.1.   At Christmas little pastries are made in each of which is put an object: a piece of sheep's foot, a piece of rope for fastening a calf, a piece of a bridle, a figure representing a bee hive, or a coin. The pastries are distributed and the object which each person finds indicates the kind of prosperity he will have. (S, 108.)

G.34.2.2.2.   At Christmas a small silver coin and a linden bark bridle are put into the holiday porridge. Whoever finds the coin will become rich; whoever finds the bridle will have good luck with horses. (H[1926], 189–90.)

G.34.3.   If you embrace a tree on which a cuckoo is singing, you can tell how many more years you will live by counting the number of times the bird cuckoos. (B, 209; J; Uj, 95; Up, 131.)

G.34.4.   On New Year's Day girls go out to the barn and stick their hands into a gap in the drying loft. The girl to whose hand it seems warm will marry an ill-tempered man. If it seems hairy or feathery, she will marry a rich man. If her hand feels cold, she will die. (Uj, 214.)

G.34.5.   A person who wishes to know the answer to a question with two alternatives can do so by trying to make his forefingers meet without looking at them. Often the question is put in such a way that an affirmative answer is given if the fingers meet and a negative answer if they do not meet. (J.)

G.34.6.   The answer to a question for which there are two alternatives can be found by burning a bit of flax. If the flax flies up as it burns the answer is affirmative; if it burns in place, the answer is negative. (Two descriptions of such divinations are given below.)

G.34.6.1.   After the uprooting of the flax a person puts a bit of flax on the table. As it is lit, the person says, "If I will get married this year, let the flame rise up; if I will not get married, let it burn low; let it not rise up." (B, 193.)

G.34.6.2.   "If I attained the age to become a soldier during Christmas, I prognosticate, I put flax on my belt, torn, rolled up, I don't press it too much together, then I say: 'If I go, let it burn and all fly up. If I don't go, let it not fly up but dissolve in the same place.' So I speak, then I light a candle and place it under the flax. Then the ball burns up about half, and it flies up. 'I'll become a soldier,' I announce. If it doesn't fly up, ' I won't become a soldier, it dissolved just there.' " (Uj, 208.)

G.34.7.   A young man or woman ties a hair on the leg of a horsefly and says, "Fly in the direction in which I will marry." In whichever direction the fly goes the person will get married (that is, the future husband or wife lives in that direction). (B, 208; Uj, 258; Up, 173.)

G.34.8.1.   If you guess which of my ears is ringing, what you think will be right; if you do not guess it, it will be wrong. (J; Uj, 190.)

G.34.8.2.   If you guess which of my ears is ringing, an acquaintance will die. If you do not guess it, an unknown man will die. (Up, 169.)

G.34.9.   On New Year's Eve boys and girls go out to the chicken coop in the dark and bring a chicken back into the house. The girl who gets a cock will marry a soldier. They put out water, bread, coal, and tobacco. Whoever's chicken pecks the bread will marry into a rich house. Whoever's chicken pecks the coal will marry into a poor house. Whoever's chicken pecks tobacco will marry a smoker. Whoever's chicken drinks water will marry a drunkard. (Bk, 82.)

G.34.10.1.   On Christmas Eve a person goes out to a fork in the road and listens with his ear to the ground. If there will be many weddings in the village, he hears the ringing of bells. If there will be many deaths, he hears chopping and hammering. If the grain will grow well, he hears the sound of threshing flails. On the way home he must not look back; if he looks back the devil (A.16.) will follow him. (B, 210.)

G.34.10.2.   On Christmas night people lie down in the field and listen. Whoever hears the sound of flails will marry a rich person. Whoever hears the sound of bells, will have a big wedding. Whoever hears nothing will die without getting married or will marry quietly without a wedding celebration. (Uj, 205; Up, 174.)

G.34.10.3.   If before midnight on Christmas Eve a person hears the sound of threshing at the barn gate, he will live; if he hears an ax, he will die; if he hears cattle low, the cattle will all live well. (Uj, 213.)

G.34.10.4.   On New Year's Eve people lie down in the middle of the field on the snow and listen. Whoever hears the sound of an ax will die next year. Whoever hears the rustling of grain or the clinking of money will become rich. A boy or girl who hears singing will get married. (Bk, 81.)

G.34.11.   A person catches a louse on a sick person and lays the louse on ashes sprinkled on the floor. If the louse crawls toward the door, the sick person will die; if the louse crawls toward the holy corner (E.6.), he will recover. (Bk, 66.)

G.34.12.   An unmarried girl stands a lighted match on end on a table. In whatever direction the match points after it has burned, in that direction she will get married. (J.)

G.34.13.1.   On Christmas young people pull stalks from the stack. The one who pulls out a stalk on which there are many kernels will marry a rich person. The one who pulls out a stalk on which there are no kernels will marry a poor person. (J; Uj, 207; Up, 172.)

G.34.13.1.   This is the same as above except that the stalks are pulled out of the stack with the teeth. (B, 212.)

G.34.13.2.   This is the same as 34.13.1. except that it takes place on New Year's Eve. (Bk, 80.)

G.34.14.1.   On Christmas Eve the young people go out to the sheep pen and grab a sheep by the foot in the dark. Whoever grabs a white sheep will marry a blonde, whoever grabs a black sheep will marry a brunet. Whoever grabs a big old sheep will marry someone big and old, whoever grabs a young sheep will marry someone young. (H, 190; P, 210.)

G.34.14.2.   On Christmas Eve the young people go out to the sheep stall and in the dark grab a handful of wool from a sheep. Whoever gets white wool will marry a blond. Whoever gets black wool will marry a brunet. (B, 213; J; Uj, 206; Up, 171; Wu, 96.)

G.34.15.1.   At the end of the harvest everyone throws his sickle. Whoever's sickle breaks will die within a year. (J; Uj, 131, 133.)

G.34.15.2.   At the end of the harvest everyone throws his sickle behind him. Whoever's sickle falls far from the others will die. (B, 192; J.)

G.34.16.1.   On New Year's Eve a boy who wishes to get married goes out to the field after everyone has gone to sleep. He strews grain three times on the ground and says, "Let the girl I will marry come to me this evening, awake me and go to harvest this grain." He goes home without speaking to anyone and goes to sleep. Around midnight his intended comes and calls him, "Come, let's go to harvest." Then he knows which girl he will marry. (Bk, 79.)

G.34.16.2.   A girl lays a lock on two pails on the night before Epiphany. When she goes to bed, she puts the key under her head. She will marry the one who asks her for the key in her sleep. (B, 158.)

G.34.17.   On New Year's Eve a girl lies down in the snow. If by morning a straw has fallen on the place where she lay, she will marry a rich man. If a leaf has fallen there, she will marry a poor man. (Bk, 56.)

G.34.18.   On the Wednesday night before Easter a spoon for each person in the family is put at the window. Whoever's spoon falls off during the night will die within a year. (B, 214.)

G.34.19.   An answer to a question for which there are a limited number of alternatives may be had by splitting the top of a small stick and placing a small crossbar in the crack. Each direction is assigned a meaning. Fire is put under the crossbar. When the crossbar has been sufficiently weakened by burning, it flies out impelled by the pressure of the two sides of the stick. The direction in which it flies indicates the answer to the question posed. (J.)

G.34.20.   A person may plant a number of trees assigning each a different meaning. A birch tree may represent wealth, a rowan prosperity in business, an apple tree prosperity in agriculture, a fir tree prosperity in carpentry, a poplar prosperity in thievery, a pine prosperity in traveling. Whichever tree thrives and grows tallest indicates the kind of prosperity which the person will have. That tree is tended for a long time. (Uj, 255.)

G.34.21. On Christmas night the girls take a piece of wood from the wood pile. Whoever gets a short piece will marry a short man. Whoever gets a long piece will marry a tall man. (Uj, 209; Up, 175.)

G.34.22. When the women cast yarn, they throw fiery coals into hot water one after the other. They say of the person whose coal sinks beneath the water, "Today it will be good for you. You start to soak first, then the yarn will be cooked." (Uj, 182.)

G.34.23. After the spring agricultural ceremony (B.2.) people stand in a group holding out their shirts and blouses as the priest throws oats over them. The one who receives the biggest share of the seed will reap the biggest harvest in the autumn. (H[1926], 178; H[1927], 242.)

G.34.24. If someone goes on a visit on *kon keča* (B.8.2.), it is possible to determine whether he is a good person or a bad person by observing the events during the year. If he is a bad person, the cattle die and misfortunes occur; if he is good, nothing happens. (Wu, 53.)

H. MAGIC

In this section are included spells and taboos. Attempts to control events by other than natural means which are described in other sections of the book are not listed here (Part One: "B. Ceremonies," "I. Cures"; Part Two: "Charms"). Magic practices recounted in folk tales have not usually been included in this section; for a motif index to magic in the folk tales, see Sebeok (1952), 78–84, and Sebeok, Balys, Roberts and Taylor, 169.

H.1.   magic affecting people

H.1.1. If, in the spring when the snow is disappearing, a person eats a small pike in cabbage soup, he will have a good life. (B, 66.)

H.1.2.1. People bathe before sunrise on Wednesday so that evil will not stick to them. (Up[S], 177.)

II.1.2.2. People bathe in the river before Easter so that their bodies will be in good condition throughout the summer. (J; Uj[S], 96.)

H.1.3.1. If a person leaves a morsel of food when he is eating, he will be left without a family. (Bk, 35.)

H.1.3.2. If noise is made on *kon keča* (B.8.2.) there will strife within the family. (Bk, 35.)

H.1.4. A love spell is cast in the following manner: Two spawning frogs are caught in the spring, wrapped in a white cloth, and placed in an ant hill. Thirty days later, after the ants have eaten the flesh of the frogs, two curved bones of the male and female frog are taken from the ant hill. A man who has these bones can make any woman he desires fall in love with him simply by touching her with the bones. (B, 71.)

H.1.5.1.   An engagement can be prevented by entangling the legs of a table with a rope. If a girl's father hears of it, he chops both the rope and the table legs to break the spell. (Usj[S], 46.)

H.1.5.2.   If, after rye is sown in the fall, a harrow is left in the field, no one in the village will get married. If the girls learn that a harrow has been left there, they go out to the field at night and chop it up. (Usj[S], 44.)

H.1.6.   If a man copulates with a woman lying on her right side, she will bear a male child. (Usj[S], 2.)

H.1.7.1.   If a woman gives birth in a sheep pen, the child will be lucky with sheep. (Uj[S], 103; Up[S], 101.)

H.1.7.2.   If a baby's umbilical cord is cut with an ax, he will learn carpentry; if it is cut with a knife, he will not learn carpentry. (B, 68.)

H.1.7.3.   If a woman eats food from which a mouse has eaten, she will learn to embroider. (Uj[S], 216; Up[S], 167.)

H.1.7.4.   If a man eats food from which a mouse has eaten, he will learn to make shoes. (Uj[S], 217; Up[S], 167.)

H.1.7.5.   If a man keeps a cat's afterbirth rolled up in a kerchief, he will not become a soldier. If he is conscripted, he will not pass the examination and will be rejected. (Uj[S], 257.)

H.1.8.1.   If a hunter eats the heart of a bear while it is still warm, he will get the bear's courage. (H[1926], 58.)

H.1.8.2.   If a child eats burned bread, he will not be afraid of bears. (J.)

H.1.9.1.   If a person's money has been stolen, he may take vengeance on the thief in the following manner: He catches a mouse and says, "As this mouse will burst, so let also the man's eye burst." Thereupon he hits the mouse so that it bursts. It is believed that the thief's eye will burst in a like manner. (Uj[S], 256.)

H.1.9.2.   To cast a spell against a thief, a person makes a candle the wick of which contains a wolf sinew. The candle is lit in church and the person says, "As the sinew in the candle is twisted, so let the feet and hands of the one who has stolen my money be twisted. As the candle burns, so also let his soul (čon) burn. Let him not keep from telling it." It is believed that the thief's hands and feet will begin to shrivel and become bent, and he will confess his crime. (B, 70; Up[S], 183.)

H.1.9.3.   If a thief while stealing money from a chest leaves behind a bit of clothing, a spell can be cast to make him confess. The piece of clothing left behind is hung on the clapper of a bell with the words, "May the thief not be able to endure the tolling of the bell." As a result of this the thief tells someone of his crime and the news spreads. (B. 70.)

H.1.10.1.1.   If a person lies on top of the stove, the stove will suck out his blood and he will become sickly. (Uj[S], 249; Usj[S], 13.)

H.1.10.1.2.   If a person lies face down on the earth, the earth will suck him. His heart will cool off and he will become phthisic. (Uj[S], 250; Up[S], 125.)

H.1.10.2.1.   A person who defiles by urinating or defecating on a former sacred spot or the place where there was once a kudə (E.1.) will become sick and may die. (Bk, 47; H[1926], 48; R, 206.)

H.1.10.2.2.   If a person urinates into a river, the *büt bodəž* 'water spirit' (A.9.1.) will punish the person with some affliction. (Usj[FB], 2.)

H.1.10.3.1.   If a person puts on a new shirt on Wednesday, his body will itch until he puts on another shirt. (Bk, 24.)

H.1.10.4.1.   If a person angers fire by spitting into it, stirring it with a dirty poker, throwing on wood very hard, or using improper language, it may send as a punishment *tul ajar,* a skin disease. (H[1926], 79.)

H.1.10.4.2.   If a person spits into fire, he will get a sore on his lips. (B, 55; Bk, 47; Uj[S], 192; Up[S], 128.)

H.1.10.5.1.   If a person angers water by making a loud noise, shouting, using bad language, drawing water with a dirty bucket, or splashing water on his clothes, he will get a skin disease called *büt ajar.* (H[1926], 62, 76.)

H.1.10.5.2.   If a person drinks directly from a spring, a sore will appear on his lips. (Bk, 46.)

H.1.10.5.3.   If a person urinates into a spring, a sore will appear on his penis. (Bk, 47.)

H.1.10.6.   If a person urinates toward the sun, either skin will come off the tip of his finger or sores will appear on his head. (B, 53; Uj[S], 191.)

H.1.10.7.   If a person eats food from which a cat has eaten, he will have lung trouble and breathe panting like a cat. (Uj[S], 174; Up[S], 124.)

H.1.10.8.   If a person eats cream which has burned while boiling, his face will be frostbitten in winter. (Bk, 41.)

H.1.10.9.   If a person stares very hard in his youth, he will lose his eyesight quickly. (Uj[S], 227; Up[S], 127.)

H.1.10.10.1.   If a person eats sour milk, his stomach will hurt. (J.)

H.1.10.10.2.   If a person swallows the leg of a fly, he will have a stomachache; if he swallows a whole fly, his stomach will not hurt. (Uj[S], 194, 195; Up[S], 126.)

H.1.10.11.   If a child walks around barefoot in the summer, people say, "The chicken will peck your foot." His foot dries out, cracks, and begins to hurt. (Uj[S], 251; Up[S], 130.)

H.1.10.12.   If a person takes up a stick or a spindle on *kon keča,* a snake will bite him the following summer. (H[1926], 38.)

H.1.10.13.   If a person drinks water from which the *büt ört* 'water soul' (A.58.2.) has left, he will become sick. (H[1926], 87.)

H.1.11.   When a girl sees her image in a mirror, she kisses the mirror and says, "Do not take my likeness." (H[1926], 84.)

H.1.12.   If children go far to play, an antlered hare will carry them off on its back. (J.)

H.1.13.   If a child eats eggs offered to the dead at Easter (B.8.3.4.), he will not grow up. (J.)

H.2.   magic affecting animals

H.2.1.   If a person works on the day before St. George's Day [April 22], wolves will eat his livestock. (Wk, 8.)

H.2.2.1.   If a horse is harnessed in the week of the Annunciation, its shoulder will be injured. (Wk, 8.)

H.2.2.2.   The sex of a foal is determined by the position of the mare when it is mounted. If the mare stands with its head toward the stable, the foal will be male; if it faces the gate, female. (Usj[S], 3.)

H.2.2.3.   A person who is angry with a bride may spoil the wedding by conjuring up a wolf or a bear to frighten the horses. This may be done by smearing bear grease on the gate and the shaft of the wagon. The bear or wolf is seen only by the horses and not by humans. (B, 71; Uj[S], 247–48.)

H.2.2.4.   Colored threads are tied in the horse's mane and tail to protect the horse against the evil eye. (Uj[S], 229; Up[S], 162; Usj[S], 4.)

H.2.3.1.   When a calf is born, the owner pours water on the stove so that the calf will grow as big as the stove. Those present for the 'cow's milk feast' (B.28.) are also sprinkled with water as a prayer is said that the cow give much milk. (H[1913], 122; H[1926], 91; H[1927], 28.)

H.2.3.2.   If cows are fed "cow grass" or "milk grass" in the spring, they will give a lot of milk. (Uj, 152; Up, 81.)

H.2.4.1.   To increase the fertility of the sheep, at Christmas (B.19.) people pull the legs of sheep and wish that they may bear twins and increase. (B, 20; H[1926], 190; S, 108; Wt, 59.)

H.2.4.2.   At Christmas time an owl is hung in the sheep stall so that the sheep will be healthy and multiply. (J; Wu, 17.)

H.2.4.3.   If a man has sexual intercourse with his mother-in-law, the sheep will multiply. (B, 68; Uj[S], 155; Up[S], 87.)

H.2.4.4.   If the sheep are not multiplying properly, an ant heap is thrown on top of the sheep pen to make the flock increase. (Usj[S], 34.)

H.2.4.5.   If sheep are shorn on Friday, they will get the staggers. (Wk, 8.)

H.2.5.   Hens are fed wheat or hemp seeds at Christmas (B.19.) with the wish that they will lay as many eggs as there are grains. (B, 69; Uj[S], 210, 211.)

H.26.   If the beehive is opened during the first week of Lent, there will be many flies which are harmful to bees. (Wk, 9.)

H.3.   magic affecting plants

H.3.1.1.   At Christmas (B.18.) piles of snow are made on the threshing-floor or in the field signifying the desired abundance of grain. (H[1926], 190; S, 108; Wt, 58.)

H.3.1.2.1.   Eggs are threshed on the threshing-floor at Christmas to express the desire that the grain be as big and as hard as eggs. (S, 107.)

H.3.1.2.2.   Hard boiled eggs taken from a girl are thrown out with the first handful of oats as sowing is begun. This brings good luck both for the crop and the girl. (H[1926], 179.)

H.3.1.3.1.   If three unthreshed sheaves are left on the threshing-floor, the grain will grow well. (Bk, 27.)

H.3.1.3.2.   If much grain is left unground in the mill in the spring, grain will grow well the next year. (B, 63.)

H.3.1.4.   If flour is ground, in the first week of Lent, the grain will not grow well. (Wk, 5.)

H.3.1.5.1.1.   If sowing is begun on Monday, the grain will grow well. (B, 64.)

H.3.1.5.1.2.   If sowing is begun on Wednesday, the grain will grow well. (J.)

H.3.1.5.2.   If barley is sown on Tuesday, it will not grow well; the stalks will be soft. (Wk, 6.)

H.3.1.5.3.   If a person starts to sow on the day of the week on which he was born, the grain will grow well. (Uj[S], 124; Up[S], 66.)

H.3.1.5.4.   If a child born with a hat and shirt [caul?] on begins to sow with them, the grain will grow well. (Uj[S], 149; Up[S], 114.)

H.3.1.5.5.   It is not good to sow or plant on the day of the week on which the Annunciation falls. (Wj, 11; Wk, 6.)

H.3.1.5.6.   Barley should be sown in the seventh week before St. Elijah's Day [July 20]. (Wk, 6.)

H.3.1.6.   While the grain is ripening, many taboos must be observed if the grain is to ripen properly. At this time no noise may be made, the *sürem* horn (F.16.) may not be blown, no hard work may be done, no building, no digging stones out of the earth, no chopping trees, no making bricks, no spinning or weaving. No bad smelling jobs such as carrying manure or making tar may be performed. It is also taboo to cross the rye fields, pick flowers, dye yarn, swim, wash clothes, move ashes, or wear startling colors. If these taboos are broken, a destructive hailstorm or cold weather may ruin the crop. It is said that grain does not like the smell of manure and dries up if the odor reaches it. (Bk, 34; H[1913], 129; H[1926], 179–80; H[1927], 246; R, 202; Wk, 4.)

H.3.1.7.   No grain should be cut before it ripens. If it is cut, the remaining grain will spoil and be ruined. (H[1926], 81.)

H.3.1.7.1.   If someone takes an ear of grain while the crop is growing and says a spell over it, the harvest will be bad. (H[1926], 135–36; P, 200.)

H.3.1.7.2.   If a person goes out to another's rye field when it is almost ripe, takes some rye home, and eats porridge made of it, the other's grain will grow poorly, but he himself will become rich. It is said that the *ia* 'devil' (A.16.) takes the grain from one storehouse to the other. To regain the luck thus stolen from him, a person must watch to see where the thief throws the first handful of grain when he starts to sow and take three grains. Then the thief will have no luck, but will become poor. (B, 19.)

H.3.1.7.3.   If a person has had bad crops for two or three years, he believes that someone has stolen the *pasu perke* 'field blessing' (A.67.14.) from his field. He finds out by means of a soothsayer (D.7.) who has stolen it. He goes secretly to that person's field late at night, puts a little earth in a bast shoe and drags the shoe by the laces to his own field. (H[1926], 89.)

H.3.1.8.   Wedding guests try to steal the bride's parents' *sürem* horn (F.16.) If they succeed, they take the *pasu perke* 'field blessing' (A.67.14.) to the groom's home. (H[1926], 182.)

H.3.1.9.1.   When people go to reap they pray for their hands and feet and ask that their bodies be as supple as straw. The one whose 'hands and feet are light' should begin to reap first. (B, 67; Uj[S], 225; Up[S], 184.)

H.3.1.9.2.   If a person begins to reap on the day of the week on which he was born, the work will go well. If not, the work will not progress and his hand will be cut off. (Uj[S], 125; Up[S], 90.)

H.3.1.10.1.   When a person builds a grain stack to last for several years, he puts a stone in the stack for mice to eat. In this way he protects the grain from mice. (J; Uj[S], 226; Up[S], 80; Usj[S], 9; Wu, 16.)

H.3.1.10.2.   When a man builds a stack, he makes not a sound until the stack is finished. If he places the sheaves with the ears toward the north, mice will not eat a single grain. (B, 67.)

H.3.2.1.   At Christmas (B.19.) people masquerading as 'Vasili old man' and 'old woman' (A.38.3.) go from house to house scattering hemp seed on the floor. They dance on it expressing the hope that the hemp will grow well. (Uj[S], 212.)

H.3.2.2.   If people go sledding down a hill or slide down a ramp at *ü arńa* 'butter week' (B.26.), flax and hemp will grow well. Sometimes they scatter hemp seed as they descend. Masqueraders called 'butter week old man' and 'old woman' say that the hemp will grow well. (B, 19; Uj[S], 212; Uj, 12; Wk, 4.)

H.3.2.3.   If a woman sows hemp on the day of the week on which she was born, the hemp will grow well and will become very white. If not, the hemp will not mature but will be grey. (Uj[S], 126.)

H.3.2.4.   If hemp and flax are sown during the eighth week before St. Elijah's Day [July 20], then they will sprout downward. They should be sown instead either in the seventh or ninth week before St. Elijah's Day. (Wj, 12; Wk, 7.)

H.3.2.5.   If a person cuts his hair while flax is being sown between Easter and Pentecost, the flax will be short. (B, 65.)

H.3.2.6.   A woman should cast yarn into the oven on the day of the week on which she was born so that the yarn will be white. (Up[S], 91.)

H.3.2.7.   A person should steep hemp on the day of the week on which she sowed it. (Wk, 7.)

H.3.2.8.   If hemp is steeped on *büt jükšəmə kečə* 'water cooling day' [in September], it will be good for spinning. (J.)

H.3.3.1.   If a person combs his hair, scratches his head or sweeps out the house on *kon kečə,* chickens will scratch up his garden. (Bk, 35; Wk, 7; Wu, 53.)

H.3.3.2.   If a person holds a needle in his hand on *radińča* (B.12.), hens will scratch up his garden. (Wj, 11.)

H.3.4.   When cabbages are stored in a tub, they are covered with a plank on top of which is placed a meteorite. This prevents the cabbages from spoiling and gives them a good taste. (Uj[FB], 74.)

H.3.5.   The water dripping from icicles is sprinkled on cucumber seeds and seedlings to make them grow well. This is done either on the Wednesday before Easter or on St. Eudocia's Day [March 1]. (Bk, 26; Wk, 7.)

H.3.6.   Old women bake potatoes in the oven at Christmas so that potatoes will grow well the coming year. (Wt, 59–60.)

H.3.7.   Some people shake the apple tree at Christmas as if shaking down apples. (H[1926], 90.)

H.3.8.   If vegetables are picked when the moon is new, they will rot. (Wk, 7.)

H.3.9.   If wood is cut when the moon is waning, there will be no new shoots. (Wk, 9.)

H.4.   magic affecting evil powers

H.4.1.   If a person looks through the hole of a big branch with his left eye, he may see a devil (A.16.). (Uj, 64.)

H.4.2.   Spoken formulas are common means of combating evil of all sorts. These formulas may be as simple as the single word *bəsməlä* or as complex as the charms (see Part Two, "Charms"). (B, 26; Be, 45, 48–49, 53–55; Uj[FB], 67; V, 60, 68, 86, 139, 245, 262, 320.)

H.4.3.   Branches of trees, especially the mountain ash and rowan, are used to drive away evil spirits. During the exorcism ceremony (B.18.), switches of mountain ash and rowan are used to beat houses, walls, fences, and women. Mountain ash branches placed over a door or at a gate prevent evil from passing through. When a person sleeps in the forest at night, he puts mountain ash twigs under his head to protect him from evil spirits. Rowan branches are put into a coffin to scare away evil spirits which might molest the deceased on his way to the under world. Brier twigs are also put into the coffin to chase away snakes which might attack him. An aspen stake driven into the ground at the grave is supposed to prevent a corpse from leaving the coffin. (Be, 48, 390, 707; Bk, 123; H[1926], 18, 40, 81, 180; S, 141.)

H.4.4.   Iron has special magical properties. The sound of the clanging of iron is believed to attract the gods and chase the evil spirits; for this reason during prayers a knife is struck against an ax. If iron is put over or under a door, evil spirits cannot enter, nor will the house be robbed. If a person makes a circle around himself or around a field with an iron object, he is said to make an "iron fence" within which evil spirits may not come. If a baby is left alone, an iron object such as a knife or scissors is put into the cradle to keep evil spirits from harming the child. A bride puts a needle or nail on the gatepost as she leaves her parents' home so that evil cannot follow her. She sometimes moves a needle from one gatepost to the other to make an "iron gate." An iron or copper object is put on the place where animals are slaughtered in the yard so that evil spirits will not remain there. An ax, knife, or other iron weapon thrown into a whirlwind causes it to disappear. Buried money appearing in the form of a person or animal can be disenchanted by striking it with an ax or other iron object. If the water spirit's daughter (A.96.2.) is touched with an iron object, she cannot escape. (B, 67–68; Bk, 50, 122–23; G, 56 [149]; H[1926], 51, 54, 59, 68, 72–73; Häm.[1915], 133; Häm.[1930a], 78; Uj[S], 231, 235–39, 242, 243; Up[S], 178, 179; Wu, 17.)

H.4.5.   Fire is used to combat evil. Smoke is believed to drive evil spirits away and attract gods. People put a firebrand in the doorway to a cattle stall so that evil will not enter; for the same purpose they place the extinguished firebrand inside the stall. Fire is used to destroy evil spirits. A tree was set on fire to prevent it from becoming a *keremet* (A.31.). A corpse which contained a *buber* (A.10.) was burned to destroy it, but the *buber* escaped in the form of a bird. Sometimes people jump over fire to purify themselves. On the Thursday before Easter each member of the family jumps three times over a burning juniper in the middle of the floor and asks the fire mother (A.1.15.) to purify him from evil. During the exorcism of evil spirits (B.18.), young people jump over a fire three times holding a firebrand and then drive the firebrand into the ground. See also the fire ceremony (B.29.). (Be, 48, 376; H[1926], 122, 151, 178; S, 153; Uj[S], 244, 255; Wu, 53–54.)

H.4.6.   The influence of Christianity is seen in the use of the cross by pagan Cheremis. Imitating the Christian practice some pagan priests cross themselves during ceremonies. Crosses are put at doors and windows to prevent evil from entering. If a person makes a cross under his feet when he gets up in the morning, he will fare well all day. Crosses are also made during a wedding ceremony (B.17.). (B, 45; Bk, 28, 44–45, 67, 72, 73; S, 193; Uj[FB], 90; S, 240, 241; Up[S], 180.)

H.4.7.   Salt is thrown into fire to chase away an evil spirit (A.11.). (B, 46.)

H.4.8.   A mirror is hung in the house so that if the devil (A.30.) enters, it will see itself and be frightened into leaving. (Bk, 48; R, 202.)

H.4.9.   A little bag of gunpowder is sewn or nailed into a baby's cradle to prevent evil spirits from harming the child. (J.)

H.4.10.   Stones from a chicken's craw put in the mouth of a corpse which contains a *buber* (A.10.) will prevent the evil spirit from coming out. (Be, 50.)

H.4.11.   The soul of the living, as well as of the dead, can fly around as a *buber* (A.10.). Its course can be stayed by tearing off the wristband of one's shirt or the band of one's bast shoes, or by splitting a wooden pitchfork. The *buber* will then fall to the ground and be changed back into a human form. (H[1926], 13; H[1927], 10.)

H.4.12.   An *obda* (A.51.) can be overcome if a person sticks his hands into its armpits. (H[1926], 55.)

H.4.13.   If a *targəldəš* (A.86.) leads a person astray in the forest, he must put his right shoe on his left foot in order to find his way home. (H[1926], 54.)

H.4.14.   A bast band wound around a tree for this purpose makes it a *keremet* (A.31.). (Be, 376–78.)

H.4.15.   A man who knew magic spit into the wind saying, "May it be a wind like the devil," and a devil (A.16.) was created. (B, 10.)

H.4.16.   If a person spits on the floor, he should step on the spittle lest a devil (A.16.) come into the house and lightning burn the house in an attempt to destroy the devil. (B, 10.)

H.4.17.   A thread drawn from a bundle of threads on top of a coffin is tied at the neck of a shirt to protect the wearer from sorcery and other evils. (H[1926], 19.)

H.5.   magic affecting the dead

H.5.1.   If a person dies on a feather bed or a felt mattress, he must count the feathers or hairs in the mattress in the next world. For this reason a dying person is usually placed on a straw pallet. (H[1926], 16; S, 137–38.)

H.5.2.   Wood left over from making a coffin is not burned lest the face of the corpse become blistered. (H[1926], 22; S, 135.)

H.5.3.   When death occurs precautions are taken to keep the deceased from harming the living. If there is a mirror in a room in which there is a corpse, it must be turned around or covered so that the dead will not select a comrade for itself among those present. Those taking part in a funeral procession must not look around. Villagers do not look at the procession from their windows, but often cover them so that they do not follow the dead. The sled used to take the corpse to the cemetery is either abandoned at the cemetery or left on the street three days before it can be used. Those returning from a burial return only to the house in which the death took place. There they bathe or at least cleanse their hands by washing or rubbing them with ashes. A pot of glowing coals, a heated stone, or ashes are put over the place where a corpse has lain in a house. (H[1926], 20, 22; H[1927], 22; S, 135, 137.)

H.5.4.   If, on the Thursday before Easter, a person puts on his clothes backwards or puts a horse bow around his neck and sits on the roof, he can see the dead wander about. (H[1926], 37.)

H.5.5.   The dead must return to the grave at cockcrow. (Bk, 122.)

H.6.   black magic

H.6.1.   Evil sorcerers (D.2.1.) go about on the Wednesday before Easter secretly collecting hair, pieces of clothing and whatever they can get. On the Wednesday before Pentecost the spell is cast. The things which a sorcerer has collected are thrown into a spring, buried in the earth, or held between the sorcerer's teeth. The sorcerer climbs to the top of a fir tree and comes down head first shouting that various parts of his body hurt him. After this the people and animals from which he stole hair and bits of clothing begin to fall sick and die. It is sometimes said that the person is enlisting the aid of a *keremet* (A.31.) in casting the spell. (B, 18; Uj[TF], 52; Wu, 67–68.)

H.6.2.   The evil activities of a *keremet* (A.31.) can be turned against one individual by another. *Jamšener* (A.19.) sends illness to those whose clothes or hair it finds buried in its territory. (S, 153.)

H.6.3.   To cast a harmful spell on someone, a handful of dirt from a grave or a human bone is left at the gate, on the stairs or at the threshold of the house of the person against whom the spell is directed. A lock of that person's hair is also left at the grave so that the dead will take vengeance on the one whom it believes to have disturbed its rest. When the person steps on the bone or dirt left near his door, he will fall ill and die. If a human bone is thrown into a well, the well will dry up; if it is thrown into a cultivated field, the field will be unproductive. (S, 154.)

H.6.4.   The wrath of a saint can be invoked by burning a candle upside down before its icon. (S, 156.)

H.6.5.   A person with an evil eye or an evil tongue can harm a person or an animal merely by looking at him or making an innocent remark about him. A person with an evil eye should look up at the ceiling to keep from harming anything. Spells are said to counteract the bad effects of the evil eyes. For the protection of a horse from the evil eye, see H.2.2.4. (B, 26; J; Uj[FB], 98; S, 184, 228; Up[S], 160.)

H.7.-15.   miscellaneous

H.7.1.   If a person begins to work on Monday, the work will be difficult the whole summer long. (Wj, 12; Wk, 9.)

H.7.2.   Work begun on Tuesday or Wednesday will not go well. (J.)

H.7.3.   If a person begins to work on Friday his work will not go well throughout the year. (J.)

H.7.4.   If a person works on a day of rest, he will lose a work day. (J.)

H.7.5.   A person should begin to work in the morning before the devil (A.15.) gets up. (J.)

H.7.6.   Work done at night will not amount to anything. (J.)

H.8.1.   At Christmas old people count kopeks as if they were rubles so that the money will increase in the following year. (H[1926], 189; Wt, 59.)

H.8.2.   If a person cooks and eats a black cat in the bathhouse at midnight, he will become rich. (Uj[S], 223; Up[S], 159.)

H.9.1.   If a person shouts, whistles, smokes too much, or dirties a house, its soul (A.58.9.) will go away and the devil (A.30.) will enter. (H[1926], 87; R, 205.)

H.9.2.   If a person chops or threshes on *kon keča*, the wind will take the roof off the house. (Wk, 5; Wu, 11.)

H.9.3.   To insulate a house well, on *pokro* [October 1], one person stuffs moss into the chinks on the outside while another lies on the floor inside. The one on the outside asks, "Is your house warm?" The one inside answers, "Very warm, it cannot be endured." (Wk, 10.)

II.9.4.   When a new bathhouse is heated for the first time, butter is put on the bench so that the steam will be good. (H[1926], 52.)

H.10.1.   Water is poured to produce rain. Sometimes this is a special ceremony (B.6.) or a part of the spring agricultural ceremony (B.2.); at other times it is simply a magic rite. Water is poured on both people and animals. In one instance it was poured on the grave of a drunkard with the words, "Do not dry up our earth Here you have water." (H[1926], 73–75, 178; H[1927], 242; J; Usj[S], 40.)

H.10.2.   If a horn is broken during a *sürem* ceremony (B.18.), there will be hail. (H[1926], 182.)

H.10.3.   For protection from a thunderstorm a person born before St. Peter's Day [June 29] throws an ax into the yard and wool from a white lamb into the fire. (H[1926], 67.)

H.11.   In the summer when it is hot and calm, people send a boy to someone for a bag of wind. He is given a bag of ashes. The bag is emptied from a height and as the ashes drift down, the wind begins to blow. (J.)

H.12.1.   A black chicken or milk from a black cow is thrown into a fire as an offering to *tul aba* (A.1.15.) to extinguish a conflagration. (H[1926], 80.)

H.12.2.   A fire started by lightning cannot be extinguished with water. A red cock, a red Easter egg, or milk from a black cow must be thrown into the fire before it can be extinguished. (Usj[S], 8.)

H.13.   If a brook is dirtied by a woman drawing water with a dirty pail, it will dry up. (H[1926], 77.)

H.14.   Miraculous powers [not specified in the source] are assigned to stags' horns (S, 161.)

H.15.   Many taboos are connected with *kon keča*. The failure to observe some brings chickens into the garden (H.3.3.1.); some result in snake bite (H.1.10.12.); no specific punishment is mentioned for others. Work must not be done on this day. Nothing may be taken in or out of the house, the oven may not be lit; cattle may not be fed with the hands, but fodder may be kicked to the animals. (H[1926], 38.)

I. CURES

Many illnesses are believed to be caused by supernaturals and can only be cured by making an offering to the one which has sent the disease. Such spirits have been discussed in Section A, some of the more elaborate offerings to them in Section B, and the method of diagnosis by seers and sorcerers in Section D. Another method of curing is by means of spoken charms and spells. For the content and structural analysis of charms, see Part Two, "Charms"; for the healer who practices this art, see D.9. This section contains cures other than those mentioned above.

I.1. A person with rheumatism or a backache should apply rubbing alcohol to the painful area. (J.)

I.2. A person who has *šem mužǝ* 'black fever' must drink three times a day a potion made of the fermented water in which black birch ament and grass roots have been boiled. (Be, 386.)

I.3. "Ant butter," a salve to heal wounds, is made in the following manner: A cream-smeared glass is placed in an ant heap. When the glass is full of ants, it is put in dough and baked in the oven. Later the ants are shaken from the glass onto a cloth. The cloth is squeezed and "ant butter" comes out. (Usj[S], 18.)

I.4.1. A bath in the bathhouse is a cure for a cold or a headache. It is said that *run kuguza* and *kuba* 'mucus old man' and 'old woman' (A.38.24.) burn their noses in the bathhouse and leave. However, it is also said that *nerge kuba* 'cold old woman' (A.38.17.) will be worse if taken to the bathhouse. For such diseases as smallpox and measles a bath is believed to be harmful. 'Smallpox old woman' (A.38.25.) becomes angry at having her nose burnt and takes the child. (B, 16; J; Uj[FB], 68; Up[FB], 16, 17, 27.)

I.4.2. If a person bathes in the river on the Wednesday night before Easter, he will not get *udǝrtǝš čerǝ* 'scratching sickness.' (Wu, 17.)

I.5. If a cow's afterbirth does not come out, any man who comes in must undo his belt. If he does not do this, the afterbirth will not come out. (Uj[S], 224; Up[S], 176.)

I.6. If a person has a stomachache, he should eat bread which has been dried out in the oven. (J.)

I.7. If a person has a hangover, he should take aspirin and apply cold compresses. (J.)

I.8. To cure a headache, water in which daisies were boiled is drunk and a bag containing the stewed daisies is put on the forehead. (J.)

I.9.1. A child with scrofula, *pi mužǝ* 'dog sickness,' must nurse a female dog and then the dog is made to jump over the child three times. (P[1948], 93.)

I.9.2. A growth on a person's body, face, or neck, called *pi ota* 'dog testicle,' can be removed by rubbing it with bread and saying, "Let the dog testicle be the dog's," and spitting. The bread is then taken outside and fed to a dog. (Uj[FB], 79.)

I.10. To prevent illness coming from the water in the spring young people along the Belaya River make rag dolls about half an ell in length. When the ice melts, they throw these into the water saying "Live well. Take sickness with you." Pieces of linen and toys are also thrown into the water. Sometimes side by side on a piece of ice are put two dolls, one called 'old man,' the other 'old woman.' The young people sing and play the accordion as they take the dolls to the river. Returning from the river, they must not turn to look back. (H[1926], 191–92.)

I.11.   A person who has tuberculosis should drink goat's milk. (J.)

I.12.   A person with a backache should apply hot compresses or use a hot water bottle. (J.)

I.13.   Milk and honey are given to a child with the whooping cough. (J.)

I.14.   A stone falling from the sky (*jumən kü* 'heaven's stone') is believed to possess curative powers. This stone is believed to be a thunderbolt, but it is not found until three years after it has fallen. It is smooth and transparent. It is able to reduce swelling by its touch. Sometimes the stone is scraped and the powder from it is mixed with water and taken internally to cure swelling. (B, 10; Uj[FB], 76.)

I.15.   To cure jaundice, *sar mužə* 'yellow sickness,' a person must boil oats in water and wash himself in the oat water three times before sunrise. (Be, 385–86.)

I.16.   A person with *jüštə mužə* 'fever' should drink quinine. (J.)

I.17.   To cure a cold, the body should be smeared with radishes. (Up[FB], 27.)

I.18.   To cure the eyes of a cow which have been "eaten" by a *buber* (A.10.), that is, are becoming blind, masticated rowan bark is applied to the eyes. (B, 7.)

I.19.   Salt is believed to possess curative power and is used especially to mitigate illness caused by supernaturals. For example, salt and groats are thrown into rivers which cause blindness, swelling, and so on. If a person becomes ill due to a fall, salt water is sprinkled on the place where he fell and the earth mother (A.1.5.) is implored to cure the sick person. (Be, 380–82; H[1926], 96.)

I.20.   Hiccoughs are cured by a scare. For example, someone starts to have a person with hiccoughs arrested; by the time he explains that he is innocent, his hiccoughs are gone. (J.)

I.21.   A stomachache can be cured "by rubbing it with another stomach," that is, by having sexual intercourse. (J.)

I.22.   Laundry soap lather should be put on a boil (*süban*). (J.)

I.23.   If a person vomits, he should eat pickles, marinated herring, or some other sour food. (J.)

I.24.   Spoken spells are used to cure a person of a stomachache caused by *asəra* (A.4.), blindness and stomachache caused by a *buber* (A.10.), rheumatism and other illnesses. (B, 8; H[1913], 124; P[1948], 6; Uj[S], 232, 233, 252, 253.)

I.24.1.   To cure an earache caused by *kož nedək* (A.47.1.), the person suffering from the earache and a friend go to a pine tree at night to beat this spirit. The one with the earache asks, "What are you beating?" The other answers, "I beat the *kož nedək*. Let the *kož nedək* belong to the pine." The person with the earache falls to the earth and rises three times as his friend beats the spirit. (B, 71.)

I.24.2.   A deaf man makes a cross and sticks his head under a bell, saying, "Gods, open my ears." Then he stands with head bowed as the bell rings some six times. He comes out and makes a cross. Then he says that his ears have been opened a little. (Uj[S], 202.)

I.25.   If a finger hurts, it should be wrapped in a spider web. (Uj[S], 218.)

I.26.   Spitting commonly accompanies charms and spells (See D.9 and Part Two, "Charms"). A horse which is unnaturally tired because of a spell can be cured by spitting twice and then striking it once with a whip. (L, 19 [36].)

I.27.   To cure a cold, people drink tea which burns the noses of *šürem kuguza* and *kuba* (A.38.27.) and causes them to go away. If a person has a stomachache he should drink a tea made from raspberry leaves or herbs. Tea is also given to those who have whooping cough. Tea made of linden flowers is used for curing a cough. (B, 16; J.)

I.28.   To relieve a toothache, tobacco tar on a piece of cotton is applied to the tooth. (J.)

I.29.   Urine is used to cure certain diseases. A person who has jaundice (*sar mužə* 'yellow sickness') must wash himself in his own urine daily three times before sunrise. A person who has *šem mužə* 'black sickness,' must drink urine from a black sheep and wash himself in it. (Be, 385–87.)

I.30.   Vodka is drunk to cure a cold and to relieve a headache. To relieve a toothache a piece of cotton soaked in vodka is applied to the tooth or vodka is simply swished over the tooth. (J.)

J. MISCELLANEOUS

J.1.   souls

In addition to his visible body, each person, according to Cheremis belief, has three unseen elements: *šüləš* 'breath,' and two souls, *čon* and *ört*. The breath of life remains within the body until death, at which time it leaves by way of the mouth with the last breath of a dying person. *Čon,* which can be translated 'life,' likewise remains in the body until the time of death. It occupies no fixed place within the body but moves about freely. If a blow is struck at the place where the *čon* is, death will ensue; on the other hand, a serious injury will not be fatal if the *čon* was in another part of the body. The *ört,* which can perhaps be roughly equated with consciousness, is much less restricted and may leave the body without causing death. It is said of an unconscious person that his *ört* has left. Similarly, it is believed that a person's *ört* actually experiences everything which occurs in dreams. The *omə uššə* 'dream seer' (D.10.1.) sends out his *ört* in search of desired information. When a person has received a great scare, he says that his *ört* was driven out. Some illnesses are caused by the fact that the *ört* has left its dwelling. If the *ört* does not return, death will occur. It is sometimes said of a dying person, "His *ört* has gone; his *čon* has not left." Sometimes the *ört* of a seriously ill person goes into the next life but later returns so that he recovers.

The word *tüs* is also used to designate the 'shadow-soul' though it properly signifies 'countenance' or 'image.'

(B, 97; H[1926], 12–14, 16; H[1927], 6, 12, 22; J; P[1909], 17.)

J.2.   life after death

After death, the *ört* 'soul' remains for a while in the vicinity of the corpse, following it to the cemetery. Often, shortly after death, it returns to wander about the village, occasionally appearing to the survivors. Sometimes it appears as a sparrow called *ört lepeñə* 'soul butterfly.' On the third, seventh, and fortieth day after death, memorial feasts (B.23.1.–3.) are held for the deceased. The fortieth day ceremony is considered to be a farewell feast after which the deceased no longer is in close contact with the living. The dead may return to the world of the living only if permitted to do so by the ruler of the dead (A.90.).

Although the dead may either help or harm the living, the fear of their power to do evil far surpasses any expectation of their aid. Numerous evil spirits are said to be especially powerful or malicious dead men (cf. A.10., A.12., A.16., A.21.2., A.31., A.44., A.51., A.64., A.66., A.86., A.90., and A.94.).

Ghost legends are also told. One such ghost, which does not interfere with the lives of humans, is that of a young woman who was drowned after falling through the ice on her way home from a party. Early in the morning her ghost appears on the bank singing a lament that she can no longer nurse her baby which is crying for her. It is believed that unmarried women return after death in the form of sickness spirits.

The tomb of a holy man is visited because of his miraculous curing powers. Offerings are made to him. His corpse does not decay.

(For folk tale motifs concerning the dead, see Sebeok (1952), 84–85.)

Objects for the deceased's use in the other world are put in the coffin. Money is supplied so that the deceased can buy himself a place to live. Tools, a change of clothes, and personal items are also put in the coffin for his use. Broken dishes and eating utensils are considered suitable for the other world. Brier and rowan branches are also given to the corpse to protect himself from dogs and snakes on the way to the underworld.

The realm of the dead, *bes tüñča* 'other world,' is located under the earth; in some regions it is believed to be to the west and graves are dug facing westward. There the dead lead a life similar to that on earth; they farm, raise cattle, keep bees, hunt, fish, and so on. Relatives live together; the first buried is the ruler of the cemetery (A.90.). After a death, dead relatives come into town to meet the most recently deceased. At funerals and memorial services, the survivors express the wish that the deceased be in a light, warm place and that the earth not weigh heavily on him. Those who die in battle or are killed by lightning go to heaven.

Superimposed on these beliefs of life after death is the Turko-Tatar concept of two realms of the dead: *bolgədə ber* 'light place' for the good and *pitškemšə ber* 'dark place' for the evil. The latter is also called *kiš pot* 'pitch cauldron' because evil souls are boiled there. In order to get to the 'bright place' each soul must pass over a narrow pole stretched across the 'dark place.' Evil souls stumble and fall into the pit. Sometimes there is a judgment by god (A.26.) or the ruler of the dead which sends the good to the right and the bad to the left. In the other world people are punished for their misdeeds and neglect of duties here on earth. There is also a belief, undoubtedly of Islamic origin, that a person dies seven times and thus passes from one heaven to another.

As a person is dying, he is laid on a pallet of straw because of the belief that a person who dies on a felt or feather mattress must count the hairs or feathers in the next life.

For burial and memorial customs which reflect the beliefs concerning the dead, see B.23. For the motif analysis of tales concerning the realm of the dead, see Sebeok (1952), 32, 68–69.

(B, 17, 160–61; Be, 391–92; Bj, 159–61, 175, 176; H⌊1926⌋, 14–16, 17–19, 61; H[1927], 22, 72, 75, 80; R, 207; S, 133–42.)

J.3.   animism

Human characteristics are frequently attributed to plants, animals, inanimate objects, and natural phenomena. Sometimes they are clearly personified as spirits (see Section A); other times they are merely treated as if human.

Forests and grain fields are clean and a person must be careful not to dirty them or use improper language. As a hunter goes through the forest, he speaks to the trees. He is careful not to hurt them in any way. At night he asks the protection of a big tree while he sleeps. In the morning, he thanks the tree and gives it his hand. The forest fears the woodcutter and shudders as he passes with his ax. There is also the belief that a tree can move from one place to another. Some trees are believed to possess the ability to whistle. Certain trees, called 'mother trees,' are especially good for bees; these trees cannot be recognized by men, but bees that make their hives there prosper. Bears understand speech and are as intelligent as men. They become angry if people speak disparagingly of them and they return after death to punish their slayers.

Life and human characteristics are often attributed to inanimate objects. Stones, clouds, and roads are considered alive. Man-made articles are also believed to be living and sentient beings. Boats, gates, axes, plows, sickles, cups, spoons, mirrors, shoes, harnesses, and many other articles are addressed as if they were human. Sickles are "fed" so that they will have strength to harvest (B.15.). Because tools are alive, the Cheremis do not like to lend them to strangers.

When such objects are no longer usable, they are not destroyed, but retired. An old gate, for example, is taken from the posts and laid in a place where it can rot in peace. When a man discards old shoes, he says, "Shoes, you have served me; you have walked on my feet. Now that you have been worn out, I hang you in a good place. Now rest in peace."

Broken eating utensils are used for offerings to the dead. When an old bowl or spoon is finally discarded, the person says "You have served us, given us food and drink; you have also fed the dead. May this be a peaceful resting place for you."

For those objects which have an *ört* 'soul,' see A.58.

(H[1926], 57–58, 80–84.)

J.4.   possession

A person can be possessed by *xuda sila* 'evil power.' Such a person travels about in the company of the devils *čort* (A.15.) and *keltəmaš* (A.30.). He has the power to make himself invisible and can float on the water like a dead man (cf. A.32.). A person with this evil power can not enter a house where a horseshoe or iron heel has been nailed up.

Once possessed by evil power, a man cannot rid himself of it. According to a tale, a man wishing to cease using this power went to live in a monastery but he was compelled to leave the church whenever a prayer was sung. He could not be restrained from leaving except by iron. When chained to his place and forced to listen to a prayer, he sank into the earth and disappeared.

For possession by a *buber,* see A.10.
(Bk, 47, 111–16.)

J.5. clothing

Some Cheremis have retained their own style of clothing on religious grounds. They say, "As god has given each people their own speech, so also he has given them their own dress."

In a time of scarcity, the Cheremis perceived the wrath of god because they had abandoned their traditional way of dressing. All factory cloth was described as the "product of an unclean spirit." The men of the region took counsel and decided to destroy all clothes made from purchased cloth. They searched for all "impure" clothing and tore it into shreds; the pieces were buried or thrown into rivers and lakes but they were not burned lest their unpleasant odor rise to the gods. A tale tells of a girl who was punished for discarding the traditional clothing by being stricken dumb.

(Manninen, 193–94.)

Elm, G.13.2.3.6., G.13.6.3.

Elopement, B.17., B.17.7.

Empty omens, G.16.3.4.2., G.23.

Enemy (sorcerer), D.2.1. *See also* Woman.

Epidemics, A.21.2., A.21.2.1., B.7.

Epiphany omens, G.15.24., G.16.5.4.3.1.–G.16.5.4.3.2., G.34.16.2.

Equisetum omens, G.12.4.1.–G.12.4.2.2.

Evening, A.15., A.30., A.36., B.4., B.5., B.7.1., B.8.4., B.12., B.16., B.18., E.2.2.; shirt donning, B.8.1. *See also* Angel, Star.

Evil: spirits, A.10., A.15., A.30., A.31., B.23.; protection against, A.1.15., A.9.5., B.1., B.7., B.8.3.2., B.23., C.1.; omens, G.3.10.1., G.3.10.5., G.3.12.2.; magic affecting, H.1.2.1., H.4.2., J.4.; possession, J.4.; souls, J.2. *See also* Day, Eye, Spirit, Strength, Tongue.

Ewe sacrifice, A.15.6., A.15.10., B.1., B.20.

Exorcism, A.9.14., B.17.4., B.18., C.5., E.3., F.15., F.16., F.20., H.4.3., H.4.5.

Expert, wax road, A.60., B.2.

Eye: evil, H.2.2.4., H.6.5.; spirits menacing, A.9.2., A.10.; soothsaying, D.7.; magic, A.16., H.1.9.1., H.1.10.9., H.4.1.; cure, I.17.; omens, G.1.6.5.–G.1.6.6.2. *See also* Seer.

Fall: ceremonies, A.21.2., A.38.23., B.2., B.5., B.7., B.7.2., B.14., B.18., B.20., B.23.5., B.23.7., F.16.; omens, G.2.5.2.2.2., G.2.7.2.1.1.1.–G.2.7.2.2., G.2.13.2.1.–G.2.13.2.3.2., G.3.2.1.2., G.3.3.2.1.–G.3.3.2.3., G.3.5.3., G.3.8.7.1.–G.3.8.11.1., G.3.14.2., G.4.1.3.2., G.4.7.1.2., G.9., G.11.1., G.13.2.3.–G.13.4.1.1., G.13.7., G.15.2.12.1., G.16.2.4.1., G.34.23.; magic, H.1.5.2.

Falling: cure after, I.19.; omens, G.1.14., G.1.14.1., G.1.23.2.2.1., G.1.23.2.2.2.

Family: deities, A.1.3., A.9.8., A.31., A.31.7., A.52.4., A.70.6., A.84.7., A.86.; ceremonies, B.5., B.8.2., B.8.3.2., B.9.1.2., B.12., B.14., B.15., B.17., B.23., B.23.3., B.23.5., B.23.7., B.32.; sacred places, E.1., E.2.; sacred tree, F.15.; omens, G.2.10.2.1.1., G.4.3.1., G.10.2.4., G.19.3.3., G.19.4., G.25.2., G.26., G.35.18.; magic, H.1.3.1., H.1.3.2., H.4.5. *See also* Blessing.

Fast: day omens, G.3.8.4.2., G.16.3.5.2., G.21.2.; half, G.34.2.1.

Fate: bee, A.27.1., B.2., B.11.; god determining, A.26.6., A.27.; grain, A.27.2., B.2., B.22.; great, B.2. *See also* Angel, Creator, God, Prophet.

Feast, A.8.6., A.9.8., B.1., B.2., B.5., B.8.3.4., B.8.6., B.12., B.13., B.17.1., B.17.6., B.17.7., B.19., B.23., B.23.3., B.23.7., B.34.; cow's milk, B.28., H.2.3.1.; memorial, A.76.5., A.94., B.23.1., B.23.2., B.23.3., B.23.5., D.1., J.2.

Fertility: spirits of, A.1.10., A.26.14., A.70., A.70.4., A.82.; rites, B.20.; omens, G.2.15.1.1.1.–G.2.15.2.2., G.4.1.1., G.4.3.1.1.–G.4.3.2.3., G.14.3.1.1.2., G.15.2.10.; magic, H.2.4.1.–H.2.4.4.

Fever, A.96.3., I.16.; black, I.2.

Field: spirits, A.9.11., A.23., A.26.13., A.31.6., A.34., A.38.18., A.38.21., A.44., A.48., A.52.7., A.56.2., A.58.7., A.67.14., A.70., A.70.14., A.84.17., A.86., A.86.2., A.93.; ceremonies, B.1., B.2., B.8.3., B.15., B.18., B.19., B.23.7., B.24., B.27., B.31.1., C.5.; sacred, E.2., E.4.; omens, G.2.1.1., G.2.9.1., G.2.11.2., G.3.3.1., G.3.11.1., G.3.11.3., G.3.16.2.1.–G.3.16.2.3., G.4.2.2., G.4.7.1.1., G.10.2.1.1., G.10.2.1.2., G.10.2.4., G.12.4.1., G.12.4.2.1., G.12.4.2.2., G.16.5.1.2.1., G.16.5.5., G.16.5.6.1., G.16.5.6.2.1., G.16.5.6.2.2., G.34.10.2., G.34.10.4., G.34.16.1.; magic, C.5., F.16., H.1.5.2., H.3.1.1., H.3.1.6., H.3.1.7.2., H.3.1.8., H.4.4., H.6.3., J.3.

Figure: lead, B.34.; pewter or tin, C.1., D.9., F.1., F.15.1., F.23.; wooden, A.9.8.

Finger, A.2., A.10., A.90., B.23., C.1., C.2.1., C.11., D.7., D.7.1., G.34.5., H.1.10.6., I.25.

Fingernails, A.90.

Fir, B.7., D.2.1., E.2., E.2.2., F.15., G.3.4.1.3., G.34.20., H.6.1.

Fire: personified, A.1.15., A.9.4., A.9.10.1., A.9.14., F.21., F.21.1.; spirits and, A.9.10.1., A.11., A.16., A.20., A.21.2.1., A.26.42., A.52.18., A.58.4., A.66.1., A.70.20., A.84., A.84.20., A.86., A.86.1.; soul of, A.58.10.; offerings, A.9.4., A.26.2., A.36., B.1., B.2., B.7., B.7.2., B.8.3.2., B.8.4., B.9.1.2.,

G.2.2.1.1., G.2.2.2.1., G.2.8.2.1.1., G.2.
9.1., G.2.11.1.–G.2.11.1.2., G.3.2.1.4., G.3.
20.1., G.4.2.1.–G.4.3.1.1., G.15.2.3., G.16.
6.2., G.16.6.3.1., G.23.1.2., G.34.2.1.,
G.34.2.2.2., G.34.22., H.1.7.1., H.3.1.2.2.,
H.3.1.7.2., H.4.6. *See also* Fortune, Prosperity.
Lung disease, H.1.10.7.

Magic, D.2.1., D.9., H.; affecting animals,
H.2.; affecting evil powers, H.4.; affecting
people, H.1.; affecting plants, H.3.; affecting dead, H.5.; black, H.6.; formulas,
A.38.8., H.4.2.; rites, B.19., H.10.1.
Maiden, pure, B.9.1.1., C.10.
Malt, B.4., B.17.2., B.17.3., B.17.4., B.24.,
C.9.; bride, B.17.2.
Man: holy, J.2.; omens for, G.1.2.1.–G.1.2.
4., G.13.2.4.2.2.2., G.15.2.3., G.34.4.;
magic for, H.1.6., H.1.7.4., H.1.7.5., H.2.
4.3., I.5.; wearing of kaftan, B.17.4.
Man (spirits), A.20., A.85.; bathhouse
old, A.38.16., B.32.1.; bridge old, A.21.2.
1., A.38.15.; butter week old, B.26., H.3.
2.2.; cattle mountain old, A.38.14.; cold
old, A.38.11., A.38.17., A.38.26., D.2.2.;
devil old, A.38.8.; drying house old,
A.38.1.; Efraim old, A.38.6.; field old,
A.38.18., A.38.21.; forest old, A.38.5.,
A.38.13.; frost old, A.38.22., B.2., B.9.1.
2., B.30.; great, A.2.1.2., A.31.; house old,
A.38.23.; hut soul old, A.38.20.; lake old,
A.38.10.; measles old, A.38.7.; mill old,
A.38.2.; money old, A.38.19.; mountain
old, A.12., A.21.2.1., D.7.2.; mucus old,
A.38.16., A.38.24., I.4.1.; Nemda Moun-
tain great, A.8., A.21.2.1.; old, A.16.,
A.16.1., A.31., A.38., A.38.9., B.17.5.,
B.18., B.23.7., D.6., D.10.1., H.8.1., I.10.;
pen old, A.38.4.; pine, A.21.1.; pine old,
A.21.1.1.; Satan old, A.75.; scabies old,
A.38.12.; smallpox old, A.38.25.; thresh-
ing-floor old, A.38.9.; Turek old, A.38.
28.; Vasili old, A.38.3., B.19., H.3.2.1.;
warmth old, A.38.26. *See also* God.
Manhood. *See* Adulthood.
Maple, B.21., G.13.2.4.5.1.1.1.1.–G.13.2.4.5.
2.1.1.2.
March, B.18.

Mare, A.67., B.9.1.2., C.1., G.14.2.5.1., G.14.
2.5.2., H.2.2.2.
Mari Turek, A.38.28.
Marriage: deity, A.1.2.; ceremonies and
practices, A.1.1., B.17., B.17.8.; omens,
G.34.4., G.34.6.1., G.34.7., G.34.9.–G.34.
10.2., G.34.10.4., G.34.12.–G.34.14.2.,
G.34.16.1.–G.34.17., G.34.21.; magic, H.
1.5.2. *See also* Bride, Wedding, Woman.
Masquerade, A.38.3., B.18., B.19., B.26.,
H.3.2.1., H.3.2.2.
Master, A.16., A.57.; bathhouse, A.38.16.;
house, A.38.23.; lake, A.51.; mill, A.38.2.;
pen, A.38.4.; spring, A.57.1.
Matchmaker, B.17.6.
May, A.94.
Mead, B.9.1.1., B.9.1.2., B.12., B.23., C.10.,
F.10.1.; *jošman,* C.10. *See also* Hydromel.
Meadow: spirits, A.38.8., A.86.; for cere-
monies, B.19., B.30., E.4., F.15.
Meal, sacrifice, A.9.8., A.21.2.1., A.36., B.7.,
B.9.1.2., B.16., B.18., B.35.
Measles, A.38.7., I.4.1. *See also* Man,
Woman.
Measurements, body, soothsaying by, D.7.1.,
G.1.4.9.
Meat, sacrifice, B.1., B.5., B.7.1., B.7.2.,
B.9.1.2., B.11., B.23., B.23.3., B.23.7.,
B.34., C.1., C.12.–C.12.3., F.3., F.7.,
F.10.3., F.21.; *šopšar,* F.3.; *šübə,* C.12.2.,
F.10.3.; whole, C.12.1. *See also* Day.
Mercy, A.26., A.34., A.78., B.34.; bee, A.78.
3.; god's, A.78.2., B.34.; livestock, A.78.
1.; money, A.78.4. *See also* Prayer.
Metal, A.81., F.1., F.20. *See also* Copper,
Iron, Lead, Pewter, Tin.
Meteorite, H.3.4.
Mice, B.23.7., G.2.10.1.–G.2.10.4., H.1.7.3.,
H.1.7.4., H.1.9.1., H.3.1.10.1., H.3.1.10.2.;
red, G.2.10.1.1.
Midnight, A.15., A.30., B.23.3., G.2.5.3.1.1.,
G.3.2.1.4.
Midsummer's Day, A.66.1.
Midwife, B.33.
Milk: spirits affecting, A.1.10.5., A.10.,
A.82.2.; offerings, A.1.15., B.8.3.2., B.12.,
B.28.; omens, G.15.2.15., G.16.3.5.1.;
magic, H.1.10.10.1., H.2.3.1., H.2.3.2.,

H.12.1., H.12.2.; cures, I.11., I.13. *See also* Feast, God.

Mill spirits, A.38.2., A.85

Miracle, A.70., H.14.

Mirror: animism, J.3.; divination, D.10.2.; magic, A.30., H.1.11., H.4.8., H.5.3.

Misfortune, A.31., A.35., B.7., B.8.6., B.9.3., C.1., D.2., D.7., D.10.1., E.1., G.1.15.2., G.3.5.1.1., G.27.2., G.35.24.

Mist spirits, A.26.45., A.70.22., A.92.

Mole, G.2.9.1., G.2.9.2.

Monday, B.5., B.8., B.8.6., H.3.1.5.1., H.7.1.

Money, A.16., A.16.1., A.38.12., A.38.5., A.38.19., A.51., A.74., A.94., B.1., B.2., B.4., B.7., B.9.1.1., B.9.1.2., B.16., B.17.-B.17.6., B.19., B.23., B.27., B.27.21., B.32., B.34., B.34.10.4., C.1., C.3., C.7.-C.7.3., D.3., F.26., G.1.6.11.–G.1.6.11.2., G.27.–G.27.2.1., G.34.2.1., G.34.10.4., H.1.9.1.–H.1.9.3., H.4.4., H.8.1., J.2.; cup, B.17.1.; guard, A.74.; sacred tree, C.7.2.; sacrifice, C.7.1. *See also* Blessing, Creator, Fructifier, Man, Mercy, Soldier, Treasurer, Woman.

Moon, A.10., B.18., G.2.15.1.1.1.–G.2.15.1.2.2., G.14., G.14.2.1.1.–G.14.2.5.2., H.3.8., H.3.9. *See also* God, Lord, Mother.

Morning, A.15., A.30., A.38.9., A.96.2., B.8., 5.1., B.12., B.14., B.17.3., B.17.4., B.17.6., B.18., B.23.2., B.26., B.30., G.1.2.4., G.2.5.3.3., G.16.2.2.1., G.16.5.4.5.2.1., G.34.17., H.4.6., H.7.5., J.2., J.3. *See also* Angel, Guard, Star.

Morning brightening, A.26.10.

Mother (spirit), A.1., A.1.10., A.21.2.1., A.26., A.26.18., B.7., C.1.; bee, A.1.6.; bee fructifier, A.1.10.6., B.11.; blessing, A.1.8., A.34.; bird fructifier, A.1.10.4.; cloud, A.1.9.; cow fructifier, A.1.10.10.; earth, A.1.5., B.2., B.9.1.2., B.23., I.19.; earth fructifier, A.1.10.5.; fire, A.1.15., A.86., B.7., B.7.2., B.8.3.2., B.9.1.2., H.4.5.; fire fructifier, A.1.10.8.; fructifier, A.1.10., B.20., B.34.; god's, A.1.2., B.2., B.9.1.2., B.34.; god's blessing, B.34.; grain blessing, A.1.8.2.; great fructifier, B.2.; great heaven god's blessing, A.27.; heaven god's blessing, A.1.8.1.1.; great heaven god's lord's, A.27.; heaven god's lord's, A.1.7.1.

1.; livestock fructifier, A.1.10.1.; man fructifier, A.1.10.2.; moon, A.1.14., B.9.1.2.; over world, fructifier, A.1.10.9.; sea, A.1.13.; sheep fructifier, A.1.10.7.; star, A.1.12.; sun, A.1.3., B.2., B.9.1.2., B.34.; warmth, A.1.11.; water, A.1.1., B.6., B.17.5., C.7.; white sun fructifier, A.1.10.3.1.; wind, A.1.4., B.2., B.9.1.2.; yard, A.1.5.1. *See also* God, Fructifier, Offering, Reporter, Tree.

Mother-in-law, H.2.4.3.

Mountain spirits, A.16.2., A.21.2., A.21.2.1.1., A.36., A.64.2., A.85.

Mountain, great, A.40.

Mucus. *See* Man, Woman.

Murder, A.3., A.9., A.66.

Mushroom, G.12.6., G.16.5.4.4.1.

Music, ceremonial, B.17.3., B.17.4., B.17.5., B.18., B.23.3., B.23.7., D.1.

Musical instruments: accordion, B.17.3., B.18., I.10.; bagpipes, A.52.7., B.8.3.2., B.12., B.17.5., B.23.3., B.27., D.1.; drum, A.52.7., B.17.5.

Naming ceremony, B.33., D.7.

Nature. *See* Spirit, God.

Neighbor, *toktal,* A.69.

Nemda Mountain, A.21.2.1., A.64.2. *See also* Man.

Nemda River, A.12., A.21.2.1.

New Year's Day, G.16.5.4.2., G.34.4.; Eve, G.34.9., G.34.10.4., G.34.13.2., G.34.16.1., G.34.17.

Night: spirits, A.3., A.9.5., A.11., A.30., A.38.8., A.38.11., A.38.16., A.46.2., A.51., A.58.9., A.85., A.86.1.; ceremonies, B.5., B.8.2., B.8.3., B.16., B.17.4., B.17.6., B.18., B.19., B.23., B.23.2.; omens, G.1.15.1., G.1.15.2., G.2.5.3.1., G.3.10.2., G.3.19., G.15.2.11., G.16.2.2.2., G.16.5.2.1., G.35.18.; magic, H.1.5.2., H.3.1.7.3., H.4.3., H.7.6.

Nightingale, G.3.9.1., G.3.9.2.

Nightmare, A.59., A.85., D.2.2.

Noise taboos, B.18., B.32., H.1.3.2., H.1.10.5.1., H.3.1.6., H.3.1.10.2. *See also* Sounds.

Noon, A.15., A.30., A.38.8.,

November, B.5., B.10., B.27.

PART TWO

STUDIES OF DREAM PORTENTS AND SACRED TEXTS

STRUCTURAL AND CONTENT ANALYSIS IN FOLKLORE RESEARCH

FROM the methodological point of view, the purpose implicit in the three studies in Part Two is to explore the possibilities of applying to a wider range of problems than has heretofore been the case, first, the formality of structural linguistics, together with, second, the quantitative approach of content analysis, to the end that the construction and stylistic characteristics of sets of texts—in these instances, folkloristic texts of magico-religious function from a single culture—be clarified.[1] These methods were introduced, in 1950, in "Cheremis Dream Portents," and developed, in 1953, in "Structure and Content of Cheremis Charms." These papers are reproduced below substantially rearranged, with several additions, and with numerous changes of both detail and emphasis, and integrated with the rest of this book. The analysis of prayers is entirely new.

STRUCTURAL ANALYSIS

Structural analysis of folklore rests on an assumption that all the products of verbal behavior may, in the last analysis, be reduced to terms of symbolic logic. Respectability is lent to this assumption by a philosophical tradition epitomized by Alfred North Whitehead, who went even further when he suggested, "Symbolic Logic, that is to say, the symbolic examination of pattern with the use of real variables, will become the foundation of aesthetics . . . when in the distant future the subject has expanded, so as to examine patterns depending on connections other than those of space, number and quantity. . . ."[2]

It has been generally recognized that the techniques whereby, in actual practice, we study verbal behavior differ, by and large, from those whereby we study

---

[1] Thus these studies differ in both aims and procedures from those of discourse analysis. The latter seeks to determine the structure of a single connected text at a time by setting up, so to speak, partial synonymity classes for it. Its procedures are akin to the formal procedures of descriptive linguistics but yield little information that goes beyond it. Cf. Harris, 1952 a and b.

The content analysis of prayers has proved too long and elaborate to be included in this book; it is hoped that these data can be published shortly in another context.

[2] Whitehead, p. 186. For some more or less successful attempts in this direction, see Empson, 1951, Johansen, and Archibald A. Hill, 1951 and 1953.

nonverbal behavior.[3] This is true in spite of occasional attempts to apply techniques of the former kind to the study of behavior which is verbal only in part, such as systems of kinship, which are in part systems of terminology (verbal) and in part systems of attitudes (nonverbal), the two parts being functionally interdependent—at any rate, such behavior is explicitly identified as being both systematic and symbolic.[4]

Among the several other possible approaches to verbal behavior, it is linguistics that studies communication systems which are symbolic par excellence, i.e., codes and messages. The method of modern linguistics may be regarded as a kind of discrete or discontinuous mathematics.[5] Folklorists, too, have of late "increasingly turned their attention to the study of patterns, forms, and devices,"[6] though these can hardly be characterized as their focal interest, since folklore has sundry pressing problems peculiar to it—such as those of transmission, and function in a natural and cultural setting—which have not encouraged the development of a rigorous technique of formal analysis.

It may be worth digressing at this point to recall that linguistics and folklore studies have common roots in the nineteenth century and were pursued with equal vigor by such scholars as Jacob Grimm, Max Müller, Theodor Benfey, and others. Linguistic preoccupation with Proto-Indo-European reconstructions naturally led the brothers Grimm to assume tales to be a detritus of early Indo-European myths, and Müller's search for tale origins by way of Sanskrit etymologies illustrates the once intimate relationship between comparative linguistics and comparative mythology.[7] Von Sydow[8] is now critical in retrospect, and stresses the distinction between the methods of philological and folklore research. But while he points to a certain lack of understanding on the part of philologists in their attitude to the work of folklorists, he nonetheless concludes that collaboration between the two fields is of supreme importance.

In more recent times, Franz Boas and some of his students have emphasized the necessity of studying the stylistic qualities of folklore texts, an impossible endeavor without a knowledge of linguistics: ". . . no one can pretend to study a people authentically without this knowledge. . . . The structure of a language and its vocabulary are so obviously fundamental for the proper appreciation and understanding of cultural and societal expressions that he who remains in ignorance of them does so at his own peril."[9]

[3] Cf. the statement of Voegelin and Harris, that "the techniques of linguistics and cultural anthropology are in general different," and the elaboration thereof, pp. 590–92.

[4] Lévi-Strauss, 1945 and 1953.

[5] Joos. On linguistics as algebra, see especially Hjelmslev, 1953. On the principal schools of structural linguistics, see Martinet.

[6] Wellek and Warren, p. 39, and corresponding references on p. 303.

[7] Thompson, pp. 368ff., and Pedersen.

[8] Von Sydow.

[9] Radin, 1949, p. ii. Boas made the same point repeatedly. For example: "It is a

The two disciplines have also crossed paths here and there with regard to certain specific methodological procedures, principally historical ones. For instance, the historic-geographic or Finnish method of folktale study[10] utilizes techniques which are in a good many particulars the same as those of a school of linguistics, rather controversial, which goes by the name of "neolinguistics.[11]

Now the interest of many linguists has shifted from historical to descriptive investigations, at least for the time being. Moreover, linguistic statements—whether descriptive or historical—tend to be exact, rigorous, compact, and internally consistent, in terms of elementary units and their patterned relations. In other words, they tend to be structural. "It seems that a major movement of this kind is now affecting many branches of science: the decline of what may be called atomism, or atomistic thought in general, and the emergence of theories based on the conception of pattern."[12] The notion of structure is thus unmistakably in the air. This is so despite the fact that as yet we do not know what exactly is meant by a "structure" in general, beyond the recognition of its being something purely formal and purely relational. Especially unclear is the connection between structures posited by the different sciences. At any rate, a structural statement is everywhere one which says something about relations rather than about the relata themselves.[13]

In folkloristic texts, too, there are certain regularly recurrent units which permit experimentation along methodological lines which might be regarded, in these broad terms, as structural. This should surprise no one who has reflected on the close analogy between the language-speech dichotomy of Saussurean linguistics, and the relationship of a given folkloristic type and its actual variations as presented by specific informants.[14] It was realized long ago, for example, that folktales and myths frequently open and close with conventional formulas. German *Märchen* formulas received attention half a century ago.[15] Bolte and Polívka assembled a great many of them.[16] More recently, a collection of fourteen Tübatulabal tale texts were explicitly examined for such formulas—in the words of the author of the article herself, "from a structural viewpoint."[17] This was also the approach of

---

precarious undertaking to discuss the characteristics of primitive poetic forms, partly because so little reliable material is available, but partly also on account of the impossibility of obtaining a fair insight into the meaning and value of literary expression without intimate knowledge of the language and culture in which they have come into being." Boas, p. 317. Cf. also Nadel, pp. 39ff.

[10] Krohn, 1926.

[11] Bonfante and Sebeok.

[12] Whyte, 1950, p. 25; cf. also Whyte, 1951, and Bertalanffy; further, for an excellent summary of this point of view, see Ruesch and Bateson, 1951, Chap. 10.

[13] Carnap, pp. 11–16.

[14] Cf. Bogatyrev and Jakobson.

[15] Petsch.

[16] Bolte and Polívka, pp. 13–36.

[17] Erminie W. Voegelin.

Vera Mae Alleman in her study of two hundred and seventy Cheremis tale texts.[18] In the Cheremis materials, two hundred and seven tales were found to have initial formulas as against sixty-three which did not, and a hundred and forty-eight final formulas, as against a hundred and twenty-two which did not. The formulas turned out to be either elementary units which could not be further meaningfully subdivided from a folkloristic point of view—only linguistically—or were simply conjunctions of the basic units. The latter were surprisingly few for such a relatively large corpus, and were easily classifiable under a small number of such headings as, attention indicators, time elements, introducers of characters (initials); termini, personal elements, and statements as to the further fate of characters (finals).

Other strikingly formulistic features in the tale have been suggested, though these have not been approached from a structural point of view. Such are: cumulative stories, where a whole series of items are repeated, plus one more; or, as in the Gaelic tales, certain recurring prose patterns known as "runs," which describe in a conventionalized fashion some series of events, in a contrasting style of speech. The Soviet folklorist V. Propp reached his remarkable conclusion that "all fairy tales are uniform in their structure"[19] on the basis of studies designed to show the laws which govern the interconnections and temporal sequence of the highly limited number of functions of the dramatis personae occurring in fairy tales. Above all, a program for a structural investigation of the folktale must include a study of the patterning of motifs. The impulse to classify them has hitherto taken precedence over the impulse to search for the manner of their workings. A linguist would ask: given a particular tale type, what relationships prevail between the motifs of which each complete tale is composed? It seems more than likely—to a linguist— that the motifs will occur in a relatively fixed order and that particular motifs will necessarily co-occur, while others will be in complementary distribution. Some motifs will occur in variant forms and such variations will be either free, or conditioned by context, or by other specific factors, and hence as predictable as any other dependent variable.

The simpler forms of folklore are particularly accessible to structural investigations, though these have but barely begun. In his work on Jabo proverbs, Herzog hinted that "certain formal features would also lend themselves to classification," and pointed out those most frequent in that language, but did not utilize such a systematization in the body of his book.[20] Bascom devised a system of symbols to represent the forms of Yoruba riddles, though the total number of his generalized formulas is slightly over a half of the total number of his riddles.[21] Reichard's analysis of the intricate structure of Navajo prayers shows especially how fruitful

[18] Sebeok, 1952, pp. 115–17.
[19] Quoted in Jakobson, 1945, p. 641.
[20] Herzog, 1936, pp. 3ff.
[21] Bascom.

such an approach can be in raising further subtle questions about the material.[22] The metric structure of the Mordvin folksong is one of the few rigorous statements available in this field.[23] Herzog has also pointed to the special problems inherent in the analysis of the folksong where the structure of the verse interacts with the musical pattern.[24]

In the chapters that follow, we shall seek out the structures underlying each of three groups of Cheremis texts: first, a body of highly stereotyped dream portents; second, a collection of charms, the magic efficacy of which is carefully guarded by strict adherence in word and act; and, finally, prayers that vary from simple to very elaborate but which yet preserve the same rigid formal outlines. Before turning to the data, however, a few comments relative to the techniques of content analysis are necessary.

CONTENT ANALYSIS

Let us discuss briefly, first, the relation of structural analysis to content analysis, and, second, the latter technique itself. We assume that structural unity is characteristic of all dream portents, charms, prayers, and other texts of that sort. "From this it follows that any quantitative approaches which overlook that unity are likely to be self-stultifying. The variables which are worth quantitative investigation will be those related to a view of the whole system. As a necessary preliminary to identifying these variables a great deal of nonquantitative work must be done. We believe that we must identify and clarify our *Gestalten* before we can intelligently measure their frequencies or even consider quantitative relations between their parts. Quantitation we regard as a postscript, a verification and testing of essentially nonquantitative hypotheses."[25]

We begin the description of a text with an exhaustive identification of its relevant elements, and with a statement of the relationship prevailing between these elements: it was found possible to state the parts of the whole and the relationship of the parts within the whole, without making statements about the nature of these component parts themselves. This procedure is what we have called structural analysis. Content analysis focuses on the component parts themselves. The distinction between the two techniques lies mainly in the presence or absence of strict criteria of relevance. Content analysis is thus on a much lower level of abstraction than structural analysis, appearing vaguer, more fluid, more arbitrary, more subjective. In structural analysis, including especially linguistic analysis, it is possible to tell what does and what does not belong to the structure, i.e., what is and what is not relevant. On the other hand, the categories of content analysis—just as the

[22] Reichard, Chap. 5.
[23] Jakobson and Lotz.
[24] Herzog, 1946 (discussion by Roman Jakobson and Morris Swadesh follows on p. 83).
[25] Ruesch and Bateson, 1949, p. 123.

elements of cultural anthropology and the motifs of the folktale—are obtainable by what has been felicitously called (with reference to culture traits) "a sophisticated awareness of their comparative implications."[26] To bring out the distinction still more clearly, but without pressing this analogy too far, perhaps one could apply the model of language study, and say that structural analysis is to content analysis in folklore research as grammatical analysis is to lexical study in linguistics.

It is generally agreed that "content analysis stands or falls by its categories."[27] The validity of the categories selected will ultimately depend on the investigator's professional skill, and may always remain arbitrary to a greater or lesser extent. The ideal content analyst of a given corpus of folklore texts will search out his categories on the basis of his knowledge of the entire cultural, and in particular folkloristic, matrix in which it is embedded, as well as of parallel corpora of texts from neighboring peoples.[28]

Content analysis is, of course, a technique well known to a variety of social sciences which has been applied to a large and diverse group of materials, as well as to a large and diverse set of problems. It is less well known to the humanities, and practically unknown to folklore. Variously defined by different workers, we may cite Berelson's definition. "Content analysis is a research technique for the objective, systematic, and quantitative description of the manifest content of communication."[29] Any sort of communication, private or "mass," can be so analyzed. While specific applications have been made in many areas, we call attention here only to the various attempts which have been made to apply content analysis to stylistic features. Berelson's bibliography of such studies includes some thirty-five references.[30]

Participants in the interdisciplinary seminar of psychologists and linguists at Cornell University in their report point to three major weaknesses of existing methods of content analysis: "(a) The units of sampling have generally been based upon expediency. . . . (b) The categories employed in deciding when a certain type of content is present or absent in a given unit have been largely arbitrary. . . . (c) Existing methods of content analysis are limited to simple comparisons of frequencies rather than measuring the internal contingencies between categories."[31] It was the feeling of this group that the transitional relations among semantic events are also important for content analysis. We wish to know: what

[26] Voegelin and Harris, p. 592.

[27] Berelson, p. 147.

[28] "Since content analysis is only a technique applicable to communication materials and since communication materials can contain almost everything people say or do, the production of relevant categories is limited only by the analyst's imagination in stating a problem for investigation and designing categories to fit the problem." *Ibid.*, p. 148.

[29] *Ibid.*, p. 18.

[30] *Ibid.*, pp. 66–72, 208–10.

[31] Carroll, pp. 26–27.

is the associational structure of the source as inferred from contingencies in its messages? Our analysis of charms, for instance, deals with their explicit content by way of a simple frequency count. In contrast, the method just referred to,[32] is designed to get at implicit content. The categories would be selected and coded as before, assuming the analyst's purpose to be constant. However, interest would now focus upon contingency, as defined by the co-occurrence of two categories within a text. Given that each category occurs in a certain percentage of units, the chance contingency is the product of the two percentages. The obtained contingencies can be evaluated against the chance contingencies in terms of the significance of differences in percentage (greater or less). By certain further techniques the web of interrelationships among the entire set of categories measured can be obtained. The final matrix analysis yields some understanding of the pattern of associations in the source, reflecting, presumably, patterns of the culture.

Although the fundamental logic of this method is very simple—in fact, nothing more than an application of the law of association by contiguity, upon which all psychologies of learning are based in one way or another—it is not yet a finished tool which can be applied to routine analyses of content. However, it is the most promising technique, with special potential value as a new research tool in folklore, as our preliminary attempts to apply the statistical contingency method to a sizeable body of Cheremis folktale motifs have shown. For example, a much higher than chance association was revealed between the notion of writing and the devil in Cheremis folktales, an insight which is as revealing as it was unexpected.[33]

In published studies of folklore texts only Bernard Wolfe, to our knowledge, has essayed something approaching quantitative content analysis of any sort, along lines reflected by this quotation. "All told, there are twenty-eight victories of the Weak over the Strong; ultimately all the Strong die violent deaths at the hands of the Weak; and there are, at most, two very insignificant victories of the Strong over the Weak. . . . Admittedly, folk symbols are seldom systematic, clean-cut, or specific. . . . But still, on the basis of the tally-sheet alone, is it too far-fetched to take Brer Rabbit as a symbol—about as sharp as Southern sanctions would allow—of the Negro slave's festering hatred of the white man?"[34] In other media of folklore, such as movies, content analyses have been made. Also, of course, qualitative content analysis of folklore materials is not uncommon, and has been preferred, perhaps because, in a sampling sense, the content under analysis tends to be too small or inexact to justify formal and precise counting, or again perhaps because its themes have appeared as *Gestalten* rather than as bundles of measurable

[32] See Sebeok, 1954.

[33] The statistical samples were prepared by J. R. Mickey, based on the motif analyses in Sebeok, 1952. One result of this research was the conclusion that motifs generally used in folktale analysis already include within them internal contingencies in different ratios. See further Sebeok, 1954.

[34] Wolfe, p. 32.

features into which such texts can be decomposed. Quantification is useful, however, when precision and objectivity are necessary or desirable, when the materials to be analyzed are many, or for the sake of a high degree of specification in comparing sets of data. Our efforts in content analysis, as exemplified by the studies that follow, should be regarded as representing three successive stages of an experiment tending in this direction.[34a]

[34a] The above chapter was written before the senior author participated in a Work Conference on Theory and Technique of Content Analysis, held in February, 1955, under the sponsorship of the Social Science Research Council at the University of Illinois. As a result of the conference his views were modified in a number of important particulars, and the analyses that follow would likely be carried out somewhat differently. The proceedings are being edited for publication.

DREAM PORTENTS

INTRODUCTORY ANALYSIS

THE typical Cheremis dream portent is highly stereotyped in form, so that a formal analysis becomes possible. For initial illustrative purposes, we will use the following sample text and translation as references:

> omo   dene muret ken,   tuj liat,   manət
> dream   with singest-thou if,   sick becomest-thou,   say-they

"If you sing in your dream, you'll become sick, they say" [Uj, 131].[35]

This text may be analyzed into three parts: I, from the beginning to the first comma; II, between the two commas; and III, from the second comma to the end. (In the transcription, "comma" marks certain specifiable syntactic constructions.)

I. This part consists of three components, which we will call (k) or constant, (±o) or optional, and (x_n) or symbol.

(k) This component must include the Cheremis morpheme corresponding to English 'sleep, dream': omə [B, Bk, J, Up, Usj], omo [Uj], in a suffixed form (omənəšto [B], omənəštə [Bk]) or followed by a postposition (omettenə~oməden [J], omo dene [Uj], omə denə [Up, Usj]). The function of (k) is to provide the *differentia specifica* whereby dream portents are distinguished from analogous structures—say, weather predictions (e.g., "If the stars are thick in the sky, there'll be snow, they say" [see Part One, G.14.3.1.2.1.3.]). With a very few exceptions, (k) is sentence initial, but this is not required.

(±o) This component is a Cheremis morpheme corresponding to English 'if': tək [B], kən [J, Uj, Usj], kiń [Up], kəńə or (verb stem+)-məkə [Bk]. In a very few instances no such form occurs, but whenever it does, it is the concluding word of part I.

(x_n) This component includes all the remaining words in I; it always occurs before (+o), and usually, but not necessarily, after (k). The symbol states the actual content of the dream, and must minimally include one nuclear verb, in the non-past tense, singular number, and, in most J, Uj, Up, Usj and some B portents, in the second person; otherwise, it is in the same tense, same number, but third person, and, in this latter pattern, always accompanied by jeŋ 'one,' 'man,' which never is found in the former. In order of frequency, the English equivalents of the nuclear verbs which occur are: see (twenty-six times); drink, wade through (three

[35] This analysis is based on a corpus consisting of published dream portents from the [B] and [Bk] collections and, for the rest, unpublished texts.

each); build, fall (into), fell, find, lose, put on, sing (two each); cross, cry, eat, fall out, feed, (cannot) get out, go (into), go (through), hear laugh, mow, rake, sow (one each). A symbol may include, in addition to the necessary nuclear verb, one or more objects which may or may not be modified by attributes of various sorts. It is also possible, occasionally, to have a second verb (or verbal noun) with parallel treatment, in which case the dreamer is shown to be a spectator of some action (e.g., x_{16}, x_{21}, x_{26}, x_{35}), rather than a direct participant in it.

II. This part will be called (i_n) or interpretation. By cultural convention or expectation, the interpretation is a function of the immediately preceding symbol; in logical terms, $f(k+x_n \pm o) = i_n$. Minimally, i_n must also include one verb, which is likewise in the non-past tense, singular number, the choice between second or third persons being optional however. The verb, or predication, which is frequently either sentence final or immediately before the optional part, may then, though need not, be modified freely in many different ways.

III. This part will be called ($\pm q$) or quotative. Its usual position is sentence final, but it may also be inserted parenthetically within the interpretation.

Applying the foregoing analysis to the sample text, we find the following five terms: (k) *omo dene* 'dream with'; ($+o$) *kən* 'if'; (x_{13}) *muret* 'singest-thou'; (i_3) *tuj liat* 'sick becomest-thou'; ($+q$) *manət* 'they-say' (the specific subscripts are from the list given below). The relations between these terms are expressed by the complete formula $[f(k+x_{13}+o) = i_3] + q$. (The constant and the optional components, and the quotative, need not be marked in future formulas.)

Most Cheremis dream portents may be sufficiently characterized by this analysis. However, occasionally an informant may juxtapose several portents, as, "If you see uncut bread in your dream, you'll live long, they say; if you see half a loaf of bread, 'I don't have much time to live,' they say [Uj, 128]. Such clusters may be analyzed precisely as the simple ones, but two things must be noted further: the symbols 'you see uncut bread' (x_{22}) and 'you see half a loaf of bread' (x_{29}) bear a special relationship to one another—here, that of a whole to a part of it; and, consequently, the interpretations 'you'll live long' (i_4) and 'I don't have much time to live' (i_5) do likewise—here they are opposites.

The foregoing analysis leads to the conclusion that the Cheremis dream portents must be classified according to their symbols, upon which the interpretation depends (all other elements being either constant or optional). The symbols must therefore be listed exhaustively. Furthermore, it must be indicated what the conventional interpretation of each symbol is. Now, since two or more symbols may be identically interpreted, it follows that the total number of interpretations is smaller than (in the corpus actually between a third and a half) the total number of symbols; hence the symbols may be grouped into a number of sets (s_n) which equals the total number of interpretations.

The theoretical possibility of a given symbol having two or more interpretations must also be explored. Such cases are encountered in the corpus: e.g., the symbol 'you see the laying of a stack' is interpreted once as 'you'll see life' [Uj, 127], and once as 'you'll grow a tumor' [Up, 125]; and the symbol 'you sing' is interpreted once as 'you'll become sick' [Uj, 131], and once as 'you'll cry' [Up, 92]. There are three explanations possible: (1) a given symbol may have two or more culturally approved interpretations, the choice between them being either entirely free, or, more likely, conditioned by certain immediate environmental stimuli not apparent from the corpus; (2) the variations are regional; (3) individual informants differ in assigning interpretations, chosen with a view to certain implicit cultural limitations. In the above pairs of examples, respectively, as the source references indicate, the portents involved come from two different speech communities, so that the second of the explanations suggests itself. In view of this, and subject to correction, we assign to the symbol 'you see the laying of a stack,' and to the symbol 'you sing,' each, two separate numbers in the list below (x_{16}, x_{21}, and x_4, x_{13}).

We shall now give a complete list of symbols which occur in the corpus; next, we shall give the list of corresponding interpretations; then we shall indicate the existing relationships between sets of symbols and their interpretations; then we shall present the corpus itself.

SYMBOLS

x_1 = 'you drink brandy' [B, 187]
x_2 = 'you sow flax seeds' [B, 174]
x_3 = 'one laughs' [B, 179]
x_4 = 'you sing' [J; Up, 92]
x_5 = 'one wades through melted snow' [B, 171]
x_6 = 'you see straw' [Uj, 141]
x_7 = 'you go into water' [Bk, 87]
x_8 = 'you cry' [B, 179; Bk, 89; J; Uj, 137; Up, 97]
x_9 = 'you wade through water' [B, 172]
x_{10} = 'you see clear (river) water' [Uj, 139; Up, 89]
x_{11} = 'you eat bread' [Bk, 86]
x_{12} = 'you wade across snow' [Uj, 130; Up, 91]
x_{13} = 'you sing' [Uj, 131]
x_{14} = 'you fall into a pit' [Uj, 133; Up, 88]
x_{15} = 'you see a fire' [Uj, 138]
x_{16} = 'you see the laying of a stack' [Up, 125]
x_{17} = 'you drink vodka' [J]
x_{18} = 'you go through a river' [J]
x_{19} = 'you put on a clean (or white) shirt (and drawers)' [J; Uj, 135; Uj, 238; Up, 94]
x_{20} = 'you put on quite new beautiful clothes' [B, 184]
x_{21} = 'you see the laying of a stack' [Uj, 127]
x_{22} = 'you see uncut bread' [Uj, 128]
x_{23} = 'you make a very nice two-story house' [J]
x_{24} = 'you fell a pine' [B, 177; Bk, 93; Uj, 142; Up, 125]

$x_{25} =$ 'you fcll a birch' [B, 178; Bk, 93; Uj, 142; Up, 125; Usj, 25]

$x_{26} =$ 'you see someone plowing' [B, 175; Uj, 88; Up, 125]

$x_{27} =$ 'one falls into water so that one cannot reach the bank' [B, 173]

$x_{28} =$ 'one loses one's boots and clothes' [B, 185]

$x_{29} =$ 'you see half a loaf of bread' [Uj, 128]

$x_{30} =$ 'you can't get out of a pit' [Uj, 132; Up, 87]

$x_{31} =$ 'you see a molar fall out' [B, 188]

$x_{32} =$ 'you build a two-story house' [Bk, 90; Uj, 185]

$x_{33} =$ 'your teeth fall out' [J; Up, 96]

$x_{34} =$ 'you lose your (inner) glove' [Uj, 136; Up, 95]

$x_{35} =$ 'you see that they are carrying manure from the stall' [Uj, 140]

$x_{36} =$ 'you find a small ax' [B, 186]

$x_{37} =$ 'you find a cap' [B, 186]

$x_{38} =$ 'you see a dead man' [B, 183; Bk, 88; J; Uj, 129; Up, 90]

$x_{39} =$ 'one sees smoke' [B, 170]

$x_{40} =$ 'you see black fish' [Bk, 92]

$x_{41} =$ 'you drink beer' [Bk, 91]

$x_{42} =$ 'you see fire' [Bk, 91]

$x_{43} =$ 'one sees blazing fire' [B, 170; J; Up, 98]

$x_{44} =$ 'you mow grass, rake hay' [B, 176]

$x_{45} =$ 'you feed hay to a horse' [B, 180]

$x_{46} =$ 'you hear the sound of a bell' [B, 189; J; Uj, 134; Up, 93; Usj, 24]

$x_{47} =$ 'you see red cows (or a red rooster)' [B, 181; J]

$x_{48} =$ 'one sees the moon' [B, 169]

$x_{49} =$ 'you see a black dog' [Usj, 26]

$x_{50} =$ 'one sees a dog' [B, 182]

$x_{51} =$ 'you see linen' [Usj, 23]

$x_{52} =$ 'you see silver coins' [Bk, 92]

$x_{53} =$ 'you see white fish' [Bk, 92]

$x_{54} =$ 'you see clean water' [J]

$x_{55} =$ 'you see a black dog' [J]

$x_{56} =$ 'you see very many little children' [J]

$x_{57} =$ 'you see a white dog' [J]

$x_{58} =$ 'you cross a bridge' [J]

INTERPRETATIONS

$i_1 =$ 'sorrow' (x_1 through x_7)

$i_2 =$ 'joy' (x_8 through x_{11})

$i_3 =$ 'sickness' (x_{12} through x_{17})

$i_4 =$ 'cure of sickness, easy, long, or good life' (x_{18} through x_{23})

$i_5 =$ 'death' (so that: x_{24} refers to the head of the family or to any male; x_{25} to a woman; x_{26} to a child or to someone in the house; x_{26}, x_{28}, x_{29}, x_{30}, to the dreamer; x_{31} to a member of the family; x_{32} to two men, one after the other, in the interval of a week, or to someone in the house; x_{33}, x_{34}, to sheep, [and x_{33} also to someone in the family]; x_{35} to cattle)

i_6 = 'birth' (so that: x_{36} refers to a male child; x_{37} to a female child)

i_7 — 'rain; fog; moist weather' (x_{38} through x_{41})

i_8 = 'clear weather' (x_{42} and x_{43})

i_9 = 'money coming in' (x_{44})

i_{10} = 'money going out' (x_{45})

i_{11} = 'news will be heard; letter will arrive' (x_{46})

i_{12} = 'not good: village will burn down' (x_{47})

i_{13} = 'a soldier will come home' (x_{48})

i_{14} = 'the dreamer will see his friend' (x_{49})

i_{15} = 'not good: the dreamer will quarrel with someone' (x_{50})

i_{16} = 'the dreamer will undertake a journey' (x_{51})

i_{17} = 'snow' (x_{52} and x_{53})

i_{18} = 'your work will be clean' (x_{54})

i_{19} = 'your friend will fool you' (x_{55})

i_{20} = 'there will be a disturbance' (x_{56})

i_{21} = 'you meet a good friend' (x_{57})

i_{22} = 'put a cross for work to be done' (x_{58})

The interpretations may be arranged, according to the frequency of their occurrence, in descending order: i_5 occurs twelve times; i_1, seven times; i_3 and i_4, six times; i_2 and i_7, each four times; i_6, i_8, and i_{17} each occur twice; i_9 through i_{16} and i_{18} through i_{22} each occur once.

Of a total of fifty-eight instances, thirty interpretations (i_5, i_1, i_3, i_{10}, i_{12}, i_{15}, i_{19}, i_{20}) are definitely unfavorable, with 'death' accounting for nearly half of the latter, or 'death,' 'sorrow' and 'disease' accounting together for twenty-five. Of the total, only eleven interpretations (i_2, i_4, i_9) may be labelled positively favorable. The remaining seventeen are neither particularly favorable or unfavorable.

Note further that the first ten interpretations may be divided into five pairs of opposites, forming these proportions: i_1:i_2=i_3:i_4=i_5:i_6=i_7:i_8=i_{10}:i_9. The remaining ones do not appear to lend themselves to such dichotomization.

SETS OF SYMBOLS

Symbols which bear identical interpretations form a set. Sets which include more than one symbol are: s_1=x_1 through x_7; s_2=x_8 through x_{11}; s_3=x_{12} through x_{17}; s_4=x_{18} through x_{23}; s_5=x_{24} through x_{35}; s_6= x_{36} and x_{37}; s_7=x_{38} through x_{41}; s_8=x_{42} and x_{43}; s_{17}=x_{52} and x_{53}. The remaining sets include only one symbol, and thus bear the same number as the symbol itself. A set may be regarded as favorable when its function equals a favorable interpretation, and vice versa. Opposite sets are such sets the functions of which equal opposite pairs of interpretations.

FUNCTIONS

All functional relations between a given set and its interpretation may be expressed now in a single formula: $f(s_n) = i_n$.

THE CORPUS

$f(x_1) = i_1$ If you drink brandy in your dream, you will have great sorrow. [B, 187]

$f(x_2) = i_1$ If you sow flax seeds in your dream, you will have great sorrow. [B, 174]

$f(x_4) = i_1$ If you sing in your dream, you'll cry, they say. [Up, 92]

$f(x_4) = i_1$ If at night you sing in your dream, you will cry, they say. [J]

$f(x_5) = i_1$ If one wades through melted snow in one's dream, one will shed many tears. [B, 171]

$f(x_6) = i_1$ If you see straw in your dream, speech will reach you; it'll be hard for you somewhere, they say. [Uj, 141]

$f(x_7) = i_1$ If you go into water in your dream, there'll be tears. [Bk, 87]

$f(x_8) = i_2 + f(x_3) = i_1$
          If one cries in one's dreams, one will have joy; if one laughs, one will have great sorrow. [B, 179]

$f(x_8) = i_2$ If you cry in your dream, it'll be well with you, they say.

$f(x_8) = i_2$ If you cry in your dream, you'll rejoice they say. [Up, 97]

$f(x_8) = i_2$ If you cry in your dream, you will be very happy, they say. [J]

$f(x_4) = i_1 + f(x_8) = i_2$
          If you sing in your dreams, it'll go badly [with you]; if you cry, you'll have joy. [Bk, 89]

$f(x_9) = i_2$ Your dream: you wade through water, thus you'll emerge from sadness, will have no sorrow. [B, 172]

$f(x_{10}) = i_2$ If you see clear (river) water in your dream, it'll be well, people say. [Uj, 139]

$f(x_{10}) = i_2$ If you see clear (river) water in your dream, you'll have joy. [Up, 89]

$f(x_1) = i_1 + f(x_{11}) = i_2$
          If you drink brandy in your dream, you will have sorrow; if you eat bread, it'll be well. [Bk, 86]

$f(x_{12}) = i_3$ If you wade across snow in your dream, you'll catch cold and will become sick, they say. [Uj, 130]

$f(x_{12}) = i_3$ If you wade in snow in your dream, you'll get sick, they say. [Up, 91]

$f(x_{13}) = i_3$ If you sing in your dream, you'll become sick, they say. [Uj, 131]

$f(x_{14}) = i_3$ If you fall into a pit in your dream, you'll become sick, they say. [Uj, 133; Up, 88]

$f(x_{15}) = i_3$ If you see a fire in your dream, your heart will ache, they say. [Uj, 138]

$f(x_{17}) = i_3$ If you drink vodka in your dream, you will catch a cold, they say. [J]

$f(x_{18}) = i_4$ If in your dream you go through a river, all your work will become easy, they say. [J]

$f(x_{19}) = i_4$ If you put on a clean (or white) shirt in your dream, your life will be good, they say. [Uj, 135]

$f(x_{19}) = i_4$ If in your dream you put on white clothes, your future life will be good, they say. [J]

$f(x_{19}) = i_4$ If a sick man puts on a clean shirt in his dreams, he'll get cured, they say. [Uj, 238]

$f(x_{19}) = i_4$ If you put on a clean (or white) shirt and drawers in your dream, life will be easy, they say. [Up, 94]

$f(x_{20}) = i_4$ If one puts on quite new beautiful clothes in one's dream, one will live long. [B, 184]

$f(x_{21}) = i_4$ If you see the laying of a stack in your dream, you'll see life, they say. [Uj, 127]

$f(x_{23}) = i_4$ If in your dream you make a very nice two-story house, your future life will be good, they say. [J]

$f(x_{24}) = i_5$ If you see yourself felling pines in your dream, if you fell the pine, the head of the family will die. [B, 177]

$f(x_{25}) = i_5$ You have a dream, you fell a birch, a woman will die. [B, 178]

$f(x_{25}) = i_5$ If you fell a birch in your dream, a woman will die in the family, they say. [Usj, 25]

$f(x_{26}) = i_5$ If you see someone ploughing in your dream, a child will die. [B, 175]

$f(x_{26}) = i_5$ If you see ploughing in your dream, someone will die in the house, they say. [Uj, 88]

$f(x_{24}+x_{25}) = i_5$

If you see a dream, the felling of a pine, that'll be a man's—a man will die, they say; if you see the felling of a birch in your dream, then that birch will be a woman's—a woman will die, they say. [Uj, 142]

$f(x_{24}+x_{25}) = i_5$

If you see a pine being felled in your dream, a man will die; if you see a birch being felled, a woman will die. [Bk, 93]

$f(x_{24}+x_{25}+x_{26}) = i_5+f(x_{16}) = i_3$

If you fell a pine tree in your dream, then that dream will show it to be a man, it'll be a man's; if you see the felling of a birch tree, that'll be a woman's; if you see ploughing in your dream, someone will die in the house, they say; if you see the laying of a stack, you'll grow a tumor, they say. [Up, 125]

$f(x_{27}) = i_5$ If one falls into water so that one cannot reach the bank, one will die. [B, 173]

$f(x_{28}) = i_5+i_5$

If one loses one's boots and clothes, one will not have a long life, one will soon die. [B, 185]

$f(x_{22}) = i_4+f(x_{29}) = i_5$

If you see uncut bread in your dream, you'll live long, they say; if you see half a loaf of bread, "I don't have much time to live," they say. [Uj, 128]

$f(x_{30}) = i_5$ If you can't get out of a pit in your dream, you'll die, they say. [Uj, 132; Up, 87]

$f(x_{31}) = i_5$ If you see a molar fall out in your dream, someone will die in the family. [B, 188]

$f(x_{32}) = i_5$ If you build a two-story house in your dream, two men will die, one after another, in the interval of a week, they say. [Uj, 185]

$f(x_{32}) = i_5$ If you see a house being built in your dream, someone will be dead [in that house]. [Bk, 90]

$f(x_{33}) = i_5$ If your teeth fall out in your dream, sheep will die, they say. [Up, 96]

$f(x_{33}) = i_5$ If in your dream your teeth fall out of your mouth, someone in the family will die, they say. [J]

$f(x_{34}) = i_5$ If you lose your (inner) glove in your dream, sheep will die, they say. [Uj, 136; Up, 95]

$f(x_{35}) = i_5$ If you see in your dream that they are carrying manure from the stall, some cattle will die, they say. [Uj, 140]

$f(x_{36}+x_{37}) = i_6$

You have a dream, you find a small ax in the dream, then your wife will give birth to a boy; if you find a cap, then she will give birth to a girl. [B, 186]

$f(x_{38}) = i_7$ If you see a dead man in your dream, the weather will be wet. [B, 183; Uj, 129]

$f(x_{38}) = i_7$ If you see a dead man in your dream, there'll be rain, they say. [Up, 90]

$f(x_{38}) = i_7$ If you see a dead man in your dream, it [the weather] will be wet. [Bk, 88]

$f(x_{38}) = i_7$ If in your dream you see a dead person, the weather will become wet, they say. [J]

$f(x_{43}) = i_8 + f(x_{39}) = i_7$

If one sees a blazing fire in one's dream, it will be clear; if one sees smoke, it will be foggy, rainy. [B, 170]

$f(x_{52}+x_{53}) = i_{17} + f(x_{40}) = i_7$

If you see silver coins in your dream, there'll be snow; if you see white fish, there'll be snow; if you see black fish, there'll be rain. [Bk, 92]

$f(x_{41}) = i_7 + f(x_{42}) = i_8$

If you drink beer in your dream, rainy [weather] will come; if you see a fire, it'll clear up. [Bk, 91]

$f(x_{43}) = i_8$ If you see blazing fire in your dream, the weather will be clear, they say. [Up, 98]

$f(x_{43}) = i_8$ If in your dream you see a fire, if the fire burns clear, the weather will be dry, they say. [J]

$f(x_{44}) = i_9$ If you mow grass, rake hay in your dream, money will come in. [B, 176]

$f(x_{45}) = i_{10}$ If you feed hay to a horse in your dream, money will go away and take another position. [B, 180]

$f(x_{46}) = i_{11} + i_{11}$

If you hear the sound of a bell in your dream, you'll receive news; a letter will come. [B, 189]

$f(x_{46}) = i_{11}$ If you hear the sound of a bell in your dream, you'll hear news. [Uj, 134; Up, 93; Usj, 24]

$f(x_{46}) = i_{11}$ If in your dream you hear the sound of a bell, there will be some kind of news, they say. [J]

$f(x_{47}) = i_{12}$ If you see red cows in your dream, this is not good; the village will burn down. [B, 181]

$f(x_{47}) = i_{12}$ If you see a red rooster in your dream, there will be a fire. [J]

$f(x_{48}) = i_{13}$ If one sees the moon in one's dream, a soldier will come home. [B, 169]

$f(x_{49}) = i_{14}$ If you see a black dog in your dream, you'll see your friend. [Usj, 26]

$f(x_{50}) = i_{15}$ If one sees a dog in one's dream, this is not good; one will quarrel with someone. [B, 182]

$f(x_{51}) = i_{16}$ If you see linen in your dream, you'll have a journey. [Usj, 23]

$f(x_{54}) = i_{18}$ If in your dream you see clean water, all your work will be clean, they say. [J]

$f(x_{55}) = i_{19}$ If you see a black dog in your dream, your friends will fool you, they say. [J]

$f(x_{56}) = i_{20}$ If in your dream you see very many little children, there will be a disturbance, they say. [J]

$f(x_{57}) = i_{21}$ If in your dream you see a white dog, you will meet a good friend, they say. [J]

$f(x_{58}) = i_{22}$ If you cross a bridge in your dream, put a cross for work to be done, they say. [J]

SYMBOLIC CONTENT

Among the several invisible inhabitants of the human body, the Cheremis count the *ört* (see Part One, J.1.). The relationship between the body and its *ört* seems to indicate a relatively low threshold between the conscious and the unconscious, and to invite attempts at translating from latent to manifest content in terms of the Freudian theory of symbolism. It is all too tempting to labor the obvious: for instance, that 'small ax' (x_{36}) is a phallic symbol ('birth of a boy,' i_6), and 'cap' (x_{37}) is a symbol for female genitalia ('birth of a girl,' i_8); or that 'felling a pine' (x_{24}) symbolizes killing the father (cf. [B, 177; Uj, 142; Up, 125]), while 'felling a birch' (x_{25}) symbolizes killing the mother (cf. [B, 178; Uj, 142; Up, 125; Usj, 25]). In this last example, four separate interpretations seem to establish 'birch' firmly as a female symbol—and yet, in the traditional Cheremis folksongs we find 'birch' the conventional symbol for 'son,' and 'to cut down a birch' means there 'to send away the son.'[36]

Lacking, unfortunately, records of informants' associations stimulated by these dream portents, "explanations" of symbolic content must remain in the realm of speculation at present. We know that the symbols are more or less stereotyped—witness their frequent recording, sometimes verbatim, from different speech communities—but we can only guess at their cultural valuation.

CHUVASH PARALLELS

Because of the extensive distribution of dream portents (with or without the allied concept of the dream-soul) the diffusion of specific portents is very difficult to trace. At best, parallels with corresponding items in neighboring cultures can be pointed out at this stage.

Cheremis culture traits are most usefully compared with Chuvash, Tatar, or Russian. All three have influenced the Cheremis language: some five hundred Chuvash and over six hundred Tatar loanwords have been identified.[37] More particularly in the field of folklore, certain end formulas in the Cheremis folktale

[36] Sebeok and Lane, p. 144 and fn. 13; also Berdnikov and Tudorovskaia.

[37] Räsänen, 1920 and 1923; Sebeok, 1952, p. 2, fn. 6.

have been assigned Chuvash origin,[38] and both Tatar and Russian folksongs have been shown to have had intensive effects upon those of the Cheremis.[39]

The deepest of these layers of acculturation is the Chuvash. The Cheremis have been exposed to the influence of the Volga Bulgars (whose modern descendants the Chuvash are) continually since about A.D. 700. For this reason, any parallel dream portents we can locate in Chuvash folklore are apt to be significant and illuminating rather than otherwise.

Among the major sources of Chuvash folklore only the collection of materials by Gyula Mészáros contains dream portents.[40] Since this is a rare book, and, moreover, provides translations only into Hungarian, we offer here an English translation of the twenty-one dream portents the collector gave, as he put it, by way of a sample:

A. If a Tatar appears in a dream, there will be an appearance of god.
B. If someone sees a Mordvin in a dream there will be a scare above water.
C. If someone sees raw meat in a dream, [it means] death.
D. Green grass in a dream [means] death.
E. If someone puts on two layers of shirts in a dream, and if one of the layers is ragged, [it means] somebody's death.
F. If someone builds a new house in a dream, somebody will die.
G. If someone is attacked by a dog in a dream, a man will attack him.
H. If a tooth falls out in a dream, something will get lost.
I. If someone beats himself with a soaked bath-switch in the bath in a dream, it means somebody's slander.
J. If someone sees a dream still in the evening, that will not soon be fulfilled; if he sees it at the break of dawn, it will be fulfilled within some days.
K. If someone drinks brandy in a dream, sorrow.
L. If someone sees a priest in a dream, there will be an appearance of the Angel of Death.
M. If someone sees a wedding in a dream, there'll be a death.
N. If someone goes into a church in a dream, that is not good.
O. If someone grinds in a dream, sorrow.
P. If someone plays with a girl in a dream, illness will arise.
Q. If a house burns in a dream, [it means] clear weather.
R. Silver-money in a dream [means] clear weather.
S. If someone is ploughing a field in a dream, someone will die.
T. If someone sees water in a dream, life.
U. If a horse gets loose in a dream, and if someone cannot catch it, if there is a sick man (in the house) he'll die, or if there is a conscripted child (in the house), he'll become a soldier.

[38] Beke, 1933.

[39] Sebeok and Lane, pp. 146–51; Karmazin, in Wichmann, 1931, pp. 380–84; and Berdnikov and Tudorovskaia.

[40] Mészáros, Vol. 1, pp. 398–400; texts with Hungarian translation are given.

A comparison of the Chuvash with the Cheremis portents yields—for such a small corpus—remarkably revealing similarities.

Five Chuvash portents resemble corresponding Cheremis portents both as to symbol and interpretation:

F.—$f(x_{32}) = i_5$ (In Chuvash, the symbol is 'new house,' in Cheremis 'two-story house,' but building either one is interpreted as 'death.')

G.—$f(x_{50}) = i_{15}$ (In Chuvash, the 'dog' specifically 'attacks,' in Cheremis he is merely 'seen,' but both are interpreted alike.

K.—$f(x_1) = i_1$

Q.—$f(x_{43}) = i_8$ (The Chuvash specifies that it is a 'house' which is burning, the Cheremis merely mentions a 'blazing fire,' but both are taken to portend 'clear weather.')

S.—$f(x_{26}) = i_5$

Two more Chuvash portents include symbols that also occur in Cheremis, but with different interpretations:

H.—x_{31} or x_{33}

T.—x_{10}

Eleven more Chuvash portents include interpretations that also occur in Cheremis, but with reference to symbols which do not occur in the latter corpus:

O. i_1

P.—i_3

T.—i_4

C, D, E, L, M, U.—i_5

R.—i_8

In all probability, only such comparisons are diagnostic when both symbols and interpretations can be matched.[41]

[41] This can in some measure be tested by comparing the Cheremis portents with a similar-sized corpus from a remote culture, for example, Aymara. LaBarre, pp. 179–80, gives thirty-five symbols and corresponding interpretations. Only one Aymara portent resembles the corresponding Cheremis portent both as to symbol and interpretation: 'the dead' or 'a person who is dead' means 'much wind or severe cold' or 'it will rain'; cf. $f(x_{33}) = i_7$. Two more Aymara portents include symbols that also occur in Cheremis, but with quite different interpretations: 'fire' or 'burning fire' means 'gossip' (contrast with x_{13} or x_{35}) and 'clean water' means 'good health' (contrast with x_9). The following six interpretations appear in Aymara also, but in reference to symbols which are not found in Cheremis: i_1 (four times), i_2 (three times), i_3 (five times), i_4 (once), i_5 (four times), i_9 (five times).

CHARMS

THE CORPUS AND ITS FUNCTION

THE word 'charm,' as used here is equivalent to the Latin phrase 'incantamentum it adjuratio magica,' or to the German word 'Segen,' which has been defined with varying emphasis; a more formal definition will be offered below, but here we adopt the definition of J. Grimm, according to whom 'Segen' are "Formeln im ausserkirchlichen Gebrauch, christlicher und nicht-christlicher Art, denen eine übernatürliche Wirkung und zwar meist schützender, heilsamer Art zugeschrieben wird."[42]

This excellent definition includes at once historical, functional, and formal dimensions, all of which are important for a complete understanding. For our purposes, however, the third aspect will be paramount. This is because the effectiveness of a charm depends on its literally exact citation, and, conversely, because any departure from its precisely set mechanism may render the magic wholly ineffective. It goes without saying that the effect depends ultimately on the psycho-cultural valuation of the charm. That is to say, it must be firmly believed in by the speaker, and a strong belief may, under certain circumstances, allow for minor variations in certain details of the text, though such variations do not, of course, alter the structural outlines of the charm.

In historical perspective, Cheremis charms are not especially problematic. They are, on the one hand, altogether different from the magic runes of Finnish folklore, both in content and in form. On the other hand, Cheremis charms are very like Russian ones, most of them sharing with the latter, among other diagnostic features, what may be called the "motif of an extremely improbable eventuality" (see below). It can be safely concluded that among the Cheremis (and also among their linguistic congeners the Mordvins and Votyaks, as well as among their close neighbors the Chuvash) the now extant charms are of relatively recent origin, having diffused in Christian times, and, specifically, from Russian sources.[43]

In the text collections which constitute our corpus,[44] charms appear under

[42] Cited after Ohrt. This comprehensive (though essentially German-based) discussion provided some suggestive hints which are followed in the course of this analysis.

[43] On the origin of the Cheremis charms, see Krohn, 1901, p. 57, and 1924, pp. 9ff.; Kuznetsov, 1904, pp. 73ff.; Mansikka, pp. 299ff. Russian charms are treated by Mansikka; (see also the discussion and bibliography in Sokolov, pp. 246–57); and Chuvash charms are treated by Mészáros.

[44] This corpus includes all the standard sources except that the seven charms occurring in V, pp. 68, 86, 139, 245, 262, and 320 are not covered here.

functional headings. These may be classified, with some inevitable overlapping, into four major categories: (1) charms having to do with medicine, both human and veterinary; (2) charms having to do with human relations, such as love or adversaries; (3) charms that are directed against witchery in general, including the Evil Eye, or certain specific spirits; and (4) charms having to do with the fauna or flora.

The Cheremis have a good many different kinds of magicians, both harmful and evil ones (cf. Part One, D.2.), and helpful and benelovent ones (D.7., D.9., D.10.). Among the latter, there is a specialist who plies his office with the help of charms. The Cheremis call him *šübedəšə*, (D.9.), the literal meaning of which is 'the one who spits.' One Cheremis word for 'charm' is *šübedəme*.[45] Both of these words are connected with the verb *šübalam* 'I spit.' The informant explains: *šübedəšə šübeden paremda al'ə šübeda* "the 'spitter' cures by spitting or spits" [Wu, 73]. This procedure undoubtedly has its root in the practically world-wide belief in the magical efficacy of spittle and spitting. The motif "magic results from spitting" (Thompson, D1776) occurs in several Cheremis folktales. In one episode, the narrator relates: "My horse became tired. A man followed me and overtook me. He came and sat upon my sled. I said, 'My horse is tired.' He said, 'Your horse has been bewitched.' He spat twice. He cracked the whip once. The horse began to run impatiently, like the wind."[46] In an unpublished tale (Uj, 43),[47] the Angel of Death (Part One, A.6.) is asked by a man, "How did you build this house?" His reply was, "If I spit once, a house grows." In still another unpublished tale (Uj, 48), a sick man spits upon the ground and from the spittle a *keremet* (cf. Part One, A.31.) springs forth.

The "spitter" may accompany his charm by various ceremonial actions to suit the occasion. Often the sorcerer holds a glass of water or brandy in his left hand, leans over it and recites the charm. Meanwhile, he may circle the rim of the glass with an object made of iron (see also Part One, H.4.4.)—a knife or a pair of scissors, for instance—and keep blowing or spitting into the water or brandy. Charm 3.1.4., for example, ends with the statement, "Let this steel penetrate into the heart, the liver of the sorcerer"; and 1.1.14.1. and 3.4.1. state, "I have with me my sharp steel sword, my sharp steel hatchet, my sharp steel knife; I chop, dismember, cut up and mangle [the spirit of the house, or some other evil spirit]." He may also blow into the patient's face through the scissors, or, as among the Chuvash, through a broom; (for iron magic, see H.4.4.).

In an interesting unpublished charm (Up, 39) the informant describes the

---

[45] Another term is *ju* (Eastern and Forest dialects), *jo* (Mountain dialects), the etymology of which is rather controversial. Cf. particularly Paasonen, 1907 b, and the literature cited in Bárczi, p. 143, *s.u.* jós.

[46] Type and motif analyses in Sebeok, 1952, p. 24.

[47] For analyses, see Sebeok, *ibid.*, p. 68.

magician's actions, and comments on the consequences. This is a charm (3.2.5.) spoken to cure a child who has been harmed by the Evil Eye and Evil Tongue:

"Phuu"—he spits into the water, casts salt [into the water], "if this salt is hurt by the Evil Eye, only then let the Evil Eye hurt the child, bite his tongue! As this salt dissolves, just so let the Evil Eye and Evil Tongue dissolve! Phuu," he again spits into the water. "If the black-eyed, red-eyed, black-currant-eyed, grey-eyed, red-fish-eyed at the bottom of the sea with his eyelids, licking with his tongue can ladle out the sand— only then let the Evil Eye hurt it, the Evil Tongue spoil! Phuu," he spits into the water again. "As the sun rises, just so let the Evil Eye go out! As the moon rises, just so let the Evil Eye, Evil Tongue depart! As the snow melts in the spring, just so let the Evil Eye and Evil Tongue dissolve! As the fog dissolves in the wind, just so let the Evil Eye and Evil Tongue dissolve! Phuu," he says and spits again into the water. Then he gives it to the child to drink, he washes him with the water into which he spit. If then the spittle does the child good, the child goes to sleep. If it doesn't do good, he doesn't then get cured, someone else will again cast a formula.

FUNCTIONAL CLASSIFICATION OF CHARMS

The following is a classification by their function of the charms which actually occur in the corpus, with some background comment in passing.

1. *Charms Having to do with Medicine*

Treatment of disease by way of charms is, of course, only one of the ways in which the Cheremis proceed against illness.

1.1.   For the cure of human ailments.
1.1.1.   Toothache. [R, 208]
1.1.2.   Burns (two variants, .1 and .2). [G, 51–52, 144; P, 76]
1.1.3.   Snakebite (two variants, .1 and .2). [G, 52, 144–45; R, 209]
1.1.4.   Hoarseness. [G, 50, 142]
1.1.5.   Bleeding (four variants, .1–.4). [G, 50, 142–43; R, 208; Wu, 72; B, 26]
1.1.6.   Syphilis (?). [G, 52, 144]
   The Cheremis word *kila* (Russian 'hernia,' 'rupture,' 'burst') is translated by Genetz as 'die von den Russen verhängte Krankheit,' which presumably means 'syphilis.'[48] (See also note to 1.1.8., below.)
1.1.7.   Swollen finger (two variants, .1 and .2). [G, 50, 142; P, 75–76]
   The Cheremis call a festering swelling on a finger a 'snake-eye'; several sayings of this sort have been recorded: "There's a 'fiery snake-eye,' they say; it must be stopped by casting a spell, they say, then one gets cured" (Uj, 239; cf. Uj, 23 and 218). Another method for curing a painful finger is to swathe it in a spider web (Uj, 149).
1.1.8.   Tumor (?). [P, 77–80]
   The Cheremis word *kela* is rendered by Paasonen as 'ein Gewächs [Geschwür?; im

---

[48] It is so interpreted by Szilasi, p. 77.

Körper überhaupt],' and, elsewhere,[49] as 'Geschwür, Beule; Beule, die als von einer Hexe verursacht gilt.' The connection, if any, between *kila* (see the note to 1.1.6., above) and *kela* is unclear.

1.1.9.   Smallpox. [Wu, 72–73]

On smallpox, see Part One, A.38.25.

1.1.10.   Sprain. [Wu, 71–72]

1.1.11.   Colic (two variants, .1 and .2).[50] [R, 208, 209]

The Cheremis word literally means 'wind.' Ordinary bellyache is caused by the intrusion of a *buber* (see Part One, A.10., and 3.3., below).

1.1.12.   Wasting of a child by a revenant. [G, 54, 147]

The Cheremis have revenants of various sorts; the most numerous among them are the *keremet* (see Part One, A.31.), which often appear in human shape and whose actions are always malevolent. It is not specified in the present context which kind of revenant is involved, but it is safe to assume that it is a *keremet*.

1.1.13.   Engrafting flesh. [R, 211–12]

1.1.14.   Alleviation of illness in general (two variants, .1 and .2). [G, 53–54, 145–47; PG, 31, 97]

1.1.15.   To stop uncontrolled sobbing. [R, 212]

The charm must be repeated until the sobbing ceases.

1.2.   Horse colic (two variants, .1 and .2). [G, 51, 143; P, 75]

Horse colic is caused by an evil spirit named *asəra* (<Tatar) (cf. Part One, A.4.).

1.2.2.   To protect horses and cattle against witchery. [B, 27–28]

2. *Charms Having to do with Human Relations*

2.1.   Against an adversary (five variants, .1–.5). [R, 209–11]

2.2.   To awaken love (two variants, .1 and .2). [PG, 31–32, 98; B, 25–26]

2.3.   To produce indifference (two variants, .1 and .2). [PG, 31, 33, 97, 99–100]

3. *Charms For or Against Witchery in General, or Against Certain Specific Spirits*

3.1.   Witchery in general (four variants, .1–.4). [PG, 30, 32–33, 97, 99; Wu, 68–71; P, 73–74]

The Cheremis call practitioners of black magic *juzə* (see Part One, D.2.); among these, the *loktəzə* 'spoiler' causes illness and damage which must be counteracted by charms.

3.2.   Evil Eye (and Tongue) (five variants, .1–.5). [G, 52, 145; PG, 30, 96; B, 26–27; P, 77; Up, 39 (see above)]

Everybody and everything can be harmed by the Evil Eye and Tongue (see Part One, H.6.5.).

3.3.   Will-o'-the-wisp. [P, 80–81]

For *buber,* see Part One, A.10.

3.4.   Spirit of the house (two variants, .1 and .2). [G, 51, 143; P, 81]

[49] Paasonen, 1948, p. 38.

[50] It is specified that the second charm is for a case of bad colic.

The *šükšöndal* (see Part One, A.85.); it is the spirit of the entire homestead, including particularly the bathhouse.

4. *Charms Having to do with Fauna or Flora*

4.1.   Protection against an attacking dog. [PG, 30, 96]
4.2.   To encourage the growth of grain. [PG, 32, 98–99]

Though functional classifications of the sort outlined above are of undoubted cultural interest, and are useful as a practical device, they do nevertheless tend to obscure the basic formal identities or similarities which underlie Cheremis charms. Furthermore, one recalls Olbrechts' criticism of Mooney's arrangement of Cherokee formulas "in a systematic sequence, in a logical order, 'logical' from the white man's point of view. . . . This classification is quite foreign to Cherokee knowledge and use. . . ."[51] Since the cultural matrix in which the Cheremis charms function is known only sketchily at best, such a classification ought not to be insisted upon. On the other hand, a structural analysis is entirely in terms of the texts being analyzed, as we hope to show in the next section.

SAMPLE ANALYSIS OF STRUCTURE

Charm 1.1.5.3. is arbitrarily selected for the purpose of this sample analysis. This charm, spoken in order to stop the flow of blood from a wound, is here reproduced first in a phonemic transcription (the bracketed numerals are for ease of reference only).

[1] *olma-pu* [2] *kuze* [3] *peledən* [4] *šińčeš,* [5] *tug-ak* [6] *tidə* [7] *püčmə* [8] *kuškən* [9] *šičšə!* [10] *buige* [11] *peledəšem* [12] *kalasaš* [13] *küleš.* [14] *büt* [15] *kunam* [16] *peled* [17] *kerteš,* [18] *tunam* [19] *ižə* [20] *məjəm* [21] *seṇe!*

Literal translation: [1] 'apple tree'; [2] 'as'; [3] 'blossoming'; [4] 'stands'; [5] 'just so'; [6] 'this'; [7] 'wound'; [8] 'growing'; [9] 3d sg. imperative of the verb 'to stand'; [10] 'all'; [11] acc. of 'blossom'; [12] 'to mention'; [13] 'it is necessary'; [14] 'water'; [15] 'when'; [16] 'blossom'; [17] 'can'; [18] 'then'; [19] 'first'; [20] 'me'; [21] 2d sg. imperative of the verb 'to overcome.'

Free translation: [1–9] 'As the apple tree blossoms forth, just so let this wound heal! [10–13] (All blossoms must be mentioned.) [14–21] When water can blossom forth, only then overcome me!'

Our analytical procedure will generally be an application of binary opposition as a patterning principle, that is, we shall repeatedly divide sequences dichoto-

---

[51] Mooney and Olbrechts, 1932, pp. 159–60, have a section on "Structure of the Formulas" among the Cherokee. The general pattern outlined there is, however, an ideal one, to which perhaps not one formula corresponds exactly.

mously until the ultimate constituents are reached, except for the first subdivision of I., where an n-termed oppositive principle will be applied.

The first operation yields two immediate constituents,[52] namely, I. [1–13] "As the apple tree blossoms forth, just so let this wound heal! (All blossoms must be mentioned)," and II. [14–21] "When water can blossom forth, only then overcome me!" Since the entire charm consists of three grammatical sentences, namely, [1–9, 10–13, 14–21], it may well be asked why the first operation yields [1–13] and [14–21] rather than, say, [1–9] and [10–21]; the reason for this will be clarified as we proceed with the analysis of the first immediate constituent.

I. The sequence [1–13] consists of two sentences, namely, [1–9] and [10–13]. Now let the symbol o represent the word 'tree,' and let further a numeral subscript represent the kind of tree involved. Thus, let the subscript $_1$ stand for "apple," then o_1 will symbolize "apple tree." The second sentence—a meta-statement about the continuation of the charm, giving a general procedural prescription on how to continue—can be regarded as equivalent to saying: "As the o_2 blossoms forth, just so let this wound heal! As the o_3 blossoms forth . . ." and so forth, until "As the o_n blossoms forth, just so let this wound heal!" Thus we have a finite number of sentences precisely alike in construction; the number of sentences is equal to the number of ethnobotanically conceived species of tree.

The internal structure of all these sentences is the same. Each sentence may be divided into two clauses, one independent and one dependent. Using sentence [1–9] as the model, the independent clause is [5–9] "just so let this wound heal," and the dependent clause is [1–4] "as the apple tree blossoms forth."

Both clauses can be further subdivided into an actor-action phrase, namely, [6–9] "let this wound heal" in the independent clause, and [1, 3–4] "the apple tree blossoms forth" in the dependent clause; and a subordinating conjunction, namely, [5] "just so" in the independent clause, and [2] "as" in the dependent clause.

Now the actor-action phrase in the independent clause differs from the actor-action phrase in the dependent clause in the construction of the verb, namely, while the former, [9] "let . . . heal" is in the imperative mode (in Cheremis), the latter, [4] "blossoms forth" is in the indicative mode. The two verbs are practically identical: they both happen to be constructed on the same base, since *sinč-* and *sič-* are allomorphs; both are singular in number, and both in the third person. However, they are opposed as to mode. We regard this contrast of indicative versus imperative as the crucial and fundamental feature which distinguishes the two actor-action phrases from one another in each sentence of this immediate constituent.

Let all actor-action phrases with a verb in the imperative mode be symbolized by S, and the particular phrase [6–9] "let this wound heal" by s. S corresponds

[52] The principal criterion for determining immediate constituents in substitutability.

to what Ohrt has called, without precise definition, the sorcerer's expression of will, or the "subjective" element in the charm.

Let further all actor-action phrases with a verb in the indicative mode be symbolized by O. O corresponds to what Ohrt has called the "objective" element in the charm which, as we have seen, consists of a magically circumspect enumeration of all the facts which are relevant. The particular phrases, i.e., the individual facts, are distinguishable only in terms of the actor, as o_1, o_2, o_3, . . . o_n, hence the entire phrase [1, 3–4] "the apple tree blossoms forth" may be represented by o_1.

Finally, let an arc symbolize both words, [2] and [5], of the subordinating conjunction "as . . . just so."

The entire first sentence can now be expressed in terms of a simple binary propositional operation, namely, implication, thus: $o_1 \supset s$. With the use of an additional symbol, namely, a dot to express conjunction, the entire first immediate constituent (i.e., the first and second sentences together) can be expressed thus: $(o_1 \supset s) \cdot (o_2 \supset s) \cdot (o_3 \supset s) \cdots (o_n \supset s)$; the first terms of the implication form the class O, the second terms, the class S (i.e., each $o_n \varepsilon O$, and $s_n \varepsilon S$), and therefore we arrive at the expression $O \supset S$. The latter is regarded as equal by definition to the sequence [1–13].

II. The sequence [14–21] consists of but a single sentence. This sentence consists of two parts: one, [18–21] "only then overcome me," is an independent clause; the other, [14–17] "when water can blossom forth," is a dependent clause.

Both clauses can be further subdivided into an actor-action phrase, namely, [20–21] "overcome me" in the independent clause, and [14, 16–17] "water can blossom forth" in the dependent clause; and a subordinating conjunction, namely, [18–19] "only then" in the independent clause, and [15] "when" in the dependent clause.

In the first actor-action phrase, the verb [21] "overcome" is in the imperative mode (in Cheremis), whereas, in the second actor-action phrase, the verb [17] "can" is in the indicative mode. This opposition is the same which we have encountered in the first immediate constituent. However, let us now compare the imperative verb [9] "let . . . heal," of the first immediate constituent with the imperative verb [21] "overcome" of the second immediate constituent. We perceive at once that there is a special relationship between these two verbs, namely, "overcome" is a negation of "let . . . heal"; it is equivalent to "let not heal." The negation of a proposition can be symbolized with a line above the expression: since "let . . . heal" was s, "let not heal" or "overcome" is $\bar{s}$. This analysis is a semantic one, but on a much lower level of abstraction than the semantic implication in the analysis in I.

The internal structure of the actor-action phrase in the dependent clause of II., that is, [14, 16–17] "water can blossom forth" is very like the internal structure of the model phrase [1, 3–4] "the apple tree blossoms forth" of I. The two phrases are not, however, absolutely identical. We must refer back at this point to the "motif of an extremely improbable eventuality" mentioned earlier in this chapter. It will be observed that an assertion such as [1, 3–4] "the apple tree blossoms forth" is true; that is, apple trees do in fact blossom forth. Contrariwise, the assertion [14, 16–17] "water can blossom forth" is—within ordinary experience—false, that is, water does not in fact blossom forth. The verb [17] "can" is the linguistic means whereby this difference in the truth-value of the two phrases is signalized. Let a superscript $^{-}$ represent the extreme improbability of such a fact as water blossoming forth. The phrase [14, 16–17] can therefore be symbolized by $\bar{o}$. These elements $\bar{o}$ and $\bar{s}$ are also members of the class O and S, respectively, i.e., they are not identical with the negation in logic.

Let an arc again symbolize the words [15] and [18–19] of the subordinating conjunction "when . . . only then."

The entire last sentence can now be expressed in terms of the same operation—implication—as all preceding sentences, thus: $\bar{o} \supset \bar{s}$. Since $\bar{o} \equiv O$, and, further, $\bar{s} \equiv S$, we arrive at the expression $O \supset S$. The latter is regarded as equal by definition to the sequence [14–21].

Since the sequence [1–13] as well as the sequence [14–21] are each equal by definition to the expression $O \supset S$, the entire charm 1.1.5.3. can be expressed thus: $(O \supset S) \cdot (O \supset S)$ which again $\equiv 2(O \supset S)$. It must be recalled, however, that in the first immediate constituent the propositional function of O is chosen so that for any O, $f(O)$ is true; and in the second it is chosen so that for any O, $f(O)$ is—within ordinary experience—false. This shows the general conformity of the sentence structure throughout the entire charm. However, the concrete structure of the charm could be more accessibly displayed by the following formula: $n_1(o \supset s) \cdot n_2(\bar{o} \supset \bar{s})$.

In sum, it appears that our sample charm is ultimately composed of two, and only two, basic elements, namely, O and S; and that these two elements are in opposition, in such a way that O implies S.

THE HISTORIOLA

The elements O and S are basic to Cheremis charms. Each of them consists of one set or a succession of sets of these two elements, and they are always related by the operation of implication.

In a few charms, however, an additional element must be taken into consideration. It will be called the "historiola" here, and symbolized by H. Such an element occurs in much fuller shapes in the magic charms of many other cultures of the same tradition, including particularly Russian, and is often referred to as the "epic motif." It is essentially an introductory reference of some sort to a past helpful deed by a beneficent power, to which the rest of the charm is anchored. In the

Cheremis texts, however, its historical origins are barely recognizable, though this circumstance does not, of course, vitiate its status in the structure.

Charm 1.1.3.1. may be used for illustration. It opens with this statement (h_1): "Upon the summit of a high mountain there is a gold chest, in the gold chest a gold goblet, in the gold goblet a silk ball," which is then immediately followed by an $O \supset S$ proposition. The charm being a cure for snakebite, this proposition reads: "If the snake can penetrate therein, bite it, grasp it, eat it up and drink it down [viz., the silk ball], then only may he bite me!" Now h_1 is repeated verbatim, except that in this second version (h_2), the word "silver" appears wherever h_1 has "gold." The identical $O \supset S$ proposition is then repeated. This is followed by a third version of H (h_3), which is the same as h_1 or h_2, except that the word "mother-of-pearl" appears wherever h_1 has "gold" or h_2, "silver." Finally, the identical $O \supset S$ proposition is repeated for the third time. The entire charm can now be expressed thus: $[(h_1 \cdot \bar{o}) \supset \bar{s}] \cdot [(h_2 \cdot \bar{o}) \supset \bar{s}] \cdot [(h_3 \cdot \bar{o}) \supset \bar{s}]$. Since, however, $h_1 \equiv H$, $h_2 \equiv H$, $h_3 \equiv H$, $\bar{o} \equiv O$, $\bar{s} \equiv S$, therefore $2[(H \cdot O) \supset S]$. We may regard an expression like $H \cdot O$ simply as an expanded variety of O itself, and symbolize it by P. Hence we arrive at the expression $3(P \supset S)$.

The symbolic content of a historiola is rather obscure, and can be partially elucidated only by recognizing historical connections and by observing the function of a given symbol in Cheremis folklore as a whole. In historical perspective, for instance, the high mountain mentioned in the historiola of charm 1.1.3.1. is a symbolic reference to Mount Calvary, that is to say, to Christ, though it seems virtually certain that the Cheremis are totally unaware of this.[53] The place where Christ was crucified is regarded, in New Testament tradition, as the temple where God meets man, hence a safe refuge, which "the snake" is unlikely to reach. As to the symbol of the silk ball, this functions conventionally in Cheremis folklore as a representation of human life. It is so used in the following folksong, for example, where its relationship to the "gold" and "silver" images is especially noteworthy:

> The morning sun emerges,
> It emerges gold-like.
> The evening sun descends,
> It descends silver-like.
> Our lives pass away,
> They pass away silk-thread-like.
> We flow and go flowing-water-like.[54]

In other words, the historiola asserts that human life is secure from evil attack under the protection of Christ, and it is, therefore, safe to set the conditions stated in O, for, within ordinary experience, they are sure to be unrealizable.

[53] Cf. Mansikka, p. 302; also Num. 21:4–9, John 3:14–15.
[54] Lach, p. 92, No. 27; a closely similar variant occurs *ibid.,* pp. 129–30, No. 118. Cheremis poetic symbols are discussed by Sebeok and Lane, p. 144.

The internal form of the historiola in the above example is one encountered frequently in a type of Cheremis folksong. Elsewhere,[55] we have called it a "spiral construction" of images: ball inside the goblet inside the chest atop the mountain. A given spiral might be spatial, as here, or numerical, pertaining to quality or family relationship, and so forth.

The proportion of h_1 to h_2 to h_3 is that of "gold" to "silver" to "mother-of-pearl." In formula 1.2.1.1.—which is absolutely identical in structure with 1.1.3.1.—the same proportion recurs: h_1 "a gold-lump comes out of the gold-furnace sparkling, sizzling"; h_2 "a silver-lump . . . out of the silver-furnace . . ."; h_3 "a mother-of-pearl lump . . . out of the mother-of-pearl furnace. . . ." Further triadic proportions which occur in the corpus are as follows: "gold" to "silver" to "copper" in 3.1.4.; "wood" to "earth" to "iron" in 2.1.1.; "great god" to "god the creator" to "thunder god" in 3.1.4. and 3.4.2. Slightly different is the historiola of 1.1.3.2., where the triadic proportion is within the same statement: "snake-khan, tree-kahn, earth-kahn." Again slightly different is the historiola of 1.1.4.: h_1 "the morning sun rises and approaches . . ."; h_2 "(the light) shines and approaches . . ."; h_3 "dawn appears and approaches. . . ." The remaining historiola-like statements in the corpus are not triadic: 1.1.2.1. "fire comes burning, rolling, like a dry tree-trunk" (ter); and 2.1.4. "there are forty-one armies behind forty-one mountains."[56]

CONTENT

Let the term "unit" be applied to any expression $O \supset S$ (or $P \supset S$). Sample charm 1.1.5.3. may thus be said to consist of two units. Our total corpus comprises forty-nine texts which have been labeled charms. Of these, all but three (which are entirely different in structure and must be considered separately) can be reduced either to one structural unit or to simple additive sequences of units. Such a reduction is, in one sense, too powerful to be serviceable. This is not because an expression in terms of units fails to indicate the *differentia specifica* whereby charms are to be distinguished from certain other kinds of texts. It is true that Cheremis weather predictions, such as, "If the wind blows from the south, there'll be rain" (Part One, G.17.1.1.), or dream portents, such as those treated in the preceding section, or certain other types of texts, can also be reduced to just two terms related by a single operation. But the verbs of each of the terms in such sentences are in the indicative, and never in the imperative mode, whereas these contrastive modes— implicit in the definition of S— are an essential feature of the charms, indeed the true source of the *mana* immanent in them. In fact, Marrett, in his famous essay, "From Spell to Prayer," called this operation "the unifying soul of the process," and conceived it to embody "the very life and soul of the affair."[57]

[55] Sebeok and Lane, p. 143.

[56] "Forty-one" is a favorite number also in the folksong; cf., e.g., the song cited by Sebeok, 1951, p. 289. See further the content of charms No. 1.1.3.2., 1.1.6., and 3.2.1.

[57] Marrett, pp. 54–55.

The symbolic expression at which we have arrived does, then, delimit charms from other kinds of texts, while it also epitomizes their fundamental unity.

On the other hand, the magnitude of the reduction obliterates individual differences: How are we to distinguish one charm from another? This broad question can be resolved into six separate and more specific questions: (1) Can a given text be reduced to one or more units, or can it not? If it can be, then, (2) Of how many units does each text consist? (3) Where the first term of a unit is *P,* what is the content of *H?* (4) What is the content of *O* in each unit? (5) What is the content of *S* in each unit? (6) By what linguistic means is implication expressed in each unit? Let us consider each question in turn.

(1) As already indicated, a given charm will fall either into a major form class—i.e., will be reducible to one or more units—or not. The major form class includes about 94 per cent of the charms in this corpus. The remaining texts are:

1.1.1.   "From the long bench to the short bench, from the short bench to the stove board, from the stove board to the stove, from the stove into the smoke window,[58] from the smoke window into the crown of the spruce, *nedək* [Part One, A.47.], begone!" This text departs from the major pattern in several respects. First of all, it contains no verb at all ("begone" translates an adverb), hence the opposition of a phrase with an indicative versus one with an imperative verb cannot be postulated. Even if it were practicable to identify the adverbial phrase "*nedək,* begone" with *S,* and the list of items which precedes it with *O,* still *O* and *S* could not be considered in opposition, since the latter merely follows the former, and the implication is nowise involved.

1.1.9.   "Old Lady, Old Man Smallpox, eat, drink, don't be angry, don't take his soul, don't hurt his eye, pass by nicely." This text contains six verbs in the imperative mode, none in the indicative, and there is nothing here that could be construed as equivalent to *O;* implication is not involved.

1.1.15.   "The sobbing around the sea, I around the mortar; the sobbing around the sea, I around the mortar; the sobbing around the sea, I around the mortar—I first!" The comment on 1.1.1. applies, *mutatis mutandis.*

Since the major form class includes such an overwhelmingly large percentage of instances, a dichotomy of major versus minor form classes does not appear to be particularly useful. It may turn out to be more advantageous to reclassify such formulas as the preceding three with other, simpler homemade spells (See Part One, H.4.2.). These spells are quite numerous, do not require the services of a "spitter," and differ entirely from the charms in form. Internal indications support this: e.g., the use of the first person pronoun in 1.1.15., of the familiar household items in 1.1.1., and the background data supplied by the informant for 1.1.9.; (in the latter, the informant uses the word *sörbalat* 'they pray,' and not *šübeda* 'he spits').

[58] See Heikel, 1888, Chap. 6, for the parts and pattern of Cheremis rooms.

This leads to a redefinition of a "charm" as distinct from a "spell," insofar as the present corpus is concerned: a "charm" is simply a text consisting of a minimum of one unit. A magic formula not including a unit may be called a "spell." Thus 1.1.1., 1.1.9., and 1.1.15. are not charms but spells, and need not be considered any further here. We are thus left with a corpus of forty-six charms.

(2) A charm, by definition, must include, minimally, one unit. The following table presents, in the left column, the number of units which occur in given charms; in the middle column, the frequency with which particular sequences of units occur in the corpus as a whole. In the right column, each figure represents the product of the figures in the left and middle columns of the same row, the total being the number of units in the entire corpus.

No. of Units	Frequency	Total Units
1	9	9
2	2	4
3	19	57
4	3	12
5	2	10
7	3	21
9	3	27
10	1	10
15	2	30
17	1	17
21	1	21
Total	46	218

The Cheremis regard the number three and multiples of three as endowed with peculiar virtue: Cheremis folktale variants, for instance, present three-headed dragons (Thompson, B 11.2.3.3.*), six-headed dragons (B 11.2.3.3.*) and a six-legged horse (B 15.6.3.1.*), nine-headed dragons (B 11.2.3.4.*), twelve-headed dragons (B 11.2.3.4.*) and serpents (B 15.1.2.9.1.*), and a twelve-legged horse (B 15.6.3.2.); the soul is located in three separate eggs (E 711.1.1.*).[59] It is unlikely to be a coincidence that a total of twenty-five charms—over half the corpus—consist of such sequences of units. Seven, and numbers which include the integer seven,[60] also possess mystic value: such sequences account for five more charms. As against these, only six charms consist of two or its multiples, and only two of five.[61]

[59] Sebeok, 1952, Section on The Folktale, Part B.

[60] The number 75 occurs in charm No. 1.1.11.2.; the number 77 in charms No. 1.1.8., 1.1.14.1., 1.2.2., 2.1.2., 2.1.3., 2.1.5., 3.1.2., 3.1.4., 3.2.1., 3.2.4., and 3.4.2. Further illustrations could be drawn from many Cheremis folksongs. See also Munkácsi.

[61] Unfortunately some of the collectors seem to have lost their patience with what must have struck them as interminable repetitiousness on the informant's part. As a result, some

Note that nine charms contain only one unit each. However, in all probability, these were repeated, in identical form, as the informant's comment after charm No. 1.1.5.2. suggests: "It is necessary to spit, speaking [this charm] three times. If it must be repeated several times, it is necessary to say it nine times."[62]

(3) For a discussion of this question see section "The Historiola," above.

(4) The categories into which the objective elements in this corpus fall are, as a whole, divisible into two distinct sets—$\bar{o}$, which consists of categories a through h; and o, which consists of categories i through o—this separation being feasible on four different levels of discourse: I. linguistic, II. rhetorical, III. logical, and IV. magical.

I. Implication is expressed throughout the entire corpus by one of two linguistic devices in a given unit: *kunam . . . tunam* 'when . . . then,' or *kuze . . . tuge* 'as . . . so' (see (6), below, and, for illustration, refer to the sample charm 1.1.5.3., above). In a unit which contains the former device, a category belonging to set $\bar{o}$ will be used; but in a unit which contains the latter device, a category belonging to set o will be used.

II. The tropes of poetry, as the principles of magic, may be divided "most relevantly into figures of contiguity and figures of similarity."[63] Accordingly, two types of units may be differentiated: those where the imagery achieves its effect by the use of metonymy and synechdoche—that is, the movement proceeds within a single world of discourse—and those where it achieves its effect by the use of metaphor and simile—that is, by joining a plurality of worlds. These correspond to sets $\bar{o}$ and o, respectively.

III. Units differ as to truth-value. When this is falsity, the category used will belong to set $\bar{o}$; but when this is truth, the category used will belong to set o.

IV. Each unit may be said to operate on the principle of sympathetic magic. But Frazer reduced this principle to what he called the "two great fundamental laws of thought," namely association by contiguity, which correlates with the categories assigned to set $\bar{o}$—"a task must be performed"; and association by similarity, which correlates with the categories assigned to set o—"like produces like."

We classify the objective elements occurring in the entire corpus in the following fifteen categories:

$$\bar{o}$$

(*a*) The magician cannot inflict harm upon his own body; hence he can be safely required to do so before he can harm anyone else.

---

of the texts end with "etc." It is not, therefore, always possible to be sure how many units a given charm would have contained had the informant been permitted to finish or had the full text been reproduced.

[62] Such identical repetitions of units are neither counted in the above table nor treated in the content analysis below.

[63] Wellek and Warren, p. 199.

(*b*) This category involves the manipulation of inanimate objects, before the victim may be harmed. We distinguish three subcategories: *b'* objects must be bled; *b''* the magician must assert his power over water; *b'''* objects other than water or those which are being bled must be manipulated.

(*c*) The magician must perform a task of considerable complexity, the various steps of which, in the given sequence, lead to a particular end, usually the serving of a meal.

(*d*) The task of manipulating heavenly bodies or phenomena which, according to Cheremis conception, lie outside the realm of human magic and are too far away from the magician's reach, is imposed upon the magician or evil force as a prior condition for harming his victim.

(*e*) Human beings, animals or animal products must be manipulated in order to make the magic effective.

(*f*) The magician or evil force must harm one or more of the gods or other supernatural creatures before he can so effect a human being. The character of some of the supernatural creatures being harmed is indicated by numerical subscripts. The subscript $_1$ refers to the (daughter of the) Great God;[64] $_2$ refers to (the daughter of) god the creator,[65] $_3$ refers to the (daughter of the) thunder god.[66] When *f* appears without a subscript, other supernatural entities were involved.

(*g*) The task of counting is imposed upon the magician or evil force as a prior condition for harming his victim.

(*h*) Other extraordinary tasks are imposed upon the source of evil, the satisfactory performance of which alone bestows the privilege of hurting the victim.

o

(*i*) A statement, involving such images as dissolving, separating, disappearing, sinking, quarrelling, mismating, breaking off, drying up, flowing away, and the like, is made as a condition for some event.

(*j*) A statement, involving such images as unifying, fusing, sticking, inseparability, piling, collecting, and the like, is made as a condition for some event.

(*k*) A statement, involving such images as blossoming, and the completion of other natural cycles, of the wind, sun, stars, etc., is made as a condition for some event.

(*l*) A statement, involving such images as motion, lightness, flying, and the like, is made as a condition for some event.

(*m*) A statement, involving the image of coldness, is made as a condition for some event.

[64] This occurs 5 times in the corpus. Paasonen, 1907a; Harva, 1926, pp. 62ff.
[65] This occurs five times in the corpus. Paasonen, 1901, p. 35, "Second Day."
[66] This occurs five times in the corpus. *Ibid.;* Harva, 1926, p. 67.

(n) A statement, involving such images as heaviness, dormancy, motionlessness, lying, and the like, is made as a condition for some event.

(o) A statement, involving the image of warmness, is made as a condition for some event.

In addition to the preceding categories, we identify an additional element frequently recurring in the corpus. Objects in the charms are often assigned the quality of certain specific metals or mother-of-pearl, which we designate as follows: a gold, β silver, γ mother-of-pearl, δ copper, and σ metals other than the foregoing.[67]

Certain obvious relations obtain among the categories. For instance, some stand in opposition: such as, i and j, l and n, m and o. Others are related trichotomously, as b, e, and f.

The table which follows presents the charms in the order of their functional classification, in terms of the content categories presented above. Each charm is listed, and the content classification of the objective element of each unit is presented.

Within the table commas separate units from each other. Furthermore, the sequence of the units within a given charm is discernible from the arrangement of the commas and lines. Thus, e.g., charm 1.1.14.1. consists of nine units, which, when classified and given their content designations, appear in the following sequence: af, f, b''', af_1, af_2, af_3, f_{123}, i, i.

CHARM NO.	CATEGORY		
	$\bar{o}$		o
1.1.2.1.	b'', b'', b'',		i, i, i, i
1.1.2.2.	b'', b'', b''		
1.1.3.1.	ea, $e\beta$, $e\gamma$		
1.1.3.2.	e		
1.1.4.	d, d, d		
1.1.5.1.	b', b', b',		i
1.1.5.2.	b'		
1.1.5.3.			k,
	b''		
1.1.5.4.	b', b', b', b', b', b', b'		
1.1.6.	b''', b''', g		
1.1.7.1.	h, h, h		
1.1.7.2.	h, h, h		
1.1.8.	ca, $c\beta$, $c\delta$, $c\gamma$, $c\sigma$, $c\sigma$, $c\sigma$, $c\sigma$, $c\sigma$		
1.1.10.	b''',		i

[67] The following frequencies obtain: $8a$, 9β, 5γ, 4δ, and 5σ. For the role of metals in magic, cf. Szendrey, 1937b, p. 166.

Charm No.	Category		
1.1.11.1.	b''		
1.1.11.2.	c		
1.1.12.	$a_1a, a_2\beta, a_3\gamma$		
1.1.13.	$j\delta, j\beta, ja$		
1.1.14.1.	$af, f, b''', af_1, af_2, af_3, f_{123},$	i, i	
1.1.14.2.		l, l, l, l, l	
1.2.1.1.	$aa, a\beta, a\gamma$		
1.2.1.2.	h, h, h		
1.2.2.	$a, g, a, a, a, a, a, a, a, a, a, a,$		
	$g, g, g, d, d, da,$	i, i, i	
2.1.1.	b''', b''', b'''		
2.1.2.	$c\beta$		
2.1.3.	b'''		
2.1.4.	e		
2.1.5.	e		
2.2.1.		$k, k, k, k, k, o, j, j, j,$	
		j, j, j, j, j, j	
2.2.2.		$k, k, k, k, k, j, j, j, j, j, j,$	
		o, i, j, j, j, j	
2.3.1.	$e, e, e,$	m	
2.3.2.		$m, m, m, m, i, i, i, i, i, i, i, i, i,$	
		i, i	
3.1.1.		n, n, n	
3.1.2.	$d, d, d, d, d, d, e, b'', ddb'''$		
3.1.3.	$c\beta, ca, c\delta, a,$	i	
3.1.4.	$c_1a, c_2\beta, c_3\delta$		
3.2.1.	$au\beta\gamma$		
3.2.2.	a, a, b''', b'''		
3.2.3.	$a, a,$	i	
3.2.4.	a, a, a		
3.2.5.	$e,$	i	
	$a,$	k, k, i, i	
3.3.	a, a, a		
3.4.1.	g, g, g		
3.4.2.	f_1, f_2, f_3		
4.1.	g, a, a		
4.2.		$j, j, k, k, k, k, k,$	
	b''', b''', b'''		

The next table presents the frequency of occurrence of the categories, arranged into $\bar{o}$ and o groups.

	FREQUENCY	
CATEGORY	$\bar{o}$	o
a	37	
b	34	
b'	11	
b''	9	
b'''	14	
c	17	
d	14	
e	11	
f	9	
g	9	
h	9	
i		28
j		24
k		18
l		5
m		5
n		3
o		2
Total	140	85

Since five units had to be classified under two categories, and one under three, the grand total in the above table exceeds by seven the total number of units themselves. The ratio of $\bar{o}$ to o in the units as a whole is of the order of 1.6 to 1, indicating the heavy preponderance of the motif of an extremely improbable eventuality.

The interest of a frequency tabulation such as we have constructed goes potentially beyond the report of the frequencies themselves. Were frequency counts available of like corpora from neighboring cultures, Russian for instance, cross comparisons would be facilitated in precise form; in addition, internal relationships in the folklore as a whole, comparisons with prayers for example, could be specified. Correlations with other aspects of the culture could be attempted as well

Two charms, 1.1.10., and 3.1.3., contain series of rather special kinds of elements which were not content analyzed. The "spitter" asserts that his magic will be effective irrespective of the time of day; no matter on which day of the week the sorcery took place; whether the sorcerer was male, a woman or a girl;[68] and whether the witchery was conveyed by means of a whirlwind, or by way of food or drink.

(5) The Danish logician Jørgensen proposes to dissolve imperatives into two factors: the imperative factor proper, which is a feature common to all im-

[68] Szendrey, 1937a.

peratives in the language, and the indicative factor, which varies from one command to another.[69]

In Cheremis, the imperative factor proper may be briefly characterized as follows, the remarks here being restricted to such forms as occur in this corpus. Two forms occur: second person (see sample charm, word 21); and third person (word 9), both singular. All the imperative forms are like the indicative forms in being unmarked as to mode, but are unlike them in being undifferentiated as to tense. The indicative forms unmarked as to tense are the imperfective ones. The contrasts to be especially considered, therefore, are: second vs. third person imperative; imperative vs. indicative second person; and imperative vs. indicative imperfective third person. The singular second person imperative is formed by a total absence of all markers—person, number, tense, or mode—that is, by the absolute stem; the third person contrasts with it by having a suffix marking person: -$z/šV$, the vowel of which varies both interdialectally and, in some dialects, according to specific morphophonemic rules. In the second person, the two modes contrast by virtue of the fact that the person is formally marked in the indicative imperfective. In the third person, both modes bear person markers, but they are quite different, the form in the imperative (given above) being identical with the nominal third person singular possessive morpheme, but the form in the indicative imperfective being a low vowel or -$eš$ (depending on which of the two conjugations is involved).

The commands differ from each other lexically, that is, as to the stems selected from among the available verbs. If content analysis were to be performed, it is this factor that would have to be analyzed. However, content analysis of S is unnecessary, since charms can already be distinguished from one another by their O-content. Let us recall, however, that S-content, too, falls into two overall categories, namely, $š$ and s. These two cannot be distinguished from each other by any formal markers, but only by virtue of their co-occurrence with one or the other form of the implication. The distribution is such that $š$ occurs in units where implication is expressed by *kunam . . . tunam* 'when . . . then,' and, consequently, where the objective element is $ō$, there is falsity, magic by contiguity, and imagery by metonymy and synecdoche; and s occurs elsewhere.

(6) As already stated, implication is expressed in a given unit in one of two ways, throughout the present corpus: *kunam . . . tunam* 'when . . . then' (see sample charm, words 15, 18), or *kuze . . . tuge* 'as . . . so' (2, 5). The two are actualizations of essentially one linguistic device: the discontinuous sequence of an interrogative pronoun, beginning with the phoneme k, located in the dependent clause, and a demonstrative pronoun, beginning with the phoneme t, located in the independent clause. Stylistic variations include the use of emphatic enclitics (as -*ak*, in word 5), or the occasional ellipsis of one of the pronouns. The

[69] Jørgensen.

distinction between the two types of expression is a crucial one, since upon this linguistic differentiation hinges the distinction between $\bar{o}$ and o, $\bar{s}$ and s, as do also the logical, magical, and rhetorical discriminations touched upon above.

Interestingly enough, pronominal elements have been used traditionally as a fundamental classificatory device of charms. So, for example, Krohn divided Votyak charms into "wenn" and "wie" varieties, with suitable linguistic subtypes.[70]

[70] Krohn, 1901.

PRAYERS

A SCHEME OF PRAYER

PRAYERS AND THEIR CONSTITUENT PARTS

"BY the regular recurrence of the occasions of prayer there was gradually formed a scheme of prayer," writes Heiler in his standard study of the subject, "the formal outlines, the succession of thoughts, and particular turns of expression became fixed, though, of course, the wording varied in accordance with the special circumstances of the moment."[71]

Our first step will be to isolate the structural, that is, relatively permanent constituents which characterize every Cheremis prayer; then we shall study the variations, governed by "the special circumstances of the moment," which lend each prayer an individuality of its own and as a result of which each prayer comes to be a separate system.

It will be convenient to decompose prayers into smaller units, each a sentence with certain characteristics, to be called "prayer-constituents," or, simply, "constituents." Let any Cheremis sentence be a "constituent" if it includes at least one instance of each of two elements, to be called, respectively, the *invocation* and the *petition*.

The *invocation* consists, minimally, of the personal name of a supernatural, but is often expanded by enumeration of its conventional attributes: e.g., *porə kugə jumə* 'good great god.'

A *petition* consists of two parts, to be called, respectively, the *entreaty* and the *theme*. Petitions vary in complexity from a simple goal plus action construction, such as *esenləkəm pu* 'health give,' to patterns of considerable syntactic intricacy.

The *entreaty* is a verb which, in the great majority of the instances, is in the imperative mode, but which may occur in the N-tense form, or, exceptionally, in the conditional mode.[72]

The remaining portion of the petition is the *theme,* that is, what the worshipper is asking for, potentially including also a statement of the conditions under which he is praying.

The range of specific formulations that can be subsumed is rather small for the entreaties and relatively larger, but limited, for the themes.

---

[71] Heiler, p. 10.
[72] This is the case in prayers No. 32–37. Cf. Kangasmaa, No. 6.1.

The invocation is frequently constituent-initial, and the entreaty most commonly petition-, and thus constituent-final. Invocation, theme, and entreaty correspond, in broad syntactic terms, respectively, to hearer,[73] goal, and action.

Consider now Heiler's remarks: "The aim of all petition is the asserting, strengthening or enhancement of one's own desire for a natural and healthy life and the satisfaction of one's deepest needs. It is partly negative when it aims at deliverance from an evil or protection against danger; it is partly positive when it has in view the granting of possessions and advantages."[74] In accordance with this distinction, we shall classify petitions, and thus their themes, into desirable, that is, those which affirmatively attract good, and undesirable, that is, those which negatively deflect evil.

Now let "prayer" be defined as any Cheremis text containing at least one constituent, or C; in brief, a prayer is composed of nC.

Within a prayer, such that n exceeds 1, the invocation may occur, it is convenient to assume, in $\emptyset$ shape; thus, the fourth constituent of Prayer 1 reads, *kajik kučaš pijalam pu* 'give luck to catch birds,' and we assume that the invocation occurs here in $\emptyset$ shape, whereas, in the first constituent, it is established that the prayer is addressed to *juma* 'god.'

A minimal C is one which contains but one petition; e.g., a woman in difficult and painful labor prays, "Fructifier mother gods, let me bear lightly" (17). A C may contain more than one invocation; thus, $C1$ of Prayer 2 is addressed to some twenty personified supernaturals.

A minimal prayer is one which contains only one C. Thus, Prayer 17 is not only a minimal C but also a minimal prayer. Elaborate prayers consist of strings of C, and may also contain other types of sentences.

RELATIVE COMPLEXITY

In our corpus, minimal prayers abound in the [B] collection (Prayers 6–26), from the District of Yaransk, Province of Vyatka, whereas prayers of the most elaborate sort come from Eastern Cheremis. In general, the most elaborate prayers of the Eastern Cheremis are also of the higher ethical level which, according to Tylor, is the "greatest of all changes which difference the prayers of lower from those of higher nations";[75] however, we can but guess whether the Yaransk type of prayer represents the basic form which the Eastern Cheremis then elaborated or whether, to the contrary, the Yaransk type is a stunted version of a more elaborate prototype.[76]

[73] Cf. Bloomfield, p. 177: "A substantive form naming a hearer is used in English as a demand for his presence or attention. . . ."
[74] Heiler, p. 17.
[75] Tylor, Vol. 2, p. 373.
[76] Cf. Itkonen, pp. 37–38.

FROM SPELL TO PRAYER?

Not only can one not distinguish stages in the religious evolution of the Cheremis in terms of the degree to which their prayers increase in elaborateness from West to East, but also one cannot draw any historical inferences from a comparison of their prayers with their charms. Webster has stated the generalization that

[the language of a charm] cannot always be separated from that of a prayer, since in both there may be personification and the use of a vocative. It is often a nice matter to distinguish between them. Everything depends, in truth, on the extent to which the object of the address is personified and endowed with human-like feelings and will. If the spiritual being is supposed always to grant a request or obey a command, [Webster continues] then the speaker's words act automatically and constitute a charm. If, on the other hand, the spiritual being retains some freedom of action and may or may not accede to the speaker's words, then these will take the form of a supplication or entreaty, that is, of a prayer."[77]

In Cheremis culture, a charm is a verbal construct having the power to produce the intended results with or without the intervention of the gods, but a prayer is cast in the form of an invocation of a deity. Thus, while the charm is an instrument of force, the prayer is simply a request; while the former is an end in itself, the latter is merely a means to an end. The scheme of Cheremis prayers, accordingly, differs from the scheme of Cheremis charms so sharply that it hardly seems profitable to argue the evolution of either from the other; rather, we prefer to regard these as two coordinate systems of magical means of controlling supernatural forces.

SAMPLE ANALYSIS OF PRAYER

The distinctions introduced above can be illustrated with Prayer 38, a not very elaborate sample. The entire text reads as follows:[78]

[1] *porə   kugə   jumə,   tazaləkəm   pu.*   [2] *esenləkəm   pu.*
good   great   god   health   give   health   give

[3] *koštməgornəm   kornanšte.*   [4] *il'məberəm   porəšte.*   [5] *tazaləkəm   pu.*
travel-road   roaded-make   living-place good-make   health   give

[6] *esenləkəm   pu.*   [7] *osal   tušmandeč   sakle.*   [8] *kürültəmə   rezekəm   pu.*
health   give   evil   enemy-from   protect   uninterrupted   food   give

[9] *osal   tušmanən   šümžəm   mokšažəm   pasəlandaren   golta.*
evil   enemy's   heart   liver   soften   send

---

[77] Webster, p. 111–12. Cf. also, Tylor, Vol. 2, p. 371; Marrett, 1914; Hauer, pp. 136–37; Toy, p. 483; Karsten, p. 271; James, pp. 273–74.

[78] The bracketted numerals are inserted before each constituent for ease of reference.

[10] *arməgəč*	*aŋgajem*	*pu,*	*manən*	*jodən*	*təlanem.*	*amin.*
everywhere-from	comfort	give	saying	asking	I wish	amen

This text can be decomposed into *10C.amin,*[79] and, further, as follows:

C1

This sentence divides into two parts, the invocation, a hearer-phrase, and the petition, an action-goal phrase.

The invocation consists of the head of the hearer-phrase, *jumə* 'god,' qualified by two conventional attributes, 'good' and 'great.' To this deity is addressed not not only to *C1,* but the entire prayer as well. Named here, *jumə* is not named again in the course of the prayer; however, we may assume that the identical invocation occurs, in ∅ shape, in each successive *C* of this prayer. Since *jumə* has been coded in Part One as *A.26.,* we shall use this expression here: *i(A.26.).*

The petition is a simple action-goal phrase, 'give health.' The entreaty, or action, is the verb *pu* 'give,' in the imperative 2 sg., and the theme, or goal, is *tazaləkəm* 'health,' in the accusative case. The initial theme of this prayer bears out Heiler's observation that "first among the subjects of primitive prayer are life and health."[80] This *t1* may be expressed as *HEA;* but the fact that *e1* shows *p1* to be affirmative need not be coded.

C2

P2 consists of *e2,* identical with *e1,* and *t2,* different in form from, but identical in meaning with *t1.* Since *t2* may thus also be expressed as *HEA,* and since it thus appears that each part of *C2* is equivalent to the corresponding part of *C1,* it follows that *C1 ≡ C2.*

C3

P3 consists of an endocentric action-character construction, 'roaded-make,' and a compound goal, 'travel-road,' the petition being in conformity with Heiler's observation that "savage man knows the dangers and difficulties of a journey by land or water, therefore, he prays for divine protection beforehand,"[81] since the sentence means, in free translation, 'make the travel-road good.'

---

[79] The following abbreviations will be used: *P* 'prayer,' *C* 'constituent,' *i* 'invocation,' *p* 'petition,' *e* 'entreaty,' *t* 'theme,' *q* 'quotative.' The symbol ≡ means 'is equivalent to'; and the symbol . 'and.' Themes are expressed, in all caps, by the first three letters of a code word, thus *NOU* 'nourishment'; a line above such an expression lends it a negative valuation. Numbers preceding expressions are to be read as cardinals; those following as ordinals: thus, *4C* 'four constituents,' but *C4* 'fourth constituent.'

[80] Heiler, p. 18.

[81] *Ibid.*

The action-character construction is *kornanšte<kornan ašte,* where the first word consists of *kornə* 'road' plus an adjectival stem-forming suffix, and the second word, *e3,* is the imperative 2 sg. form of the verb 'to make,' the two words having been given by the informant in close sandhi. *T3,* a compound goal in the accusative case, may be expressed as *TRA,* an affirmative petition being the case.

C4

Syntactically, *p4* is equivalent to *p3,* consisting of an endocentric action-character construction, 'good-make,' and a compound goal, 'living-place.'

The action-character construction is *porašte<porə* 'good' and *e4≡e3. T4* is again a compound goal in the accusative case. Both *t3* and *t4* are deverbal noun stems (*košt-mə, il'-mə*), compounded with a second noun, each in the accusative case (*kornə-m, ber-əm*).

The petition being affirmative, *t4* may be expressed as *LIV,* in accordance with the quotation from Heiler under *C1,* for it falls in the class of themes having to do with the protection and improvement of the conditions of living, in the wider sense.

C5, C6

$C1 \equiv C2 \equiv C5 \equiv C6.$

C7

In *p7,* the worshipper asks for protection against *tušman,* 'enemy.' The action, or *e7,* is *sakle* 'protect,' in the imperative 2 sg., rendering *p7* to be negative; and the goal, *t7,* consists of an attribute-head construction with the postposition required by the verb. This *t7* may be expressed as *ENE,* and the fact that *p7* is negative marked by a raised line; thus: $\overline{ENE}$.

C8

". . . acquisition of food and drink . . . occupy a prominent place in primitive prayer,"[82] and a request for uninterrupted nourishment is the theme of *p8.* This is again an actor-goal construction, where *e8≡e1,2,5,6;* and *t8,* to be expressed *NOU,* consists of a qualified noun in the accusative case.

C9

A free translation of *p9* is, 'cause the enemy to have a change of heart.' *Pasalandaren* is said for curing bad wounds, and to extinguish fire; when an enemy is planning evil deeds, his heart and liver—seats of the soul—burn. Thus, *t8* may be expressed as $\overline{ENE}$, and therefore, *C9≡C7.*

[82] Heiler, p. 19.

C10

This sentence divides into two major parts, *p10* and the phrase *manən jodən tɔlanem;* the latter is a conventional quotative, *q.*

P10 consists of $e10 \equiv e1,2,5,6,8$; and *t10,* which conforms to this observation of Heiler's: ". . . we find that the subject of the prayer is sometimes quite generalized."[83] This we shall express as *GEN.*

Formula for Prayer 38. Summing up, we see that Prayer 38 consists of ten constituents plus the word *amin;* that the entire prayer is addressed to *jumɔ;* that six themes are sounded, one of them four times, one of them twice, and the rest each once; that one theme is negatively valued, the others all affirmatively; and that a quotative occurs in the final constituents. The foregoing analysis can be transformed into the following formula which contains all the essential information: $P38 \equiv 10C.amin \equiv [i(A.26.)] \cdot [t(4HEA) \cdot (2\overline{ENE}) \cdot (TRA) \cdot (LIV) \cdot (NOU) \cdot (GEN)] \cdot q \cdot amin.$

CONCLUDING OBSERVATIONS

A technical distinction is sometimes introduced by content analysts between the context unit and the recording unit. The context unit is "the largest body of content that may be examined in characterizing a recording unit," which is defined, in turn, as "the smallest body of content in which the appearance of a reference is counted" (a reference is a single occurrence of a content element).[84] In this study, the prayer corresponds to the context unit, and the constituent to the recording unit.

Of the two fundamental elements of a prayer-constituent, the invocation presents no special problems from the point of view of content analysis: all that needs to be stated is the name, or, if several, the combination of names—arranged, for a particular complex, in a certain conventional order—of the supernaturals being invoked.

"The heart of all prayer," however, "is petition";[85] and petition, in Aldous Huxley's simple definition, is "the asking of something for ourselves."[86] In Cheremis, what we have called the entreaty is Huxley's "the asking," and what we have called the theme is his "something." The Cheremis suppliant, in unembarrassed importunity, may heap petition upon petition and, as Heiler complains, "the few thoughts which could be expressed in two or three sentences are again and again repeated with small formal variations,"[87] at least in the more elaborate prayers of the native repertory. As even a single sample has shown, the theme is the term with maximal variability—that is, the worshipper asks, with an economy

[83] *Ibid.,* p. 10.
[84] Berelson, p. 135.
[85] Heiler, p. 17.
[86] Huxley, p. 219.
[87] Heiler, p. 11.

of verbs, for relatively many and varied things. The particular form in which the entreaty is cast yields little information, except the implication that the theme represents a desirable or undesirable state of affairs. On the other hand, the themes are essentially symbolic devices which can provide indices of the ideals of Cheremis dogma, and when we discover what the principal themes are that the Cheremis sound in their prayers, and what the relative frequencies are with which they sound them, we may have gained information about their attitudes of preference that are likely to be centrally characteristic of their culture. First, however, we shall discuss how the Cheremis pray, and give a survey of the prayers upon which the analysis has been based.

THE CORPUS AND ITS FUNCTION

HOW AND WHEN THE CHEREMIS PRAY

This is a generalized description of how the Cheremis pray, based on miscellaneous sources. First, before important ceremonies, they bathe in clean water, sometimes in the bathhouse, at other times in a brook in the vicinity of the prayer grove. Having thus cleansed themselves, they put on fresh white clothing, not worn on any other occasion; they also change their footgear. While praying, they face east or, more commonly, southeast, regardless of the time of day. The group expresses their common wishes and cares through the mouth of the priest who stands in front of the congregation; beside, or just behind, him stand his assistants. The other members of the group express wishes silently, by bodily posture: the men form rows behind the functionaries, kneeling; and, if there are women present as well, these kneel behind the men. (Members of the *kugu sorta* sect never kneel in the course of prayer; they stand facing southeast and bend the upper part of their bodies; they raise their hands, palms forward, in a gesture of greeting the 'white great god.') The priest and his helpers may wear their caps, but the other men pray bareheaded. As the priest prays, he sometimes circles the fire or sacrifice tree in a clockwise direction. Sometimes the priest brandishes a burning stick, and sometimes he strikes a knife against the blade of an ax. As he says "amen," he bows, nodding his head, or prostrates himself altogether, his forehead touching the ground. The congregation follows suit. After the prayer is over, many of the men go to the priest to thank him for the service.

The occasions for prayer are many and varied, some private and some public, and some both in close succession. Private prayers are said by the devout individual throughout the course of regular, daily activity. The Cheremis may thus pray in the morning, after he has washed his face, and then again before and after his morning meal; likewise, he prays both before and after his noon and evening meal; he prays, finally, before he goes to sleep. Travel induces frequent prayer, which the Cheremis may be impelled to pronounce as he leaves his room, again as he emerges from the house into the street, as he enters a neighbor's house, when he goes out to the fields, on approaching a forest, when crossing a river, on arrival in another village, and so forth. Prayer is especially intense on Friday.

Communal prayer takes place every seventh week, as well as at certain regularly recurring occasions around the calendar.[88] Often, after the communal prayer at the village grove, prayer is continued in each home. Yearly occasions for prayer include: the times of the equinoxes and solstices; when the cattle are let out to graze, when rounding up the flocks, and again when about to slaughter them; the times of seeding oats, hemp, and rye, and the times of reaping these same staples; when one is about to break bread baked of new produce; when about to remove honey from the hives; when beginning to fell trees; and so forth.

The rites of transition call forth prayer: the Cheremis woman prays in labor; several prayers are said before birth, and several after. When a child is named, on the twenty-first day after birth, the ceremony in the prayer grove is accompanied by prayer. When a young Cheremis man goes off to find a bride, his father prays in his home, and when the girl has consented, the bridegroom and his bride pray in her house, and continue to pray daily until the wedding, and throughout the entire wedding ceremony they pray at various intervals till the couple is bedded. After a Cheremis dies, his family say prayers before, at, and after the burial, for example, at the memorial feast forty days after death, and the Thursday preceding Easter at the feast of the candles. Prayers are also a part of the rites of increase, the agricultural ceremonies of *aga pajram,* planting, harvesting, and fructifying. Prayers accompany sacrifice ceremonies, as for example those of the *küsə* (Part One, B.9.) and *keremet* (Part One, B.7.), the vows (Part One, B.4., B.16.) a Cheremis makes in lieu of a sacrifice, the sacrifices which are made to cure certain illnesses, and so forth.

PRAYER TEXTS

This analysis of Cheremis prayers is based on thirty-eight of the somewhat larger number of available prayer texts. These texts come from the following collections, listed here in chronological order of their publication:

1. This prayer was first published in Kazan, in 1840, among the letters of Aleksandra Fuks, and was then republished in Pest, in 1864, by Budenz, with corrections of the text and a Hungarian translation; (see also "Introduction: Primary Sources"). The

[88] "The definite occasions of prayer repeat themselves again and again, the needs impelling to prayer remain constantly the same. Thus it happens that primitive man does not wait until he falls into distress or cherishes a wish, but he regularly brings to the higher beings in a general comprehensive form his permanent needs and wishes. And so, besides the extraordinary occasions of prayer there are the regular, customary ones suggested by seasonal changes, sunrise and sunset, the changes of the moon, seedtime and harvest." *Ibid.,* p. 4.

prayer was said to be spoken at a Cheremis *sürem* festival, as was also Prayer 28. The text consists of seventeen sentences. It was evidently recorded in Tsarevokokshajsk as indicated both by the internal evidence of the Cheremis dialect group which the text represents, and our knowledge of the whereabouts of Mme. Fuks.

2. This lengthy and elaborate prayer may be found on pages 55–61 of the [G] collection (with German translation on pages 148–57). It was recorded from the District of Krasnoufimsk, Province of Perm, 1887, and published two years later. In the course of this prayer, the priest summons the gods to hear him by striking a knife against an ax.

3. This prayer was recorded, in 1885–1886, in the District of Tsarevokokshaisk, Province of Kazan, as spoken by the Cheremis priest Gavril Jakovleff, of the village Unsha. It may be found on pages 15–18 (German translation on pages 76–80) of the [PG] collection, published in 1895.

4. This prayer was probably recorded from the same informant as Prayer 3, and may be found on pages 18–20 (80–83) of the same collection.

5. This prayer appears in the same collection as Prayers 3 and 4, but was given by a different informant, Vassili Fadejeff, as assistant priest *(polykart')* of the village Morki. The text is on pages 20–21; the translation on pages 83–84.

6. This prayer, and the twenty more which follow, are each from the [B] collection, pages 22–24, recorded during World War I, from a Cheremis prisoner of war, one Dimitrij Rybakov, from the District of Yaransk, Province of Vyatka. Each text is quite short. The collection appeared in 1931. Prayer 6 (=[B1]) is addressed to 'earth great god' (cf. Part One: A.26.25.).

7. See 6, above. This prayer (=[B2]) is addressed to 'grain gods' (cf. Part One: A.26.16.).

8. See 6, above. This prayer (=[B3]) is addressed to 'grain blossom god' (cf. Part One: A.26.34.1.).

9. See 6, above. This prayer (=[B4]) is addressed to 'blossom great god' (cf. Part One: A.26.34.).

10. See 6, above. This prayer (=[B5]) is addressed to 'grain angel' (cf. Part One: A.84.13.).

11. See 6, above. This prayer (=[B6]) is addressed to 'blessing mother god' (cf. Part One: A.26.1.3.).

12. See 6, above. This prayer (=[B7]) is addressed to 'bird god' (cf. Part One: A.26.14.).

13. See 6, above. This prayer (=[B8]) is addressed to 'chicken god' (cf. Part One: A.26.8.).

14. See 6, above. This prayer (=[B9]) is addressed to 'bee god' (cf. Part One: A.26.28.).

15. See 6, above. This prayer (=[B10]) is addressed to 'bee mother god' (cf. Part One: A.26.1.2.).

16. See 6, above. This prayer (=[B11]) is addressed to 'wind god' (cf. Part One: A.26.24.).

17. See 6, above. This prayer (=[B12]) is addressed to 'fructifier mother gods' (cf. Part One: A.26.1.4.).

18. See 6, above. This prayer (=[B13]) is addressed to 'man fructifier mother' (cf. Part One: A.1.10.2.).

19. See 6, above. This prayer (=[B14]) is addressed to 'tree lord' (cf. Part One: A.52.13.).

20. See 6, above. This prayer (=[B15]) is addressed to 'water mother' (cf. Part One: A.1.1.).

21. See 6, above. This prayer (=[B16]) is addressed to 'grain blessing mother' (cf. Part One: A.1.8.1.).

22. See 6, above. This prayer (=[B17]) is addressed to 'grain blessing mother god' (cf. Part One: A.26.1.3.1.).

23. See 6, above. This prayer (=[B18]) is addressed to 'cattle fructifier' and 'cattle fructifier mother' (cf. Part One: A.82.2. and A.1.10.1.).

24. See 6, above. This prayer (=[B19]) is addressed to 'sheep fructifier' (cf. Part One: A.82.10.).

25. See 6, above. This prayer (=[B20]) is addressed to 'sheep fructifier' and 'sheep fructifier mother' (cf. Part One: A.82.10. and A.1.10.7.).

26. See 6, above. This prayer (=[B21]) is addressed to 'earth fructifier mother' (cf. Part One: A.1.10.5.).

27. This prayer is spoken in the course of the celebration of the *aga pajram* festival (cf. Part One: B.2. for a description of this ceremony), as are also Prayers 30 and 36. This version was recorded from a young farmer, Ivan Nagorskich, in 1906, in the District of Urzhum, Sernur village, but not published till 1931; see the [Wu] collection, pages 27–28.

28. This prayer, spoken by the same informant as 27, but in the course of the description of the *šürem* festival, like Prayer 1, occurs on page 29 of the [Wu] collection.

29. The [Be] collection, all of a religious character, contains several descriptions of miscellaneous rituals, and the appropriate prayers are embedded in the texts as a whole. These materials were dictated, like texts 6–26, in Budapest, during World War I, (published in 1934), by a different Cheremis prisoner of war, one Vasilij Andrianov, who came from the Eastern Cheremis District of Birsk, Province of Ufa. The prayers are important because the Eastern Cheremis were the last of this people to come under Christian influence; the informant still described himself as a believer in what he called "Cheremis religion." From this collection, we select three prayers, one an Easter prayer, on pages 704–5.

30. See 29, above. Several prayers are spoken in the course of this *aga pajram* festival (cf. also Prayer 27 and 36), and we select the one on pages 708–9, said in the course of the sacrifice.

31. See 29, above. This lengthy prayer is embedded in a splendid description of the *küs'ə* festival (cf. Part One: B.9.), in several sections throughout the text, pages 710ff.

32. The [P] collection, gathered from the District of Birsk, Province of Ufa, in 1900 (published in 1939), contains this long prayer, dictated by the principal mulla of Čhurajeva village (pages 34–48).

33. See 32, above. This prayer was given by a mulla named Almakaj, from Staro-Kulchubajeva village (pages 49–67).

34. See 32, above. This prayer is spoken at the conclusion of spring plowing, by

the seeder (pages 68–69), preferably on one of the days the Cheremis consider lucky—Sunday, Monday, or Wednesday. The seeder scatters upon the ground, besides the seed, some ten eggs, which he then recovers. After he is through with the seeding, the basket which had contained the seed is turned upside down, covered with a cloth, and a whole loaf of bread and the eggs are placed upon it. Then this prayer is spoken, and as he says the final constituent, the worshipper slices off a piece of the bread and buries it in the ground with one of the eggs.

35. See 32, above, pages 68–69. Some person *(učo)* other than the mulla besprinkles and then slaughters the sacrificial ram, while the mulla himself speaks the first constituent. Then while the meat is cooked, at the outset of the meal, the mulla repeats the same sentence, and continues the prayer to its end. The prayer is addressed to a *keremet* (cf. Part One: A.31.).

36. See 32, above, pages 69–70. The principal mulla speaks this prayer at the *aga pajram* festival (cf. also Prayers 27 and 30).

37. See 32, above, pages 70–72. This prayer is spoken by a wedding guest who knows it well, in the house where the wedding takes place, after the arrival of the bride and after the pancake is set upon the table. Everyone stands during the prayer.

38. This is a prayer recorded from Mr. Iwan Jewskij, rather typical in style of the rest of his repertoire. It is reproduced above in its entirety, as our sample text.

PART THREE
THE TEXTURE OF RELIGIOUS LIFE

THE PAGAN BASE AND CHRISTIAN
SUPERSTRUCTURE

THE PAGAN BASE

NATIVE Cheremis religion is based entirely on oral tradition and, therefore, the beliefs and practices vary slightly from one region to another. However, essentially they are alike throughout. In Part One and Part Two an extensive analysis of native Cheremis beliefs and practices has been set forth; for our present purposes a brief resumé of them is given here.

Animism is the all-pervasive concept of Cheremis religion. Souls or, more exactly, soul-powers, are believed to be possessed by almost everything. The Cheremis pantheon contains literally several hundred personified supernaturals, ranging from a supreme god to ghosts. Nature, in practically all its aspects, is personified, and there may be a separate deity or spirit for almost every phase of it. In addition to the numerous family gods, household spirits, spirits of the forest, the water, the fire, the earth and vegetation, in addition to the gods of sky and air, of birth and death, there are a number of witches and demons which cause harm to man and his property. The most important, most powerful, and most dreaded of these "lower spirits" are the *keremet,* held in even greater awe than the high gods are themselves. These *keremet* were originally human, some of them former rulers, or heroes, or the founders of specific clans. A peculiar feature of the fenced sanctuaries dedicated to these *keremet* is that no foreign language may be spoken within its confines, since the spirit dwelling there "hates foreign tongues." Worship of nature gods and spirits is usually directed to the east and south; worship of *keremet* is often to the north or occasionally to the west. The realm of the dead is sometimes believed to be in the west.

Worship of the gods and spirits consists largely of sacrifices accompanied by prayers for blessing. Sacrifices include animals, grain products such as bread, pancakes, and porridge, and drink offerings of mead, beer, and vodka. Animal sacrifices are made outside the town in a grove in which each god has its own special tree.

Most important sacrifices consist of a large animal to the deity being worshipped plus other small ones to his helping spirits. The most precious sacrifice animal is the horse, which is seldom offered and then only to gods and to the *keremet* spirits. Cows are sacrificed to female deities; and sheep, goats, ducks, geese, and chickens to less important spirits. The meat of the sacrificed animal is cooked in the grove, and, after small pieces of various parts have been offered up, the people eat the remainder. Often the pieces dedicated to the gods are thrown into the fire, and the fire spirit is asked to take the sacrifice to the god in question.

General sacrifices take place either periodically—for instance, at the great festivals in honor of the nature gods, generally held during the most beautiful time of the summer, either annually or after the lapse of three or five years—or they are held as a consequence of some calamity. At the *küsə* ceremony, which is the annual sacrifice in honor of the gods, the number of animals offered may run into the hundreds, depending on the gods worshipped and the number of people participating in the sacrifice. An individual who has suffered disease or other misfortune may also be called on to make a sacrifice, although usually on a smaller scale than the general sacrifices. A seer is consulted as to which god or spirit has been the cause and, therefore, should be propitiated with a sacrifice. If a person is not financially able to make the sacrifice, he makes a sacrifice vow which he fulfills later.

Agricultural ceremonies are held in the field, but no animals are killed. Sacrifices to the family gods are put on a special corner shelf, held sacred, usually in the *kudə,* the summer hut. After her marriage, a Cheremis woman will, for some time to come, return to the *kudə* of her former home to sacrifice, especially in case of illness or some other misfortune diagnosed by the seer as having been caused by the spirit of the 'old place.' In this way, the 'little family' continues to depend on the 'great family.' Sacrifices are also made to specific spirits in the place where they dwell—the sacrifices to a water spirit, for example, are made on the bank of a river, as when the fishermen offer bread or brandy to urge the spirit to drive fish into their tackle.

The Cheremis honor a dead person with a rather elaborate funeral ceremony and remembrance feasts on the third, seventh, and fortieth day after his death. In addition, there are yearly ceremonies at which all the dead are remembered. During the memorial ceremonies, the dead person is considered to be an invisible guest to whom the living talk, offer a seat, give food, and so forth, as if he were alive. These ceremonies are characterized by feasting, drinking, dancing, and singing. People believe that the enjoyment of the living is an index of the extent to which the dead person is also enjoying himself. Life after death is considered a continuation of life on earth; consequently, at the time of burial, things that the person may need, such as tools and money are put in the coffin. In the case of an unmarried girl, for example, materials for her wedding clothes in the next world are also included.

A person who has led a good life on earth goes to a good place in the other world which is always characterized as being light. According to the beliefs in some places, torment in a vat of boiling pitch awaits those who have lived wickedly. At funerals and during memorial ceremonies, surviving relatives and friends pray to the ruler of the dead, *kiamat töra,* not to torture the deceased but to allow him to live happily in the light.

Uneven numbers occur frequently in Cheremis religious practices, the most common being three, seven, and nine. Many religious acts are repeated three times. The number three is extremely frequent in ceremonies for the dead but also figures in other ceremonies. In addition to having a seven-day week, in some districts there is the belief that there are seven heavens and hells. The belief also exists that there are in the world seventy-seven religions given by god. Frequently the numbers seven and nine have similar uses so that what may be nine in one region is seven in another. A deity's retinue may consist of seven or nine helping spirits. The number of times water may be poured on a sacrifice animal to make it shudder may be seven or nine. Nine seems to be common in ceremonies: there are usually nine loaves of bread, nine bowls of mead, nine spans cut at a sacrifice. Nine people make offerings into the fire at the sacrifice ceremony. The numbers seven and nine are frequently used in prayers when asking for blessings. There is a formula asking for such abundance that seventy-seven friends may be fed from the harvest. Nine sons and seven daughters are requested in one prayer. Another asks that the livestock be driven into the stall from "seven times nine paths."

The number seven appears quite frequently in Cheremis religious practices. In addition to having a seven-day week, gods are often believed to have seven helpers. In some districts there is the belief that there are seven heavens and hells. The number seventy-seven appears frequently in prayers, especially in the formula asking for such abundance that seventy-seven friends may be fed from the harvest. The number nine also occurs frequently, but not so often as seven.

Women rarely take an active part in ceremonies, and frequently they are not present. They are not permitted to enter the *keremet* grove or to touch the things in the holy corner of the *kudə*. They are, however, permitted to attend sacrifices in *jumən otə* 'god's grove.' Many women attend *aga pajram* (B.2.), fewer attend the sacrifice ceremonies. At one *mükš jer* four women were present by invitation because it was thought that their presence would bring a greater blessing. A woman may assist her husband as he makes a *sorbalmə* vow (B.14.). When women attend a ceremony they kneel behind the men or to one side. Women prepare the pancakes and other baked goods and brew the beer used during ceremonies. They also occasionally help cook the meat of the sacrificed animal.

The life of the Cheremis is governed by a large body of folk beliefs. The bulk of these have to do with predicting, from the movements of animals and other natural occurrences, weather, crops, sickness, and death. There are certain taboos connected with specified times of the year. For instance, on the Wednesday before Easter no work may be done without unfortunate consequences. If a person even combs his hair on that day, chickens will scratch up his garden. There is also the belief that if any bad smells are made while the grain is in bloom, the crop will be poor. Consequently, people do not move manure or make pitch during this season. Some beliefs are associated with evil spirits. Both iron and mountain ash twigs are effective in keeping the devil away. Some devils are believed to originate from spittle; therefore, when a person spits, he must be sure to step on his spittle to prevent it from becoming a devil.

Cheremis weddings, although a few prayers are said, are, by and large, social affairs. The betrothal takes place when the young man, usually accompanied by an older friend, formally asks and receives permission from a girl's father to marry her. The girl gives her consent by drinking mead which the young man offers her. At that time, or shortly after, arrangements are made for the wedding. On the day of the wedding friends gather at both the house of the groom and of the bride where there is a plentiful supply of food and drink. After everyone has had his fill, the groom and his friends go to fetch the bride. At the bride's house there is more eating, drinking, and merrymaking. The couple receive the blessings of the bride's parents; and then go to the groom's home. After a similar blessing from the groom's parents, they are considered to be man and wife. The headdress of a married woman is put on the bride; and she distributes gifts of towels and shirts to the groom's relatives who in return must promise to give the young couple something. After that there is more revelry, with singing and dancing, accompanied by music. The festivities last for three days.

The Cheremis sacrifice a white sheep at the birth of a child to the deity of birth, and there are other ceremonies connected with the cult of procreation. For example, Harva describes the festival that is proclaimed when the sheep have not increased satisfactorily. Boys and girls are invited.

> As a sacrifice a wild bird is shot, but for lack of this a hen may be used. The host takes the bird and the hostess the implements necessary at the sacrifice, and a journey to the sheepfolds is made, the boys and girls following them, creeping on all fours. The hostess induces the children to keep after her, enticing them like sheep, the movements and voices of which the children seek to imitate. The boys butt at the girls, imitating rams. Arrived at the sheepfold the host makes a fire, round which the so-called sheep crawl baa-ing three times, following the hostess. They then rise, and the bird is cooked and eaten in the sheepfold, the bones being thrown on to the roof of the fold and prayers offered up to the 'sheep-fructifier.' [It is not customary to invite many boys to this ceremony] but chiefly girls, lest too many rams be born in the flock.

Before eating, a devout Cheremis offers part of his food to the gods by placing it on the floor near the door or by an open window facing the sun. If he is traveling, he puts the food on the ground. If he passes a place dedicated to a supernatural, he leaves a small offering of money or bread.

THE CHRISTIAN SUPERSTRUCTURE

From the beginning of the Russian domination of the Cheremis attempts were made to Christianize them. No force was used, but the special inducement of

---

[1] Harva, 1927, pp. 259-60.

freedom from taxes for a few years was offered to those who would become baptized. This resulted in a large number of persons joining the Russian Orthodox Church for economic reasons but without sound convictions. In the middle of the nineteenth century, there were whole settlements living in the deep forest who officially counted themselves as pagans. Instead of going to church, many Cheremis continued to go to their holy birch woods where they said their pagan prayers. The people always felt that their existence as a coherent group would be endangered if they abandoned the old faith. Accordingly, they used to say, "If we cease to go to the woods, our whole people will perish."

The Church realized this and redoubled its missionary efforts, establishing schools and training Cheremis-speaking priests.[2] By the end of the nineteenth century, census figures indicate that almost three-fourths of the Cheremis were members of the Russian-Orthodox Church. However, for many this was still in name only, and pagan beliefs and customs remained deeply rooted. Many Cheremis did not actively resist Christian priests but tolerated their views while secretly maintaining their own beliefs. In order not to be involved in religious discussions they often agreed with whatever the priests said, thus giving an impression of being orthodox Christians. It was inevitable that a certain amount of intermingling of the two competing systems should take place. Christian priests cast prayers into the pagan form and attempted to identify Christian figures with pagan supernaturals in order to make the new religion more acceptable to the Cheremis. This resulted in confusion in the minds of many Cheremis who were unable to distinguish between Christian and pagan rites. It was expedient for the Cheremis to adopt certain outward forms of Christianity in order to avoid trouble from Church authorities. It was easy for Cheremis to add the Christian God and saints to the already imposing list of pagan supernaturals. In some places, the distinction between "Cheremis deities" and "Russian deities" was retained only to the extent that when a petition was to be made a seer was consulted as to whether a prayer should be addressed to a Russian or Cheremis supernatural.

The available published sources give no indication as to the religious practices or statistical importance of the Christian Cheremis in recent years. However, our informant has given a description of the religious life of his village which is probably representative of the merging of Christian beliefs with older traditions. Although everyone is nominally a Christian and is baptized as a child, this religion is not important in the culture. Moreover, it is unwise for a person with political ambitions to participate in religious activities. Services are attended more often by older people than by the young.

2 There are also Cheremis saints. One of the most popular of them is a martyred girl, Maria, who, legend has it, suffered death at the hands of her pagan stepmother in the seventeenth century. Her cult is especially strong among Cheremis women and their female Russian neighbors.

In contrast with the pagan Cheremis who are polytheistic and sacrifice animals to the supernaturals, the Christian Cheremis are superficially monotheistic and practice baptism. The informant reports that there is only one god, *jumə;* nevertheless, prayers are addressed to *šočən aba* 'birth mother,' *kinde perke* 'grain blessing,' *tul bodəž* 'fire spirit,' and other minor deities to whom the non-Christians make regular sacrifices. Both Christian and pagan Cheremis believe in angels, *šukčə,* and devils, variously called *čort, ia,* or *šajtan.*

Administratively, there is little difference between a pagan and a Christian congregation. Each village is autonomous in religious matters, and there is very little formal organization. Occasionally, a group of Cheremis villages unite to hold joint services in much the same way as is done in pagan areas. Each village has at least one priest who is called *molla* or *pop.* Some Cheremis use the word *pop* only for a Russian priest, but this distinction is not made in the informant's village where there is no contact with Russian priests. In other regions the priest is called *kart.* Usually, the native priest is an older man of little literacy but forceful personality who is able to read or quote a bit from the Bible and to deliver sermons. One important qualification is a good memory for the long prayers which he must recite. He is also expected to live a good life, and may keep his position until incapacitated by the weakness of old age or death. He wears no special dress and is not set apart from the rest of the community in any way. The function of the priest is to lead public ceremonies. However, if he is not present, someone else may do so. The priest rarely officiates at weddings, baptisms, or funerals. A *kart* is often selected from among a priest's former assistants. When there are several priests, the senior one is called the 'great *kart,*' the others being 'small *kart.*'

There are no churches in Cheremis villages. Public services are held in a house large enough to accommodate the worshippers. Agricultural ceremonies are held in appropriate fields, or sections of them, set aside for the purpose; for example, the spring seed festival offerings are sacrificed at so-called 'pure spots' in the fields. Prayers are sometimes said in a sacred grove, the *küs otə,* while facing to the east, or 'upward.'

The ordinary service lasts about two hours and consists mainly of prayers recited by the priest to which the people respond, "Amen." In keeping with the old Cheremis tradition, everyone wears white to religious services. During prayers everyone except the priest kneels, the women either behind the men or to the side. Services for worship are held on Fridays at irregular intervals throughout the year; they are most frequent in May and June, the time between planting and harvesting, which is also a time of intense religious activity among the non-Christian Cheremis. The spring agricultural ceremony, *aga pajram,* is substantially the same for the Christians and pagans including even the throwing of food offerings into the fire. Weddings, funerals, and memorial feasts for the dead follow closely the old Cheremis traditions. Oftentimes the family holds services in the home—reminiscent of an American prayer meeting. The Christian Cheremis, like the non-Christians, have no holy image in their houses.

The only ceremony which appears to be specifically of Christian origin is baptism, a rite performed by a godparent who is chosen by chance. The parents who wish to have their child baptized may secretly decide that the first person to enter their house on a certain day will be the godparent. Another way of choosing a godparent is to pass out little cakes in one of which a silver coin has been hidden; the person who finds the coin becomes the godparent. In either case, the choice is independent of the personal preference of the parents or the person chosen for the role. The godparent immerses the child in water three times and gives him a new name. The child already has a name which has been given by its parents and which is used for official purposes. The name given by the godparent, often similar to that given by the parents, is the one by which a person is usually called. A few days after baptism the godparent presents the child with a shirt and supplies food and drink for a celebration at the home of the parents. Once baptized in this manner, a person is never called on to reaffirm his faith. As he grows to adulthood, he gradually assumes religious responsibilities at the same time as he takes over his social and economic obligations.

KUGU SORTA, 'BIG CANDLE'—
A NATIVISTIC MOVEMENT

HISTORY OF THE SECT

THE national religious movements among the Cheremis became particularly lively towards the end of the nineteenth century, by virtue of the foundation of a new influential sect, the *kugu sorta*, literally, 'big candle.' Strictly speaking, this is not a single, uniform movement, but, almost from the time when it first came to public attention, there have been several factions within it. There is, however, an ascetic group the beliefs and practices of which are quite distinct and, though its members are fewer in number than those who belong to more traditional factions, their importance is far greater as a focus for the preservation of fundamental Cheremis cultural values. Supporters of the *kugu sorta* sect resisted the Czarist regime and the "capitalistic order of society" by boycotting factory-produced goods and by their refusal to serve in the war. The new religious movement gained numerous adherents and spread rapidly. Its best known advocates were the Jakmanov brothers in the Jaransk area, in the 1880's. Although some attempts have been made to trace the origins of the sect back to the beginning of the nineteenth century, claiming that it began as a protest against the missionary activities of the government-supported Russian Orthodox Church, which became especially vigorous at about that period, we have little information about it until towards the end of the century. We know that in 1878 there was a meeting of sect members on which occasion their beliefs were discussed. A lack of agreement caused a split into two factions, one choosing to follow the traditional, pagan pattern of sacrifices and prayers, and the other advocating reformed beliefs and practices. A principal point of disagreement involved animal sacrifice: The traditionalists held that the sacrifice of animals was the most fitting offering to god; the reformers felt, on the other hand, that all destruction of life must displease god, since he is the source of life.

In the 1870's and 1880's, the movement spread rapidly in Jaransk, and hence to the Uržum district and to Kazan, in spite of the fact that sect members made little deliberate effort to attract converts, since they believed that, if god so willed, the sect would grow without their actively proselytizing. A large number of the supporters of this new movement were nominally Christian. At first, the Russian Church ignored the movement. However, as it became increasingly apparent that sect members were neglecting their Christian obligations, after some peaceful attempts to draw them back into the Church had failed, the Church began, with Government backing, to persecute them. In the 1890's, *kugu sorta* followers were forcibly taken to church and put through the motions of worship. They were forbidden to work or sell their own property without official consent. In 1893, after involved legal procedures, ten of the sect leaders were exiled to Siberia. In 1906, regulations were somewhat relaxed, however, and the exiles permitted to return to their homes. Because, intermittently, the government prevented sect members to own land or work upon what they did own, they had difficulty supporting themselves. Their economic life was seriously disrupted, for they were forced to become merchants and peddlers temporarily; however, they returned to farming as soon as conditions allowed. Even in the absence of government persecution, they often suffered economic hardships because dishonest Russians and others took advantage of their religiously scrupulous honesty and trust. Because of, first, the persecution and, later, the ridicule which continued even after the official persecution was suspended, *kugu sorta* members kept their activities secret, and strangers were but seldom suffered to attend their religious services. It is this subversive, underground character of their pursuits that make data about the sect relatively scarce, even though two leaders bought a printing press and, for a short while, published information about the movement with which they were associated.

After the October Revolution, the *kugu sorta* experienced a considerable boom, since many of the Cheremis, when the Orthodox Church was deprived of its official backing, promptly abandoned Christianity.[3] Some Cheremis Communists—of whom, however, there were then not more than a few hundred—lent their moral support to the reformed wing of the sect, stressing its revolutionary character. But the leading Party organs soon came to consider the *kugu sorta* the most dangerous anti-Soviet organization among this people. The sect opposed to the Russian state, Czarist and Bolshevik, its own dream of a Cheremis nation without Russians, and produced a historical myth depicting the past of the Cheremis in splendid colors. Thus, one of the Cheremis folktales which has been traced back to *kugu sorta* influence starts with the words, "And there was a time when the Mari ruled over half the Russian land; and its capital was *Maska Ava,* or Moscow as the Russians called it, when our forefathers had been driven away. . . ." These Cheremis believed that their ancestors had founded Moscow, a name which they said was derived from *maska aba* meaning 'bear mother.' The defeat and consequent subjugation of the Cheremis are said to have resulted from their neglect to worship god.

In the late 1920's Vasiliev, a native Cheremis student of his people's customs and language, reported that the number of adherents had diminished, giving as the principal reason that the strict ascetic life prescribed by the sect had lost its appeal

[3] One sect member even suggested that a law be passed making all Cheremis officially *kugu sorta* members, even as during the Czarist regime all Cheremis living in certain regions were declared Christian. This proposal was not, of course, adopted.

to Cheremis youth. Zykov reported in 1932 that, although the *kugu sorta* members said that almost all Cheremis were *či mari* 'genuine Cheremis,' the masses did not follow the teachings of the sect. In areas where the sect was strong, it successfully opposed collectivization and all attempts to change the older way of life. Zykov states, however, that these protests came from the older people and that the younger generation was more receptive to Soviet reforms. Yet, however, information from other sources indicates that, not only was the sect very much alive in the 1930's, but also that it seems to have formed some sort of a united religious front with other groups, ranging from devout Christians to outspoken pagan traditionalists, for the purpose of resisting Bolshevik pressures. To counteract these and similar nationalistic ideas current among the Cheremis, Soviet authorities disseminated their own version of Cheremis-Russian relations in the past, the only version which can legally be circulated in the Mari A. S. S. R. today.[4] It is difficult to assess to what extent the Cheremis genuinely accept the official ideology, although, in 1946, a majority of the adult population of the Mari Republic signed a letter to Stalin, which, composed of two hundred and eighty-eight lines in verse, said, among other things:

> From times immemorial we believe, we know
> That the Russian is our friend and brother. . .
> This friendship has lasted four centuries
> From the very days when Akpars, the hero,
> Led the Mari people into the Russian camp
> And went into battle against the Tatar Khans.

The story of the Cheremis princeling, Akpars, who participated in the Russian conquest of Kazan, is borrowed from Cheremis folklore; but it contains only part of the historical truth since the more nationally conscious Eastern Cheremis, at any rate, supported the Tatars in their fight against the Russians.

BELIEFS AND PRACTICES

Although the members of the sect say that they follow the ancient beliefs of their forefathers, the way in which they do so is largely limited to material things. They display marked hostility to technical progress, try to live as their ancestors did, and to use only those things which their ancestors had before Russian acculturation began. Members of the sect show, for example, strong dislike for the railways passing through their territory. They call them 'fire serpents,' a concept possibly derived from Cheremis folklore's *buber,* a demon somewhat akin to the will-o'-the-wisp (see Part I, A.10.), and claim that the railways would destroy the Cheremis people. However, the spirit of the *kugu sorta* religious beliefs is quite different from that of the old pagan religion. The old religion concerned itself

---

[4] *Pravda,* June 22, 1945, no. 147 (10229), p. 2.

with the way in which the people could propitiate the gods in order to secure bless-ings and ward off misfortune and disease. The *kugu sorta* member, on the other hand, is interested in living a life which is completely pleasing to god and in obtaining god's forgiveness when he fails to do so.

Kugu sorta is a name given to the movement either by the Russian missionaries or the Christian Cheremis because a large candle is used in the course of the cere-monies. The name is appropriate because an enormous candle occupies a central place in the service. The big taper is reported to have assumed its importance at a meeting of some seven hundred believers in 1877. While the congregation was discussing the type of sacrifice that would seem fitting, a solar eclipse occurred. This so frightened the participants that, after it had passed, each contributed his small candle to make a single large one. From this time on, it was held that candles are among the preferred offerings. These candles, burned at the ceremonies, are handmade by the men. The wax used for them is taken from living bees only. If a man must buy wax, he does so only from a person he knows so that he can be sure the wax is pure and acceptable. Most candles are small and slender; however, many are quite large. In instances where there are a large number of worshippers, the big candle may weigh up to sixty pounds. If the candles used during a ceremony have not burned half-way down, they are used again at the next service; otherwise, they are melted and made into new candles.

The sect does not call itself *kugu sorta;* rather, its members refer to themselves as 'god's soldiers,' or *ži mari* 'genuine Cheremis,' and to their religion as 'the beliefs of our forefathers,' 'the original beliefs of our forefathers,' 'the old beliefs,' and 'god's right beliefs.' Sect members are also called *oš mari kalək* 'white Cheremis people' and their beliefs *kugarńa bera* 'Friday beliefs.'

Members of the *kugu sorta* recognize one supreme being, *jumə,* who is ad-dressed in prayers as 'the one origin and source of life, the white great god.' He is both father and mother, and is addressed by a variety of names according to his different attributes: thus, he is the creator of the world and the judge of mankind; he is omniscient, omnipresent, merciful, and kind. After he created the universe, in which our solar system is but one of many, he did not abandon it but, rather, continues to guard and protect his creation. The names by which he is addressed are those used for separate deities by non-*kugu sorta* pagans. Significantly, sect members are opposed to earthly leaders because they want to be ruled by *jumə* alone.

The earth was created in the framework of the Pleiades. At the same instant when he created man, *jumə* also created seventeen 'sources,' *tüŋ,* in each of which there are both male and female components. Ten of these are in heaven, the rest on earth. Those in heaven—*küšəl tüŋ* 'upper source'—rule the whole world, at the same time acting as intermediaries between man and god. To the first group be-longs the *tüŋ* of the sun which is lord over all the others. The seven earthly ones—*üləl tüŋ* 'lower source'—which maintain life on the earth, are the 'sources' of mankind, hemp, grain, trees, bees, animals, and grass, and also act as intermediaries between god and the 'upper sources' on the one hand, and the earth and mankind, on the other. Fire and air are original elements which are in everything. Old men tell of three "creators" who are not generally known to *kugu sorta* members. These supernaturals, who have the appearance of middle-aged or elderly men, act as intermediaries between god and the earth; the first is about seven feet above the earth, the second above him, and the third higher still. The lowest of the three orders things on earth and passes up a report to the second, who in turn passes the report to the third, who tells it to god. Likewise, god's blessings are passed down to earth through these intermediaries.

There are good spirits, guardian angels (*šukšə*), which protect each person from birth to death, and help him even in the afterlife. They are called 'the living angel protecting the spirit' and 'the angel bringing the living spirit.' In his daily prayers, a person always prays to his angel as well as to god. God has an army to which the angels, thunder, lightning, and the clouds belong; and with their help he fights the evil powers, his worst enemy being the devil, *osal,* who tries to harm the whole of creation. Heaven is located above the earth, in seven successively better layers, and under the earth there are seven layers of hell.

On earth, god created man first. So that man could clothe himself, hemp was created next. In the beginning men lived in a golden age. However, they fell into sin, and, as a consequence, they now suffer heat, cold, night, and death. God knows all the failings and sins of mankind and will judge them. People must pray for forgiveness and strive to live according to god's commandments; but man is naturally stubborn and fails to live as god desires him to. The absolution of sins lies in god's hands alone. To obtain forgiveness, men must repent of their sins; and this repentance must be evident not only in words but also in deeds. Good works save the soul. Some day, the earth will return to the Pleiades where it was created, and at that time there will be a final judgement. The evil will be sent to hell, but the good will be permitted to live on the earth where there will again be a golden age. According to one source, the sect members also hold that the earth will pass through seventeen epochs, being in the ninth epoch now. When the tenth epoch comes, the earth will be uninhabitable, except for the sect members who will save themselves by clinging to the roots of the trees in the prayer groves, and continue to live there happily. After death, each soul is judged by god and assigned either to a warm, light, and pleasant place, or banished to a dark place. The position of a soul in the other life is not permanent, since god may move it from heaven to hell or vice versa.

Members of this sect recognize such religious leaders as Mohammed, and regard them as prophets, among whom Christ is considered the greatest. Of course, Christ could not be divine, since there is only one *jumə*. Christian figures permeate *kugu sorta* beliefs. Noah, "the terrible grandfather," is depicted as the judge of the dead who is not far above the earth. Good *kugu sorta* members are sent to paradise but sinful souls are sent to hell where they are beaten by demons with whips and thrown into *kiš pot* 'resin pot.' More sinful souls are sent deep into hell where they are punished by Satan. Noah also figures in the following legend related by *kugu sorta* members:

When Noah began to build the ark according to god's instructions, the devil became curious. He tempted Noah's wife to make wine. Noah got drunk on the wine and revealed god's intentions. The devil hid in the ark, escaping destruction in the deluge. Noah's wife was left on earth stuck in the mud as a warning to others.

Legends are also told about Adam and Abraham who are believed to be the forefathers of the Cheremis. Also, the *kugu sorta* have saints. One such is Old Man (*kuguza*) Philip, who knew the secrets of all gods, communed with the "creators," saw spirits, and the like.

Brotherly love is perhaps the most essential doctrine of this movement. Members believe that all men are brothers and that consequently they must love and help each other in all possible ways. This applies not only to friends and fellow believers but to all mankind. *Kugu sorta* adherents are tolerant of all other religions. They say that there are seventy-seven religions, all of them good, and that a person can be happy in any, depending upon his sincerity.

All nature is considered to be alive and have a soul; since god has given it life, man should not harm or offend it. Animal life, however, is more highly valued than vegetable. Nature is believed to be pure, unspoiled, and free of sin, spending all its time in praise of god, an example which man should follow. The truest servant of god is the sun which warms people, causes things to grow, and acts as an intermediary between god and man. The stars take the sun's place at night. The moon, however, is under god's curse because, according to a legend, death in the form of a witch was captured and hidden by a man and the moon did not report this event to god. It is punishable by god to misuse or destroy anything in nature, and is a sin even to think about such things, since god knows the thoughts of man. In order to survive, it is often necessary for man to destroy life, as when he reaps grain or slaughters an animal for food. However, when he must take a life, man must pray to god for forgiveness explaining that the act is necessary. Their abhorrence of killing manifested itself, for example, in 1907, when they publicly buried weapons and prayed to god for their destruction; and is further shown by their firm attempts at evading military service. The followers of *kugu sorta* recognize the need for having certain tools such as knives, sickles, and axes; but they hope that a time will come when they will no longer be necessary. The bees, because they sustain themselves without destroying anything else, live an ideal existence.

In addition to showing the greatest consideration for all creatures, *kugu sorta* members practice self-discipline and restraint. They prohibit hate, persecution, conflict, intolerance, laziness, and luxury; they encourage peace, love, harmony, tolerance, diligence, and simplicity. Killing—both murder and suicide—stealing, adultery, fraud, covetousness, lying, boasting, gossiping, quarreling, cursing, idleness, are all sins. A person must not set himself up to judge that which he has not himself seen or heard. He should not do to others that which he does not want done to himself. He should not cause trouble between a married couple. Towards his forefathers he ought to show respect and he should attempt to follow their customs, advice, and commands, which stress brotherly love. The importance of avoiding the destruction of god's creations is so much emphasized that people take care, while going through the forest, not to break any branches unnecessarily. They are forbidden to be idle and must work constantly. In the morning, a person may not eat until he has done some work. Work is believed to be the foundation of existence, and anyone who attempts to make life easier is really shortening his life. The accumulation of money is negatively valued, since money itself neither feeds nor clothes people. Rather, a person should share his blessings with others. Further injunctions are the following: the believer must not worship images; he must, at certain times, abstain from sexual intercourse; he is forbidden to dance and sing in an unseemly manner.

On the positive side, a person must exercise brotherly love to the fullest extent. He should do as many good works as he can without expectation of thanks, and repay evil with good. If one receives evil from another, he should pray for god's protection and examine himself to see whether the act is punishment for some sin of his own. A person should honor and obey his parents. He should show hospitality to all people.

In addition to these ethical and moral laws there are some beliefs which are less clearly in the domain of the sacred: a person should walk along the middle of the street and not under windows, and he should look back over his right, rather than his left, shoulder; he should not hold his hands behind his back; if he spits, he should not fail to step on his spittle.

For the strictest members of the sect there are severe dietary laws. Grains, peas, a certain species of beans (*šira lodak*), cabbage, nuts, plums, grapes, raisins, berries, beef, veal, domesticated geese and ducks, dairy products, honey, mead (*mü pürə*), and hopless beer (*uməladəmə sra*) are permitted. Forbidden foods include certain other kinds of beans, cucumbers, potatoes, carrots, turnips, onions, apples, mushrooms, horse meat, pork, chicken, eggs, sugar, sweets, vodka and other alcoholic beverages, narcotics, coffee, tea, and tobacco. Wild animals, birds, and fish are not eaten. If, after death, god finds remains of some forbidden food in the body, he punishes the soul. Excessive eating and drinking are forbidden, but there are no complete fasts. For many of these taboos there are rationalizations: the pig is not eaten because it is a dirty animal; only that which one raises can be used for food, therefore wild animals are not to be eaten; onions are not used because they grow from tears shed over the dead; and so forth.

In theory, medicine, too, is forbidden, since disease is thought to be caused by spirit instrusion of wicked persons, so that the only treatment for illness consists of prayer to god for recovery. In practice, however, when seriously ill, many *kugu sorta* followers will go to doctors and take medicine.

Cleanliness—of body, clothing, and of the home—is extremely important. Sect members must wash themselves every morning, at mealtimes, and before ceremonies. The floors, and sometimes also the walls and ceiling, are washed every fourteen days. Holiday clothes are made of homespun white linen and kept spotlessly clean.

A person wishing to join the *kugu sorta* must undergo a probationary, preparatory period which may last seven weeks but may be shortened to forty days. During this time the proselyte must follow closely the teachings of the sect. He must take only the prescribed food and drink, and he must exercise great moderation. He must wash his entire body daily and say an appropriate prayer. He must not quarrel, say anything improper, or dance. He must shun all luxuries and amusements. During this period he makes special prayer clothes from cloth obtained from another member of the *kugu sorta*. A person who fails to live up to the regulations of the sect may be expelled and not permitted to attend services. If such a person repents, he is readmitted to the sect but sometimes must again undergo the probationary period required of a proselyte.

CEREMONIES

The sect has no rigid, formal religious organization. Indeed, there are no priests. In the home, the father leads the family in prayer; at public ceremonies, one of the older men acts in the capacity of prayer leader. All members participate in the praying, though young children are not usually brought to services. They stand facing east or southeast as they pray, older children to one side, men and women together. At times, they raise their palms out, as high as their shoulders. Between prayers a *gusle,* a zither-like stringed instrument, is played. While praying, they thank god that he has protected and preserved both man and nature. A very important function of prayer is to ask god for forgiveness of sins. People also pray for god's blessing, but they do not ask for specific material benefits because god knows their needs better than they. Prayers are said daily before and after work, before and after eating, and before going to sleep. They also make offerings of food to god. Among the strictest members of this sect, offerings consist of honey and grain products, since bloody animal sacrifices are strictly forbidden. (Some groups do, however, continue to make animal sacrifices in much the same way as other pagans, though these offerings and sacrifices are made only to god and his helping spirits, never to propitiate the numerous evil spirits which loom so important in the lives of the other Cheremis.) In the home, candles are

the most common offering. At the important ceremonies in the grove, they sometimes burn the small table upon which the offerings have been placed.

The weekly sabbath is Friday. Services are never held on the Jewish Sabbath,
on the Christian Sunday, or on a Tuesday. Every seven weeks members assemble
for a general town service, which may be held outdoors or in a home, depending
on the weather. Before the service, the people wash and put on clean clothes. Before
important holidays, on the seventh, seventeenth, and sometimes even the hundred
and twenty-seventh morning, they must bathe in cold water. For Friday they bathe
and put on their holiday clothes the evening before because they must not undress
on Friday. On other, less important, days this is done on the same morning.

The holiday clothes, which are all white, are worn only on religious occasions.
Commercially manufactured clothing is not used at all. In fact, no manufactured
goods of any sort may be used by sect members, who try to live entirely by their
own means. Thus, light is supplied by splinters of resinous wood, and fire made by
friction. In particular, all objects used in religious services must be handmade.
These are kept on a shelf in the right-hand corner of the house along with some
other household items. Opposite the door to the house there is a special oak or birch
table used for prayer.

No churches are erected, since it is believed that the best place to worship
god is in nature. (However, some people have a special building on the farm for
prayers.) Outdoor services are usually held before a prayer tree (*ona pu*) in a
grove. No representations of god are made, since it is believed that to bow down
before a material object is idolatry.

During the ceremony in the grove, the prayer tables are put in front of a
prayer tree, usually a linden or birch. Sometimes the table is covered with a cloth
so that crumbs from the offering will not fall off and be stepped on. On the table
there are five to seven containers made of linden or birch bark. In the center box
are rye, oats, and hemp seeds, and candles standing upright in the grain. In the
middle of the box there are three large candles dedicated to the three creators
(*püirəšo*); the six candles around the edge are dedicated to their angels (*šukšə*)
of which each creator has two. To the right of this box there is another box in
which there are seven candles, one of which is the same size as the big candles in
the first; this candle is dedicated to the mother of life, and the others to her six
angels. According to the number of worshippers and the importance of the prayer,
there may be more such boxes of candles. More than one table may be necessary.
If there are two tables, one may be birch and the other linden, or both may be
birch. The box of nine candles is placed on the birch table. To the left of the two
boxes is placed, during the family prayer, a container for candles for the well-
being of the members of the family; as many candles are lit as there are members
of the family. During the ceremony, fire is made by friction to light the candles.
Each person brings a candle which he lights from the candles on a certain table.

Containers are also placed on the table to hold food and drink offerings which are brought by those attending the service. After the prayer there is a meal and then the candles are snuffed out between two pieces of pine wood.

Amulets believed to bring a blessing to all their agricultural activities are worn by *kugu sorta* members while planting. The men wear a little bag of rye around their neck and women, oats.

There are a number of yearly ceremonies—having to do with phases of the calendar or with agricultural activities—which come at the winter solstice and spring equinox: when the cattle are turned out to pasture in spring and brought back in the fall; when the grain is sowed and harvested; when new grain is first used during haymaking; when, in September, they begin cutting wood; when, in June, they slaughter animals, and when honey is gathered.

At certain times during a person's life special prayers are said. For example, before a baby is born, they are said two or three times, as well as on the day of birth. After the birth the people pray five times, on the seventh, fourteenth, seventeenth, nineteenth, and twenty-first days. The first four prayers are held at home on the twenty-first day they go to the grove to pray. At that time, the baby is named by the parents' simply telling their friends the name they wish to give the child and the friends' replying, "May god grant it." They also pray on the child's seventh, fourteenth, seventeenth, nineteenth, and twenty-first birthdays. It is the father's duty to see that his child gets married.

BETROTHAL AND MARRIAGE

Girls usually marry a the age of sixteen and boys at eighteen. Marriage is permitted only between sect members; if a marriage is desired with a person who is not a member of the sect, he must join. By and large, however, the betrothal and marriage ceremonies of the *kugu sorta* follow the general pattern of the traditional Cheremis betrothals and marriages, though they have been modified to be in harmony with the sect's general principles of sobriety and its greater emphasis on prayer.

When a father who is a member of *kugu sorta* decides that it is time for his son to get married, he calls to his house a friend who will help make arrangements for the marriage. The two men pray to god for a blessing on the marriage and then set out to find a suitable bride. When they find a likely girl, they go with the son to her house. There they light a candle, and the young people pray that they may get married according to god's commandment.

In the betrothal ceremony the young man brings to the girl, who is standing in the middle of the floor, a winnowing basket containing a sieve, bread, two cups of mead, a birch bark container, rye and oat grains, and candles. The girl takes these and hands them to the friend of the boy's father who puts them on the table. The kernels of the grain are put into the birch bark container: seven for god, seven for the angel of the day, and one for each person present. The young man says, "I have no one to sew my clothes and bake my bread. May god give me someone." The he tastes some of the bread and mead. The girl replies, "I have no one to sow the field. May god give me someone." She also tastes bread and mead. Now the girl gives the boy seven, seventeen, or nineteen pieces of linen as a symbol of her consent, and they are betrothed.

After the betrothal both bride and groom pray every day (in their parents' home) for god to bless the marriage. On the morning of the wedding—usually a Friday—friends assemble at the house of the groom where they pray to the accompaniment of the drum and *gusle*. The father of the groom sends his son and the guests to the bride's house. The groom carries a candle in his bosom.

At the bride's house the groom takes his candle in his right hand and a mead cup in his left. The bride comes out of her house with a candle in her left hand and a mead cup in her right. Having exchanged greetings, they touch cups and bring their candles together. Everyone goes inside the house where the bride's parents are seated at the table. They exchange greetings by touching cups. Then everyone puts his cup on the prayer table; and the bride and groom also put their candles there in a special container. Then a prayer is said and the bride and groom stand next to each other while the bride's parents give the couple their blessing. The bride changes her clothes and distributes gifts of linen. After this, they all set out for the groom's house and then for the grove. If the grove lies between the bride's house and the groom's they may go directly to the grove.

In the grove (called *kuerla* 'birch grove,' a term used even if there are no birch trees there), before the sacrifice tree, they place seven tables seven paces apart. The tables are made of materials that represent the seven *tüŋ*. On each table are placed candles and offerings for each of the seven *tüŋ*. The candles are lit during the long prayer. At this time the bride and groom and chief wedding attendants carrying lighted candles circle the tree and tables seven times from east to west. After the seventh time, the bride gives the groom her candle, and the headdress of a married woman is put on her. Then she stands to the right of the groom and takes her candle. The bride and groom kiss each other seven times. During the ritual meal which follows, the candles on the tables as well as those that people are carrying are put out with a special snuffer, a little shovel.

After the meal they go to the groom's house. When they arrive, they get out of the cart, and the father of the groom holds in his hand a birch bark box in which there are nine candles. During the reception ceremony, the young couple touch candles and kiss each other seven times. Finally, they enter the house, the newlyweds in the lead with candles in their hands. Inside, the father and mother of the groom go around the table from east to west, after which the father places the candle box in the place where the prayer objects are kept. When the young bride and groom are led to bed, a prayer is also said to god to bless them.

Sometimes anniversary offerings are made in the grove on the twenty-sixth, twenty-eighth, thirtieth, thirty-second, thirty-sixth, thirty-ninth, sixty-ninth, and eighty-ninth wedding anniversaries. Divorces are seldom granted, and then only on the grounds of unfaithfulness.

FUNERAL CEREMONIES

When a person dies (*kudəš kaimə* 'going to the hut'), the corpse is washed, dressed in clean white linen clothes, and put in the coffin. The coffin, made of fir wood, is shaped so that the end for the head is wider than the end for the feet. The inside of the coffin is seared with fire, and the bottom strewn with birch leaves; and a piece of linen is laid on top of the leaves. Into the right hand of the corpse is put a piece of linen which is said to enable the corpse to hold a candle. The corpse is covered with linen. A prayer is said to the guardian angel and the survivors kiss the corpse on the lips or cheek. A birch bark box in which seven candles are fastened is put on the table. One of the candles, thicker than the others, is dedicated to the person's guardian angel. These candles are taken to the grave with the coffin.

The burial usually takes place on the third day after death. The uncovered coffin is carried to the grave which has been dug before the coffin is brought. The grave, which is six feet deep, runs northwest to southeast with the head at the northwest. At the grave, the lid is put on the coffin, and it is lowered into the ground while the wish is expressed that the deceased be warm. A handful of earth is thrown on the coffin and the dead person is urged to be unafraid. Those at home, in the meantime, have washed and buried things belonging to the deceased. When those who have gone to the burial return, the house is clean and the bath prepared. They bathe and partake of a meal. Whatever is left of the candles is used to remember the dead at regular prayer meetings.

A remembrance ceremony, attended by friends and relatives, is held for the dead on the seventh day after his death. Seven candles are lit and a prayer is said to the guardian angel to intercede with god for the forgiveness of the sins of the dead person. The sect members believe that there is torment after death for the sinful. Even if a soul goes to heaven, this does not mean it is completely pure. A soul in heaven can go down to hell; but it may later free itself and rise once more to heaven. Therefore, the survivors pray to god that the dead person may not be in torment. Lastly, a fortieth day memorial ceremony is held for the deceased in the prayer grove. If the family so desires, and is able to afford it, additional memorial ceremonies may be held in the grove, and a sacrifice made, on the first, third, and seventh anniversaries of the death of a person.

THE SECT AS A NATIVISTIC MOVEMENT

Like so many other field and document-based studies of acculturation, the above report was an essentially descriptive account of the rise of a religion, its course over one or two generations, and of the details of its beliefs and practices. At the start of the movement, the Cheremis people had been exposed to the impact of three other cultures: for at least eleven centuries, they had been in intimate contact with the Volga Bulgars; in 1236, they were subjugated by the Mohammedan Tatars, and the latter also had profound effects upon their culture over their six centuries of contact.[5] And, finally, in the thirteenth to fifteenth centuries, the Moscovian state began the conquest and gradual assimilation of the Cheremis tribes, who were rapidly being encircled by Russian—and hence Christian—landowner and peasant colonization. The Cheremis, prior to their subjugation by Moscow, clung to a seminomadic clan existence of hunting and trapping, as shown, for example, by their original payment of tribute to Moscow in the fur products of their hunting. By the fifteenth and sixteenth centuries, they began, however, to adopt a settled mode of life and agriculture. After the fall of Kazan, on October 2, 1552, their adaptation steadily increased in intensity, though it was not until Elizabeths' twenty years' reign (1741–1761), that some behavior patterns and inner values of Christianity found a certain degree of permanent acceptance among them.[6]

Our first task was to disentangle, insofar as still identifiable, what L. P. Mair called the "zero point of what can be discovered of the independent native system," [7] the pagan base of Cheremis religious life, with its polytheistic outlook and emphasis upon animal sacrifice.

By contrast, we next attempted to describe the religious culture of those Cheremis whose outlook is, superficially, at least, monotheistic, and who practice

[5] Cf. the following remarks by Vernadsky: "Whatever the ethnic origin of the tribes populating Mongolia in the twelfth century, they all were similar in their way of life and social organization and thus may be said to have belonged to the same cultural sphere. There was no generic name at that time, however, to denote the totality of these tribes and clans. The name Mongol originally referred to only one small tribe. That tribe came to prominence early in the 12th century, but in the middle of the century was defeated by its neighbors, the Tatars, and all but disintegrated. The Tatars then became in their turn one of the leading tribes in Mongolia" (pp. 11–12). "In religious belief the forest tribes were essentially shamanists; the steppe people, although influenced by shamanism, were primarily worshippers of the Sky. . ." (p. 13). The "Mongols" didn't interfere with the religion of their subjects. It was stated in the Great Yasa that Chingis-Khan "ordered that all religions were to be respected and that no preference was to be shown to any of them" (quoted on p. 102). In 1313, with the enthronement of Özbäg, "Islam became the official religion at the khan's court and gradually was adopted by most of the khan's Mongol and Turkish subjects. The conversion proved final this time" (p. 195). On the "Mongol" impact on spiritual life in Russia, see also Section 5, Chapter 5, and passim, in Vernadsky.

[6] The classic account in Russian literature is S. T. Aksakoff's Family History, first published in 1846. This remarkable work depicts with vivid charm the cultural contacts between the Russian settlers in the region of Ufa with the Finno-Ugric and Turkic speaking indigenous population during the reign of the Empress Catherine (1762–96).

[7] Mair, in Beals, p. 631.

baptism—in other words, of those members of the group who have successfully combined into a more or less harmonious whole portions of their original culture with traits of Russo-Christian provenience. As D. Mackenzie Wallace, a Western traveler in these regions in the 1870's observed, contact between the Russian peasantry and what he called "the pagan Finns . . . naturally led to a curious blending of the two religions. . . ." Their "simple-minded eclecticism often produces a singular mixture of Christianity and paganism. . . . Thus a Tscheremiss, on one occasion, in consequence of a serious illness, sacrificed a young foal to Our Lady of Kazan!" This he explains, "without taking into consideration the inherent superiority of Christianity over all forms of paganism," by the fact that peoples like the Cheremis "had no organized priesthood, and consequently never offered a systematic opposition to the new faith; the Russians, on the contrary, had a regular hierarchy closely allied to the civil administration . . . and some of the police-officers vied with the ecclesiastical officials in the work of making converts. . . . The ecclesiastical authorities were extremely moderate in their demands. They insisted on no religious knowledge, and merely demanded that the converts should be baptized. As the converts failed to understand the spiritual significance of the ceremony, they commonly offered no resistance, so long as the immersion was performed in summer. So little repugnance, indeed, did they feel, that on some occasions, when a small reward was given to those who consented, some of the new converts wished the ceremony to be repeated several times." [8]

The forces of acculturation finally resulted in a contra-acculturative movement,[9] the rise and spread of the reactionary *kugu sorta* sect. As Kluckhohn remarked, ". . . in psychological language the generalization is that human beings are so constituted that, particularly under conditions of extreme stress, they will often react in roughly similar ways to the same pressures. Nativistic movements constitute a case. . . . Details vary widely in accord with the pre-existing cultures, but the broad patterns are very much alike." [10] The *kugu sorta* movement is no exception to this generalization, but it behooves us to inquire now somewhat more closely into the specific cultural conditions and processes involved, and then to assign this sect a place in the typology of nativistic movements at large.

"For years it has been the custom for most anthropologists," wrote W. W. Hill in 1944, "to revert to economic determinism for an explanation of messianic phenomena." [11] Now it cannot be denied that, in explaining the development and

---

[8] Wallace, pp. 154–56. Wallace, who later became a famous newspaper correspondent, remained in Russia from 1870 to 1875, in a private capacity. His book, first published in 1877, served for many years as a standard authority in the west on pre-revolutionary Russia. For an interesting parallel in America of converting natives by bribery, see Kelly, p. 65: the Navaho "had only allowed water to be 'thrown upon' their children because the parents who brought children were rewarded with gifts of hoes and picks."

[9] "A fresh vision of a moral order," as Redfield so elegantly phrases it (p. 81).

[10] Kluckhohn, p. 514.

[11] W. W. Hill, p. 523.

growth of the *kugu sorta* sect, economic factors must weigh very heavily. In the 1860's, it will be remembered, the peasants of Russia achieved emancipation from serfdom; but they had to pay exorbitant prices to their landlords for both land recently purchased and holdings previously allotted. It was just in the decade in which the religious movement in question gained impetus that "land crowding" in the village became extreme. The Soviet economist P. I. Lyashchenko summarized the situation as follows:

> During 1880–1890, in an atmosphere of general political reaction and a fear of revolutionary activity by the peasantry, the privileged nobility undertook new pressures with a view to strengthening its social-political hegemony and, above all, its enslaving financial power over the peasantry. In the late eighties there began a long period of a policy of increased official protection of the nobility and its "trusteeship" over the peasantry. The establishment of "firm rule" by the rural officials, the raising of legal class barriers against the peasantry, the limitations upon family subdivisions . . . the restriction of communal redistribution of land . . . the transformation of the peasants allotted property into an "inalienable class fund" by prohibiting the alienation or mortgaging of peasant allotments . . . the prohibition and limitation of resettlement by the peasants in the interest of retaining locally a labor supply for the landowners . . . these were the chief measures adopted during this dark era of aristocratic reaction.[12]

In 1889, for example, under the immediate stimulus of increase in taxation, Cheremis peasants from four volosts of the Uržum district revolted. Their rebellion was soon crushed, hundreds of them were flogged, and their property sold at auction for a mere trifle to Cheremis landowners.

This was the economic milieu in which the *kugu sorta* doctrines flourished. Members of the sect experienced a particularly severe economic crisis, since they were punished by the government for their participation by being completely prevented from owning land and thus forced to turn peddlers, hired hands, and laborers in commercial enterprises. Their response to the industrial expansion in the last decades of the century was unmistakably economic in form, if not in rationalization. Their hostility to technical advances was "explained" by their attempts to live as their ancestors did; their refusal to wear commercially manufactured clothing—or, indeed, to use any factory-produced goods (not even matches)— by their desire to use only such objects as were used by their ancestors in olden times; and their lack of money—since it neither feeds nor clothes a person—was turned into a virtue. Since the industrial upsurge of the 1890's was due in large measure to the expansion of railway building, sect members tore up tracks passing through their territory, and identified the railways—calling them "fire serpents"— with one of the most dreaded demons of the Cheremis pantheon, a will-o'-the-wisp named *buber,* which must be destroyed by true believers.

[12] Lyashchenko, p. 471.

While it thus seems clear that economic considerations must loom prominently in any realistic interpretation of this particular nativistic movement, these cannot be thought of as uniquely determining the inception and growth of the sect, as is shown, for instance, by the fact that the successful peasant revolt of 1917 coincided not with its decline, but, quite the contrary, with its extraordinary blossoming. Social factors must be given at least equal weight, for, as Barber emphasized, "deprivation may arise from the destruction not only of physical objects but also of sociocultural activities." The essential function of the sect that appeared in reaction was then "to proclaim a *stable order,* one which will define the ends of action . . . [and whose] doctrines describe men's former life, meaningful and satisfactory." [13]

The cult of the Big Candle, in response to merciless exploitation on the part of the dominant Russians, and in the face of the frustrations attendant upon rapid social change—in particular, the ever increasingly severe disruption of the patterns of Cheremis family life—crystallized (rather like the Peyote movement than like the Ghost Dance) around passive acceptance and peaceful resignation.[14] Thus, for example, members of the sect resisted the military service required of them by their Russian masters, rationalizing this in terms of their horror of killing, but acting only to the extent of a public burial, in 1907, of all weapons at hand, accompanying their action by prayer to god that he annihilate these weapons.

As Linton showed, "what really happens in all nativistic movements is that certain current or remembered elements of culture are selected for emphasis and given symbolic value," and "the more distinctive such elements are with respect to other cultures with which the society is in contact, the greater their potential value as symbols of the society's unique character." [15] The values most prominently stressed in *kugu sorta* doctrine are, in the first place, those which favor social cohesion [16] and, in the second place, those which condemn the violence of the larger society surrounding them.

Social cohesion is achieved, in the more general sense, by the secretly, and

---

[13] Barber, p. 665.

[14] Toynbee, in whose unusual terminology the Cheremis would be classed among the internal proletariat of our modern Western society, asks whether "we find the two veins of violence and gentleness reappearing in our Western internal proletariat's reaction to its ordeal" (p. 398), and finds, by and large, manifestations of the militant temper in the ascendant.

[15] Linton, p. 232.

[16] "The standard work on Russian geography published before the First World War said about the Mari, or, as they used to be called, Cheremiss: 'One meets but seldom a nationality which notwithstanding its low level of development has such a fully crystallized national self-consciousness and which is so much attached to its national existence.'" Quoted by Kolarz, p. 51, from *Rossiya, Polnoye geograficheskoye opisanie nashego otechestva* [=*Russia, Full Geographical Description of Our Homeland*], vol. 5, p. 207 (St. Petersburg, 1914).

therefore uniquely, shared knowledge and experience on the part of all members of the sect (the dietary laws, for example) which set them off not only from the surrounding foreign population, but, perhaps equally significant, from their fellow-Cheremis who, on the one hand, have not yet emerged from the darkness of paganism and animal sacrifice and who, on the other, have embraced Christianity and thus given up their identity as a distinctive group. Like the Vailala Madness of Papua, the *kugu sorta* doctrine rejected certain of their own key rituals from earlier times as much as certain foreign traits. Social cohesion is achieved, in the more specific sense, by virtue of certain ethical mandates, the most important of which assert that all men are brothers and must be loved and helped in every way possible; which encourage, in addition to love and good works, such virtues as peaceful behavior, harmony, tolerance, hospitality toward all comers, and diligence for the common good. Violence is explicitly condemned and the practice of restraint and self-discipline in the face of adversity fostered. The animal sacrifice so characteristic of the pagan Cheremis is abandoned with abhorrence. The rule of earthly leaders is rejected. Action is replaced by prayer. Believers must imitate the life-ways of their ancestors until the arrival of the millenium—the tenth and next of the seventeen epochs—almost at hand, when the earth will be inhabited only by sect members, saved by clinging to their sacred trees. The Big Candle stands as the central, shining symbol of the people's unity. The huge candle—product of the labors of the society they consider the most perfect one of all, that of the living bees—is molded into one from the slender, individual contributions of each participant, lovingly hand-produced by the men of the sect, pointing the way to heaven in the midst of ceremony and prayer.

It remains to ask where the *kugu sorta* sect belongs in Linton's illuminating multi-dimensional scheme of nativistic movements in general. In terms of Linton's first distinction—there are attempts, always conscious and organized, on the part of the members of a society either to revive or to perpetuate selected aspects of its culture—it is quite clear that the Cheremis movement tends far more towards perpetuative than towards revivalistic nativism. That their efforts were conscious and organized is certain, for it is known that it was at a meeting of sect members, in 1878, that the reformed wing, which then and there rejected the pagan custom of animal sacrifice, deliberately chose to go its separate way. Among the culture traits which they selected for perpetuation might be mentioned, for example, the distinctive Cheremis cult of the dead, a well-defined and elaborate complex of general and individual memorial feasts, funeral and remembrance ceremonies. In spite of the fact that sect members explicitly claim to be teaching the beliefs of their forefathers, their sub-culture is actually an amalgam of old pagan beliefs which, though they underwent some modifications, never did disappear, plus Christian and Mohammedan traits.[17]

[17] While it is less easy to demonstrate the presence of Buddhist traits, there are some interesting parallels that could be drawn. It will be recalled that Kubilay was converted to

Linton's second feature contrasts nativism which is essentially magical with nativism which tends towards the rational. In this sense, the Cheremis sect is rational rather than magical, for it does not lean very heavily on the supernatural, or upon a magical formula. On the contrary, it relies mainly on perfectly rational mandates, such as good works and hard work. These are essentially realistic choices, for it is not impossible, even under current conditions, for such mandates to be carried out.

In Linton's fourfold typology, then, the *kugu sorta* movement is a relatively pure instance of perpetuative-rational nativism. (In his other typology of possible situations for contact groups, the Cheremis belong, with respect to the Russians, under the category of dominated but superior, a situation which may be so universal that this classification, while true, is probably trivial.)

In passing, it may be worth noting that, in addition to *kugu sorta,* there was also another form of national opposition to Communism. This took shape among Cheremis intellectuals who chose to adhere to Pan-Finnic ideas and to be more inclined to look to bourgeois Helsinki than to proletarian Moscow for cultural guidance. "Finnish bourgeois culture" appeared to them desirable as a pattern for the cultural revival of the Cheremis and their other sister Finno-Ugric peoples of the Soviet Union. The emergence of these Pan-Finnic ideas is the more interesting since the Cheremis had been for some twelve centuries under Turkic and Slavic influences, and shows that the *kugu sorta* movement was merely one of several alternative responses at the disposal of this society, thus bearing out Barber's theory.

It was just fifteen years ago that Herskovits called for research in the field of acculturation, pointing out that "an entire series of problems directed toward a similar end is available for study in the contacts of the primitive tribes of the U. S. S. R. with the European modes of life of the Russians" [18]—an opportunity which has as yet not been, for it could perhaps not properly be, explored. And yet it is worth repeating, with Linton, that the study of nativistic movements has ceased to be a matter of purely academic interest, and this is particularly true in this area swarming with multifarious "imperialized folk"—to use Redfield's apt expression [19]—who came to be dominated by both the political rule and the social and economic exploitation of Russian civilization.

Buddhism and that the lama Pagspa of Tibet extended his blessing to the Yuan—the reigning Mongol—dynasty in China.

[18] Herskovits, p. 123, n. 1.

[19] Redfield, p. 45.

APPENDICES

APPENDIX A. ETYMOLOGICAL NOTE ON RUSSIAN LOAN WORDS IN CHEREMIS RELIGIOUS TERMINOLOGY. By Felix J. Oinas

IN this list the Cheremis words are given in the form in which they appear in various sources; their grammatical characterization is not included in the translation. The transcription is phonemic; to this end, the transcription of some sources has been simplified. The Russian equivalents are in square brackets. Cross references to Part One of this volume are in parentheses after the translation.

ad, adə (Sz.), *adəškə* (Bk 146.), *at* (R. Wju 253.), *xat* (R.) [ad] 'hell'; *xadəškə keäš* (R.) 'to die out of grace'

adam (Bj 143.) [Adam] 'Adam'

amen (P 1948.), *amin* (P 1948. Sz.), *amin'* (Be 705. J.) [amin'] 'amen'

amin'itlat, amin'itlen (Bu 47, 45.) 'to cross oneself (lit. to say amen)' [cf. amin' 'amen']

banjuška [Vanjushka] (man's name); *oš-buj-banjuška* (S 149.) 'blond Vańuška' (A.97.)

basli [Vasili] (man's name); *basli-kuba, basli-kuguza* (H 1926.189.) 'Vasili old woman,' 'Vasili old man' (A.38.3.)

batuška, batuško (L 20, 3.), *paička* (R.) [batjushka] 'father (priest)'

bečern'a (Sz.), *bečern'ä* (R.) [vechernja] 'evening service'

bedən (H 1926.195.) [vedun] 'sorcerer' (D.2.3.)

bedən' (V.) [vedun'ja] 'witch'

benčaijen (L 39.), *benčajem* (Sz.), *benčäem* (V.), *benčäjäš* (Bk 110.), *b'enčajalt* (Sz.), *menčajem* (V.) [venchat' (sja)] 'to marry; get married (in church)'

bera (J. Sz. V.), *berä* (R.), *ber'a, b'era* (Sz.) [vera] 'faith, belief, religion'; *marij bera* (V.) 'adherent of the Mari (Cheremis) religion'; *rušla bera marij* (V.) 'adherent of the Christian religion'

berbənəj (Wk 5.) [verbnoe (voskresen'e)] 'Palm Sunday'

bijnamat, bijnamate (Sz.), *binamat* (J. Sz.), *binamato* (Sz.), *bujnamat* (R.), *bujnomat* (Sz.) 'guilty; sinful' [vinovat(yi) 'guilty']

bjes (Sz.) [bes] 'devil' (A.7.)

blagobešen'je (J.), *blagobešən kecə* (Wj 11.), *plašin* (Wk 6.) [blagoveshchenie] 'the Annunciation, Lady-day'

blagodat (Sz.) [blagodat'] 'grace'

blagoslabi (L 43.), *blagoslobajaš* (R.), *blagoslobajem* (Sz.), *blagoslobajen* (Bk 118.), *blagoslobi* (R.), *loslobitlə* (Bu 328.) [blagoslovit'] 'to bless'

blagoslobenja (Sz.) [blagoslovenie] 'blessing'

bolxbə (Sz.) [volkhv] 'cláirvoyant, soothsayer'

bolšennəj sila (Bk 111.) [cf. bol'shaja sila] 'greater power'

bol'a [volja] 'will'; *jəmən-bol'a* (R.) 'God's will'

338

bošemnikše (L 61.) [? volshebnitsa] 'sorceress, witch'

božaš (R.) [bozhit'sja] 'to swear (in God's name)'

b'enčajamə tajn- (Sz.) [cf. tainstvo venchanija] 'marriage sacrament'

cäšökn'ä (V.), *cäšomn'a* (R.), *časamla* (V.), *časanik* (Sz.) [chasovnya] 'chapel'

cerka, cerkba (Sz.), *cerke* (B 25. V.), *cerkə* (R. W 1923.112.), *cerkəš* (B 32. Bj 166.), *c'erke* (Sz.), *čerke* (P 1948. Sz. V.), *čerkeš* (Bu 46.), *čerkə* (W 1923.112.), *čerkiške* (L 39.), *čer'ke* (J.) [tserkov'] 'church'; *cerkəbičə* (R.) 'cemetery'; *cerkəšk keäš* (R.) 'to go to church'; *čerkan agulvško* (L 43.) 'village with a church'; *čerkan jaləštə* (Bu 257.) id.

čort (Bk 47. J. R.) [chort] 'devil, deuce' (A.15.) ; *čort-pört* (Bk 110.) 'devil's house'

čurpan [churban 'stump']; *čurpan-širt* (S 160.) 'stump devil' (A.15.1.)

diabol (Sz.), *d'abəl* (J.), *jabəl* (R. Sz. V.) 'devil; prankish or playful person' (A.18.) [d'javol 'devil']

duxobnaj (Sz.) 'will, testament,' *tuxobnəj* (R.) 'clergyman' [dukhovnaja 'will,' dukhovnoe litso 'priest']

dusa (Sz.) [dusha] 'soul'

əres (Sz. V.), *kəres* (P 1948.), *kres* (J. Sz.), *krest* (Sz.), *kreste* (B 25. V.), *krestə* (R.), *krestəm* (Bj 190. Bk 28.), *krestn* (L 59.), *kres'* (V.), *kres'e* (Sz.), *res* (Sz. V.), *rese* (Sz.) [krest] 'cross'; *kolešedem-grestə* (R.) 'grave-cross'; *krestel* (R.), *šian əres-kəl* (Wu 38.) 'cross worn around the neck by the Orthodox'

eresl (Sz.), *əreslem, kreslem* (V.), *o[k] kreslən* (B 67.), *krestaltam, krestem* (V.), *krestäš* (R.), *krestät-ät* (Bk 72.), *krest'it'staš* (J.), *kres'ta* (Bu 114.), *kr'estl-* (Sz.) [krestit' (sja)] 'to baptize, christen; to cross oneself'

gospodə (R.), *gospodi, gospod'i* (L 15, 43.) [gospodi] 'Oh, Lord!'

gaspot' (J.), *gospod'* (Sz.), *ospod'* (Sz.) [gospod'] 'God, the Lord'

ikon (R.), *ikona* (J.), *ikončəm* (Bk 73.) [ikona] 'icon'

ilin-gečə (Wu 13.), *il'an kece* (B 68.), *il'jin-geče* (J.), *il'jin kečə* (Bk 28.) [Il'in den'] 'St. Elijah's day'

il'ša [Il'ja] 'Elijah'; *il'ša-jumo* (S 191.) 'Elijah god' (A.26.9.)

ispobedaš (Sz.) [ispovedat'] 'to confess'

israjlski narot, izrajlski narot (R.) [izrail'skii narod] 'Israelites'

istukan (Sz.) [istukan] 'idol'

izuš kristos (Wt 153.) [Izus Khristos] 'Jesus Christ'

jabəlgən (V.) adj. 'playful, frolicsome' [cf. d'javol 'devil']

jačok (Sz. V.), *ječok* (V.), *tiäčok* (R. V.) [d'jachok] 'sexton'

jakən (V.), *jäkən* (Bk 260, R.) [d'jakon] 'deacon'

jebam (Bj 143.) [Eva] 'Eve'

jeret'ək (R.) [eretik] 'heretic'

jerəs (R.) [eres'] 'heresy'

judeješ (R.) [iudei] 'Judaic people'

jürje . . . gečə (Wk 8.) [Jur'ev den'] 'St. George's day'

kadən (Bk 99.), *kajilä* (R.) [kadilo] 'censer'

keldjä (R.) [kel'ja] 'monastic cell'

kibot (R. Sz.) [kivot] 'ark for holy objects; ark of the covenant' *kladbišä* (R.), *klanpišša* (T. 52.), *klatbišä* (R.) [kladbishche] 'cemetery'; *kladbišäškə cikäš* (R.) 'to bury'

klotkam (B 31. Bj 159.), *koladka* (Sz.), *kolatka* (Häm. 1930a. 133. Sz. V.), *kolatkam* (Be 50. Wu 48.), *kolotka* (H 1926.16. Sz. W 1923.64.) [kolodka] 'coffin'; *mügär-kolatka* (V.) id.

kobejäš (R.) [govet'] 'to prepare for the communion; to fast'

koldun (B 18. Bk 231. Bu 155.) [koldun] 'wizard, sorcerer' (D.2.1.)

kolokolnəm (Bk 110) [kolokol'nja] 'bell tower, belfry'

kres, krest, etc., see *əres*

kres-ačažə (Wu 37.), *kresm[e] at'až, kresm[e] at'aže* (B 36, 38.), *kres'-ačam* (Bu 78.) [krestnyi] 'godfather'

kresm[e] abaž[e] (B 36.), *kres'-aba* (Bu 78.) [krestnaja] 'godmother'

kres'n'ik ergəžə (Bu 81.) [krestnik] 'god-child'

kreščenja (Sz.), *krešen'e* (J. V.), *krešen'e keče* (V.), *krešen'elan* (L 32.), *krešen'jä* (Bk 28.), *krešen'jä gečə* (Bk 28. Wk 5.) [kreshchenie] 'baptism, christening; Epiphany'

krešən (V.) [kreshchenyi] 'baptized'

kriləs (R.) [kliros] 'choir, gallery (in the Russian church)'

kristos (Bj 141.), *xristos* (R.) [Khristos] 'Christ'; see also *izus kristos; xristos ələžən* (R.) 'Christ has arisen!'

korop (R.), *kropšəm* (Bk 122.) [grob] 'coffin'; *koropmastar* (R.) 'coffin maker'

kum (Bu 78. J. R.), *kuma* (J. R. Sz.) [kum, kuma] 'godfather, godmother'; *kumäbä* (R.) 'godmother'; *kumät'ä* (R.) 'godfather'

xerubiməm (Bu 47.) 'cherub (a prayer)' [kheruvim 'cherub']

xuda (Bk 28.), *uda* (B 67.) [khudo] 'the evil one, the devil'

xuda sila (Bk 47.) [khudaja sila] 'the evil power' (J.4.)

ladən (Bk 99. R.) [ladan] 'incense'; *ladən-donə tetəräš* (R.) 'to spread incense'; *ladənšekšəm əštäs* (R.) id.

lampat (Sz.) 'lamp, lantern' [lampada 'icon-lamp']

lešak (Bu 37.), *l'ešak* (B 11. Bj 187.) [leshak] 'wood spirit' (A.43.)

l'eši (R.) [leshii] 'wood spirit (swear-word)' (A.11.)

makar [Makar] (man's name); *makar-keremet* (S 149.) 'Makar-keremet' (A.44.)

manak (J. R. Sz. V.) [monakh] 'monk, friar'; *manakeš keäš* (R.) 'to become a monk, to enter a monastery'; *šapki-manak* (V.) 'neither a monk nor a layman'

manastər (J. V.), *monastir* (R. V.), *monaser* (Sz.), *monastirəškə* (Bk 114.) [monastyr] 'cloister, monastery, nunnery'; *ədərämäš-mənastir* (R.) 'nunnery'; *püergə-mənastir* (R.) 'monastery'

manašən'kə (R.), *manaška* (J.) [monashenka, monashka] 'nun'

mer, mir [mir 'world']; *mer-jumə* (Wu 27.), *mer-jumo* (H 1926.64, S 191.) 'world god' (A.26.27.); *mer kugo jumo* (V.) 'great god of the world'; *mer küsö* (H 1926.104. V.), *mer-küsotə* (H 1926.104.) 'sacrificial grove for several villages; the sacrificial festival' (B.9.; E.2.1.); *mer-küsö kumaltəš* (V.) 'public prayer conducted by several villages in June'; *mir-kumaltəš* (P 1948.) 'big sacrificial festival; grove where the festival is held' (B.9.; E.2.1.)

mən'inik (R.) [imeninnik] 'the one whose name-day it is'

mətar (Sz.) [mytar'] bibl. 'publican'

mikolə gece (B 65.), *mikolo, mikolo-keče* (V.) [Nikolin den'] 'Michaelmas'

mikola-jumə (H 1926.141.) 'Michael god' (A.26.26.)

mogilä (R.) [mogila] 'grave'; *mogilä kapajəšə* (R.) 'grave-digger'

molebən (Sz.) [moleben] 'public prayer'

molitbu (R. Sz.), *molitbum* (Bu 46.), *molitbä* (Bk 114.), *mol'itba* (J.) [molitva] 'prayer'

nadər (H 1926.166. Sz. V.) [nadar] 'money for offering' (C.7.3.)

naloj (R.) [analoi] 'lectern (in the Orthodox church)'

obdokim keče, obdokin keče (V.), *obdoxi gečə* (Wk 7.) [den' Evdokii] 'Eudocia's day'

obden'a (Sz.), *obetn'ä* (R.) [obednja] 'noon mass'

okna [okno 'window']; *okna-sakčə* (H 1926.94) 'window angel' (A.84.16.)

oltar (Sz.) [altar'] 'altar'

paravoj [parovoi adj. 'steam']; *paravoj-ia* (H 1926.53) 'ship devil' (A.16.3.)

pasxa (Sz.) [paskha] 'Easter'

petro-gečə (Wk 243.), *petro kečəleč* (Be 709.), *petrof* (J.), *petrop* (W 1923.81.), *pötren kece* (B 59.) [Petrov den'] 'St. Peter's day'

pərcäš (R.), *pričaš, pričašč, pričašlək* (Sz.) [prichastie] 'communion, sacrament'; *pərcäšəm podəlaš* (R.) 'to go to Holy Communion'

pərcäšäjäš (R.), *pričašajaš, pričašajektak* (Sz.) [prichashchat'(sja)] to 'administer or to receive Holy Communion'

persak (P 1948. V.), *pric'aga* (Sz.), *pričak* (V.), *prisaka* (Sz.), *prisäk* (V.), *pris'agm* (L 32.), *pris'aka* (Sz.) [prisjaga] 'oath'

pobedäjäš, pobedäjaktäš (R.) [ispovedovat'(sja)] 'to confess one's sins'

pokro (B 57. Bk 41. Sz. V.), *pokro-gece* (B 57.), *pokro-geče* (J.), *poxro* (R. V. W 1923.84.), *poxro-gečə* (Wk 4.), *poxrogəc* (Wk 5.) [pokrov] 'feast of the intercession of the Holy Virgin'; *pokro pajrem* (Sz.) id.

pokronnoj listm (L 56.) [pokhoronnyi list] 'death-certificate'

pomən'ga (R.) 'celebration in memory of someone dead' [pominki 'wake']

pomiluj (L 15.) [pomilui] 'have mercy'

ponomar (Sz.) [ponomar'] 'sexton, sacristan'

pop (B 32. Bj 167. Bk 118. Bu 101. J. L 1. Sz. W 1923.84) [pop] 'priest, pope'; *kogo bopet* (Bk 115.) 'high priest'; *pelbop* (R.), *pelpop* (V.) 'deacon'; *pop solaštəšə* (Bk 54.) 'village with a church'; *samoj kogo popšə* (Bk 114.) 'highest priest'

post (R. Sz.) [post] 'fast, fasting'; *postəm ajaš* (R.) 'to celebrate a fast, to fast'

postaš (Sz.) [postit'sja] 'to fast, keep the fast'

prazdnik (Sz.), *praznek* (Bk 84. R. Wk 193.), *praznəkem* (Bk 266.), *praznəket* (B 33.) [prazdnik] 'holiday, feast'; *prazdnekəm ajaš* (R.) 'to celebrate a festival'

prazdniklem (Sz.) 'to celebrate a holiday' [cf. prazdnik 'holiday, feast']

prestol (Sz.) [prestol] 'throne, altar'

prixot-kəcən (Bk 60.) [prikhod] 'parish'

proročica (Sz.) [prorochitsa] 'prophetess'

proročestbobajem (Sz.) [prorochestvovat'] 'to prophesy'

prorok (J. Sz.) [prorok] 'prophet'

radin'ťa (Wu 56.), *räden'iцə geцə* (Wj 11.) [radonitsa] 'festival, on Tuesday after Quasimodo' (B.12.)

raj (J. Sz.), *rajəšt* (Bk 145.), *rajəštə* (Wju 111.) [rai] 'paradise, heaven'

rašta (Sz.) [rozhdestvo] 'Christmas'

rešetka (P 1948.) 'fence around a grave' (reshetka 'railing, grating']

ruš [cf. russkii] 'Russian'; *rušärn'ä* (R. V.) 'Sunday'

saba (W 1923.88) [savva] 'Sabbath; Sunday, Lord's day'

sbaga-bata (Häm. 1930a.86.) 'bride's maid, "woman match-maker" ' [svakha 'match-maker']

sbatajjen, sbatajšna (L 39.) [svatat' (sja)] 'to seek in marriage, woo'

sbatitel, suatlanaš (Sz.) [svjatit'] 'to consecrate'

sbätoj (Sz.), *sbätöj* (R.), *sb'atoj* (J.), *sb'etoj, suat* (Sz.) [svjatoi] 'holy, saint'; *sbätöj šüləš* (R.) 'Holy Ghost'; *sbätöjät'äbälä* (R.) 'the saints'

sbätöj-dux (R.) [svjatoi dukh] 'Holy Ghost'

sbet [svet 'world']; *be[s] sbetəš* (B 31.), *bes sbetəšte* (Bj 167.) [tot svet] 'the other world, the life to come'

semək (B 9. J. P 209. R. Sz. V.), *semik, s'emek* (Sz.) [semik] 'festival on the 7th Thursday after Easter' (B.13.)

smört (Bj 158. R.) [smert'] 'death'

sotana (B 96.), *sotona* (B 96. Sz.) [satana] 'Satan' (A.75.) ; *kogo sotonažə* (Bk 147.) 'great Satan'; *samoj kogo sotonalan* (Bk 147.) 'greatest Satan'; *sotona-koba* (B 9.) 'Satan-woman'; *sotana-kuguza* (B 10.) 'Satan-man'

spas (J.) [spas] 'a holiday'; *kogo-spas kečə* (Wk 4.) 'the Assumption of Mary'; *spaš jumo* (V.) 'savior god' (A.26.35.)

strastnoj (Wk 5.) [strastnaja] 'Holy Week'

suatən adv. (Sz.) [svjato] 'piously'

sut [sud 'court of law, court']; *jəmən sut-tenə* (Wju 111.) 'before God's judgment'

svaga batə, see *sbaga batə*

tajn, tajnstbo (Sz.) [taina, tainstvo] 'sacrament'; see also *b'enčajamə tajn-*

truška (B 38.) [druzhka] 'best-man'; *izi-truška* (Häm. 1930a.86.) 'little best-man' (B.17.3.) ;*kugu-truška* (Häm. 1930a.86.) 'big best-man' (B.17.3.) ; *üdər-truška* (Häm. 1930a.88.) 'bride's best-man' (B.17.4.)

tux (R.) [dukh] 'spirit'; *tuxat* (R.) 'by God'

üstel (H 1926.119.) 'fresh linden branches laid on the ground, on which the offering-breads are placed' [stol 'table'] (F.22.) ; *kolšə üstel* (H 1926.119.) 'a small one-legged table, on which the feast for the dead is spread' (B.23.3.)

van'uška, see *banjuška*

zabet (R. Sz.) [zavet] 'covenant, testament, will'; *toštə-zabet* (R.) 'Old Testament'

zakon [zakon] 'law'; *toštə zakon* (R.) 'Old Testament'

zapobed (Sz.) [zapoved'] 'commandment'

zautrən'a (R.), *zautr'en'a* (Sz.) [zautrenja] 'early mass, matins'

zbon'aš, -em (R.), *zbon'it'* (J.) 'to ring (the church bell)' [zvonit' 'to ring']

zloj-dux (R.) 'ghost' [zloi dukh 'evil spirit']

žerətbä (R.), *žertba* (J. Sz.) [zhertva] 'sacrifice'

žertbennika (Sz.) [zhertvennik] 'sacrificial altar'
žertəbajaš (R.), *žertəbət'staš* (J.) [zhertvovat'] 'to sacrifice'
žezəl (R.) [zhezl] '(bishop's) crozier'

APPENDIX B: GAZETTEER

Aganur (town)—56°38′N, 49°10′E.

Apšat-jal—app. same as Balayev.

Arino (town)—56°22′N, 48°50′E.

Asli-Kul (lake)—54°20′N, 56°35′E.

Balayev (mill)—55°23′N, 55°37′E.

Bashkir A.S.S.R.—app. 51°35′–56°30′N, 53°10′–60°E; center app. Ufa.

Belaya River—882 mi. long; rises in Ural Mts.; flows generally SW then NW into Kama River at 55°54′N, 53°33′E.

Bir River—app. 50 mi. long; flows generally SW then NW into the Belaya River at 55°29′N, 55°30′E.

Birsk (city)—55°25′N, 55°32′E.

Birsk (city district)—area surrounding city of Birsk, corresponds roughly to administrative division of township; formerly in north central Ufa government district (which see), now in north central Bashkir A.S.S.R.

Bol'shaya Amzya River—app. 30 mi. long; flows E into Tulva River at 57°2′N, 55°36′E; Tulva flows N into Kama River at 57°18′N, 55°33′E.

Bol'shaya Kokshaga (river)—135 mi. long; rises 25 mi. NW of Yaransk; flows generally S into Volga at 56°8′N, 47°47′E.

Buraveyo (town)—55°50′N, 55°25′E.

Buy River—app. 65 mi. long; flows generally WSW into Kama River at 56°13′N, 54°12′E.

Bystry Tanyp River—app. 95 mi. long; flows generally WSW into Belaya River at 55°42′N, 54°34′E.

Cheboksary (city)—56°9′N, 47°14′E.

Chembulatova (town)—exact location unknown.

Cherlak (town)—55°43′N, 54°42′E, ca. 39 mi. WNW (305°) of Birsk, ca. 7 mi. N of the Belaya River, on the left bank of its tributary stream, the Bystry Tanyp.

Chkalovsk (city)—formerly called Vasileva Sloboda (until 1927) and Vasilevo (1927–37); 56°47′N, 43°15′E.

Churajeva—see Churakayevo.

Churakayevo (town)—55°25′N, 53°50′E.

Elnet River—see Yelnet River.

Ener-Muchash (town)—56°N, 49°11′E.

Galich (city)—58°21′N, 42°21′E.

Gor'kiy (city)—56°20′N, 44°E; also center of oblast of same name.

Kama River—1,262 mi. long; rises in central Urals; flows generally SW into Volga River at 55°10′N, 49°20′E.

Kandry-Kul (lake)—54°30′N, 56°5′E.

Kazan (city)—55°47′N, 49°7′E.

Kazan (government district)—administrative division under the Empire, extended from
app. 46°30'–52°E and 54°–57°N; in 1920 NW portion made into Mari Autonomous
Oblast (see Mari A.S.S.R.), remainder into Tatar A.S.S.R.

Kiebakova (town)—55°58'N, 55°E on Kiyabak River.

Kirov (city)—formerly Vyatka (1780–1934); 58°36'N, 49°41'E.

Kokshaga River—see Bol'shaya Kokshaga and Malaya Kokshaga.

Kokshayskoye (town)—56°9'N, 47°49'E.

Kostroma (city)—57°46'N, 40°56'E.

Koz'modem'yansk (city)—56°20'N, 46°35'E.

Krasnokokshaisk—see Yoshkar-Ola.

Krasnoufimsk (city)—56°37'N, 57°46'E.

Krasnoufimsk (city district)—area surrounding city of Krasnoufimsk, corresponds roughly
to administrative division of township; formerly located in extreme S of Perm government district (which see), now in SW Sverdlovsk Oblast.

Kubyan (town)—56°18'N, 49°23'E.

Leningrad—formerly St. Petersburg (1703–1914) and Petrograd (1914–1924);
59°57'N, 30°16'E.

Malaya Kokshaga (river)—app. 125 mi. long; rises app. 57°N, 48°15'E; flows generally
S into Volga at 56°7'N, 47°52'E.

Malmyzh (city)—56°30'N, 50°45'E.

Mari A.S.S.R.—app. 55°35'–57°20'N, 45°35'–50°15'E; center app. Yoshkar-Ola; first
formed as Mari Autonomous Oblast from Kazan government district in 1920, incorporated into Nizhegorod Territory 1929–36, made A.S.S.R. in 1936.

Mari Turek (town)—56°46'N, 49°36'E.

Mishkino (town)—55°28'N, 55°57'E.

Molotov (city)—formerly Perm (1791–1940); 58°N, 56°15'E.

Morki (town)—56°27'N, 48°59'E.

Moscow—55°50'N, 37°34'E.

Moskovo (town)—55°19'N, 55°6'E.

Nemda River—app. 75 mi. long; flows generally N into Vyatka‾River at 57°38'N,
49°3'E.

Nemda River (Urzhum area)—app. 45 mi. long; rises 57°33'N, 50°26'E; flows generally
S into Vyatka River at 57°3'N, 50°20'E.

Nizhegorod Territory—Nizhegorod contracted form of Nizhni Novgorod (now Gor'kiy),
former administrative division incorporating several present A.S.S.R.'s, remainder now
Gor'kiy Oblast.

Nizhni Novgorod—until 1932, name for Gor'kiy Oblast, which see.

Oka River—918 mi. long; rises app. 250 mi. SSW of Moscow; flows generally N then
NNE into Volga at Gor'kiy.

Perm—see Molotov.

Perm (government district)—administrative division under the Empire, extended from
app. 53°–65°E and 55°30'–62°N; changed to Ural Oblast (1923–34), then to
Sverdlovsk Oblast; in 1938 W section separated to form Perm (since 1940, Molotov)
Oblast.

Ruš-roda (town)—exact location unknown.

Saint Petersburg—see Leningrad.

Sanchursk (town)—56°57'N, 47°16'E.

Shor-Unzha (town)—56°27'N, 49°30'E; probably the Unzha mentioned in connection
with village of Morki, but it should be noted that there is an Unzha (58°1'N, 44°E)
on the Unzha River which flows into the Volga near the Yelnet River.

Staro-Kucherbayevo (town)—55°54'N, 54°51'E.

Staro-Kulchubajeva—see Staro-Kucherbajevo.

Stary Zeleny Dol (city)—55°51'N, 48°32'E.

Sverdlovsk (city)—56°50'N, 60°39'E.

Sviyaga River—245 mi. long; rises app. 53°35'N, 47°30'E; flows generally N, parallel
with Volga and then into Volga at 55°48'N, 48°47'E.

Tanyp River—upper tributary of Bystry Tanyp, which see.

Tatar A.S.S.R.—app. 54°–56°40'N, 47°20'–54°15'E; center app. Chistopol.

Toktay-Belyak (town)—56°53'N, 48°56'E.

Tsarevokokshaisk—see Yoshkar-Ola.

Tsarevokokshaisk (city district)—area surrounding city of Tsarevokokshaisk, corresponds
roughly to administrative division of township; formerly located in extreme N of
Kazan government district (which see), now as Yoshkar-Ola in Central Mari A.S.S.R.

Ufa (city)—54°44'N, 55°56'E.

Ufa (government district)—administrative division under the Empire, extended from
app. 52°–60°15'E and 52°45'–56°30'N; in 1919 became Bashkir A.S.S.R. except for
NW section, which was included in Tatar A.S.S.R.

Ufa River—599 mi. long; rises on N slope of S Urals; flows generally NW then SSW
into Belaya River below city of Ufa, at 54°41'N, 56°3'E.

Unsha—see Unzha.

Unzha—see Shor-Unzha.

Urzhum (city)—57°5'N, 50°E.

Urzhum (city district)—area surrounding city of Urzhum, corresponds roughly to administrative division of townships; formerly in S central Vyatka government district
(which see), now in S central Kirov Oblast.

Vasileva Sloboda—see Chkalovsk.

Vasilevo—see Chkalovsk.

Yelnet River—app. 50 mi. long; flows generally SE then NE into Volga River at
56°20'N, 46°28'E.

Volga River—2,290 mi. long; rises app. 200 mi. SE of Leningrad; flows generally E
then S into north Caspian Sea.

Vyatka (city)—see Kirov.

Vyatka (government district)—administrative division under the Empire, extended from
app. 46°30'–54°E and 55°45'–53°N; in 1929 incorporated into Nizhegorod Territory
(which see), made Kirov Oblast in 1936.

Vyatka River—849 mi. long; rises app. 120 mi. NW of Kirov; flows generally SE then
W and S into Kama River at 55°35'N, 51°32'E.

Yaransk (city)—57°15'N, 47°50'E.

Yaransk (city district)—area surrounding city of Yaransk, corresponds roughly to administrative division of township; formerly located in SW Vyatka government district (which see), now in SW Kirov Oblast.

Yelnet River—app. 50 mi. long; flows generally SE then NE into Volga River at 57°22′N, 42°52′E.

Yoshkar-Ola (city)—formerly Tsarevokokshaisk (until 1918) and Krasnokokshaisk (1918–29) 56°38′N, 47°55′E.

Yurino (town)—56°18′N, 46°15′E.

BIBLIOGRAPHY

SOURCES FOR THE TEXT [1]

AGAFONOV, N. J.
1901   "Aleksandra Andreevna Fuks," *Russkij Biograficheskii Slovar,* vol. 21. St. Petersburg. [In Russian.]

AHLQVIST, A.
1859   "Nachrichten über Tschuwaschen und Tscheremissen," *Archiv für Wissenschaftliche Kunde von Russland,* vol. 18, pp. 39–64.

AKSAKOFF, SERGHEI.
1923   *A Russian Gentleman* (trans. J. D. Duff). London.

BARBER, BERNARD.
1941   "Acculturation and Messianic Movements," *American Sociological Review,* vol. 6, pp. 663–69.

BÁRCZI, GÉZA.
1941   *Magyar Szófejtő Szótár* [=Hungarian Etymological Dictionary]. Budapest.

BASCOM, WILLIAM R.
1929   "Literary Style in Yoruba Riddles," *Journal of American Folklore,* vol. 62, pp. 1–16.

BEALS, RALPH.
1953   "Acculturation," in A. L. Kroeber, chairman, *Anthropology Today,* pp. 621–41. Chicago.

BEKE, ÖDÖN.
1926   "Az Új Cseremisz Irodalom" [=The New Cheremis Literature], *Magyar Nyelvőr,* vol. 55, pp. 52–55.
1927   "A Pogány Cseremiszek Vallása" [=The Religion of the Pagan Cheremis], *Magyar Nyelvőr,* vol. 56, pp. 14–17, 52–55.
1931   *Tscheremissische Texte zur Religion und Volkskunde.* Oslo Etnografiske Museum, Bulletin 4. Oslo.
1933   "Cseremisz és Csuvas Mesevégek" [=Cheremis and Chuvash Tale Endings], *Ethnographia,* vol. 44, pp. 75–76.
1934   "Texte zur Religion der Osttscheremissen," *Anthropos,* vol. 29, pp. 36–69, 371–89, 703–37.
1937   "Tscheremissische Märchen aus dem Kreise Jaransk" *Opetatud Eesti Seltsi Aastaraamat,* vol. 2, pp. 133–92.

[1] This bibliography covers (with a few exceptions) only such items as are actually cited, and is not meant to be an exhaustive list of works in the field which forms the subject of this book.

1938   "Tscheremissische Märchen, Sagen und Erzählungen," *Mémoires de la Société Finno-Ougrienne,* vol. 76.

1949   "Szómagyarázatok" [=Etymologies], *Nyelvtudományi Közlemények,* vol. 52, pp. 119–29.

1951a   *Volksdichtung und Gebräuche der Tscheremissen (Maris).* Budapest.

1951b   "Cseremisz szómagyarázatok [=Cheremis Etymologies], *Nyelvtudományi Közlemények,* vol. 53, pp. 249–51.

1954   "Ősi temetkezés emléke a mari nyelvben" [=A Trace of Ancient Burial Customs in the Mari Language], *Nyelvtudományi Közlemények,* vol. 56, pp. 283–85.

BERDNIKOV, V. M. AND TUDOROVSKAIA, E. A.

1945   *Poetics of the Mari Folksongs.* Yoshkar-Ola. [In Russian.]

BERELSON, BERNARD.

1942   *Content Analysis in Communication Research.* Glencoe, Ill.

BERTALANFFY, LUDWIG VON.

1950   "An Outline of General System Theory," *The British Journal for the Philosophy of Science,* vol. 1, pp. 1–32.

BLOOMFIELD, LEONARD.

1933   *Language.* New York.

BOAS, FRANZ.

1927   *Primitive Art.* Oslo.

BOGATYREV, P. AND JAKOBSON, R.

1929   "Die Folklore als eine besondere Form des Schaffens," *Donum Natalicium Schrijnen,* pp. 900–13. Nijmegen-Utrecht

BOLTE, JOHANNES AND POLÍVKA, GEORG.

1930   *Anmerkungen zu den Kinder- und Hausmärchen der Brüder Grimm,* vol. 4. Leipzig.

BONAFANTE, GIULIANO AND SEBEOK, THOMAS A.

1944   "Linguistics and the Age and Area Hypothesis," *American Anthropologist,* vol. 46, pp. 382–86.

BUDENZ, JÓSZEF.

1864   "Erdei Czeremiszség. Mondat- és Szövegközlés" [=The Forest Cheremis. Sentences and Texts], *Nyelvtudományi Közlemények,* vol. 3, pp. 97–156.

CARNAP, RUDOLPH.

1928   *Der logische Aufbau der Welt.* Berlin-Schlachtensee.

CARR, EDWARD HALLETT.

1951   *The Bolshevik Revolution, 1917–1923.* New York.

CARROLL, JOHN B., AGARD, FREDERICK B., NEWMAN, STANLEY S., OSGOOD, CHARLES E., AND SEBEOK, THOMAS A.

1951   *Report and Recommendations of the Interdisciplinary Summer Seminar in Psychology and Linguistics.* (Mimeographed.) Ithaca.

COON, CARLETON S.

1939   *The Races of Europe.* New York.

DIMANSHTEIN, S. M., ed.

1930   *Revolution and the Nationality Question: Documents and Materials,* vol. 3. Moscow. [In Russian.]

EMPSON, WILLIAM.

    1951   *The Structure of Complex Words*. London.

FUKS, ALEKSANDRA ANDREEVNA.

    1840   *Notes of Aleksandra Fuks about the Chuvash and the Cheremis of the Government of Kazan*. Kazan. [In Russian.]

GENETZ, ARVID.

    1889   *Ost-Tscheremissische Sprachstudien*. I. "Sprachproben mit deutscher Übersetzung," *Journal de la Société Finno-Ougrienne*, vol. 7, pp. 1–181.

HARRIS, Z. S.

    1952a "Discourse Analysis," *Language*, vol. 28, pp. 1–30.

    1952b "Discourse Analysis: A Sample Text," *Language*, vol. 28, pp. 474–94.

HARVA (HOLMBERG), UNO.

    1913   "Die Wassergottheiten der finnisch-ugrischen Völker," *Mémoires de la Société Finno-Ougrienne*, vol. 32.

    1914   *Tscheremissien Uskonto* [=Religion of the Cheremis]. Porvoo.

    1925   "Der Todesengel," *Studia Orientalia*, vol. 1, pp. 72–77.

    1926   *Die Religion der Tscheremissen, Folklore Fellows Communications*, no. 61.

    1927   "Finno-Ugric Mythology," in *Mythology of All Races*, vol. 4. Boston.

HAUER, J. W.

    1923   *Die Religionen, ihr Werden, ihr Sinn, ihre Wahrheit*. Stuttgart.

HEIKEL, A. O.

    1888   "Die Gebäude der Čeremissen, Mordwinen, Esten und Finnen," *Journal de la Société Finno-Ougrienne*, vol. 4.

    1910–15 *Die Stickmuster der Tscheremissen*. Helsingfors.

HEILER, F.

    1937   *Prayer*. Oxford.

HERBERSTEIN, SIGISMUND VON.

    1851–52 *Notes upon Russia: being a translation of the earliest account of that country, entitled Rerum Moscoviticarum Commentarii*. London. (First edition, Vienna, 1549.)

HERSKOVITS, MELVILLE J.

    1938   *Acculturation, the Study of Culture Contact*. New York.

HERZOG, GEORGE.

    1936   *Jabo Proverbs from Liberia*. London.

    1946   "Some Linguistic Aspects of American Indian Poetry," *Word*, vol. 2, p. 82.

HILL, ARCHIBALD A.

    1951   "Towards a Literary Analysis," in *Studies in Honor of J. S. Wilson*, pp. 147–65.

    1953   "A Sample Literary Analysis," *Report of the Fourth Annual Round Table Meeting on Linguistics and Language Teaching*, pp. 87-93. Washington, D. C.

HILL, W. W.

    1944   "Navaho Indians and the Ghost Dance of 1890," *American Anthropologist*, vol. 46, pp. 523–27.

HJELMSLEV, LOUIS.
    1953   *Prolegomena to A Theory of Language, Indiana University Publications in
            Anthropology and Linguistics,* Memoir 9, Bloomington, Indiana.
HUXLEY, ALDOUS.
    1945   *The Perennial Philosophy.* New York and London.
HÄMÄLÄINEN, ALBERT.
    1908a   "Tšeremissien uhritapoja" [=Sacrificial Customs of the Cheremis], *Journal
            de la Société Finno-Ougrienne,* vol. 25, no. 3, pp. 1–17.
    1908b   "Matkakertomus" [=Report of Journey], *Journal de la Société Finno-
            Ougrienne,* vol. 25, no. 5, pp. 19–22.
    1909   "Tšeremissien mehiläisviljelyksestä" [=Cheremis Apiculture], *Journal de
            la Société Finno-Ougrienne,* vol. 26, no. 1, pp. 1–16.
    1915   "Mordvalaisten tšeremissien ja votjakkien kosinta- ja häätavoista" [=Mord-
            vin, Cheremis, and Votyak Courting and Marriage Ceremonies], *Journal de
            la Société Finno-Ougrienne,* vol. 29, no. 1.
    1925   "Tšeremissien tuohitorvet ja niiden käyttö" [=Cheremis Birch Bark Horns
            and Their Use], *Kalevalaseuran Vuosikirja,* vol. 5, pp. 99–110.
    1928   "Tšeremissien ja votjakkien periodiset paholaisten karkoitusemenot" [=
            Cheremis and Votyak Ceremonies for Exorcising the Devil], *Kalevalaseuran
            Vuosikirja,* vol. 8, pp. 26–46.
    1930a   "Beiträge zur Ethnographie der Ostfinnen," *Journal de la Société Finno-
            Ougrienne,* vol. 44, no. 1, pp. 1–160.
    1930b   "Tšeremissien ja votjakkien keremeteistä" [=Cheremis and Votyak
            keremets], *Kalevalaseuran Vuosikirja,* vol. 10, pp. 43-57.
    1933   "Mordvalaisten ja tšeremissien asumuksista ja kotipalvonnasta" [=Mordvin
            and Cheremis Houses and Dedications], *Virittäjä,* pp. 331–38.
    1936–37 "Das kultische Wachsfeurer der Mordwinen und Tscheremissen," *Journal
            de la Société Finno-Ougrienne,* vol. 48, no. 1, pp. 1–158.
    1945   "Über den Namengebungsbräuche bei den Mordwinen und Tscheremissen,"
            Mitteilungen des Vereins für finnische Volkskunde, vol. 3, pp. 1–9.
ITKONEN, ERKKI.
    1953   "Materialveröffentlichungen aus dem Gebiet der tscheremissischen Sprache,"
            Finnisch-Ugrische Forschungen Anzeiger, vol. 31, pp. 36–47. Helsinki.
JAKOBSON, ROMAN.
    1945   "On Russian Fairy Tales," *Russian Fairy Tales,* pp. 631–56. New York.
JAKOBSON, ROMAN, AND LOTZ, J.
    1952   "Axioms of a Versification System Exemplified by the Mordvinian Folk-
            song," *Acta Instituti Hungarici Universitatis Holmiensis,* Series B, Lin-
            guistica 1, pp. 5–13. Stockholm.
JAMES, E. O.
    1938   *Comparative Religion.* London.
JOHANSEN, SVEND.
    1949   "La notion de signe dans la glossématique et dans l'esthétique," *Travaux du
            Cercle Linguistique de Copenhague,* vol. 5, pp. 288–303.

JOOS, MARTIN.
    1950 "Description of Language Design," *Journal of the Acoustical Society of America,* vol. 22, pp. 701–8.

JØRGENSEN, JØRGEN.
    1937–38 "Imperatives and Logic," *Erkenntnis,* vol. 7, pp. 288–96.

KANGASMAA, EEVA.
    1953 "The So-Called Past Tenses in Cheremis." (Mimeographed.) Bloomington, Indiana.

KARSTEN, RAFAEL.
    1935 *The Origins of Religion.* London.

KELLY, HENRY W.
    1941 "Franciscan Missions of New Mexico, 1740–1760," *New Mexico Historical Review,* vol. 16.

KLUCKHOHN, CLYDE.
    1953 "Universal Categories of Culture," in A. L. Kroeber, chairman, *Anthropology Today,* pp. 507–23. Chicago.

KOLARZ, WALTER.
    1952 *Russia and Her Colonies.* New York.

KROHN, KAARLE.
    1901 "Wo und wann entstanden die finnischen Zauberlieder?" *Finnisch-Ugrische Forschungen,* vol. 1, pp. 52–72, 147–81.
    1924 "Magische Ursprungsrunen der Finnen," *Folklore Fellows Communications,* no. 52. Helsinki.
    1926 *Die folkloristische Arbeitsmethode.* Oslo.

KUZNETSOV, S. K.
    1893–97 Über den Glauben vom Jenseits und den Todten-Cultus der Tscheremissen," *Internationales Archiv für Ethnographie,* vol. 6, pp. 89–95; vol. 8, pp. 17–23; vol. 9, pp. 153–61; vol. 10, pp. 41–52.
    1904 "The Cult of the Dead and Beliefs about the Afterlife of the Meadow Cheremis," *Ethnograficheskoe Obozrenie,* vol. 16, no. 60, pp. 67–90; vol. 61, pp. 56–109. [In Russian.]
    1908 "The Cheremis Sect *kugu sorta,*" *Ethnograficheskoe Obozrenie,* vol. 29, no. 4, pp. 1–59. [In Russian.]

LABARRE, WESTON.
    1948 *The Aymara Indians of the Lake Titicaca Plateau, Bolivia.* Menasha, Wisconsin.

LACH, ROBERT.
    1929 "Tscheremissische Gesänge," *Gesänge russischer kriegsgefangener,* vol. 1, no. 3. Vienna and Leipzig.

LÉVI-STRAUSS, CLAUDE.
    1945 "L'analyse structurale en linguistique et en anthropologie," *Word,* vol. 1, pp. 33–53.
    1953 "Social Structure," in A. L. Kroeber, chairman, *Anthropology Today,* pp. 524–53.

LEWY, ERNST.
    1925–26   *Tscheremissische Texte.* I. Text; II. Übersetzung. Hannover.
LINTON, RALPH.
    1943   "Nativistic Movements," *American Anthropologist,* vol. 45, pp. 230–40.
LOWIE, ROBERT H.
    1948   *Primitive Religion.* New York.
LYASHCHENKO, PETER I.
    1949   *History of the National Economy of Russia to the 1917 Revolution.* New
        York.
MAIR, L. P.
    1934   "The Study of Culture Contact as a Practical Problem," *Africa,* vol. 7, pp.
        415–22.
MANSIKKA, V. J.
    1909   "Über russische Zauberformeln mit Berücksichtigung der Blut- und Verren-
        kungssegen," *Annales Academiae Scientiarum Fennicae,* Series B, vol. 1,
        no. 3.
MARRETT, R. R.
    1914   *The Threshold of Religion.* London.
MARTINET, ANDRÉ.
    1953   "Structural Linguistics," in A. L. Kroeber, chairman, *Anthropology Today,*
        pp. 574–86. Chicago.
MÉSZÁROS, GYULA.
    1909   *A csuvas ősvallás emlékei* [=Remnants of the Ancient Chuvash Religion].
        Budapest.
MOONEY, JAMES AND OLBRECHTS, FRANS M.
    1932   *The Swimmer Manuscript. Cherokee Sacred Formulas and Medicinal Pre-
        scriptions.* Bureau of American Ethnology, Bulletin 99. Washington D. C.
MÜLLER, GERHARD FRIEDRICH.
    1759   "Nachricht von dreyen im gebiete der Stadt Casan wohnhaften heidnischen
        Völkern, den Tscheremissen, Tschuwassen und Wotiacken," *Sammlung
        Russischer Geschichte,* vol. 3, no. 4. St. Petersburg.
MUNKÁCSI, BERNARD.
    1921   "Sechzigerrechnung und Siebenzahl in den östlichen Zweigen der finnisch-
        magyarischen Sprachfamilie," *Keleti Szemle—Revue Orientale,* vol. 9, no. 1,
        pp. 1–24.
NADEL, S. F.
    1951   *The Foundations of Social Anthropology.* Glencoe, Ill.
OHRT, FERDINAND.
    1935–36   "Segen," *Handwörterbuch des deutschen Aberglaubens,* vol. 7, pp. 1582–
        1620.
PAASONEN, HEIKKI.
    1901   "Beiträge zur Kenntnis der Religion und des Kultus der Tscheremissen,"
        Keleti Szemle—Revue Orientale, vol. 2, pp. 30–38, 122–33, 198–210. [Also
        in "Tscheremissische Texte," 1939, pp. 181–215.]

1907a "A finn és a cseremisz isten-nérvől" [=Concerning the Finnish and Cheremis Name of God], *Nyelvtudományi Közlemények,* vol. 37, pp. 14–21.

1907b "M. jós, javas, javos" [Hungarian etymologies], *Nyelvtudományi Közlomények,* vol. 37, pp. 335–36.

1908   *Vocabularium Linguae Čuvašicae.* Budapest.

1909   "Über die ursprünglichen Seelenvorstellungen bei den finnisch-ugrischen Völkern und die Benennungen der Seele in ihren Sprachen," *Journal de la Société Finno-Ougrienne,* vol. 26, no. 4, pp. 1–27.

1914   "Mythologisches, etymologisches," *Mémoires de la Société Finno-Ougrienne,* vol. 35, no. 11, pp. 1–10.

1939   "Tscheremissische Texte," Paavo Siro, ed., *Mémoires de la Société Finno-Ougrienne,* vol. 78.

1948   *Ost-Tscheremissisches Wörterbuch,* Paavo Siro, ed. Helsinki.

PEDERSEN, H.
1931   *Linguistic Science in the Nineteenth Century* (trans. J. Spargo). Cambridge.

PETSCH, R.
1900   *Formelhafte Schlüsse im Volksmärchen.* Berlin.

PLATANOV, S. F.
1929   *History of Russia* F. A. Golder, ed., (trans. E. Aronsberg). New York.

POKSHISHEVSKIĬ, V. V.
1951   *Along the Volga: from Gor'kiy to Astrakhan.* Moscow. [In Russian.]

PORKKA, VOLMARI.
1895   "Volmari Porkka's tscheremissische Texte mit Übersetzung," Arvid Genetz, ed., *Journal de la Société Finno Ougrienne,* vol. 13, no. 1, pp. 1–140.

PRÖHLE, VILMOS.
1908   "Tatár nyelvjárási adalékok" [=Tatar Dialect Data], *Nyelvtudományi Közlemények,* vol. 38, pp. 63–110, 330–63.

RADIN, PAUL.
1937   *Primitive Religion, its Nature and Origin.* New York.

1949   "The Culture of the Winnebago: As Described by Themselves," *Indiana University Publications in Anthropology and Linguistics,* Memoir 2. Bloomington, Ind.

RAMSTEDT, G. J.
1902   "Bergtscheremissische Sprachstudien," *Mémoires de la Société Finno-Ougrienne,* vol. 17. Helsinki.

REDFIELD, ROBERT.
1953   *The Primitive World and Its Transformations.* Ithaca.

REICHARD, GLADYS A.
1944   *Prayer: The Compulsive Word.* New York.

REICHENBACH, HANS.
1947   *Elements of Symbolic Logic.* New York.

ROUDENKO, M.
1920   "Recherches sur la religion paienne des Tscheremisses," *Revue d'Ethnographie et des Traditions Populaires,* vol. 1, pp. 32–50.

RUESCH, JURGEN AND BATESON, GREGORY.

  1949   "Structure and Process in Social Relations," *Psychiatry*, vol. 12, pp. 105–24.

  1951   *Communication*. New York.

Russia, Full Geographical Description of Our Homeland.

  1914   Vol. 5. St. Petersburg. [In Russian.]

RÄNK, GUSTAV.

  1949–51   *Das System der Raumeinteilung in den Behausungen der nordeurasischen Völker*, vols. 1–2. Stockholm.

  1949   "Die Heilige Hinterecke im Hauskult der Völker Nordosteuropas und Nordasiens," *Folklore Fellows Communications*, no. 137. Helsinki.

RÄSÄNEN, MARTTI.

  1920   "Die tschuwassischen Lehnwörter im Tscheremissischen," *Mémoires de la Société Finno-Ougrienne*, vol. 48.

  1923   "Die tatarischen Lehnwörter im Tscheremissischen," *Mémoires de la Société Finno-Ougrienne*, vol. 50.

  1928   "Osttscher. *kəzər-pijambar*," *Mémoires de la Société Finno-Ougrienne*, vol. 58, pp. 214–16.

SEBEOK, THOMAS A.

  1950a   "Cheremis Dream Portents," *Southwestern Journal of Anthropology*, vol. 6, pp. 273–85.

  1950b   "A Cheremis Autobiography with Remarks on Other Uralic Personal Documents," *Hoosier Folklore*, vol. 9, pp. 17–24.

  1950c   "Concerning Cheremis Names," *Language*, vol. 26, pp. 276–78.

  1951   "Levirate Among the Cheremis as Reflected by their Songs," *American Anthropologist*, vol. 53, pp. 285–89.

  1952   *Studies in Cheremis Folklore*, vol. 1, *Indiana University Publications, Folklore Series*, vol. 6. Bloomington, Indiana. [With others.]

  1953   "The Structure and Content of Cheremis Charms," *Anthropos*, vol. 48, pp. 369–88, 760–72.

  1955   "On Christiansen's Review of *Studies in Cheremis Folklore*," *American Anthropologist*, vol. 57, pp. 863–64.

         "Toward a Statistical Contingency Method in Folklore Research," *Studies and Papers in Honor of Distinguished Service Professor Stith Thompson on the Occasion of His Seventieth Birthday*. (Forthcoming.)

SEBEOK, THOMAS A., AND LANE, EVELYN.

  1949   "The Cheremis Folksong: A Soviet Viewpoint," *Slavonic and East European Review*, vol. 28, pp. 139–51.

SEBEOK, THOMAS A., BALYS, JONAS, ROBERTS, WARREN, AND TAYLOR, ARCHER.

  1952   "Addenda to *Studies in Cheremis Folklore*, vol. 1," *Journal of American Folklore*, vol. 65, pp. 167–77.

SEBEOK, THOMAS A. AND INGEMANN, FRANCES J.

  1954   Review, with comparative notes, of Uno Harva, *Die Religiösen vorstellungen der Mordwinen, Journal of American Folklore*, vol. 67, pp. 214–17.

SMIRNOV, JEAN N.
    1898   "Les Tschérémisses," in Paul Boyer, ed. and trans., *Les populations finnoises des bassins de la Volga et de la Kama,* pp. 1–214. Paris. (First ed., 1889.)

SOKOLOV, Y. M.
    1950   *Russian Folklore.* New York.

SYDOW, C. W. VON.
    1948   "Folk Tale Studies and Philology Some Points of View," *Selected Papers on Folklore,* pp. 189–219. Copenhagen.

SZENDREY, ZSIGMOND.
    1937a "A varázslócselekvések személye, ideje és helye" [=Performers, Times, and Places of Magic Acts], *Ethnographia,* vol. 48, pp. 13–24.
    1937b "A növény-, állat- és ásványvilág a varázslatokban" [=The World of Plants, Animals and Minerals in Magic], *Ethnographia,* vol. 48, pp. 154–66.

SZILASI, MORICZ.
    1901   *Cseremisz Szótar* [=Cheremis Dictionary]. Budapest.

THOMPSON, STITH.
    1946   *The Folktale.* New York.

TOY, CRAWFORD H.
    1924   *Introduction to the History of Religions.* Cambridge.

TOYNBEE, ARNOLD J.
    1947   *A Study of History* (abridgement of vols. 1–6 by D. C. Somervell). New York and London.

TYLOR, EDWARD B.
    1874   *Primitive Culture.* Boston.

VASILJEV, V. M.
    1915   "Attitude of the Cheremis Toward Sexual Immorality," *Izvestija Obščestva Archaeologii Istorii i Etnografii pri Kazanskom Universitete,* vol. 29. Kazan. [In Russian.]
    1926   *Marij Muter* [=Cheremis Dictionary]. Moscow.
    1927   *The Cheremis Religious Sect kugu sorta.* Krasnokokshaisk. [In Russian.]

VERNADSKY, GEORGE.
    1953   *The Mongols and Russia.* New Haven.

VOEGELIN, C. F. AND HARRIS, Z. S.
    1947   "The Scope of Linguistics," *American Anthropologist,* vol. 49, pp. 588–600.

VOEGELIN, ERMINIE W.
    1948   "Initial and Final Elements in Tübatulabal Myths," *Southwestern Journal of Anthropology,* vol. 4, pp. 71–75.

WALLACE, D. MACKENZIE.
    1878   *Russia.* New York.

WALLIS, WILSON D.
    1918   *Messiahs: Christian and Pagan.* Boston.
    1939   *Religion in Primitive Society.* New York.

WEBSTER, HUTTON.
    1948   *Magic, a Sociological Study.* Stanford.

WELLEK, RENÉ AND WARREN, AUSTIN.
  1949 *Theory of Literature*. New York.
WHITEHEAD, ALFRED NORTH.
  1937 "Remarks," *The Philosophical Review*, vol. 46, pp. 178–86.
WHYTE, LANCELOT LAW.
  1950 "Simultaneous Discovery," *Harper's Magazine*, Feb., pp. 23–26.
  1951 (Ed.) *Aspects of Form. A Symposium on Form in Nature and Art*. London.
WICHMANN, JULIE.
  1913 *Beiträge zur Ethnographie der Tscheremissen*. Helsinki.
WICHMANN, YRJÖ.
  1923 *Tscheremissische Texte mit Wörterverzeichnis und grammatikalischem Abriss*.
        Helsingfors.
  1931 "Volksdichtung und Volksbräuche der Tscheremissen," *Mémoires de la
        Société Finno-Ougrienne*, vol. 59.
  1932 "Über eine Reformbewegung der heidnischen Tscheremissen," *Journal de la
        Société Finno-Ougrienne*, vol. 45, no. 7, pp. 21–46.
WOLFE, BERNARD.
  1949 "Uncle Remus and the Malevolent Rabbit," *Commentary*, vol. 3, pp. 31–41.
ZSIRAI, MIKLÓS.
  1939 "Reguly Antal emlékezete" [= In Memory of Antal Reguly], *Magyar Nyelv*,
        vol. 35, pp. 1–8.
ZYKOV, N. V.
  1932 *Religious Trends among the Mari*. Nizhni Novgorod. [In Russian.]

SOURCES FOR THE GAZETTEER

Authority for Transliteration

Permanent Committee on Geographical Names, Royal Geographical Society. 1942.
London.

Maps Consulted

European Russia 1:1,500,000. Army Map Service 5307, Reprint of Russian Series, 1938:
Sheets 11 and 12.

Europe 1:1,000,000. Army Map Service 1301, Reprint of Geographical Section, General
Staff (British) 2758, 1943–47: Sheets NN–39, NN–40, NO–40. Army Map Service
1301, Geographical Section, General Staff (British) 2758, 1940–42: Sheets NO–38,
NO–39. Geographical Section, General Staff (British) 2758, second edition, 1943:
Sheet NM–40. Geographical Section, General Staff (British) 2758, provisional
edition: Sheet NN–40.

United States Air Force World Aeronautical Charts 1:1,000,000. Third edition, 1947:
Sheet 164. Third edition, revised: Sheets 155, 156, 235, 237. Fourth edition:
Sheet 236.

General Stab d. Heer Operationskarte Russland 1:1,000,000, 1942: Sheet 4.

General Stab d. Heer Osteuropa 1:300,000, 1941: Sheets. Zusammendruck Wotkinsk-
Birsk (H/58–I/56), D56, 57, 58, H55, L55.

Eastern Europe 1:250,000. Army Map Service N501, first edition, Intelligence data to
     1946: Sheets NN–38–2 and 3, NN–39–1, NO–38–8 and 9, 11 and 12, NO–39–7
     and 8, 10 and 11.
Russian General Staff, Military Topographic Section. Spetsial'naya Karta Evropeyskoy
     Rossiy. 1:420,000. Sheet 128, 1872.

Additional Sources

GORKIN, A. F., AND OTHERS, EDS.
     1938   *Great Soviet World Atlas,* vol. 1. Moscow.
The Columbia Lippincott Gazetteer of the World.
     1952   New York.